D1199260

The Urban Life of the Yuan Dynasty

Written by Shi Weimin
Translated by Liao Jing and Zhou Hui

Paths International Ltd

湖南人民出版社

General Preface

by Ji Xianlin (1911~2009)

An obvious fact has been ignored by scholars both at home and abroad (it seems that that Hegel noticed it): For five thousand years and thousands of miles across the globe, among all nations, the Chinese nation has been one that loves history most and has the most ancient, most complete and most systematic collection of historical classics. From the Yellow Emperor (2697~2599 B.C.) to the People's Republic of China today, Chinese history has progressed in a continuous flow, generation after generation, for several thousand years. *The Records of the Grand Historian* by Sima Qian (145 or 135~86 B.C.) of the Han Dynasty was the first systematic Chinese historical text. Ever since Ban Gu (32~92), dynastic histories have been written one after another. In fact, in the early years of every dynasty, one of the most important tasks was to compile a history of the previous dynasty. These history books constitute the so-called "official history". In addition, China has numerous "unofficial" history books. Historical literature was thus listed as an independent branch in *The Complete Library of the Four Treasuries*.

There is no way to ensure whether or not all the above-mentioned history books are authentic and reliable. This is impossible, for no country, in any period of its development, can boast a history that is 100 percent authentic. When one dynasty overthrows another and compiles a history of it, how can it possibly tell the truth all the time? Lu You (1125~1210) once wrote, "Who can stop rumors after he dies?" However, it also goes too far to call these classics "war records" or "court records". Anyhow, in my opinion, compared with other ancient countries such as India, China's historical classics are more reliable, because they do not contain too many mythologies or lies.

What are the benefits of possessing a complete collection of historical classics, or in other words, what is the significance of having a history?

There are many benefits and great significance. We always say that we must draw lessons from other people's mistakes and from the past. There are many such sayings in Chinese. Sima Guang (1019~1086), a great historian of the Song Dynasty, composed a great book of general history called *Zizhi Tongjian or The Comprehensive Mirror for Aid* in Government, in which "zizhi" means "aid in government". His intention in writing the book was obvious. History can also bring about truth. Whatever the truth is, just let it be. We must not distort it, exaggerate it, or tell lies, intentionally or otherwise. Facts show us the process and rules of development of human history and as well as the direction where it is heading for. History can guide our actions, make us confident, and enable us to avoid detours and mistakes. "Mountains multiply, streams double back — I doubt there's even a road; willows cluster darkly, blossoms shine — another village ahead!" Finally, we aim at arriving at a world of great harmony. Is this not significance enough?

However, it is not an easy task to acquire historical knowledge. We can simply "draw lessons from our past". In the past, historical studies were classified into various levels. History experts (I also want to include postgraduates here) must read the Twenty-four or Twenty-

five History Books of China and even the "unofficial history books".
Zhang Xuecheng (1738~1801) claimed, "The Six Classics are all about
history." If so, the Six Classics must also be read. Famous systematic
historical texts, naturally, must not be ignored. It is enough for high and
mid-level intellectuals, who are less professional than historians, to read
history books like *The Comprehensive Mirror for Aid in Government and
A Concise Account of China's General History.* At the lower level are
people who are illiterate or can read only a little, probably they have little
have little interest in history. But their knowledge of history is amazing.
This is probably attributable to the wide spread of fiction and drama.
The novel The Romance of the Three Kingdoms alone teaches people
much about history. There are few people in China who do not know the
stories of Liu Bei, *Guan Yu and Zhang Fei*, the three sworn brothers in
that book. Zhuge Liang's name is even better known. General Yue Fei,
another popular novel, tells the story of a patriotic general Yue Fei in the
Southern Song Dynasty. *The Romance of the Tang Dynasty*, similarly, tells
us much about the Tang Dynasty. In China, there are many such books.
What is more, various types of dramas have been produced on the basis
of such books. As a result, even ordinary people have rich knowledge
of history. As for the question of whether the information is reliable or
not, there is no need to answer it. Many events are indeed recounted
without confirming them in the first place. Therefore, getting misleading
information becomes inevitable as long as we obtain historical knowledge
in that way. These novels have misled not only the common people but
also scholars. Wang Yuyang (1634~1711), a famous poet in the early
Qing Dynasty, wrote elegies for Pang Shiyuan, a literary figure that never
existed in reality. Of course, Wang was laughed at by his peers.

After the founding of the People's Republic of China in 1949,
Chinese culture has witnessed dramatic progress. More and more history
books targeting at common readers have been published. The days are

gone, to my delight, when one had to learn history through fiction and drama. Now people have a variety of channels for learning history. In relation to the significance of history I have mentioned above, this is really a welcome phenomenon.

Now the Hunan People's Publishing House adopts a new way to acquaint its readers with Chinese history and society. By focusing on the capital city and the major cities of different dynasties, this book series draws a panoramic picture of the urban politics, economy, culture, religion and customs so as to help us better understand ancient China. It deftly integrates history and general interest, not merely presenting dull facts, but trying to entertain the readers in a relaxing manner. The authors in this series write on the basis of historical facts. This is a much better approach to attain the knowledge of history compared with that in the past when people learned history through fiction and drama. I feel very gratified at this on behalf of Chinese readers.

This book series will be published soon and I wish it every success. I am confident that it will be hugely popular with its readers. A nation that does not know its history would not love its own country. This has always been my conviction, and with it I conclude this preface.

元 代 城 市
生 活 长 卷

The Urban Life of the
Yuan Dynasty

Table of Contents

Part Four

Part Five

Part Six

元代城市
生活长卷

The Urban Life of the
Yuan Dynasty

Part One

The Nomadic Chieftains' Blueprint of the City

The Mongols, whose life featuring migrating to wherever the water and grass are available, had entered the city for the first time. Entranced by its wealth and lifestyle, the new rulers began to construct palaces with high walls on the steppe. And soon a megacity that was to awe the whole world was built.

1

In the spring of 1206, white nine-tailed banners were raised on the northern Mongolian steppe by the Onon River. Temüjin of the Kiyad was honored Chinggis Khan and became the first monarch of the Great Mongol Empire.

The Empire was a nomadic one through and through, for its people were both warriors and producers. "On horseback they can fight battles; off horseback they are good graziers." (Preface to Great Institutions of Statecraft, Vol. 41, YWL) Chinggis Khan's magnificent palace tent or ordo was the power center of the country, for the immense steppe nullified the necessity of the city or even too many fixed structures.

Chinggis Khan was beyond doubt the most awe-inspiring military leader, under whose command thousands of brave and fierce horsemen raided the agricultural lands from time to time. He crushed forty countries!

(Biography of Emperor Shizu, Vol. 1, YS) Chinggis Khan's armies could not only be found in the Central Plains, northwest and northeast of China, but also in Central Asia and the vicinity of Europe.

Wars were devastating. The city especially bore the brunt. "In areas covering thousands li in the Yellow River Valley, Yangtze River Valley and east of the Taihang Mountains, the population was decimated; gold, cloth, children and livestock were plundered; houses were burnt down; the city walls were damaged and deserted." (LCGMBY, Vol. 4) "The city was in ruins. Grass took over the damaged city walls. And only howls of foxes could be heard there." (QDLG, Vol. 1)

However, the most intimidating thing was the "wholesale massacre" carried out by the Mongol troops. Chinggis Khan decreed that any city that had put up resistance should be massacred once captured. "All the inhabitants, young and old, pretty and ugly, rich and poor, submissive and unyielding, should be exterminated without mercy, except the craftsmen, doctors and prophets." (MDBL) Taking Baozhou (modern Baoding in Hebei Province) for example, when the city was occupied, all the inhabitants were driven out of the city by the Mongols and the old were killed first. "Two days later, it was ordered that all regardless of age should be killed." (JXSSWJ, Vol. 17) "The number of corpses surpassed a hundred thousand. If piled up, they could probably reach the top of the city wall." (LCWJ, Vol. 35) After twenty years of war, "counties and towns in Hebei, Hedong and Shangdong were almost deserted." (JXSSWJ, Vol. 16) Cities and towns in northwest and Central Asia were afflicted by wars as well.

Having nomad in their blood, the Mongol cavalry found it hard to adapt to the sedentary life. Thus they just left in autumn and return in the next spring every time after they intruded the agricultural lands, seldom staying to station the captured cities or areas. Some Mongols even claimed that "The Han Chinese were useless to their country. We may as well

元代城市
生活长卷

The Urban Life of the
Yuan Dynasty

drive them away and turn their lands into pastures." (Biography of Yelü Chucai, Vol. 146, YS)

Did the city really amount to nothing for the nomadic Mongols?

Confucians, religions personage and generals of other ethnic minorities in Mongol service rose to its defense.

Among them was Muqali, the Mongolian general designated by Chinggis Khan to be in charge of the war against the Jin Dynasty, and was called "Prince of State". Shi Tianni from Zhengding pledged loyalty to Muqali and became one of the most important Han generals in his army. One day Shi purposefully advised to Muqali, saying, "The Central Plains were generally pacified, but we still wink at the sack of the cities. I don't believe that is included in Your Highness's purpose of punishing those unruly people. In addition, Your Highness was dispatched by the Khakhan to eliminate the rebels and bandits. How can Your Highness follow the acts of those unworthy ones?" Liu Xiang'an, a commander under Shi Tianni, also advised to Muqali, "Since time immemorial, every newly founded country has taken special care of its people and their livelihood. But now areas east of the Yellow River have been sacked and eradicated. Then who would transport supplies for our troops next time? It is high time that we took care of the survivors and comforted the dead." Muqali agreed and enjoined his troops that "he who abuses or rapes the captive should be punished according to the military law." (Biography of Shi Tianni, Vol. 147; Biography of Liu Xiang'an, Vol. 150, YS)

Qiu Chuji, titled Master Changchun, was a Taoist master of the Complete Realization Sect. He once accepted the invitation of Chinggis Khan and traveled all the way to Central Asia to meet with him. Chinggis Khan consulted him about the methods of achieving immortality and ways of ruling the country. And he told Chinggis Khan to respect heaven and love the people, and to purify the heart and reduce the desires. Qiu Chuji also added, "Whenever one says he wants to unify all under heaven, he would never be addicted to killing." (Biography of Qiu Chuji, Vol. 202, YS)

Of all the advice the most useful piece was from a Khitan named Yelü Chucai. He read a lot and was especially good at astronomy, geography, calendrical sciences and astrology and had entered an official career during the Jin Dynasty. Impressed by his erudite learning, Chinggis Khan appointed him Scribe. After the death of Chinggis Khan, his successor Ogedei Khan, the second emperor of the Great Mongol Empire, inherited his trust in Yelü Chucai. With the new Khakhan's consent, Yelü Chucai sent court officials to collect taxes on items like land and commerce in the Central Plains, and had tribute like foods, gold and cloth poured in without even leaving Ogedei Khan a step. That really pleased the Khakhan and opened his eyes to the importance of the agricultural lands. When the Mongol forces marched south out of their steppe, the emperor of the Jin Dynasty hastily moved the capital from Zhongdu (present-day Beijing) at the foot of the Yanshan Mountain to Nanjing (modern Kaifeng in Henan province). In 1234, the Mongol troops conquered Nanjing and their generals demanded a wholesale massacre in the city, for according to their usual practice, "The enemy that had ever resisted with stones or bow and arrow was regarded as defying the order and should be killed once defeated." At that critical moment, Yelü Chucai stormed to Ogedei Khan to dissuade him from the massacre by saying that "what our generals and soldiers wanted from our decades' long pacification campaigns was nothing but a land with people living on it. If all the people were executed, the land was but a waste. Then what's the use of it?" Ogedei Khan began to waver in his decision. Yelü Chucai further pointed out that "the city was dwelled by the deftest craftsmen and the greatest noble families in the country. If they were all killed, what would we get out of an empty city?" Only until then did Ogedei Khan agree to ban the massacre and a population of 1.47 million was thereby

元代城市
生活长卷

The Urban Life of the
Yuan Dynasty

spared.

The decrease and eventually the termination of the massacres was a major turning point. After the fall of the Jin and Western Xia Dynasty which located west of the Yellow River, the battlefield was switched from the Yellow River Valley to the Huaihe River Valley and the Yangtze River Valley. The Central Plains as well as the cities and towns in North China began to recover from war.

2

The rising empire in North China had no fixed capital, which was inconceivable for people of the Central Plains who had been used to a sedentary life and a monarchal reign. Therefore they kept urging Ogedei Khan to build a capital city. After meticulous consideration, Ogedei Khan decided to locate the capital in the heartland on the northern steppe by the Orkhor River (currently Erkun River in Mongol). This arrangement was fairly sensible as it was the birthplace as well as the power center of the Great Mongol Empire. The newly built capital was named Qara-qorum.

The construction of the new city began in the spring of 1235. The person in charge of the project was a Han Chinese named Liu Min who was the Head of Artisans in Yanjing. When the major structure of Qara-qorum was completed in the next lunar New Year, Ogedei deliberately hosted a grand banquet to feast the Mongol imperial princes there for celebration. In 1237, he ordered the Muslim craftsmen to build the Saolin City (City for Spring Hunting) and the Gegen Cagan Ordo 70 li north of Qara-qorum. In 1238, Toshu Lake City and Toshu Ordo which were located 30 li south of Qara-qorum were successively established.

The advent of the city on the Mongolian steppe was really something noteworthy. It marked the acknowledgement of the significance of the city on the part of the nomadic ruler— the Khakhan who began to make efforts to construct new cities.

The construction of Qara-qorum lasted for nine years—from 1251 to 1259. It wasn't finished until the era of Mongke Khan, the fourth Khakhan of the Great Mongol Empire.

Mongke Khan's younger brother Qubilai, later titled Shizu, "had a precocious ambition to serve all under heaven", and was thus in contact with a wide circle of "literati from all over the country" to consult ways of ruling a country. In 1251, Qubilai was sent by Mongke Khan to lead the pacificaiton campaigns in the Han territory south of the Gobi Desert, and together with him went a large group of advisers of diverse ethnic backgrounds. Qubilai then rebuilt the Wuzhou City (modern Zhangbei County in Hebei Province) to temporarily house his entourage. In the spring of 1256 he asked Monk Zicong to select a place appropriate for a new city as their home base. Zicong finally chose the Dragon Hill on the north bank of the Li River as the site of the new city. The Dragon Hill was backed by the Nanping Mountain in the north, and surrounded by vast plains in the east and west. It also faced the summer resort of Jinlianchuan of the Jin Emperor in the south. Its location and flat terrain made it an ideal site for a city. And this new city, named Kaiping, was located right in the place where today's government office of Plain Blue Banner stands, 20 miles north of Yellow Banner Camp, in Inner Mongolia Autonomous Region.

It took three years to build the Kaiping City. And the supervisors of the construction were all Han Chinese. They were Dong Wenbing from Gaochen, Jia Juzhen from Huolu and Xie Zhongwen from Fengzhou.

The construction of Kaiping City caused a sensation in the local area, and left behind a legend about Qubilai borrowing land from a dragon. "According to the legend, when Grand Guardian Liu Zicong relocated the capital, the land couldn't be drained dry because of the nearby dragon pond. Zicong then advised Emperor Shizu to borrow the

元代城市
生活长卷

The Urban Life of the
Yuan Dynasty

land from the dragon, and Emperor Shizu agreed. In the same midnight, the dragon ascended to heaven with thunders roaring in the sky. And foundation of the city was successfully laid with earth in the next day." (ZZZJ, Vol. 1) Later a poet named Yang Yunfu wrote a poem about the legend.

With the advent of His Majesty the magnificent capital was built,

Wind whirling and thunder rolling, the dragon was panicking.

When the moon shone above the sea all mountains were bathed in the brilliance,

When the sun rose above the Fusang trees all under heaven was illuminated.

The legend of the dragon is, of course, incredible, but it revealed the fact drainage was a hard nut in the construction of the Kaiping City. And it was under the common efforts of both the designers and the artisans that the new city was finally erected on the steppes south of the Gobi Desert.

On April 28, 1260, Qubilai ascended the throne, making himself the fifth Khakhan of the Great Mongol Empire. And his coronation was held right in the Kaiping City.

3

Qara-qorum appeared far-flung as a capital when the monarch needed to rule the densely populated Central Plains. And some Mongol aristocrats had already been aware of the problem. Before the accession of Qubilai, Ba Tulu, the grandson of Muqali, once advised to Qubilai, pointing blank, "Yanjing is a place full of elites and talents. It is well located, with the Yangtze River and the Huaihe River on the south and the steppes and desert on the north. In addition, every heavenly destined emperor would dwell in the heartland of the country to receive the tribute from all around the world. Had Your Majesty wanted to rule the entire state, Yan is the most suitable place to work and rest." (Biography of Ba Tulu, Vol. 119, YS) Though Qubilai spent most of his days in Kaiping after his accession, he paid great attention to Ba Tulu's proposal and send his ministers and advisers discussing over the site of the capital.

Qara-qorum obviously lost the eligibility for a capital. Qubilai wintered in Qara-qorum in 1260, and he realized it was very difficult to meet the basic needs of a huge central administration, the armies and a rapidly increasing population with the foodstuffs and goods that were to be delivered over a distance of thousands of li from across the steppes, the Gobi Desert and the Central Plains. And meanwhile he knew that the ruling foundation of the Great Mongol Empire over the Central Plains has been solidly laid, all he needed to do was to be an aboveboard emperor of a legitimate Chinese dynasty. If he persisted in setting the capital in the north of the Gobi desert and refusing to move the political center to the south, his empire would still be treated as a small country huddled up in the corner of the steppes, which would not only affect the further unification of the ruling classes of the Mongols and Han Chinese, but also hinder the governance of the Central Plains from stepping into the right path. Thus Qara-qorum was no longer eligible for a capital in terms of the geographic location, economic conditions and political situation.

Options for the new sites of the capital actually narrowed down to only two: one is Yanjing, the old capital of Liao and Jin dynasties; the other is the newly built Kaiping.

According to the Han advisor Haojing who represented the majority, Yanjing fit requirements of the seat of the Mongol imperial administration in North China and deserved the status of the capital with its excellent geographical location. It faced Eastern Liao in the east and the Great Plain to the north of the Yellow River in the south. It bordered Shaanxi in the

west, and was backed by the great mountains and impregnable pass in the north. Then what should the Mongol ruler do with Kaiping? It was simply suggested that there should be two capitals in the country, with Yanjing as the primary one and Kaiping the auxiliary one.

After discreet consideration, Qubilai agreed with the proposition of two capitals. On June 16, 1263, he renamed Kaiping Fu Shangdu, which was usually called Shangjing or Luanjing in the history. On September 5, 1264, Yanjing was renamed Zhongdu and was later renamed Dadu on March 4, 1272. Thus Dadu was the primary capital, and Shangdu the auxiliary one.

4

The construction of Zhongdu or Dadu and the extension of Shangdu started almost at the same time.

Zhongdu or Dadu was designed by Zicong with the assistance of Confucians like Zhao Bingwen. The capital was redesigned and was relocated to the northeast of Yanjing instead of building on its old site, which was out of two reasons. For one thing, Yanjing was too dilapidated and its former imperial palace had worn away over one thousand years. Thus it would be easier to build a new city than to renovate the old one. And then it was the water source of Kangping. The major water supply of Kaiping— the Lotus Pool in the west of the city was insufficient and poor in water quality. Thus it could hardly meet the needs of the development of the city. And the question of water supply could easily be solved by moving the new capital to the northeast of Yanjing where the new city could be watered by the lakes around the Qionghua Island which were connected with the Gaoliang River.

The construction of Zhongdu or Dadu was carried out in the following steps:

First was to restore the Qionghua Island and Guanghan Palace which are now located in Beihai Park, modern Beijing. The construction started in the spring of 1264 and a new palace was built in the same year. The renovation of the other structures on the island lasted until after 1266.

In 1266 started the construction of the imperial city, the palace city and the imperial palace. In the spring of 1272, the palace city was completed. In the next year the major palace Daming Hall began to be built and was finished at the end of the same year. On February 9, 1274, the first day of the first lunar month in the eleventh year of Zhiyuan, Qubilai held the court assembly to celebrate the lunar New Year's Day in the new Daming Hall where the Heir Apparent, the imperial princes and all the court officials came to pay their respects and extend their congratulation to him.

Last was the construction of the city walls and the other city facilities and they were completed in 1276.

People in charge of the construction of the capital included the Han commander Zhang Rou and his son Zhang Honglüe, Minister of the Ministry of Works Duan Zhen, the Mongol Yesu Buhua, the Jurchen Gao Wei, and the semuren Yeheidie'erding. Among others, Duan Zhen played the most prominent role, for he not only engaged in the whole construction of Dadu, but also assisted in the maintenance of Dadu. As the Regent in Dadu, he was in charge of the renovation and extension of the city walls, imperial palace, the government offices, and river channels in Dadu for a long time.

By 1285 residents and government officials had almost moved to Dadu.

The extension and restoration of Shangdu which started in 1267 lasted for about five or six years. The major structures of the imperial palace like Da'an Pavilion, Confucian Temple and Town God's Temple, and a group of new government offices were built during that

元代城市
生活长卷

The Urban Life of the
Yuan Dynasty

time.

Qubilai went in for large-scale construction of palaces and cities, which afflicted himself with the reproach from the Mongol tribes. The Mongol imperial prince in the northwest especially sent an envoy to question Qubilai. "Our customs are different from those of the Han Chinese. Your Majesty now settled on their land, established capitals and cities, and even adopted their rites and institutions. What was the reason for that?" (Biography of Gao Zhiyao, Vol. 125, YS) Qubilai's determination to implement his two-capital policy didn't waver at such censure. With Dadu as the primary capital, the Mongol regime in the Central Plains could be strengthened and its status as the legitimate Chinese dynasty could be erected and guaranteed, which in turn paved the way for the unification around the whole country. With Shangdu retaining its status as the capital, the bulk of Mongol traditions and customs could be preserved and the ties with other Mongol chieftains and aristocrats could be maintained through regular hunting activities, which was also beneficial to the development of the Mongol ethnic group.

5

In 1271 Qubilai changed the title of the state from "the Great Mongol Empire" to "Da Yuan" (Great Yuan). In 1276 the Mongol troops captured Lin'an (Modern Hangzhou), the capital of the Southern Song Dynasty. In 1279, the last Song holdout was defeated. After the unification of China, the territory of the Yuan Dynasty "expanded northwards across the Yinshan Mountain, westwards to Liusha, eastwards to the border of the former Liao Dynasty, and southwards to the sea".
"In terms of the extent of territory, it equaled the Han and Tang dynasties in the east and south, but far surpassed the latter in the west and north,"

covering an area twice the size of present-day China including modern Mongolia, Russian Siberia and parts of Thailand and Burma. (Section one, Treatise on Geography, Vol. 58, YS)

To efficiently run such a bulky country, the sovereign of the Yuan Dynasty adopted Xingsheng (branch Secretariat or province) as the administrative unit, "dividing the country into eleven provinces, among which Hebei and western Shangdong, designated as the Central Region, was governed by the Secretariat, while the rest were governed by Branch Secretariat." (Cities, Vol. 40, YWL) There were a total ten Branch Secretariats in the Yuan Dynasty.

1. Liaoyang Xingsheng with Liaoyang (currently belongs to Liaoning Province) as its seat of government. Under this came present-day Liaoning, Jilin and Heilongjiang provinces as well as the areas to north of the Amur River and to the east of the Usuri River.

2. Henan Jiangbei Xingsheng with Bianliang (modern Kaifeng of Henan Province) as its seat of government. Under this came present-day Henan Province and parts of Hubei, Anhui and Jiangsu provinces that were to the north of the Yangtze River.

3. Shaanxi Xingsheng with Fengyuan (modern Xi'an of Shaanxi Province) as its seat of government. Under this came present-day Shaanxi Province and parts of Inner Mongolia and Gansu Province.

4. Sichuan Xingsheng with Chengdu as its seat of government. Under this came most of present-day Sichuan Province as well as parts of Shaanxi and Hunan provinces.

5. Gansu Xingsheng with Ganzhou (modern Zhangye of Gansu Province) as its seat of government. Under this came present-day Gansu Province, Ningxia Hui Autonomous Region and part of Inner Mongolia.

6. Yunnan Xingsheng with Zhongqing (modern Kunming of Yunnan Province) as its seat of government. Under this came present-day Yunnan Province, and parts of Sichuan and Guangxi provinces, as well as parts of

Thailand and northern Burma.

7. Jiangzhe Xingsheng with Hangzhou as its seat of government. Under this came present-day Zhejiang and Fujian provinces as well as parts of southern Jiangsu and Jiangxi provinces.

8. Jiangxi Xingsheng with Longxing (modern Nanchang of Jiangxi Province) as its seat of government. Under this came most of present-day Jiangxi and Guangdong provinces.

9. Huguang Xingsheng with Ezhou (modern Wuhan of Hubei Province) as its seat of government. Under this came most of present-day Hunan, Guizhou and Guangxi provinces as well as southern Hubei Province.

10. Lingbei Xingsheng with Qara-qorum (renamed Hening, to the north of modern Kharkhorin of ?v?rkhangai Province, Mongolia) as its seat of government. Under this came present-day Mongolia, the Inner Mongolia of China, parts of Xinjiang Province and Russian Siberia.

Apart from the above ten administrative units, a parallel institution—the Commission for Buddhist and Tibetan Affairs was installed in the central government to govern the "Tubo Area" (region where the Tibetan inhabited) which included modern Tibetan Autonomous Region and parts of Sichuan and Qinghai provinces.

Below the level of Xingsheng, there were such political divisions as Route (lu), Superior Prefecture (fu), ordinary Prefecture (zhou) and District (xian).

In 1266, Qubilai decreed that ordinary Prefectures in North China should be ranked into three grades: large (shang), middle (zhong), and small (xia), depending on their registered populations. The dividing lines between categories were drawn at 15,000 and 6,000 households. There were also three grades of Districts: large (shang), middle (zhong), and small (xia), with the dividing lines between categories drawn at 6,000 and 2,000 households. In 1283, he also categorized those ordinary Prefectures and Districts in Jiangnan Region. The ordinary Prefectures were classified into three grades: large (shang), middle (zhong), and small (xia) with the dividing lines between the categories drawn at 50,000 and 30,000. Districts were classified into three grades: large (shang), middle (zhong), and small (xia). In 1295, he revised the ranking criteria of those ordinary Prefectures in Jiangnan with the corresponding figures changed to 100,000 and 50,000.

In 1283, Routes were also ranked into two grades: large (shang) and small (xia). "The registered population of the large Routes exceeded 100,000 households, and that of the small Routes fell short of 100,000 households. In those areas of strategic importance, the ranking standard of large Routes could be lowered to below 100,000 households". (Section seven, Monograph on Offices, Vol. 91, YS)

According to the statistics of 1293, there were altogether 169 Routes, 43 Superior Prefectures, 398 ordinary Prefectures and 1165 Districts in the country. (Section fourteen, Annals of Emperor Shizu, Vol. 17, YS) After some amendments, the final data in the Di Li Zhi (Treatise on Geography) of Yuan Shi (History of the Yuan) was that there were "185 Routes, 33 Superior Prefectures, 359 ordinary Prefectures, 4 Military Prefectures (jun), 15 Pacification Commissions (an fu si), and 1127 Districts" around the country.

There's no denying that the city played a positive role in administration. Under normal circumstances, the seat of a Branch Secretariat would be installed in big cities or at least in medium cities; the administrative center of a Route would be installed in at least medium cities; the government offices would be installed in small cities and town, or sometimes in medium cities.

Cities were also ranked in three grades, large (shang), middle (zhong) and small (xia), according to the population density and the size of the urban area.

The census given by the Ministry of Revenue under the Secretariat in 1291 showed that "the population of the inland cities was 999,444; that of Yangtze-Huaihe Valley and Sichuan was 11,430,878; and that of the coastal areas was 59,848,964. The floating population reached 429,118." (Section 13, Annals of Emperor Shizu, Vol. 16, YS) Judging from the statistics of population of the Routes recorded in Treatise on Geography of the History of the Yuan, in the Yuan Dynasty four fifths of the population was distributed in Jiangzhe, Jiangxi and Huguang Xingshengs which were located to the south of the Yangtze River, and a good half of the rest one fifth dwelled in the Central Plains with only a few scattered in areas like Shaanxi, Sichuan and Eastern Liaoyang Xingshengs.

The proportion of the urban population to that of the whole country was unknown due to the lack of statistics. Thus we could only provide the population of some principal cities here.

The registered population of Dadu Route was 147,590 households, 401,350 individuals. So the line "there were one hundred thousand households in the capital" was usually used by people to refer to the residents in the capital. (Wang Hui, Poem on the Solar Eclipse, Vol. 8, QJJ) However, if every household consisted of four or five people, then the total population of the capital should be between 400,000 and 50,000.

The registered population of Shangdu Route was 41,061 households, 118191 individuals. About half of the population dwelled in the city, while the rest lived in the ordinary Prefectures and Districts under Shangdu Route.

Except Dadu, Routes that were concurrently the seats of the principal cities in north and northwest China and Sichuan with a population over 200,000 included Fengyuan (modern Xi'an with a population of 270,000), Gongchang (modern Longxi with a population of 360,000), Chengdu (with a population of 210,000). Routes with a population above 100,000 included Baoding, Zhengding, Shunde (modern Xingtai), Daming, Huaiqing, Weihui, Dongchang, Caozhou, Dezhou, Yidu, Jinan, Datong, Jining (modern Taiyuan), Jinning (modern Linfen), Bianliang (modern Kaifeng) etc. And Routes with a population about 100,000 included Chongqing, Yan'an, etc.

Jiangnan Region and the Huaihe River Valley were densely populated. And people there mainly dwelled in the cities. Route in those areas with a population above 1,000,000 included Hangzhou (1,830,000), Jiaxing (2,230,000), Yangzhou (1,470,000), Changzhou (1,020,000), Wuzhou (modern Jinhua, 1,070,000), Taizhou (modern Linhai, 1,000,000), Ningguo (modern Xuancheng, 1,160,000), Jiqing (modern Nanjing, 1,070,000), Raozhou (modern Boyang, 4,030,000), Fuzhou (3,870,000), Longxing (modern Nanchang, 1,480,000), Ji'an (2,220,000), Yuanzhou (modern Yichun, 1,000,000), Fuzhou (in Jiangxi, 1,090,000), Changde (1,020,000), Lizhou (modern Lixian, 1,110,000), Tianlin (modern Changsha, 1,080,000), Jingjiang (modern Guilin, 1,350,000), Guangzhou (1,020,000) etc.

Routes with a population about 500,000 included Huai'an, Zhongxing (modern Jiangling), Jiande, Qingyuan (modern Ningbo), Shaoxing, Quzhou (modern Quxian), Wenzhou, Chuzhou (modern Lishui), Huizhou (modern Shexian), Xinzhou (modern Shangrao), Jianning (modern Jian'ou), Quanzhou, Ruizhou (modern Gao'an), Linjiang (modern Qingjiang), Gongzhou (modern Jiujiang), Chaozhou (modern Chao'an), Wuchang, Yuezhou, etc.

Routes with a population about 300,000 included Pingjiang (modern Suzhou), Luzhou (modern Hefei), Anqing, Huzhou, Ganzhou, Hengzhou (modern Hengyang) etc.

In North China, a city with a population above 200,000 could be

ranked as big city, while in South China the figure was 1,000,000. That was also true of a medium city. A northern city with a population above 100,000 could be ranked as medium city, while in the south the figure should be above 300,000.

Such a difference between the north and the south was also reflected in the size of urban area. According to the historical records, Dadu "was 60 li in circumference" (Section one, Treatise on Geography, Vol. 58, YS), almost of the same size as Chengdu and Pingjiang (both of the two cities "were 32 kilometers in circumference" (MKBLYJ, pp. 138 & 174) Whereas Hangzhou "160 kilometers in circumference" was almost five times the size of Dadu. Another sharp contrast could be drawn between the northern cities—Shangdu and Qara-qorum and the southern cities—Shaoxing and Zhenjiang. The urban area of Shaoxing was 45 li in circumference and that of Zhenjiang was 26 li in circumference. Both were much bigger than that of Shangdu about 10 li in circumference and that of Qara-qorum about 12 li in circumference.

The construction of Dadu and Shangdu was the largest urban construction undertaken in the Yuan Dynasty, while that of other cities was much smaller and was mainly the restoration of the old city facilities. Those cities, though most were installed with complete facilities such as city walls, streets, bridges, gardens and water delivery and shipping facilities, were no longer as grand, tidy and splendid as the newly-built Dadu due to the lack of maintenance over years.

7

The citizenship of the Yuan cities was somewhat miscellaneous.

Ever since the establishment of the "two-capital" system, the lifestyle of the Mongol Emperor, the Heir Apparent and their wives greatly changed. They "had had no fixed residence", but now they became sedentary, and settled in cities. Only when during the imperial inspection tour to Shangdu or on a large-scale hunting expedition would they temporarily stay in "nabo" (seasonal camp) or tents.

The Mongol imperial princes and their families dwelled in cities as well. They either had residence in Dadu or Shangdu, built mansions in cities that belonged to their appanage in the Central Plains or Jiangnan Region, or established towns in their appanage on the steppes.

There was a large Palace Guard called "Keshig" in the Yuan imperial palace. Keshig in Mongolian meant "imperial bodyguard". It was, on the one hand, the imperial bodyguard responsible for the safety of the imperial palace. On the other hand it attended to the affairs of the royal family and thus played a crucial role at the Yuan imperial court. The members of the Keshig or the Keshikten enjoyed a high political status and were extremely well paid in the Yuan Dynasty. The Keshig had originally a force of 10000 guards but it was later often overstaffed. After many times of elimination, it had expanded to a force of over 13,600 men by the reign of Emperor Wenzong. And most of the Keshikten dwelled in Dadu or Shangdu.

Officials and Subofficial Functionaries as well as their families were generally the permanent residents of cities and towns. According to the statistics of 1293, "there were a total 2,733 government offices, 221 of which were based in the capital. Of all the 16,425 officials in the country, 1,684 served at the imperial court." (Section fourteen, Annals of Emperor Shizu, Vol. 17, YS) After 30 years, the number of the officials increased by 10,000. "There were altogether 26,690 officials in the country, 22,490 of which were ranked. Of the 2,089 court officials, 938 were semuren and 1,151 were Han Chinese. Of the 506 capital officials, 155 were semuren and 351 were Han Chinese. Of the 19,895 outer officials, 5,689 were semuren and 14,236 were Han Chinese. Of the unranked 4,280 officials, 876 were Confucian Instructors, 232 were Medical Instructors, 921 were

Mongolian Instructors, 73 were Yin-Yang Instructors, and 2,106 were of no fixed positions". (Section one, The Ministry of Personnel, Vol. 7, YDZ) And there were over 100,000 Subofficial Functionaries serving in over 30 different positions throughout the country.

As an agrarian country, the peasants constituted the bulk of the entire population of the Yuan Dynasty. But there also thrived other professions irrelevant to agriculture in the city, such as "Confucians, Buddhist monks, Taoist priests, doctors, sorcerers, artisans, craftsmen, archers, warriors, official receptionists, acrobats, superfluous Subofficial Functionaries, those working in the redundant government offices, entertainers, merchants, prostitutes, beggars, soldiers, posts, waiters in teahouses and taverns, attendants of stores, pharmacists, fortune-tellers, story-tellers, geomancers, Buddhist disciples, odd-job men like messengers and temple officials, salt dealers, hawk raisers, hunters, manufacturers, gold diggers, workers and servants of the wealthy or influential families." (ZSDQJ, Vol. 22) And a considerable group of people of the above occupations dwelled in cities and towns.

In the Yuan Dynasty, Buddhist monks were called monks, Taoist priests were called masters, Christians were called Erkeun (or Arkaim) and the Muslim preachers were called Danishmand. They together with the Confucians, physicians, and fortune tellers were exempted from military service and taxation.

The censuses in the Yuan Dynasty were carried out according to the hereditary occupational groups (huji). There were many different hereditary occupational groups in the Yuan Dynasty, such as the military households, postal relay households, hunting households, salt households, artisan households, in addition to the Buddhist and Taoist households, Confucian households, medicine households which were respectively consisted of the above mentioned Buddhist monks, Taoist masters, Confucians, and doctors. Among all these hereditary occupational groups, the artisan households had the largest urban population. In the Yuan Dynasty, the artisans working for the government were grouped into the artisan households, which consisted of the captives or the artisans captured during the war and the craftsmen recruited from the civilians. The number of the artisan households in the Yuan Dynasty exceeded 200,000. And the members of the artisan households served hereditarily for the government.

Apart from the artisans belonged to the artisan households, there were another large group of artisans in cities and towns who were grouped to the civilian households. According to a popular book about blacksmith published between the Yuan and Ming dynasties, the artisans in the Yuan Dynasty engaged in such occupations as "material supply, large civil engineering, small civil engineering, timber sawing, bricklaying, rock crushing, laborer, handymen, construction, palace construction, rock punching, silver forging, arris making, street paving, well digging, drum making, bell making, forging and polishing, barrel hooping, shoe making, mirror polishing, scissors sharpening, knife sharpening, water proofing, Buddha sculpturing, gilding, painting, jade grinding, pleaching, knotting, embroidering, modeling, etc" It is worth mentioning that of the artisans belonged to the civilian households, some were truly craftsmen making tools, some engaged in the service trade like barbers, and some were in fact folk artists making artistic handicrafts.

Merchants, entertainers and prostitutes mostly dwelled in cities due to the nature of their occupations.

8

The city was also a residential area of an assortment of ethnic groups.

After Chinggis Khan unified the tribes on the steppes and established the Mongol Empire, those nomadic tribes once with distinctive ethnicity

gradually evolved into a single one with "Mongol" as its name and the Mongolian as its language. However, the names of some old clans were still in use in the new tribe, for example, the clan of Chinggis Khan, which was then called the "Golden Family" and became the nucleus of the Mongol ethnic group. Based on the documents and paintings of the Yuan Dynasty, we can roughly depict the appearance of the Mongols. They were mostly of average build. "With a maximum height of five feet and two inches or five feet and three inches, the Tartars were probably not very tall, nor every fat. They had a broad but flat face, cheekbones, single eyelids and thin hair and beard." (MDBL) According to the Europeans, "the eyes and cheeks of the Mongols separated much farther apart than other ethnic groups. Their cheeks protruded high above their mouths. Their noses were small and flat, and the eyes were tiny with eyelids turning upwards to the brows. A majority of them had slim waists with only a few exceptions, but almost all were of medium height. They seldom wore long beard, though some had thin beard above the upper lip and in the chin, which they never trimmed. (CSMGJ, Vol.7)

Of all the ethnic groups in the Yuan Dynasty, the Han Chinese was the most populous and the most widely dispersed one. And most of the inhabitants of the former Jin and Song dynasties were Han Chinese. The Khitan and Jurchen, immigrated to the Central Plains during the Jin and Liao dynasties, were almost "sinicized" and assimilated into the Han Chinese in the Yuan Dynasty. The Khitan, Jurchen, Bohai people, and Korean in Northeast China were all considered Chinese in a broad sense. The Europeans used to call China "Cathay", and the indigenous Chinese "Seres". According to the records of the Westerners, "the Khitan were of short stature······like all the Orientals, they had tiny eyes; they didn't wear beard and their faces resembled those of the Mongols, though not as broad as them." (CSMGJ, pp. 160-162)

From the Mongol Empire to the Yuan dynasty, ethnic groups in

Northwest China and the merchants from the Western Regions, all subjugated by the Mongols through military means, immigrated to East China in large numbers where they formed their own habitations in areas south of the Gobi Desert, the Central Plains, and Jiangnan Region, etc. Among them the most influential ethnic groupes included the Uighurs, the Qauluqs, the Kipchaks, the Qanglis, the Asuts, the Tanguts, the Argyns, the Muslims, etc.

The Uighurs, namely the Uyghurs in Gaochang, were the ancestors of the modern Uygur ethnic group. The Qauluqs were the descendants of the Karluks in the Tang Dynasty. The Kipchaks were a branch of the Turks. The Qanglis were the descendants of the ancient Gaoche people, and also a branch of the Turks. The Asuts were the descendants of the Ancai people in the Han Dynasty. Tangut or Hexi was an appellation used by the Mongols to denote the people of the Western Xia Dynasty. The Muslims in the Yuan Dynasty mainly referred to the Turks in Central Asia, Persians and Arabs who believed in Islam. They were the ancestors of today's Hui ethnic group in China. Of the ethnic groups immigrated from the Northwest to the east, the Muslims were the most widely distributed and outnumbered other ethnic groups.

The ethnic groups in Northwestern China were generally called "semuren", who had relatively distinctive physical features. For example, the Tanguts were strongly built and dark-skinned; the Uighurs were of medium height and had a protruding nose and sunken eyes; the Kipchaks also had a protruding nose and brown hair; the Asut had green eyes.

Besides, some other ethnic groups were also grouped into semuren. They included the Tubo people (ancestors of the modern Tibetans), the Bai people (ancestors of the modern Bai ethnic group), the Luo-luo people (ancestors of the modern Yi ethnic group), the Jinchi and Baiyi peoples (ancestors of the modern Dai ethnic group), the Mexie people

元代城市
生活长卷

The Urban Life of the
Yuan Dynasty

022

(ancestors of the modern Naxi ethnic group), the Hanni people (ancestors of the modern Hani ethnic group), the Pu people (ancestors of the modern Blang ethnic group), the Tuliao and Tong people (ancestors of the modern Zhuang ethnic group), the Miao people (ancestors of the modern Miao ethnic group), the Yao people (ancestors of the modern Yao ethnic group), etc.

After the unification of China, the Mongols imposed a strictly enforced class system on all of society. The four ethnic classes, in order of descending privilege, consisted of the Mongols, the semuren, the Han, and the southerners.

The Mongols, being the "people of the state", belonged to the first class.

The semuren in the second class designated all peoples who immigrated from the west of China, the western region and Europe. They included the aforementioned the Uighur, Qarluq, Kipchak, Qangli, Asut, Tangut, Argyns, Muslim, Tubo, Naiman, etc. The term "semu" appeared in the Tang Dynasty, meaning "various sorts". It was later adopted by the Yuan people to designate the western immigrants due to their diversified nationalities. Sometimes, the semuren were also called "peoples from various countries".

The Han in the third class generally referred to various peoples in the former Jurchen Jin territory in northern China, including the Han Chinese, the Jurchens, the Khitans, the Bohai people, and the Koreans. Most inhabitants in Yunnan and Sichuan Xingshengs that had been submitted to the Mongols were also assigned to the Han.

People in the fourth class were called "southerners". They were all subjects of the former Song Dynasty and were sometimes dubbed "manzi", "xinfuren (newly submitted people)", etc. For southerners, people of the three ranks were "North Chinese". Thus the Han ethnic group was slipped into two separate classes by the Mongols with different prescribed political status and treatment. The Mongols advocated racial discrimination and persecution during their reign. In perspectives of promotion within the bureaucratic system and the imperial civil examination, the Mongols and the semuren were received preferential treatment. And they were also protected judicially, for people from the other two lower ranks were more severely penalized and were forbidden to bear arms and to travel freely. There was no denying that the four-class system implemented by the Yuan imperial court exerted an impact on the city life of the Yuan Dynasty, which will be elaborated on in the following chapters.

The cities of the Yuan Dynasty were dwelled by a multiracial citizenry, which was first reflected in the Yuan harem. Intermarriage was permitted in the Mongol royal family (for more details please refer to the following chapters), thus it was easy to find the Mongols and semuren and sometimes the Han Chinese and Koreans in the imperial consorts concubines. Even the Palace Women were of different ethnic origins, which could be verified by the palace poems of the Yuan Dynasty.

Tailored clothes of brocade from the court indicated royal favor,
At dawn the results of the imperial civil examination were proclaimed at the Gate of Heaven.
The old Palace Woman in the imperial palace was from Jiangnan,
Rejoicing at the southerner's winning first place in the examination.

Without any make-ups and having her hair worn only in a bun,
The young beauty from the south entered the imperial palace.
Upon the scene the hu Palace Women all dissolved into laughter,
All crowding around to apply rouge and powder to her face.

元代城市
生活长卷

The Urban Life of the
Yuan Dynasty

The two poems told the story of the Palace Women from Jiangnan.

The Emperor returned to his spacious tent in Qara-qorum for the hunting,

The Korean Palace Women served in the Palace of the Lady of Handsome Fairness.

The new Palace Women were selected from among a thousand Jurchen households,

Aged only thirteen they were barely able to articulate the word "tea".

These lines talked about the Korean and Jurchen Palace Women.

The Tibetan dancing girls were as if fairies in heaven,

From their tender hands falling the epiphyllum and intoxicating glamour.

The Tangut girl was eighteen years old,

With her long gown opened on the left.

Wearing a bun an inch high above the forehead,

She was ridiculed upon entering the imperial palace.

These lines indicated that there were many Palace Women of the Tibetan and Tangut origins. The attendants waiting upon the royal members and the imperial consorts and concubines were also of different ethnic backgrounds. Besides, the Imperial Preceptors who were the eminent Tibetan Buddhist monks, Taoist personages and the Confucian advisors also haunted the imperial palace.

People of different ethnic backgrounds could also be found in

Dadu City, such as officials, religious personages, soldiers, servants or handicraftsmen engaging in all kinds of trades and merchants from different regions and even countries. The commercial activities could best demonstrate the characteristics of a multiracial citizenry. The following poem was a very good example.

> Vendors bargained over cents,
> Their voices penetrated the silence of the muddy lane.
> Crying their wares they peddled all day long,
> An assortment of dialects could be heard.
> (Poems on Life in the Capital, Vol. 2, CBZLG)

It was also true of Shangdu. "The Han Chinese and people of different ethnic backgrounds lived together, making Shangdu a magnified marketplace." In the downtown area of Shangdu, one could easily find "people fighting and cursing against each other with their own dialects". (Ten Poems on Kaiping, Vol. 16, QRJSJ)

The situation of the other cities was almost the same as that of the two capitals, except that the number of the Mongols and semuren from North China dropped as the city moved southward. We may as well take Zhengjiang and Guangzhou for example.

According to the official census of the Yuan Dynasty, the population of indigenous residents of Zhengjiang was 160,065 households, 613,578 individuals. The population of the "immigrants" was 3,845 households, 10,555 individuals, including 163 Mongols (29 households), 93 Uighurs (14 households), 374 Muslims (59 households), 106 Erkehüns (23 households), 35 Tanguts (3 households), 116 Khitans (21 households), 261 Jurchens (25 households), and 9,407 Hans (3,671 households). (Registered Permanent Residence, Vol. 3, ZSZJZ)

According to the census of 1304, the total population of the

元代城市
生活长卷

The Urban Life of the
Yuan Dynasty

Guangzhou area was 180,873 households, including 180,323 households of the southerners, and only 550 households of the North Chinese. The population of the North Chinese in the urban area of Guangzhou was 372 households, and the figure in Fanyu District, Dongguan District, Zengcheng District, and Xiangshan District was respectively 151, 4, 2, and 21. In Districts like Nanhai, Xinhui, Qingyuan, however, there were no North Chinese. (Registered Permanent Residence, Vol. 6, DDNHZCB) Under the rule of the nomadic emperors, the number of cities, including the newly built and the captured, was no less than that of the Song Dynasty. The nomads who eventually settled in the city were to usher in a new era of the city with other city dwellers.

Part Two

Chapter One | **Ordo (the Palace Tent) in the City**

Along the course of the history, we toured from ordo to the sumptuous palace.

1

For those Southern Song envoys and European Christian missionaries sent to the Great Mongol Empire during the period between 1130s and 1150s, those looming and lofty ordos and complexities of tents on the steppe were something quite impressive.

Ordo was a Mongolian word meaning "palace tent" or "temporary imperial abode" in Chinese.

According to the Southern Song envoy Xu Ting, ordo, the gigantic and round structure, "was literally a magnified felt tent on the steppe, which was covered with two layers of felt with lattice sections made of willow trees built in to get light. It was set up with a door and fastened to the ground with thousands of thongs. With the gilded threshold and columns," it was also called "the Golden Tent" (HDSL). A wooden fence painted with all kinds of patterns and designs was erected around the great tent. It usually contained two or three doors with the biggest one exclusive to the Emperor, for which a Western missionary Rubruck once commented that "though it always remained open, it was not guarded

元代城市
生活长卷

The Urban Life of the
Yuan Dynasty

because no one dared to walk through it." Those who were permitted to enter the ordo were to use the other door (or doors) guarded by soldiers armed with swords, bows and arrows (CSMGJ, pp. 60 & 99).

The exterior of ordo was usually covered with white felt or "white velvet", sometimes with "red velvet", or with hide of lion or leopard of alternate strips of white, black and red. The roof and the walls of the tent were lined with brocade or marten hide. No one was allowed to touch the threshold as well as the ropes holding the tent, or he or she would be severely punished. Within the tent there were a few supporting pillars that were either gilded or elaborately carved and were attached to the crossbeams with gold nails. There had been no compartment within an earlier ordo. But later a corridor was usually separated from the main hall by the pillars, and sometimes, the rear of the main hall was compartmentalized into the imperial bedroom.

The floor of ordo was covered with thick rugs. There was a high wooden platform decorated with gold and silver facing due south, upon which there stood the Emperor's throne. The platform was approached by four stairways with three in the front and one at the back. The middle one in the front was reserved for the Emperor and the other two on its sides were for the nobles and those of lower status. During an imperial feast, those who proposed a toast to the Emperor walked to the throne through one side of the flight and down through the other. The stairway at the back of the platform was reserved for the mother, wife and relatives of the Emperor. The major wife of the Emperor was seated next to but a little lower than him on the platform. His sons and brothers sat on his right on couches in lines down the platform with his other concubines and daughters seated opposite. Stools were provided for the nobles and officials, but the officials of lower ranks were to sit on the rugs. There used to be benches at the doorway of the tent to keep beverages and foodstuffs. They were later used to keep the large royal dinner service.

Such an ordo was especially designed for the Emperor to deal with the state affairs and hold court audiences. The ordo always situated in the center and faced the south on every campground and therefore it always appeared the most "magnificent". It was followed on both sides by the tents of the Imperial Consorts and Concubines with that of the most prestigious Empress on the extreme west side (the Mongols honored the west direction) and that of the lowest rank on the extreme east side. These tents again were followed on both sides by those of the guards and officials together with their families with an interval of about 30 meters.

The tents dwelled by the Imperial Consorts and Concubines were relatively smaller. However, if seen through the eyes of the common people, they were already grand and fabulous enough. The whole tent was lined with golden cloth with a stove burning in the center. In addition, two or more beds could be found in these tents. Whenever the Emperor paid a visit to these tents, he would be seated together with the matron on one of the beds, with their children sitting behind them on the other beds.

About a stone's throw away from the great tent, there was a stable. Nearby there parked hundreds of wagons that kept all sorts of tributes and gifts presented to the Emperor and stuff like gold, silver and silk to be distributed among the nobles. Both the stable and the wagons were properly guarded and were not access to irrelevant people.

A variety of tents were scattered around the great tent, which could be reflected by the line "the white tents strewn over the earth were stars twinkling in the sky". Anyway such gigantic tents employed by the emperor and his wives to deal with the state affairs and live in were limited in number, and most of the other tents were very small. Thus there came the line "laugh not at the small tents with low roofs, for there dwelled either aristocrats or Imperial Concubines." (Yang Yunfu, LJZY)

元代城市
生活长卷

The Urban Life of the
Yuan Dynasty

2

There were two types of ordo. One was movable and the other immovable with the size of the latter much larger than that of the former.

Those constantly migrating ordos were directly loaded onto the carts. Someone had caught sight of a 30 feet wide tent being transported by a cart. The width between the wheel-tracks of the cart was 20 feet, and when the tent was on the cart it projected beyond the wheels on either side 5 feet. Such a cart was driven by 22 oxen, eleven abreast across the width of the cart, and the other eleven before them. The axle of the cart was as large as the mast of a ship. A man stood at the entry of the tent on the cart driving the ox, while those in the tent could either sit or sleep. Such a combination of tent and cart was called "tent on board", at which people would sigh with wonder: "seen from afar, the cart loaded with the tent looked so solemn that its magnificence even eclipsed that of the most great chanyul in ancient times". "Each corner of the cart was installed with either sticks or boards" to stabilize the huge tent. The transportation of the ordo was called qiying; while pitching a camp in a chosen site was called dingying. The procession of the migrating tents was appeared exceedingly great in formidable array, "reminiscent of the circuitous swarms of ants. It stretched for about 15 li and spanned a width nearly half of that of the length." Almost all the other tents were to move with the ordo. Travelling at the front of the fleet were usually the professional sorcerers who were in charge of picking an ideal site for camping and were to prepare for the religious rituals to greet the owner of the ordo who traveled after them. Only when all such preparations had been made would the ordo and other tents be unloaded and erected in the campground in order. The campground would usually situate on the northern side of a slope "to shelter from the wind". The ordo migrated at no fixed time, either every month or every quarter, all depending on the will of the owner. However, it would not move in the dead cold of the winter until the arrival of the next spring (HDSL & CCZRXYJ).

During the reign of Chinggis Khan four major Ordos, in addition to others, were erected in places of Avarga near Luju River (near the modern Kherlen River), Black Forest of the Tuul River (regions in the upper reaches of the modern Tuul River), Salih Plain (situated between the upper reaches of the Kherlen River and the Tuul River) and on the northern side of Hanghai Mountain Ranges. All of these ordos were movable.

In 1236, Ogedei Khan built an enormous tent which could accommodate one or two thousand people in the summer camp Ormaktoua. It was said to be a "permanent tent" and was called "Shira Ordo", meaning "the yellow tent". It was what the Southern Song envoy called the "golden tent". This fixed ordo later provided an important venue for the assembly of the aristocracy and the chieftains summoned by the Mongol Khakhan. In addition to the immovable Ordos, Ogedei and his successors Güyük Khan and Mongke Khan also constructed movable ones.

Qara-qorum ceased to serve as the capital after the accession of Qubilai Khan. As a result, its surrounding seasonal camps, including the Shira Ordo, were forsaken and later reduced to the residence of the Mongol princes defending the northern borders of the Gobi Desert. But soon a new Shira Ordo was put up among the hills on the steppe to the west of Shangdu by Qubilai who then turned it into a fixed architectural complex through the adding palaces to it. The imperial feasts such as "the Jamah Banquet" were usually held it. It was therefore also designated as the Cane Palace.

There were permanent Ordos in Dadu as well. According to CMZ (Book II, Vol. 3) "An exceptionally lavish palace tent, named ordo, would be erected at the coronation of the Yuan Emperor. After his demise, it would then be loaded onto the cart." Such Ordos situated within the palace city of Dadu. After the decease of the Emperor, it would continue to be inhabited by his widows and its name would be changed into

"huo-shi-fang-zi" from then on. "Since Emperor Shizu, the word 'huoshi' in Mongolian had designated the title of the widows of the deceased Emperors. Each of them was allotted a palace tent where they were to offer sacrifices to their late husbands. Every huo-shi-fang-zi was also allotted a Keshig and a group of maids. And its annual expenses and festival gifts and awards were also guaranteed." "Thus 'huoshi', in short, referred to the Empresses of the deceased Emperors." However, huo-shi-fang-zi could also be interpreted as "the carts of the imperial widows", due to the fact that all the imperial widows were to follow the reigning sovereign to Shangdu for the summer holidays in their exclusive wagons. (XJZJY, pp. 216-218) Huo-shi-fang-zi were usually parted to the east of the Daming Palace (which would be mentioned later) within the Donghua Gate of the imperial city of Dadu. A Yuan imperial poem once mentioned the huo-shi-fang-zi:

> Widows of the deceased Emperors lived in the east,
> Sufficed with food and clothing;
> Their tents were guarded by soldiers with flags and weapons,
> Who served the deceased with the old rites.

Until the late Yuan Dynasty, there were altogether "11 Ordos dwelled by the former Empresses".

Some permanent tents and houses, called "nabo", were set up along the traffic arteries between Dadu and Shangdu for the Emperor and his entourage to rest. Nabo, the transliteration of Khitan in Chinese, meaning "field headquarters", "temporary abode" or "temporary tent", originally referred to the imperial tent of a Liao Emperor during the imperial inspection tour. It was later adopted by the Yuan people to denote "the abode of the emperor on tour" (Zhou Boqi, HCJ). Taiping Village located about 10 li due north of Dadu, for example, "was the campground of Emperor Shizu"; Longhu Tai and Bangchui Dian respectively situated to the south and north of the Juyong Pass "were both strewn with the imperial tents called nabo" (Section three, Record of Warcraft, Vol. 100, YS; XJZJY, p. 252) Along the boulevards between Dadu and Shangdu, there were altogether 33 permanent nabo that were smaller than ordos.

In addition to the above fixed ordos and nabo, the Yuan emperors never all together gave up the use of "field headquarters" — the movable tents, especially during the hunting expedition or their expedition to the steppe to the north of the Gobi Desert.

The ordo pitched near or even within the city only symbolized an effort on the part of the Mongols to preserve their traditional customs. The royal members since Qubilai, however, had already lived in palaces.

3

There was a palace city in Qara-qorum, as well as Dadu and Shangdu in later times. All these palaces, though similar in style, were of different regional and temporal characteristics.

In Qara-qorum, there was no imperial city but only the palace city that was situated in the southwest corner of the city and was walled with walls of earth about two li in circumference. The palace city had four gates. "One was reserved for the Emperor, one for his sons and relatives, one for his wives and daughters and one for the populace" (SJZFZS, P. 277) According to the traditional customs of the Mongols, the Emperor used the southern gate, the Imperial Princes and the Imperial Consorts and Concubines the eastern and western gates, and the others the northern gate.

Different from Qara-qorum, the palace city in Dadu and Shangdu was enclosed by the imperial city.

元代城市
生活长卷

The Urban Life of the
Yuan Dynasty

The imperial city of Dadu was located in the center of the southern part of Dadu and its city walls, over twenty li in circumference, were called the screen wall or Lanma Wall, and were lined with thick and lofty trees at the outside. The fifteen gates of the imperial city, with Lingxing Gate in the middle of the southern wall as the front gate, were usually referred to as the red gates since all of them were painted red. Over ten paces within Lingxing Gate there flew the Jinshui River, across which there spanned three white stone bridges named "Zhou Bridge". The bridges were all engraved with auspicious patterns of dragons, phoenixes, and clouds, and appeared as resplendent as jade. Besides, four marble dragons crouched under each bridge which was also surrounded by tall willows. The imperial city was home to not only the palace city, but also the palaces of the Heir Apparent and Empress Dowager, such as Longfu Palace and Xingsheng Palace, the imperial garden, and the Taiye Pond (modern Beihai and Zhonghai in Beijing).

Shangdu was much smaller than Dadu. Its square imperial city, located in the southeast of Shangdu, measured 1,400 meters on each side with its east and south walls overlapped with those of the outer city. The walls of the imperial city were made of mud planks and located and coated with stones. They were about 6 meters high, 12 meters wide at the bottom and 2.5 meters wide at the top. At the four corners of the imperial city walls there were four turrets towering high above the city. Six gates, one on the south and north walls and two on the east and west walls, allowed access. Mingde Gate, the southern gate of the imperial city, was the front gate. Outside of the each gate of the imperial city there was a wencheng (earthen jar city) which was either square or U-shaped. The imperial garden was not included into the imperial city of Shangdu, which was different from that of Dadu.

The palace city of Dadu was located in the east of the imperial city. It was a rectangle measured 480 bu from east to west and 650 bu from south to north. The walls, 35 chi high, was built of bricks and had altogether six gates: three in the south wall with Chongtian Gate, or the Meridian Gate, in the middle and Xinggong Gate and Yuncong Gate on the two sides, one in the east, west and north walls, namely Donghua Gate, Xihua Gate and Houzai Gate. All of these gates were decorated with glazed tiles, vermilion doors, red pillars, red walls and painted ceiling, etc. The entire palace city was overlooked by the turrets standing at its four corners.

The layout of the palace city of Shangdu was similar to that of Dadu. It was located in the center of the imperial city near the east, and was 570 meters wide from east to west and 620 meters long from south to north. The city walls, about 5 meters high, were made of mud planks and coated with stone bars of half a meter thick at the bottom and with gray bricks at the top. And an additional layer of broken bricks was sandwiched between the gray bricks and the mud planks. The palace city of Shangdu had only three gates, with one on the south, east and west walls. The southern gate was called Yutian Gate, and the eastern and western gates Donghua Gate and Xihua Gate. There were also four turrets on the palace city.

Chongtian Gate and Yutian Gate played an important role in the life of the Emperor in that they were where the emperor issued the imperial edicts, which could be demonstrated by the following lines: "At Chongtian Gate amnesties were proclaimed; From the throats of the thousands gratitude was acclaimed." And "Upon the declaration of the imperial edict at Yutian Gate; came a post horse galloping to Dadu like a lightning." (Zhang Yu, Songs under the Imperial Carriage, Vol. 2, ZGBSJ; Hu Zhu, Ten Poems on Luanyang, Vol. 14, CBZLG.) The place beside the two gates was called Saoling and it served as the venue of assembly for the officials waiting to attend the court audience. "Swarms of courtiers crowded before the Yutian Gate" was the line that depicted the scene of the courtiers attending the court audience. (Zheng Yanzhao,

元代城市
生活长卷

The Urban Life of the
Yuan Dynasty

036

4

The main hall in the palace was the place where the Emperor held audiences, hosted feasts and received foreign dignitaries, and it served as the major imperial sleeping quarters as well. Wan' an Palace in Qara-qorum, Daming Hall in Dadu and Da' an Pavilion in Shangdu were such structures with different characteristics in the era of the Mongol Empire and the Yuan Dynasty.

Wan' an Palace was located in the center of the palace city of Qara-qorum. It measured 55 meters from south to north and 45meters from east to west. There were nine lines of pillars from south to north and eight lines from east to west, in all, seventy-two pillars with thirty built into the walls. The palace was a structure with three stories. The first floor was for the Khakhan, the second for his wives and the third his retainers. Two wing halls adjoined it on its both sides, which were especially reserved for the Imperial Princes and the imperial bodyguards. As the first palace built by the Mongol rulers, Wan' an Palace, though considered extremely magnificent at the time, was actually rather simple and crude, and couldn' t bear comparison with the later Daming Hall and Da' an Hall.

Daming Hall, or Changchao Hall, was located in the south of the palace city of Dadu. It measured 200 chi long, 120 chi wide and 90 chi high. It has three gates, with Daming Gate, the main entrance, exclusively for the Emperor and the other two side entrances Rijing Gate and Yuehua Gate for the officials attending the court audience. The hall was raised on a base of three stories and it was surrounded by a marble balustrade carved with the images of dragons and phoenixes. Each vertical post of the balustrade rested upon a sea turtle with head protruding beyond the edge of the terrace, which added an air of magnificence to the hall. A kind of nutgrass grew in front of the hall. It was imported from the hometown of Chinggis Khan to the northern of the Gobi Desert by Emperor Shizu, Qubilai, to remind his children of the hardships in establishing the empire.

As the main audience hall, Daming Hall was designed for the Emperor to "be crowned, celebrate the lunar New Year's Day and have an audience with the courtiers during the festivals and his birthdays". It was elaborately constructed and decorated. For example, its pillars were gilded and carved with coiling dragons. On the each side of the hall was red mullioned window. The ceiling panel was painted in gold and adorned with Yan stones. "The pillars were square, about five to six chi in width, and decorated with raised flowers, golden dragons and clouds. In the center of the ceiling there is a pair of coiling dragons." And the stones used for paving the floor were all "made of piebald stone transported from Junzhou, which were all polished with nuts and shone like the mirror".(Regulation for the Imperial Palace, Vol. 21, NCZGL, sic passim)

Daming Hall was connected with the imperial sleeping quarters with a colonnade which was 240 chi long, 44 chi wide and 50 chi high". The imperial sleeping quarters was commonly known as Nutou Hall. It measured 150 chi long, 50 chi wide and 70 chi high, including 11 bedrooms and 3 shrines of Buddha. Daming Hall, colonnade and the imperial sleeping quarters together formed an I-shaped architectural complex, which was then further surrounded by over a hundred side buildings of 35 chi high. Besides there was a small hall on the other three sides of the imperial sleeping quarters, namely Wensi Hall, Zitan Hall and Baoyun Hall.

Da'an Pavilion, located in the center of the palace city of Shangdu, was actually "moved" from the Northern Song capital Bianliang, where it had been called Xichuan Pavilion. "Because there was not a main hall in the palace city of Shangdu, the magnificent Da'an Pavilion was then

used as the main hall" (Annotation on the Painting of Da'an Pavilion, Vol. 10, DYXGL) Xichuan Pavilion originally measured 220 chi in height and was a three-story structure except for the foundation. "It got slightly damaged during the transportation and was later renovated" in Shangdu. Today among the ruins of the palace city of Shangdu, we could still find a palace base, three meters high and sixty meters long, which was approached by a stairway in the front and was adjoined by an eight-meter wide pavement on the east, west and north sides. It is, beyond any doubt, the site of Da'an Pavilion.

Da'an Pavilion was fairly grand and imposing. Its magnificence and elegant architectural style were vividly revealed in the following lines written by the Yuan poets.

Loftily yet gracefully stood Da'an Pavilion;
Soaring into the sky it towered high above Shangdu.

Da'an Pavilion was the Moon Palace on the earth,
Against the blue sky it invited winds from all the directions.

Da'an Pavilion was in fact Yanchun Pavilion.
Long existed were its tall tower and painted walls.
Shrouded in the misty foliage and veiled by pearl curtains,
It was usually visited by the Emperor in the early summer.

There was a sarira sculpture of Sakyamuni on the top floor of Da'an Pavilion, where the Imperial Preceptor would conduct Buddhist ceremonies. To warn his children against the extravagant and wasteful lifestyle, Emperor Shizu deliberately left his trunk for keeping the clothes on the second floor of Da'an Pavilion, admonishing: "pass it down to my children and grandchildren, hoping it would remind them of my thriftiness, and keep them immune to the prodigality so commonly found among the Chinese." (Biography of Li Bangning, Vol. 204, YS) Just as the nutgrass planted in front of Daming Hall, the truck was the embodiment of Emperor Shizu's high expectations for his descendant. The first floor of Da' an Pavilion was place where the Emperor had the coronation, held an audience with the Imperial Princes and officials, and hosted feasts.

There was also a colonnade and the imperial sleeping quarters attached to Da' an Pavilion, for one could find the remains of the base of a palace, probably the imperial sleeping quarters, of two meters high, thirty meters long and twenty-five meters wide, lying to the north of the ruins of Da' an Pavilion.

Daming Hall, Da' an Pavilion and Wan' an Palace were almost decorated in the same as the ordo. Taking Daming Hall for example, in the center of the hall there was an "exquisite screened platform in the shape of the Chinese Character '山' (mountain), painted in gold and red, which was approached by a stairway and surrounded by red railings". On the platform there set the throne and the seat for the Empress which were flanked by the couches for the Imperial Princes, courtiers, and Keshikten to sit during the feasts."

In summer, "thin sheets of silk painted with dragons and phoenixes" were hung on the walls of the main hall, while in winter they would be changed into "the hides of yellow weasel, and the floor would be covered with those of sable to keep warm. And the shrine of Buddha would also be decorated in the same way to keep warm with the hides of snow weasel on the walls and those of sable on the floor."

The imperial sleeping quarters were also elaborately decorated. The bedchamber was usually furnished with two or three beds lying parallel to one another. Its floor was covered with red and yellow rugs with mats made of fine pieces of bamboo padded beneath". "Golden flowers were

元代城市
生活长卷

The Urban Life of the
Yuan Dynasty

attached to the window lattice that was lined with transparent oilpaper with a floral design and covered with silk coated with tallow which would be changed into felt coated with tallow in winter."

5

In addition to the above architectural complexes, the palace city and imperial city of Dadu and Shangdu were home to other palaces, such as Yanchun Pavilion, Longfu Palace and Xingsheng Palace in Dadu; and Hongxi Hall, Shuijing Hall and Muqing Pavilion in Shangdu.

Yanchun Pavilion, of 150 chi long, 90 chi wide and 100 chi high, was located to the north of the sleeping quarters of Daming Hall. It consisted of two stories, with the first floor named Yanchun Tang and the second Yanchun Ge, connected with a staircase in the east of the Yanchun Tang. A colonnade of 140 chi long, shorter than that of Daming Hall, was attached to Yanchun Pavilion. It connected Yanchun Pavilion with the imperial sleeping quarters, which were of 140 chi long, 75 chi wide and 75 chi high, larger than those of Daming Hall. Yanchun Pavilion was built in the same architectural style as that of Daming Hall. There were also an auxiliary palace on its east, west and north sides, namely Cifu Hall or the Eastern Warm Hall, Mingren Hall or the Western Warm Hall, and Qingning Hall. And the entire architectural complex was also surrounded with over a hundred "side buildings". Yanchun Pavilion usually served as the place to hold Buddhist and Taoist ceremonies.

Apart from the two major structures—Daming Hall and Yanchun Pavilion, there were two other architectural complexes in the palace city of Dadu. Both were located to the west of the right side buildings of Yanchun Pavilion, namely Yude Hall (flanked by two shrines of Buddha) and Chengqing Hall (flanked by two locker rooms). Above Houzai Gate of the north wall of the palace city, there was a pavilion with a stage where entertaining performances would be put on whenever the emperor arrived. The stage was adjoined by an observatory in the east and a bathroom in the west. The "side buildings" of Daming Hall and Yanchun Pavilion were the residence of the imperial consorts and concubines. They were decorated with "flora and rock formations. And each chamber was furnished with three embroidered beds and embellished with patterned sheets of silk on the walls."

Longfu Palace and Xingsheng Palace were located outside of the palace city but within the imperial city, with the former in the south and the latter in the north. The major structure of Longfu Palace was Guangtian Hall, while that of the Xingsheng Palace, the Xingsheng Hall. The architectural layout and the décor of the two halls were similar to that of Daming Hall and Yanchun Pavilion. Both were connected with the imperial sleeping quarters by a colonnade and were surrounded by side buildings. Longfu Palace, originally called the Eastern Palace or the Palace of the Heir Apparent, had been the residence of the Heir Apparent Jingim. It was later renamed Longfu and was dwell by the Empress Dowager after the demise of both Jingim and Emperor Shizu. The Xingsheng Palace was built for the Empress Dowager during the reign of Emperor Wuzong. Some smaller palaces were scattered around Longfu Palace and Xingsheng Palace. For example, Kuizhang Pavilion, the imperial library, was built within the Xingsheng Palace. It was later renamed Xuanwen Pavilion and Dunanben Tang in the late Yuan times when it was changed into the school for the Heir Apparent.

The palaces in Shangdu, such as Hongxi Hall, Shuijing Hall, and Xuanwen Hall, were built in the similar architectural style to that of palaces in Dadu. They mainly served as the place where the Emperor conducted state affairs, studied, and hosted feasts. On the north wall of the palace city of Shangdu there was also a giant pavilion, called Muqing Pavilion. It "consisted of hundreds of rooms", and could rival the one

that was situated above Houzai Gate in the palace city of Dadu.

6

Both Dadu and Shangdu were featured in imperial gardens where the royal members played and relaxed. There were two imperial gardens in the imperial city of Dadu. One was in the north of the palace city where all kinds of exotic flowers and rare herbs grew. In the garden there was a patch of land of eight qing, which was especially reserved for the Emperor to till and plant. The other one was located to the west of Longfu Palace where there were such scenic spots as rockeries and the Liubei Pond. The imperial gardens in Shangdu was located in the north of the imperial city which largely preserved the scenery of the steppe with "tall elms and short willows; garden lotus and purple chrysanthemums".

The famous Taiye Pond was situated in the west of the palace city in Dadu and to east of the Longfu Palace and Xingsheng Palace, including the modern Beihai and Zhonghai. It was filled with lotus, with dragon boats boarded by the Emperor and his wives shuttling in between. There were two isles in the lake—the south one and the north one. The south isle was called "Yingzhou" (the present-day Tuancheng) which was capped with Yitian Hall or Yuan Hall; the north isle was Qionghua Island which was renamed Longevity Hill or Wansui Hill in 1271. The Longevity Hill that measured "tens of zhang in height" was studded with exquisite rock formations. "It was approached by trails in all directions and dressed in lush green vegetation which was dotted by shade of tall trees, reminiscent of the fairyland." On the top of the hill stood a palace called "Guanghan Hall", which was 120 chi long, 62 chi wide, and 50 chi high. In Guanghan Hall there was a chamber called Xiaoyu Hall, within which there was a throne and a couch for the Emperor and his attendants to rest while touring in the hill. Guanghan Hall was endowed with a spectacular view because it was situated at the highest point of Dadu. From the palace one could either gaze at the West Mountain shrouded in clouds afar or get a bird's eye view of the Dadu city. A marble bridge over 200 chi long connected Longevity Hill to Yingzhou which was also winged by two long bridges extending to the land. The east bridge was a common wooden one while the west one was a wooden suspension bridge. In addition, Longevity Hill and Yingzhou were also installed with such facilities as hot spring resorts, toilets and dressing room where "the imperial consorts and concubines freshened their make-up". To the east of the Taiye Pond, there situated the imperial game park where all kinds of rare animals were raised.

In addition to the imperial gardens situated in the capitals, hunting parks also dotted the vicinity of the Yuan capitals, especially Shangdu, for the emperor to "practice hunting". "700 li northwest of Shangdu there was the North Pavilion"; "The East Pavilion and West Pavilion, respectively situated 50 li east and west of Shangdu, were rich in water and grass, poultry, fish and other animals. An imperial abode was established there and whenever the Emperor passed there on his hunting expedition, he would always stop to practice falconry." There was another hunting preserve in Changanor (white lake) to the south of Shangdu. It was installed with the imperial abode called "Hengjia Hall", which was as tall as yet more formidable than the palaces in Shangdu".

The palaces built in the Yuan Dynasty emphasized symmetry and decoration. They were mostly wooden structures embellished with bright colored glass. Although most of them were built in the traditional Chinese architectural style, some were constructed with great originality by absorbing the Mongolian architectural elements. For example, the I-shaped architectural complex consisted of the main audience hall and the sleeping quarters with a colonnade spanned in between was obvious a product

元代城市
生活长卷

The Urban Life of the
Yuan Dynasty

of the Ordo system. The décor of the palaces was also very Mongolian. All the main audience halls were furnished with a throne, couches and drinking vessels, and all the bedchambers were plainly decorated with rugs and animal skins. Even when the Mongol Emperors had settled in the spacious palaces, they still refused to give themselves up to the Chinese living style and always endeavored to preserve Mongolian rituals and customs.

Chapter Two | The Hu bed, Elephant-drawn Carriage and the Goat Cart

Since the unification of China, the barriers to the interflow of commodities between the south and the north had been completely removed. Therefore, a variety of household goods flew into the imperial palace and the residence of prince as tributes or commodities either made by imperial artisans or sold by the merchants, which greatly enriched the life in the imperial palace.

1

During the era of the Mongol Empire, the throne of the Khakhan in ordo was long and wide, just like a bed. It was made of ivory and was painted gold, with exquisite carvings and lavish decorations of gold, precious stones and pearls. Such a throne was, in fact, the hu bed decorated with gold and gems, and was designated as "the gilded hu bed with the dragon head" in Jiangnan Region (areas south of the lower reaches of the Yangtze River) or the "imperial couch" in north China. After Qubilai established the capital in the Central Plains (the middle and lower reaches of the Yellow River), it continued to be used in the main audience halls, such as the imperial couch carved with seven dragons in Daming Hall which was installed with a seat for the Empress and was padded with a white cushion sewn with gold threads, the imperial couch inlaid with a jade dragon wrought in gold in Guanghan Palace, and the

元代城市
生活长卷

The Urban Life of the
Yuan Dynasty

imperial couch of camphorwood engraved with golden dragons in Longfu Palace etc. Such imperial couches, or thrones, however were widely used in the imperial palace as seats instead of beds. The imperial couch was usually flanked by lines of couches for the Imperial Princes and courtiers to sit on.

The "imperial bed" or "dragon bed" in the bedchamber of the Emperor, though sometimes also referred to as "the imperial couch", was used as a bed in its real sense. They were usually made of different materials like marble, nanmu, red sandalwood, camphorwood etc. The bed for imperial consorts and concubines was designated as "the silver bed" or "ivory bed". Such beds were usually installed with a golden screen made of nanmu in the front. There was a built-in wardrobe in most imperial bedchambers and those of the imperial consorts and concubines.

The imperial couch for the Emperor and Empress was always padded with a cushion. The most commonly used cushions in the imperial palace were square and were called "kejim" in Mongolian. Such cushions were often made of golden brocade; they were thus also referred to as "the square cushion of golden brocade". Beneath the square cushion there was usually a green cushion which was also made of golden brocade. The only difference between the square cushion and the green cushion was color, for that of the square cushion was yellow.

The bedding used on the imperial bed in every imperial bedchamber included several mattresses and a quilt made of nas i j. Whenever the Emperor was to sleep, golden petals sprayed with exotic perfume would be scattered over the bed. According to the record, there were several kinds of mattress used in the imperial palace, such as Jihua mattress, mattress sewn with gold threads, long mattress, silk long mattress, narrow mattress, and thick mattress, etc. (XJZJY, P221; Section one, Record of Vehicles and Garments, vol. 78, YS) Nas i j, a Persian word, denoted a kind of precious golden brocade from the Central Asia. It was usually used by the royal members to make quilts. Besides, there were also embroidered pillows and canopies on and above the imperial bed.

Qubilai, who advocated thrift, was against the use of golden brocade in the imperial palace. One day he went to visit his ailing son Jingim who was then sick in bed. When beholding his son lying under a quilt of golden brocade, he immediately criticized his daughter-in-law Bairam-Egechi: "I always considered you a virtuous woman. When did you become so extravagant?" Bairam-Egechi knelt down and answered: "I have never used it before. But now the Heir Apparent was sick in bed, and I thought it would help expel moisture in the quilt." With those words, she immediately changed the bedding. (Section two, Biography of the Imperial Consorts and Concubines, vol. 116, YS)

When the Mongol Emperor held an audience or hosted a feast in the palace or ordo, he seated himself on the imperial couch with the aristocrats on the couches and the officials on the rugs. Meanwhile there was an engraved ivory wine table or wine table with Raden beside the entrance. Such wine tables were about eight chi long and seven chi and two cun wide with a tall gold pitcher standing on them. So tables and chairs were not required on such occasions. But when the Emperor read over and commented on official documents, read books and crowned Empress and Heir Apparent, he would need tables and chairs. There were also a wide range of tables in the imperial palace, such as the imperial desk, red-lacquered lamp table, red-lacquered incense table, table for imperial edict, table for imperial edict to confer nobility titles, table for imperial seal, table for memorial, and table for tribute etc. The imperial desk was for the emperor to deal with the daily state affairs. It was covered with a gold-sprinkled red silk table cloth with dragon and cloud design with a gold-sprinkled red Mongolian silk lining. Beside the imperial desk there were four iron balls and two poles capped with a dragon head from which dangled a tassel. The red-lacquered lamp table and red-lacquered

incense table were used to hold the incense burner, incense container and candlestick. They were respectively covered with a gold-sprinkled yellow silk table cloth with dragon and cloud design and a gold-sprinkled red silk table cloth with dragon and cloud design. The table for imperial edict, table for imperial edict to confer nobility titles and table for imperial seal were used to hold respectively the imperial edicts, imperial edicts to confer nobility titles and imperial seal. They just looked the same as the incense table and were covered with the same table cloth as that of the incense table. The table for memorial and table for tribute were used to hold respectively the memorials to the Emperor and the tributes presented to the Emperor. They were also covered with a table cloth and would be placed with a potted orchid on top. The chairs used in the imperial palace were mostly the gilded folding roundback armchairs which were thus referred to as "the golden chairs". Besides, stools, especially those short gilded ones, were also used in the imperial palace.

Whenever the Emperor made an imperial inspection tour, the imperial desk, incense table, golden chairs and golden stools as well as the table cloth and its lining would also be carried along with the Emperor.

2

The imperial cities of the capital were installed with bathrooms and toilets, among which the Wenshi Bathroom in the willow woods of the Longevity Hill in the Taiye Pond of Dadu was the largest. "It was a maze of nine interconnected caves with good lighting. In the central cave, there was a coiled dragon with its head cocked to the left and its mouth holding a bead. When the cave was filled with hot spring water, the water would spread to other eight caves, and then a strand of fragrant mist would rise from the mouth of the dragon, which was fairly wonderful." It was an ideal place for the royal members to bathe in the hot spring (Regulation for the Imperial Palace, Vol. 21, NCZGL)

The sanitary wares often used by the Emperor included the golden basin, golden water bottle, well-pulley, golden towel, golden incense burner, golden incense container, golden spittoon in the shape of a kettle, golden spittoon, and golden duster etc. The golden basin was a gilded basin decorated with silver. The golden water bottle was a silver soup bottle with a lid, a handle and a spout, and it was decorated with gold." The well-pulley was used for fetching water from a well. It was a gilded X-shaped object with its top ends coiled up to which attached a red silk rope. The golden towel was a lined gold-sprinkled red silk with dragon and cloud design. All these objects were used by the Emperor when washing his face the rinsing his mouth. The golden incense burner and the golden incense container were also made of silver and gilded. The former was a pedestaled lotus censer covered with an iron ball engraved with dense wavy patterns. And the latter was a round case seven cun in diameter. The golden spittoon in the shape of a kettle and golden spittoon were made of also made of silver and gilded. The former had a wide mouth, a hollow belly and a lid; and the latter was lidded and was as round as a fou2. These two objects were indispensable in ordo and imperial palace, because spitting was banned there. The golden duster which was made of the tail of red yak or "white and fine soft cattle-hair" was used to drive away the mosquitoes and flies. "The end of its gold handle was carved with a dragon head and it was dyed into different colors". A special person was put in charge of these sanitary wares, and he had to carry them along with the Emperor when he was on a tour. (Section two & three, Record of Vehicles and Garments, Vol. 79 & 80, YS)

Toilet paper had long been used in the toilets of the imperial palace. A typical case was that when Bairam-Egechi was waiting on the Empress, "she served the Empress wholeheartedly. She would even test the toilet paper for softness with her own checks before sending it to the toilet.

(Section two, Biography of the Imperial Consorts and Concubines, Vol. 116, YS)

There were also a wide range of fans in the imperial palace, such as the round red fans for escorting the emperor, the feather fans of big, medium and small sizes for cooling the air, and round green fans, etc. Fans were especially desired during the hot summer days in the imperial palace. The Ministry of Rites of the Secretariat had to provide the imperial palace with fans three days before the Dragon Boat Festival. "The covering of such fans were unprecedentedly exquisite with such delicate kesi embroideries of people, stories, trees and flowers, plumes, landscape." Apart from the covering, the other parts of these fans also reflected the artisans' esthetic judgment and fantastic skills. Some fans were with jade handles and others were sewn with silver threads." The Imperial Manufactories Commission also had to send fans to the imperial palace as tributes, such as the painted fans, emerald fans and fans painted with landscape. All the fans would be distributed among the imperial consorts and concubines as well as the Imperial Princes for the summer.

During the era of the Mongol Empire, when the khakhan and the aristocrats rode outside, they protected themselves from the sun with an umbrella or "a mini tent" tied to a long stick. Later sunshades studded with precious stones were invented for the Khakhan. After the accession of Qubilai, the varieties of the imperial umbrellas and canopies were gradually completed, such as the large umbrella, square purple umbrella, square red umbrella, canopy, crank umbrella, red umbrella, yellow umbrella, feather canopy and peacock canopy. "All the imperial umbrellas and canopies of the Yuan Dynasty were capped with a golden stupa, while those before the Song Dynasty were flat at the top." And only the round-bottom canopies were used on the imperial chariots.

3

Candles were the major lighting material in the Yuan imperial palace, which were made by artisans supervised by the Supervisorate of Candles under the Ministry of Works of the Secretariat. The Imperial Regalia Service which supervised the Candles Service was established in the imperial city of Dadu as well as Shangdu to "take charge of the candles and the keys to the bathrooms and halls in the imperial palace." Candle Keepers in the Imperial Regalia Service were responsible for the candles in the imperial palace. Hence there was the saying "the Imperial Regalia Service controlled the major provision for the palace; their candles were as chunky as a rafter." The candlesticks in the imperial palace were almost made of silver and were usually designated as "the silver candlesticks". The Yuan Palace poems had recorded the scene when the candles were lit in the palace.

Candles burned out on the silver candlesticks and incense vanished in the thurible,
Leaning against the screen the dancing girl was divesting herself of the costume.

The candles has extinguished on the silver candlesticks by the morning,
Yet she still indulged in her dreams by the window.

When the Emperor made an imperial inspection tour, the lantern instead of candle would be used during the trip. Emperor would leave Dadu for Shangdu in the summer, and he had to pass through the Jugong Pass at night every year. When "the imperial procession crawled between two extended lines of lanterns", the people were greatly impressed by "the city over lit by thousands of lanterns and torches". Usually, when the Empress and the imperial consorts and concubines returned to the imperial palace of Dadu, it was already dark. They would then be welcomed by "guards of honor holding large red lanterns with long red-lacquered rods coated with silk with golden dragon design." (XJZJY, P. 222) Lanterns were also used by the imperial concubines and consorts at night, as was revealed by the palace poem:

> I lit the lantern to illuminate my courtyard in the snowy night,
> Hoping the goat cart would turn up from the darkness.

In addition to the red lanterns, lanterns with white shade, or "silver lantern", were also used in the imperial palace.

Firewood, charcoal and coal were used to cook and get warm in the Yuan imperial palace. And they were provided by such government agencies as the Fuels Service and the Firewood Office in both Dadu and Shangdu. One thing needs to be mentioned is that coal has already been widely used in the North China by then. Marco Polo also mentioned coal in his famous book.

"Throughout this province there is found a sort of black stone, which they dig out of the mountains, where it runs in veins. When lighted, it burns like charcoal, and retains the fire much better than wood; insomuch that it may be preserved during the night, and in the morning be found still burning. These stones do not flame, except a little when first lighted, but during their ignition give out a considerable heat.

It is true there is no scarcity of wood in the country, but the multitude of inhabitants is so immense, and their stoves and baths, which they are continually heating, so numerous, that the quantity could not supply the demand; for there is no person who dares not frequent the warm bath at least three times in the week, and during the winter daily, if it is in their power. Every man of rank or wealth has one in his house for his own use; and the stock of wood must soon prove inadequate to such consumption; whereas these stones may be had in the greatest abundance, and at a cheaper rate."

Coal was also produced in the vicinity of Dadu. "There were over thirty coal pits in the Dagu Mountain forty five li west of Wanping District, and over ten anthracite pits in Taohua Gou fifty li southwest of Wanping." "The merchants in and out of Dadu would go to the West Mountain to buy coal with ox carts in the ninth lunar month and then sell it in the markets in Xin' an or outside Dadu before the arrival of the spring, for it would be very difficult of the ox carts to travel on slushy roads. In the past the government taxed the coal, and hundreds of ox carts of coal would shuttle between the coal pits and the city every day. After the second or third lunar month, merchants came to sell inferior coal in the city on ox carts. Later coal was found in the North Mountain but it was considered inferior and was seldom bought by the residents in the capital. And therefore was very cheap." (XJZJY, P. 209) Coal was also widely used in the imperial palace in the Yuan Dynasty, which could be proved by the following line:

When returning to the east of the palace at night,
I saw coals still glowing in the ashes of incense.

4

In the past when the Mongol Khakhan made an imperial inspection tour, he would travel, as has been mentioned before, in the movable ordo which, however, was substituted by "the elephant-drawn carriage" since the accession of Qubilai Khan.

元代城市
生活长卷

The Urban Life of the
Yuan Dynasty

His Majesty capture Yunnan with his horse rod,

From which he brought the elephant to China.

(Watching the Elephant, Vol. 1, QYJ)

"On the first day of the first lunar month of the dingyou year (1237), the elephant was brought to the capital. Although it appeared sluggish at the first sight, it, in fact, strode at a high speed, and only the horse could catch up with it. Towered above all the houses in the capital it was distinguished from all the other elephants by its height" (XJZJY, P. 232) The elephants were originally imported from Yunnan which was later joined by Burma, Champa, Jiaozhi, Chenla, Jinchi (southwestern Yunnan), and Cheli. But transporting the elephants involved great danger. In 1280, a soldier named Lao Yin was strangled to death by an elephant when he went past Ansu Prefecture with the elephant sent to the court as tribute from Yunnan. The tamed elephants in Dadu were kept and raised in the tall and spacious elephant house situated to the south of the Southern Park in Xijin Ward, or of the modern Jishuitan and Qianhai and Houhai of Shichahai in Beijing. "Whenever the Emperor made an imperial inspection tour, the elephant-drawn carriage was always driven by a foreign official." (Section two, Record of Vehicles and Garments, Vol. 79, YS)

The "elephant-drawn carriage" was actually a large wooden sedan chair carried by four elephants, each with a driver on it. The sedan chair was installed with a canopy and decorated with flags. It was padded with a cushion sewn with gold threads and coated with lion hides. The Emperor would change to ride an elephant or on a chariot drawn by two elephants on the narrow mountain paths or in mountain passes. The elephant-drawn carriage was also called "elephant sedan chair" or "elephant chariot". It started to be manufactured in 1280.

Because people in the Central Plains had never seen an elephant before, they were regarded it with great curiosity. And the poets praised them unanimously:

His majesty arrived in Shangdu,
In a tent carried by the elephants.
(Zhang Yu, NXQ)

Imposingly marched the golden tent,
The moving mountain of jewelry on the back of elephant.
(Ke Jiusi, GXSS)

The imperial abode in Changanor,
Looking forward to the arrival of the elephant-drawn carriage.
(Yang Yunfu, LJZY)

Although the imposing elephant-drawn carriage looked majesty, it was not as safe as it was comfortable to ride. In 1282, Liu Haoli, Minister of Personnel, reported to the Secretariat: "His Majesty had a predilection for the elephant-drawn carriage to travel on between the two capitals. Powerful as the animal was, it was, however, not easy to control. If there should crop up any accident, even if there was a large group of escort at hand, to whom could His Majesty turn for help?" Just as Liu had expected, soon there happened an incident in which some attendants narrowly escaped from being trod by a frightened elephant. (Biography of Liu Haoli, Vol. 167, YS) Several years later, another accident happened on Qubilai's way back to the imperial palace after he finished hunting, in which the elephant of the imperial carriage was frightened into a stampede by an "entertainer" performing a lion dance. Fortunately, a tragedy was averted by an attendant named He Sheng who timely stopped the elephant with his own body. Dangerous as it was, Yuan Emperors never truly gave

元代城市
生活长卷

The Urban Life of the
Yuan Dynasty

up this means of transport.

In addition to the elephant-drawn carriage, there were a wide range of two-wheeled imperial chariots with different colors. And the color the chariot depended on its material. The jade chariot, for example, was green. Its saddle, bridle, and harness were all green and it was even pulled by a green horse. Whereas the golden chariot was red, the ivory chariot yellow, the leather chariot, white, the wooden chariot black. In the chariot there was an armchair with continuous yoke back padded with a square cushion and a cushion of golden brocade and a rug on the floor. In the area enclosed by the carved balustrade there were all kinds of bedding prepared for a rainy day. The ceiling of the chariot was "painted with a green dragon in the west, a white tiger in the east, a rosefinch in the north and a tortoise in the south". At the entry there hung "a door curtain with dragon and cloud design". In addition, each chariot was also installed with a red-lacquered cupboard to hold such objects as golden incense burner and golden incense container.

Sedan chair and goat cart were the major means of transport for the Emperor to travel in the imperial palace.

The sedan chair, made of agalloch eaglewood, "had a back in the shaped of the Chinese character '山' and a bejeweled screen with dragon and cloud design in the front." Behind the screen there was an imperial couch carved with dragons and clouds with a footrest lying in front. And the imperial couch was also padded with a cushion. The Emperor usually drove a goat cart to visit his wife or concubine at night. The goat cart thus played an important role in the imperial harem, which could also be mirrored by the following lines.

The goat cart traveled through the palace at midnight,
Leaving the lonely boudoir trembling in the cold autumn.

Divine were the palaces bathed in the moonlight,
Shadows of parasol trees climbed up the screened windows.
Not would I insert salty bamboo branches in front of the door,
In bed I only listened to the sound of the passing goat cart.

Later, "the five cloud chariot" was invented for Emperor Shundi to travel in the imperial palace. "The chariot had five compartments, with the central one reserved for the Emperor and the others for his wives. Its railings were made of delonix regia and its hubs of ebony. A luminous pearl was hung in at the top of the chariot which saved the Emperor the trouble of lighting the lantern when driving in the imperial palace at night." (YSYTJ)

5

When the emperor made an imperial inspection tour, he would be accompanied by a large entourage including the Empress, imperial consorts and concubines, Heir Apparent, Imperial Princes and the courtiers who mainly travelled on "palace carriages" or sometimes by horse. Thus it was not difficult to imagine what a spectacular it was when all these palace carriages drove together on the road.

From Changping the palace carriages set out in order,
Two extended lines of lanterns illuminated the city in the dark.

In palace tents the windows of the later emperors,
Arrived in Shangdu following the imperial edict.
Constant streams of carts flew by with stong yaks
And fine white horses of saddle wrought in gold.

The "palace carriage" was, in fact, the carriage used by the nomads on the steppes. Such carriage could be divided into two kinds according to their functions. One was the passenger carriage, and the other freight cart.

The passenger carriage on the steppe was called "the black carriage" or "felt carriage". It was a kind of elaborate wagon covered with waterproof black felt and drawn by oxen or camels. Married women usually embellished their carriages with embroidery works. Some even placed a statue of Buddha in a decorated felt carriage parked before the tent. Those who travelled on the steppes would find the felt carriage a good substitute if they couldn't ride the horse.

Freight carts on the steppes were subdivided into two categories: the large ones for carrying the tents and the drays for carrying other things. The cart for carrying the tents was called gerlugs (tent cart) in Mongolian. The tent cart, as we have mentioned before, was one of such carts. However most tent carts on the steppes were those small ones pulled by only one or several oxen or camels instead of those giant ones drawn by tens of oxen. Although people could also travel on the tent cart by staying in the tent on it, they still prefer the felt carriage to it during the migration.

There were also a wide range of drays on the steppes, such as the dray for carrying wool and the lockable dray. The lockable carts were used for carrying coffers. We could find a detailed description of such coffers in the books written by some western missionaries. "They weave light twigs into squares of the size of a large chest, and over it from one end to the other they put a turtle-back also of twigs, and in the front end they make a little doorway; and then they cover this coffer or little house with black felt coated with tallow or ewe's milk, so that the rain cannot penetrate it, and they decorate it likewise with embroidery work. And in such coffers they put all their bedding and valuables, and they tie them tightly on high carts drawn by camels, so that they can cross rivers(

without getting wet) , such coffers they never take off the car. When they set down their dwelling-houses, they always turn the door to the south, and after that they place the carts with coffers on either side near the house at half stone' s throw, so that the dwelling stands between two rows of carts as between two walls." "A single rich Mongol or Tartar has one or two hundred such carts with offers." (CSMGJ, pp112-113) Such carts with coffers were obviously lockable though it was not always necessary to do so. Most freight carts used for transporting foodstuffs on the steppes were, like those flatbeds or horse-drawn carts in the Central Plains, uncovered.

Vehicles travelled slowly on the steppes. A woman alone could lead twenty or thirty such carts pulled by oxen or camels. The driver would tie the carts one after the other and then sat on the front one driving the ox, and all the others followed after with the same gait. Should it happen that they came to some bad piece of road or a river, he would untie them, and take them across one by one. Even those huge carts pulled by over ten oxen were driven by only two men—the owner and his servant, for "the tame oxen easily submitted to their command." A shaft was placed horizontally in front of the cart to keep balance. Thus even the imperial concubines or the palace maids could drive the palace carts without any difficulty.

There is a vast steppe lying between Dadu and Shangdu. To cross the steppe, one needed to travel in a carriage or by horse. Thus the Yuan imperial palace was always equipped with light but firm saddlery to facilitate driving and riding. And such saddlery was no different from what the ordinary nomads had used. "The saddle and rein weighed no more than eight jin, and the horses wouldn' t be burdened when galloping on the steppes; the saddle rose vertically at the front while flat at the back, so the rider would not get hurt from a sudden turnaround; the stirrups were round on the top while wide at the bottom, so it was easy to

元代城市
生活长卷

The Urban Life of the
Yuan Dynasty

step on and fix the feet while riding. The stirrup leather, being coated with tallow, was durable and waterproof; it was also convenient to use during the riding as it only measured one cun in width and less than four zong in length." (HDSL) Apart from the saddle and stirrups, one also needed reins, a stumbling rope, a lasso pole, and a horsewhip, etc. in riding. In the Yuan Dynasty, it was also a popular practice to decorate the saddlery with gold, silver or precious stones.

When the Emperor went for an outing, especially hunting, he would sometimes ride. So a special group of people would follow him to help take the saddlery. The saddlery the Emperor used included a horsewhip container, the Mongolian saddle, and a small gilded and four-legged table decorated with silver which was used for the Mongol Khakhan and Yuan Emperor to mount the house.

6

Apart from the daily necessities, the Emperor also needed timepieces to keep the time.

In Daming Hall of Dadu, there was the lotus clepsydra, a large water clock designed by Guo Shoujing, an eminent scientist in the Yuan Dynasty. The water clock was a four-tiered structure of gold measured one zhang and seven chi in height. "It was decorated with pearls outside and powered by a machine inside, which transported the liquid from one container to another." There were twelve small wooden idols in the water clock, each representing a deity holding a tablet that told the hour. "An idol would pop out of the clock at each hour to announce the time." Another wooden idol would stand inside the clock "with a finger pointing to the minutes of the time". At the each corner of the clock, there also stood an idol carrying a bell, a drum, a zheng3, or a cymbal. The bell rang at the first quarter of the hour, and the drum was beaten at the second quarter of the hour, zheng at the third quarter and cymbal at the fourth quarter. (Section one, Record of Astronomy, Vol. 48, YS)

Later Toghun Temür, Emperor Shundi, devised another clepsydra. "It is six or seven chi high, and half as broad. It contained a wooden case, concealing a number of jars for the water to trickle into. On the top of the case was the model of the Hall of Three Saints and in the middle of the chest a fairy holding up bits of stick showing the time. At each hour she floated up to perform her task. At each side were two saints in golden armor, one with a bell, the other with cymbals, with which they struck the hours during the night most punctually; and a lion and phoenix flapped or capered about to accompany the music. East and west of the case were the halls of the sun and moon, with six flying fairies standing in front. At midday and midnight the fairies came in pairs, and crossed a fairy bridge to the Hall of Three Saints, after which they went in again. Never had such an elaborated machine been made in the past." (Section six, Annals of Emperor Shundi, vol. 43, YS)

Smaller clepsydras could also found in the other halls of the imperial palace. "Apart from bronze clepsydras, there were also exquisite lamp clepsydras and hour glasses." (Section two, Vol. 3, CMZ)

Two Supervisors of Water Clocks served in Daming Hall to take care of the clepsydra and record the time. And two Timekeepers waited outside the hall to announce the time, with one crowing like a cock on the top of the left tower and the other "kneeling beside the steps of the tower to announce the time with a tablet in hands." The Water Clock Section under the Directorate of Astronomy was in charge of the water clocks in the palace. And it was usually the Timekeeper that announced the beginning of the day in the palace.

There were four types of calendars in the Yuan Dynasty. They were the State Calendar, Uighur Calendar, Muslim Calendar and Shoushi Calendar, of which the Shoushi Calendar developed by Guo Shoujing was

元代城市
生活长卷

The Urban Life of the
Yuan Dynasty

the most simple and accurate. Every Winter Solstice was the day when the Astrological Commission distributed the new calendars of the next year in the court, so it was also called "the Calendar Day". The calendar presented to the Emperor was printed on white paper with colorful paintings of Chinese Zodiac, and its title was written in Mongolian. The Muslim calendar presented to the Emperor was printed on the purple paper. Besides, the new calendars would also be presented to the Heir Apparent, Imperial Consorts and Concubines, Imperial Princes, and also to the Secretariat, Bureau of Military Affairs, Censorate and other government agencies. From following palace poem we could take a look at the scene when the calendars were distributed in the palace.

> Feasts ushered in the auspicious day,
> With the sun shining from high above.
> Officials of the Astrological Commission presented calendars
> To every Imperial Prince in front of their couches.
> (Ke Jiusi, GCSWS)

Chapter Three | Layout of Dadu

As a typical Yuan city, Dadu was well installed with such basic infrastructures as city walls, city gates, bell tower, drum tower, streets, bridges, wards, markets and taverns. Besides, the new city was also featured in many scenic spots and historical sites.

1

It was considered a privilege to enter the imperial palace through the red city gates of the imperial city of Dadu. But here we were more willing to take you to tour around the urban area of the Dadu city.

Upon arriving in Dadu, one would be awed by the imposing city walls, city gates, the Bell Tower, and Drum Tower.

According to the archaeological studies, the outer wall of Dadu measured 28,600 meters in perimeter. The east wall was 7,590 meters, west wall 7,600 meters, south wall 6,680 meters, and north wall 6,730 meters. The outer city was a rectangle, covering an area of about 50 square kilometers. The city walls tapered all the way from the foundations upward and they were built in accordance with the general technological standard of the Yuan Dynasty. The walls measured 24 meters thick at the foundation, 16 meters high, 8 meters thick at the top, approximately in the proportion 3:2:1.

The city walls of Dadu were made of pounded earth in the traditional

元代城市
生活长卷

The Urban Life of the
Yuan Dynasty

way by using board frames and ramming. Such mud walls were prone to collapse in rainy days. Someone had proposed to change them to brick ones, and some were even willing to supply the bricks to coat the walls, which, however, restricted by economical conditions, was only realized on a small scale by "a short brick wall" at the west corner of the city. In early Yuan times, reeds were used to prevent the walls from being soaked by rain. "Every year the mud walls of Dadu would be thatched with reeds to protect it against the rain." "Thus an abundance of reed beds were developed and every year millions of reeds could be harvested. The reeds would then be woven together and piled on the walls in the proper order." It was not until the reign of Emperor Whenzong that this annual practice was canceled for fear that enemies should capture the city by setting the inflammable reeds on fire. (XJZJY, p. 1) In fact, coating the city walls with reeds not only was ineffective in protecting the walls, for the rain could still penetrate the need sheets and thereby corrode the mud walls, but also greatly burdened the state finances. For example, in youyuan period, an abundance of labor and money were dumped on restoring the city walls.

There were 11 city gates in Dadu: three on the east wall, namely Guangxi Gate, Chongren Gate, and Qihua Gate; three on the south wall, namely Wenming Gate or Hada Gate, Lizheng Gate, and Shuncheng Gate; three on the west wall, namely Pingze Gate, Heyi Gate, and Suqing Gate; and two on the north wall, namely Jiande Gate and Anzheng Gate.

Why was this carefully planned, highly symmetrical and perfectly rectangular city installed with only 11 gates instead of an even number, such as 12, 8, or 10? Actually it was deliberated arranged by its architect, Zicong or Liu bingzhong, to invite the protection from tutelary deity Ne Zha, by comparing the three gates on the south wall to Ne Zha's three heads, the six gates on the western and eastern walls to his six arms, and the two gates on the north wall to his two feet.

The axis of Dadu started from Lizheng Gate in the south, and then ran straight to Zhongxin Pavilion, the landmark indicating the center of the city, through Lingxing Gate of the imperial city and Chongtian Gate and Houzai Gate in the palace city. Fifteen bu west of Zhongxin Pavilion there was Zhongxin Tower. It was indeed the first time in the history of urban architecture that the center of a city has been determined through the on-the-spot survey and marked during the phases of design and construction.

The avenues were lined with tall houses and towers,
The peals and drumbeats shook the air of the capital.

The Bell Tower and the Drum Tower, both situated to the west of Zhongxin Tower, were built separately. The Drum Tower, or Qizheng Tower, was located in the south of the city. It was where the timepieces and chronophers—water clock, drum and horn were kept. The Drum Tower was in the north, directly facing the Bell Tower. But different from the capitals of the succeeding dynasties, although the Bell Tower and Drum Tower were located in its central area of Dadu, they were not on the axis of the city.

2

Marco Polo, the Italian traveler, who had stayed in Dadu for a long time, pointed out that "the boulevards of the capital were such that from one city gate there was an uninterrupted view across the city to the opposite city gate" The streets of Dadu were indeed orderly laid out, just like a chessboard. "The streets that ran from south to north were called 'meridian', while those east-west ones 'parallel'. Among them the wide ones measured 24 bu in width (about 372 meters) and the narrow ones 12 bu in width (about 18.6 meters). In addition, there were 384 fire lanes and 29 alleys." The alleys measured 6 bu wide. (XJZYJ, p. 4) Another scholar named Huang Wenzhong also mentioned in his Dadu Fu (Ode to Dadu) that "as for its road system .It had crisscross streets and maze of lanes, with the wide ones permitting about 50 horses to gallop side by side, and the narrow ones four wagons." (Section one, Vol. 16, TXTWJ) However, there were a "T-shaped" intersection and a diagonal road in Dadu as well.

Except a few flagstones, most streets in Dadu were dirt roads due to the lack of stones, which were, therefore, always dusty.

Between the shuttling the horses and carts,
Danced in the wind the brown dusts.

Gusts of wind swept along the road,
Sending the dusts whirling into the sky.
(Poems on Life in the Capital, Vol. 2, CBZLG,)

These dirt roads could become muddy in rainy days.
Muddy and bumpy the road was,
In between of nowhere stuck horses and carts.
Pervasive were ponds of water on the road.
Waterlogged was the entire land.

Therefore someone sighted "the Yanshan Mountain became drenched mire in rainy days." (Preface to Feng's Poem of Praying to Heaven for Clear Days, Vol. 43, QJJ; Songs of the Trip, Vol. 14, WSXSWJ)

To cope with this problem some local government chose to pave the roads with slabstones and some even raised the flagstones tens of centimeters above the ground to drain the water and mud, which could not only keep the road surface clean, but also help to nourish the trees lined aside. The roads in the meadow of the imperial garden in Dadu were also the raised flagstones.

Dadu was watered by two major water supply systems. One was for transporting grains. It consisted of the Gaoliang River, the Haizi Lake, and the Tonghui River. The other provided water for the imperial palace. It composed of the Jinshui River and the Taiye Pond. As for the ordinary inhabitants in Dadu, they mainly relied on the wells for water and sometimes they would also do the washing in Hazi. Hazi was actually a lake which was located in the north of the imperial city and to the south of the Wanshou Mount. It was thus named because it was a boundless lake where the springs in the northwest of the mountain converged. Women who lived nearby or near the Bridge of the Bureau of Military Affairs would usually come here to do the washing. There were seventeen public wells in Dadu for the residents to fetch water and water their livestock as well. Water in these wells was drawn through a kind of newly designed noria. "Such noria fit all kinds of wells in that it was flexible in length to ensure the two wheels geared to each other. A chain of wooden bailing buckets was slung to the vertical wheel and the buckets hung down into the well. When one was to fetch water from the well, he only needed to push the horizontal wheel above the well which geared to the vertical one and thereby drive it as well as its buckets to move. The water held in bailing buckets would then to be poured into the stone water pipe, and water would then flow to the stone trough outside of the railings around the well. From dawn to dusk, the noria would always be at work to meet the needs of the inhabitants and their livestock." (XJZJY, p. 110)

In addition, the drainage system in Dadu was also highly developed. Ditches lined on the both sides of the south-north avenues were discovered during the archaeological excavation of Dadu. These ditches measured one 1 meter wide and 1.65 meters deep and were made of long slabs of stone with some also covered with slabs of stone. All these ditches ran from north to south according with the terrain of Dadu. Besides, there were stone culverts beneath the city walls to drain the sewage produced by the city.

There were many bridges in Dadu as well. Among them, the number of the recorded ones has already exceeded 100. The majority of these bridges were made of stone. These stone bridges were mostly "decorated with balustrades and ornaments of divine animals carved out of marbles in the West Mountain, paved with polished grey stone, and were made in a style that was typical of Jiangnan Region." And "ingots of cast iron were used to fill the seam of the pavement." (XJZYJ, p. 208)

3

In Dadu there were a total of 50 wards among the crisscrossing streets, where residences, markets, and government offices were situated. And each ward was installed with an archway, on which the name of the ward was inscribed. Now let's make a tour of these wards from south to north under the guidance of the books Yuanyi Tongzhi (Record of the Unification of Yuan Dynasty) and Xijin Zhiji Yi (Collection of Scattered Writings of the Record of Xijin).

Passing through Longjin Bridge or "the first bridge under the heaven" one could see the main entrance of Lizheng Gate in the south of Dadu. Lizheng Gate has three entrances. The one in the middle was reserved for the Emperor; the left one usually remained closed; only the right one allowed access.

Right across Lizheng Gate was Lingxing Gate of the imperial city with a wide and straight approach called Qianbu Corridor lying in between.

To the east of Qianbu Corridor there was Wuyun Ward where the office of the Secretariat was situated. Its name "wuyun" meaning auspicious clouds of 5 colors was derived from a Tang poem in which there was a line "shrouded in the auspicious clouds of five colors were the triple constellations". The "triple constellations" in the line were usually used to indicate the three most powerful administrative organs in the Chinese history, namely the Secretariat, the Chancellery and the Department of stage affairs. On the west side of Qianbu Corridor was another ward called "Wanbao Ward" whose name literally meaning "all the most precious things" came from the line "All the most precious things were harvested in autumn".

The Secretariat was the top administrative organ in the Yuan Dynasty whose office was originally set in the northern city while the office in Wuyun Ward was then belonged to the Department of State Affairs. Thus the two administrative bodies were dubbed as "the northern department and "the southern department". After the merger of the two administrative organs, the office of the Secretariat was moved over to the southern city leaving its old office to the Hanlin Academy.

The new office of the Secretariat was a walled compound with three etiquette doors, namely the outer etiquette door, the middle etiquette door and the inner etiquette door. "Huge gates and tall walls, it was very imposing". The outer etiquette door was near to the eastern city gate-tower of Lizheng Gate with a board inscribed two bold Chinese Characters "Du Sheng" meaning "the Secretariat" hung over it. The east-west thoroughfare ran right across the middle etiquette door which connected Wuyun Ward with Wanbao Ward. As for the inner etiquette door, it was further divided into three doors, with one in the central and the others on each side.

Passing through the inner etiquette door one could find five large chambers referred to as the "Main Audience Hall of the Secretariat".

They were "spacious and bright with ornate beams and walls." The main audience hall was then flanked on the east and west by side rooms which were "elaborately decorated with landscape paintings". Five flora-lined Zhishe or breezeways radiated from the main audience hall to the five houses called "the Chamber of the Secretariat" or "the Chamber of the Capital" which were also flanked by several side rooms. These annexes were the working place of the Principal Officials of the Secretariat. In the spring and winter they would work in the eastern annexes, while in the summer and autumn they would move to the western ones. The seat for the head of the Secretariat, the nominal highest official of the Secretariat (usually the Heir Apparent), was placed in the center of the chamber and was flanked by those for the Grand Councilor of the Right, the Assistant Director of the Left, Managers of Government Affairs and other officials in descending seniority. Behind the chamber there were rockeries "shrouded with foliage and flowers" adjoined by a little pavilion. In addition, the entire architectural complex also included the Hall of Judges, and the Hall of Consultant in the Secretariat, etc.

Wenmig Gate was also called "Hada Gate, for behind it there was the residence of Prince Huda. Near the Residence of Prince Hada there situated Muqin Ward and Leshan Ward. These wards respectively derived their names from the book Shangshu (Classic of History) and the historical allusion of "Pince of Dongping in the Han Dynasty who found great ecstasy in doing good deeds".

The office of the Censorate, the central supervisory institution, was in the third lane of Hada Gate. It was also an architectural complex including etiquette doors, the main audience hall, breezeway, as well as the main chamber. To the west of the office of the Censorate was Chengqing Ward whose name was derived from the phrase "set all under heaven in order."

To the west of Chengqing Ward stood Qilu Ward which was

adjoined by the Court of Imperial Entertainment, the imperial winery, on the west. Qilu ward got its name from "its adjacency to the official wine cellar" because in Maoshi (Classic of Poetry) the word "qilu" alluded to wine.

The office of the Astrological Commission, which dealt with astrology and calendrical science, was located at the south eastern corner of the capital, not far away from Wenming Gate. The ward near to the office of the Astrological Commission was called Mingshi Ward, because in Zhouyi (Book of Changes) there was the line "men of noble character should work on accurate calendars to precisely keep the time."

Fucai Ward was located to the west of Taida Street within Shuncheng Gate. It was thus named because it was adjacent to the official storehouse. To the east of Taida street there was Shiyong Ward whose name came from Shangshu (Classic of History) meaning "the populace were more coherent in great upheavals". To the north of Shiyong Ward was Anfu Ward whose name "anfu" in Mengzi (Mencius) meant peace and happiness.

According to the traditional Chinese architectural style, the Ancestral Temple was in the east of the capital while the Altars of State were in the west, which was also inherited by the Yuan capitals. Thus Ancestral Temple, built in 1280, located to the north of Qihua Gate in the eastern wall of Dadu. The Altars of State, built in 1293, located between Pingze Gate and the Yi Gate in the western wall of Dadu.

North of the Ancestral Temple there was Muqing Ward whose name was derived from Maoshi (Classic of Peotry), while to the south of the Ancestral Temple was Huanghua Ward.

West of Muqing Ward there situated Yinbin Ward, Renshou Ward and Penglai Ward. Renshou Ward was thus named because it was adjacent to the Imperial Dispensary, while Penglai Ward got its named from "the Penglai Mountain abode of immortals", for it was situated right across

the Taoist Temple Tianshi Gong.

Sicheng Ward, Mingzhao Word and Baoda Ward were situated to the west of Huanghua Ward. Baoda Ward was thus named because it was near to the Bureau of Military Affairs. The office of the Bureau of Military Affairs was located to east of the Yuhe River outside of the eastern wall of the imperial city of Dadu. Across the Yuhe River there was Chaoyang Bridge which was also called the Bridge of the Bureau of Military Affairs.

Passing through Pingze Gate one could find Jincheng Ward and Xianyi Ward in the south, and Xicheng Ward, Futian Ward, Mingyu Ward and Jiqing Ward in the north.

Beside the Zhongxin Pavilion there was Wufu Ward which derived its name from "Five Happiness started in Shangshu (Classic of History). When walking along the street extending from the east of the Zhongxin Pavilion to Chongren Gate, one could find Jinggong Ward, Zhaohui Ward and Juren Ward on the southern side of the street, and Jintai Ward, Lingchun Ward and Juxian Ward on the northern side.

The offices of the Route Command and Police Commission of the Dadu Route were situated to the east of the Zhongxin Pavilion. And to northwest of the office of the Route Command was the Confucius Temple and the office of the Directorate of Education.

Passing through Heyi Gate, one could find Youyi Ward, Taiping Ward, Faxiang Ward, Yongxi Ward and Fengchu Ward in the south and Xijin Ward right next to the Haizi Lake in the north.

On the other side of the Haizi Lake, there was the diagonal road. Fengchi Ward and the Yuxuan Ward were located to the north of the road. The names of these two wards had something to do with the Secretariat, for the office of the Secretariat was originally situated to the north of Fengchi Ward. "Fengchi Ward was near to both the Haizi Lake and the old site of the Secretariat, hence the name 'fengchi' meaning phoenix pond." The name of Yuxuan Ward came from Zhouyi (Book of

Changes), according to which a tripod carried by jade hooks symbolized great harmony. The hooks to carry tripods were later used to refer to the three high-ranking officials in the imperial court, one of whom was the head of Secretariat. And as the ward was adjacent to the office of the Secretariat, it was thus named Yuxuan.

To the east of Fengchi Ward lay the street of the Bell Tower. On the Bell Tower one could see Liren Ward and the Zhaoxian Ward in the northwest and Dangui Ward in the northeast. And on the Drum Tower, one could see Qinghua Ward in the south, beside the bridge of Hazi.

Passing through Guangxi Gate in the eastern wall of Dadu one could find Qiansi Storehouse. And within Suqing Gate in the western wall was Wanyi Storehouse, to the east of which there was Yongfu Ward.

In addition, there were Shansu Ward, Gantang ward, Qianshan ward, and Kefeng ward within Jiande Gate in the north wall, Huaiyuan Ward, Qianning Ward, and Qingyuan Ward in the northwestern corner of the city, and Taiheng Ward in the northeastern corners of the city, not far from Anzheng Gate.

4

There were two major commercial areas within Dadu. One was near to the Bell Tower and the other was in Yangjiao Market in Anfu Ward within Shuncheng Gate.

Around the Bell Tower there was the most important and the most bustling commercial district in Dadu. In front of the Bell Tower, There huddled not only the rice market, the wheaten food market, the poultry market where foodstuffs could be bought, the silk market, the hat market where clothes were sold(for example, groceries like the needle shops all crowded at the southeastern corner of the city), but also the timber market selling the building materials such as wooden barriers, wooden pillars

元代城市
生活长卷

The Urban Life of the
Yuan Dynasty

with crossing grooves at the bottom, all sorts of sandalwood rafters, worn-out hempen sandals, bricks and tile, plaster, hemp-fibred plaster, hemp bits, etc. The hemp-fibred plaster sold in Dadu came from the West Mountain and was also called "true hemp-fibred plaster" because it was made of hempen sandals that had been washed, dried, and chopped up instead of coal ash. And the shredded hempen sandals could substitute ramie as a building material. Besides, there were luxury markets, for example, the pearl market and the coral market in the first lane to the west of the street before the Bell Tower. "The whole lane was packed with gold, silver, pearls and rare objects" and a wide range of rare curios and precious gadgets could be found there.

In addition, there were a total of five "Qionghan Markets" or employment markets where people found jobs in Dadu. The biggest Qionghan Market was in the street right behind the Bell Tower. It, in turn, gave birth to three other markets, namely the firewood market, the ironware market and the boot market where "soles of shoes, shoe-pads, and other parts of shoes were sold".

Beside the diagonal road near the Haizi Lake, there stood Wanghu Pavilion, one of the famous scenic spot in the capital, whose high visit rate making the diagonal road a street "packed with taverns and stages". The doors of the taverns were usually painted with the portraits of the Four Lords of the Warring State (Lord Chunshen of Chu , Lord Mengchang of Qi, Lord Pingyuan of Zhao, and Lord Xinling of Wei), fenced by red-lacquered railings, and roofed by delicate eaves, like that of the palace." The walls with doors were "painted with horses and wagons with grooms, umbrellas and flags." "The door leaves of some taverns were also painted with the portraits of Zhongli of Han and Lü Dongbin of Tang", both of whom were among the Eight Immortals. In front of the doors of taverns there usually stood "a golden three-layered tablet in the shape of the Character "山" (mountain)" called

"Huanggong Lu".

There was also a livestock market called Yangjiao Market or "Yangshi Jiaotou" in Dadu. The word "Jiaotou", meaning "the place where people from the four directions under heaven converged", was the synonym for "market". The livestock market could be subdivided into many smaller markets, including the sheep market, house market, ox market, camel market, donkey and mule market, etc.

Apart from the one situated behind the Bell Tower, another two Qionghan Markets were located near Shuncheng Gate, with one near the southern street of Shuncheng Gate, and the other in a place called "Caodar" within Shuncheng Gate.

In the early Yuan times, there had been a slave market in Yangjiao Market where livestock as well as slaves were sold. It was later banned by the Yuan Court, but its premises were preserved "for the later generations to take warning from it".

Apart from the markets in the two major commercial areas, there were other specialized markets in and around the Dadu city.

The high demand for vegetables and fruits in the city gave birth to such markets as the vegetable market, fruit market and fish market. There were several vegetable markets in Dadu, all of which were strewn around the city gates, such as the third bridge of Lizheng Gate, the T-shaped street of within Hada Gate, and the area outside of Yi Gate. The fruit markets were respectively distributed outside of Shunyi Gate, Anzhen Gate and Yi Gate. Among them only one was next to a vegetable market. One may find that all the vegetable markets and the fruit markets was installed around the city gates, which was quite reasonable in that the proximity of the markets to the suburbs could greatly facilitate the transportation and storage of the vegetables and fruits. One li outside Wenming Gate there was a pig market and a fish market.

Fuels, or in modern terms, the resources was a thorny problem in

元代城市
生活长卷

The Urban Life of the
Yuan Dynasty

Dadu, for the large population in the city would consume a staggering amount of fuels every year. Although coal had already been found and used as fuels in Dadu, as has been mentioned before, the coal produced by the state-owned coal pits were mainly supplied to the imperial palace instead of the markets. And even the coal and charcoal brought into the city by the brokers were mostly sold to the merchants and traders instead of the populace. Thus the reed and firewood remained the major source of fuels for the inhabitants in Dadu. Even the imperial palace used the reed as fuel in addition to the coal. Part of the reeds harvested from the reed fields outside of Dadu were used to coat the city walls and part were supplied to the imperial kitchen. In Dadu there was a Shaofan Bridge which led to the imperial kitchen. Every day the firewood and reed would be transported to the imperial kitchen through the bridge, which attested to importance of reeds in the palace. The populace also relied heavily on the firewood and reed to cook meal and get warm.

> Rooted in the cold soil were the white reeds,
> Flickering in the wind like torn brooms.
> Yet millions of households in the capital,
> Take thou as the firewood to cook meal.
> (Ten Poems Composed in the Boat, Vol. 3, QRJSJ)

Thus reeds were indispensible to the populace. In addition to the firewood and charcoal market lying behind the Bell Tower there were another three scattered in Dadu. One was located outside of Shuncheng Gate; another was near Qiansi Storehouse; a third was near to the office of the Bureau of Military Affairs. Besides, there was a coal market in front of Xiuwen Ward, and hay markets outside of every city gate. Even with all these markets, the price of the firewood and reed was such that not only those ordinary citizens but also those medium and low-ranking officials couldn't afford the firewood and reed. Wang Hui, an official served in the Yuan court, for example, was forced to suffer from coldness in the winter because the he could not afford either firewood or reed. He then made a poem to express his depression.

> Firewood was sold at the price of cinnamon and pearls,
> Alas! Coldness still lingered on even in the middle of February.
> (Songs of Dadu, Vol. 28, QJJ)

In the late Yuan times, someone proposed to fetch coal from the West Mountain through waterway to alleviate the fuel shortage in Dadu. In 1342, the Grand Councilor of the Right and the Assistant Director of the Right of the Secretariat submitted a memorial to the throne in which they say "the population of the capital was now well over a million. Thus it was insufficient to solely rely on the peasants to supply the hay and firewood. The only solution to our fuel shortage was the coal in the West Mountain which could be accessed by boat if we connect our waterway in the capital with the Jinkou River." Emperor Shundi adopted their proposition and sent laborers to lengthen the Jinkou River. However, all the efforts went in vain due to a failure design. (Section one, SGWS)

The stationery stores clustered around Qilu Ward. "The marketplace was packed with shops for carving and engraving documents, writing letters, and making ivory spoons and chopsticks, and red bridles, reins, and gold and silver tablets for horses, and brands such as red braids, four-colored braids, and blue tablet braids for scholar officials. There were also shops selling all kinds of asparagus walking-sticks." In front of the office of the Secretariat, one could find the book market and the paper market. Besides, there was a wagon market in eastern Dadu within Qihua Gate and a timber market in the western city.

In addition to the shops in the marketplace, there were a good

元代城市
生活长卷

The Urban Life of the
Yuan Dynasty

number of others strewn in Dadu. Among them many were mobile ones. "Often the peddlers would rent half a house which faced south on a high street to sell fruits, vegetables, give a haircut, tell the fortune, and mill rice."

"Ever since the reign of Emperor Shizu, every district has started to celebrate the Imperial Birthday by setting up a shed to hold lavish banquets and put on plays." (CMZ) In fact, other festivals, such as the Spring Festival, the Lantern Festival and the Dragon Boat Festival, were also observed throughout the country. "During the festival, merchants would set up sheds made of reed mats in the marketplace. In the sheds they would hang paintings of landscape and paintings featuring birds and animals." foodstuffs and daily necessities were also sold in such shops. And the goods sold in these sheds as well as the paintings hung in them often changed according to the festivals. But such kind of sheds were different from those housing the banquets in the counties, because they were, by nature, temporary booths set up by urban merchants. But the latter were also very common in Dadu. Once there was a big festival, "high-ranking officials in the court and wealthy families would set up large sheds" to feast their relatives and friends. Paintings would be hung and "fruits, wine, cakes, vegetables, and meat products would be provided" in these sheds.

The storehouses in Dadu served as the supply stations in the city. Some of the storehouses were owned by the government, while some belonged to private owners like merchants and officials. Most of the state-owned storehouses were walled to prevent from being raided by thieves and robbers. Bazuosi Storehouse in Dadu, for example, was fortified by a circumference of high and thick walls except the main entrance. Besides, an additional protection of thorn-like devices was added to the walls, making it impossible for the thieves to climb over the walls. Its cache was built of bricks with its windows and doors firmly locked. "In addition, the storehouse was also guarded by the gatekeeper.

5

Temples and religious structures also played a vital role in the urban life.

The Town God's Temple of Dadu was situated at the southwestern corner of the city, not far from Shuncheng Gate. The Temple of Guan Yu was located to the east of Haizi Bridge and to the south of Zhaohui Ward. Dukang Temple where god of wine was worshiped was located in the Court of Imperial Entertainment. Wenchang Temple was situated to the north of Luqi Ward which was adjacent to the Court of Imperial Entertainment. And Dongyue Palace where God of Mount Tai was worshiped was located two li outside of Qihua Gate. Sacrificial ceremonies and other relevant activities would be held in these temples every year.

The Yuan emperors believed in Lamaism. And every Yuan Emperor would go in for large-scale construction of temples after they mounted the throne. When the Dadu city was planed, it was found that Daqingshou Monastery where the dagobas of Monk Haiyun and Monk Ke'an were situated just sat on the line of the future south wall. To protect the monastery, Qubilai ordered to bend the city wall so as to include the monastery and the dagobas into the city. Therefore, Daqingshou Monastery was later situated within Shuncheng Gate. Among the new monasteries in Dadu, four were most representative. They were Dahuguo Renwang Monastery built by the Empress of Qubilai which was located by the Gaoliang River in the western city, Dashengshou Wan'an Monastery (the modern Baita Monastery) built by Qubilai which were located with Pingze Gate, Datianshou Wanning Monastery built by Emperor Chengzong which were located near Zhongxin Pavilion, and

Dachengtian Husheng Monastery built by Emperor Wenzong which were located at the foot of the Yuquan Moungtain, in the west suburb of Dadu.

As the famous Taoist monastery, Changchun Palace was the most important monastery of the Quanzhen Sect. It was located in the old city of Yanjing. In the new city Dadu, a branch monastery of Changchun Palace was built in Sicheng Ward within Qihua Gate. After the unification of China, the head of Zhengyi Sect in Jiangnan Region was summoned by the Emperor for an audience in the north. He then built a Taoist monastery— Chongzheng Wanshou Palace in Penglai Ward in Dadu.

There were two Christian Churches in Dadu. Both were built by a Roman Catholic missionary during the years between 1293 and 1305. One was situated "in front of the imperial palace of the Khakhan" (CSMGJ, p. 229), probably in Wanbao Ward; the other was two and a half li away from the former.

There were several Islamic mosques in Dadu as well. They were generally referred to as Libai Temple.

6

In Dadu there were "Eight Great Sights of Yanshan Mountain", respectively the Autumn winds on Taiye, the Qionghua Island in shady springtime, the Great Wall surrounded by lush Greenery at the Juyong Pass, the Rainbow Floating over the Jade Spring, the Golden terrace in the Glow of the setting sun, the Moon over the Lugou Bridge at dawn, the western Hills shimmering in Snow, and Drifting Rains at the Ancient City of Jizhou.

The Taiye Pond and the Qionghua Island were situated in the imperial city. Therefore their beauty could only be gazed by the commoners from afar through the red gates.

The Juyong Pass, extending for over 30 li, was situated between two mountains in the northwestern of Dadu. The red gates of the entrance and exit were guarded by armed soldiers. In the years between 1342 and 1345, three pagodas were added to the Juyong Pass. The gates under the pagodas allowed access. And the walls of the gates were inscribed with Buddhist scriptures in six languages, namely the Sanskrit, Tibetan, The phags-pa Script, Uigur Script, Western Xia Script and Chinese. The purpose building these pagodas was to "convert the pedestrians to Buddhism and had them bathed in the mercy of the Buddha".

The mountains in the west suburb of Dadu were generally referred to as the West Mountain Ranges, which included the Yuquan Mountain, the Shouan Mountain, and the Fragrant Mountain. The Yuquan Mountain was already a scenic spot usually visited by the Jin emperors. The lake lying before the Yuquan Mounntain, called the West Lake or Wenshan Lake, was the predecessor of today's Kunming Lake in the Summer Palace. The Shouan Mountain, or Wuhua Mountain, lay to the west of the Yuquan Mountain. During the reign Emperor Yingzong of Yuan, the Dazhaoxiao Monastery (modern Wofo Temple) was built in mountain. The Fragrant Mountain was situated to west of the Shouan Mountain. Half way up the mountain there was the Dayongan Moonestary built in the Jin Dynasty. After revamped in the Yuan Dynasty, the monastery became more magnificent. Every autumn, citizens of Dadu would surge to the West Mountain to appreciate the red maple trees, which had become a custom among the populace.

The Lugou Bridge in the southern city of Dadu was built in the Jin Dynasty. It was a beautiful stone bridge with eleven segmental arches. The balustrades of the bridge were caved with hundreds of lions of different gestures and sizes. Liu Binzhong, the designer of Dadu was also deeply impressed by the beautiful bridge.

Jimen was originally in the old Jin capital Yanjing. After Dadu was built, Yanjing was referred to as the old city. As the new city was located

元代城市
生活长卷

The Urban Life of the
Yuan Dynasty

082

to the north of the old city, Dadu was also called the northern city and Yanjing the southern city.

The prosperity of northern city was beyond measurement,
While the southern city was packed with forsaken edifices.

Most of the former residents of the southern city moved to the northern city, leaving behind a skeleton of city whose houses were either deserted or torn down, and whose city walls and moat were totally destroyed. Only those Buddhist monasteries and the Taoist temples were preserved in the southern city. They were later visited as scenic spots by people of Dadu.

Although there were many gardens and places of historic interest in Dadu, they were not open to the commoners. "Only those who had power could get access to the famous gardens installed with exquisite ponds and beautiful flowers. When the flowers were in full blossom the gardens would be packed with horses and wagons, making these places the paradise of the privileged" (Cheng Lü, The Autumn Pavilion, Vol. 9, AYTWJ)

7

The houses of the citizens in the capital varied greatly from district to district and from the poor to the rich.

The size every house in the city was restricted by many elements, such as the size of the urban area, the layout of the district, and the population. After Dadu completed, the Yuan court decreed that "all the imperial relatives and officials of merit should build their residences within the land granted to them. And every piece of land measured eight mu." However, the residences of the privileged often outgrow their allotted appanages and some would even extend to occupy the street. The court, therefore, had to impose a ban on such unauthorized occupation of streets, decreeing "he who violate the decree should be punished and the houses occupied the street should be torn down". (Miscellaneous Rules, Vol. 27, TZTG) The wealthy and powerful families, however, turned a deaf ear to the decrees. There were still quite a few squatter buildings in Dadu.

The residences of the officials, aristocrats, and business tycoons clustered together, forming a special housing area in the city. The area around Lizheng Gate was generally known as "the land of gentry", for it was the residential area of the aristocrats and court officials. The land around Shuncheng Gate and Pingze Gate provided temporary lodging for the merchants in the capital. In addition, the northern street behind the West Palace was occupied by the central government offices, and most high-ranking officials lived there. Every residence had gatekeepers who were either old men or young children. They stuck to their posts from morning till dusk to lead the horses for their masters. In front of Huanghou Tavern there a group of breweries. All the taverns on the street were built in different styles and featured in different wine and dishes.

There were many magnificent structures in these residential areas. For example, within Shuncheng Gate, there was Qingyuan Tower standing right across Lichun Tower, which was the former residence of the Grand Councilor Bayan in the late Yuan times. And to the north of Qingyuan Tower there was Chaoyuan Tower. By the Haizi Lake, there stood Wanghai Tower which was the residence of another powerful courtier El-Temür. And in the southwestern city there situated a garden which belong to Ahmad, the Chancellor of the Exchequer of Qubilai.

The relics of Houying Mansion discovered during the excavation of Dadu showed that the mansion consists of three compounds, a main one and two side ones. All these three compounds spanned a width of

nearly 70 meters. The northern house in the main compound measured 13.47 meters in width. Elaborately constructed, it was furnished with exquisite articles for daily use, like porcelain and lacquer ware, and such rare objects as crystal and agate articles. The mansion was believed to be the residence of people of middle or upper classes. Besides, there were many additional facilities in and out of the mansion, such as the stone or iron lions and the "leather-hat" houses. It was a common practice in Dadu to put a pair of stone or irons lions beside the door of the courtyard.

"Those noble or wealthy families in the capital would put a pair of lions beside the main gate, while marble lions would be installed at the two side gates." "Leather-hat houses could be found within the outer gate of the residence of a high-ranking official. They were thus named because they resembled the two ears of a leather hat worn by the officials."

The residents in Dadu mainly lived in the central and southern parts of the urban area, and only very few lived in the northern city. The restraint imposed on the size of the house in Dadu resulted in high land price and rents. Burdened by the high rental expenses, people from outside Dadu often "found it uneasy to live in the capital". They sighed: "the wealthy families owned rows of mansions, while I only complain about the days being fading too quickly". "The days are fading two quickly" became a catchword in Dadu because the rents were collected at the end of the month. The housing conditions of the craftsmen, vendors, low-ranking officials, servants in the government offices, Confucian scholars and vagrants differed greatly from that of the dignitaries. For example, after the fall of the Southern Song Dynasty, the Song eunuchs were brought to Dadu to serve in the Yuan palace. One of them was allowed to move of the palace to recuperate. The house where he lived in Dadu, however, had only one room "in which he ate and slept", and two pieces of furniture—a table and a stove. (ZZZJ, Vol. 1) Coincidentally, during an archeological excavation in Beijing, a shallow foundation of a

Yuan house was discovered at No.106 High School. And the foundation showed that this house was similar to that of the Song eunuch: there was only a stove, a kang (heatable brick bed) and a stone mortar in the house; the walls were made of broken bricks and the floor was very damp. Thus could be inferred that most commoners in Dadu must have lived in such houses. Since Liao and Jin dynasties, kang has been widely used in north China. Therefore, it was not too difficult to find a kang in a Yuan house.

元代城市
生活长卷

The Urban Life of the
Yuan Dynasty

Chapter Four | **The City on the Steppe and the Old Capital in Jiangnan**

The simplicity of Shangdu contrasts sharply with the prosperity of Dadu. And Hangzhou, though stripped of the city walls, was still considered "the paradise on earth" by the whole nation. However, no one had expected that it would soon be changed into "the living hell" by the Yuan troops.

1

If one was to travel from Dadu, a flowery city, to Shangdu, a city on the steppe, one would experience a sharp change in both the climate and people's lifestyle.

Situated on a land of continental temperate grassy climate, the winter of Shangdu was long and freezing. People often had fingers or toes bitten off by the extreme coldness. Some would even be frozen to death on the steppe in winter. There was not much snow in winter and snowstorms that lasted for several days were few and far between. The wind on the steppe was not very strong but it grew to freezing gusts in April. The short but windy spring was followed by the long summer which often lasted for two to three months. In summer the temperature changed greatly from day to night, and the frost-free period was quite short. It frosted even in June. Thus the morning in July was very chilly, and one would often one feel cold at both hands and feet. In midsummer the steppe was frequently visited by fierce bolts and lightning. It often rained but the precipitation was small. Due to the effect of the cold air, rain was often turned into hail and sometimes the hail stones would be as large as eggs. The autumn on the steppe was also quite short. During the autumn, the climate was mild, the sky was high and the air was brisk, and winds grew light in most areas on the steppe. Thus it was an ideal season for the monads to go hunting. It snowed all year round on the steppe, "in every May and June" and "usually in April and August". According to the modern scientific survey, the regional temperature of the whole year averaged out to be 1.2℃ and that of July 18.5℃, making the steppe an ideal summer resort for the Mongol emperors.

Shangdu was much smaller than Dadu. Though it was also a square city with a circumference of outer walls measuring 2,200 meters, it expanded for only less than 5 square kilometers, almost ten times smaller than Dadu. And though its city walls were built in the proportion 3:2:1, the same construction standard as that of the city walls of Dadu, they were much shorter than those of Dadu. The remained city wall relics were 5 meters high, 10 meters wide at the bottom and 2 meters wide at the top. The walls were also made of rammed earth and part of the southeastern wall, coated with stone, belonged to the imperial city.

Shangdu had altogether seven city gates, one west gate and two gates at each of its other faces. And each of the gates was installed with a wengcheng, either rectangular or U-shaped. A deep and wide city moat circled around outer city walls. As the imperial city was constructed in the southeastern corner of the outer city, two eastern gates (respectively referred to as the eastern gate and the little eastern gate) and the southern gate (Mingde Gate) provided direct access to the imperial city. Thus there were, in fact, only four gates in the outer city.

The outer city of Shangdu was divided into two separate parts by an east-west earthen wall of about two meters wide. The northern part was

元代城市
生活长卷

The Urban Life of the
Yuan Dynasty

the imperial hunting park, while the southern part was the residential area.

The roads of Shangdu were all dirt ones. Thus every time after rain "the streets would be too narrow to ride horses and two muddy to drive carts" (Poems on Shangjing, Vol. 15, QRJSJ) It was often the case that "hardly had the rain stopped when the sun came out", but the streets were already filled with "muddy puddles impossible to wade through". So the pedestrians had to prolong their journey by walking under the eaves on skinny horses". (Poems on Shangjing, Vol. 7720, YLDD)

2

In Shangdu, edifices like government offices and monasteries were almost situated in the imperial city, which was very different from Dadu. The Confucius Temple, for instance, was situated in "the southeastern part of the capital", (Tablet Inscription in the Confucian Temple of Shangdu, Vol. 44, ZZJ) obviously within the bounds of the imperial city.

Except the north wall, all the other three faces of Shangdu were installed with a neighborhood outside of the city gate. The western neighborhood was believed to be the commercial area of Shangdu, which could be proved by the fact that the horse market was once located there. The eastern neighborhood was usually packed with yurts for the retinues of the princes and aristocrats who came to the capital to have an audience with the Emperor, because it was close to the imperial city. Thus there was the poem:

> The western neighborhood was packed with wagons,
> While the eastern one was dotted with yurts.
> (Poems on Shangjing)

Apart from neighborhood, there was a large storehouse outside of the eastern and western gates of Shangdu respectively. They were Wanying Storehouse and Guangji storehouse.

The markets in Shangdu were not clearly subdivided as those in Dadu, but one could find almost everything there, such as foodstuffs, clothes, groceries, and livestock. Shangdu were also featured in taverns with streamers flying in front of the doors.

Beside the Luan River, and west of the imperial road,
Streamers of taverns blowing under the low eaves.
(Zhang Yu, A Song for Those at the Border, Vol. 3, ZGBSJ)

By the side of the Luan River liquor was sold at the price of gold,
Still I dismounted from the horse to drink, giving no thought to money.
Beckoning streamers beckoning pedestrians on the imperial road,
Young were all the drunkards lying in the taverns.
(Ma Zuchang, The Traveling Carriage, Vol. 5, STWJ)

Street traders peddling all sorts of things could also be found in Shangdu. However most of them were impoverished because their incomes totally depended on the season and the market. For example, the following poem just depicted the hardship a veteran underwent when selling the firewood.

A bundle of firewood on back the veteran peddled around the market,
Following the direction of the sun he moved with a hundred back.
Hands cracked as a turtle back and clothes like rags,
He doggedly carried his bundle braving the piercing north wind.
Yet the market was already parked with carts of firewood, large and

元代城市
生活长卷

The Urban Life of the
Yuan Dynasty

small,

Worthless was my bundle of firewood, even inferior to the earth under the feet.

Smoke curled up from restaurants teeming with customers,

All poked fun at me but none showed sympathy.

At dusk I carried the bundle back to my adobe house,

Lying on bed, I was choked up when I sang to the moon.

(Yuan Jue, Selling the Firewood, Vol. 16, QRJSJ)

The houses of ordinary citizens in Shangdu was rather shabby, most of them lived in adobe houses which were low and small. And most of these houses were caves by nature. An adobe house was actually a thatched burrow of about one zhang deep. It was floored with wooden boards, and walled by earthen walls. Vegetables and wheat were planted outside the house. And a hole was made in the house to serve as a chimney. (Yan Guangda, Journey of the Peace Mission) It was very uncomfortable to live in such adobe houses, for "the mud house was changed into a prolonged kang when a fire was made" ; "although there was a fire burning in the kang, the house was still very cold" . Such adobe houses, however, were not very strong. In winter it iced over while in spring it usually get deformed, dilapidated and unsightly after the ice melted.

In the dead cold of water spring was frozen and land humped up like tomb,

While in spring the mounds melted into puddles of slush.

All the cracks formed in coldness were eradicated off the walls,

Leaving only the dilapidated houses slanting here and there.

(Poems on Shangjing)

Every year the emperor would spend his summer in Shangdu. Therefore many important affairs took place in Shangdu. As for the particulars, they will be revealed in the following chapters.

3

June 25, 1275 was supposed to be an ordinary day.

In Lin'an, the capital of the Southern Song Dynasty, the morning market was closed and the shops lining the streets were opened, starting to drum up business. And the West Lake was already teemed with throngs of tourists.

With the sun shining high above the head, Zhou Mi, keeper of Fengchu Storehouse, wandered along the street together with his friend Zeng Zhaoyang, who had told him about a magical snake charmer in the capital and took him to have a look at the conjuror.

There were quite a few performers putting on animal shows in the streets. With a few drumbeats, there jumped out a little monkey doing somersaults and performing martial arts. Before long, it was joined by other monkeys, and they together formed a pyramid which won them a lot of acclamations from the crowd. Then the little monkey took the opportunity to running around, asking for a gratuity with a little bamboo hat. This show had no sooner ended than another one was staged. With the sound of gongs, in a big sink several hatted fish of about one chi long surfaced to water and danced. After a while, a tortoise appeared followed by four hatted little ones. After they circled around the tank for three times, the big tortoise stopped at the edge of the tank and the other little tortoises immediately crawled over to pile themselves one upon another on the back of the big tortoise. The little tortoise on the top then shook its head and wagged its tail, as if bowing to people. Its funny gestures really amused the spectators.

But Zhou Mi's attention was attracted by a big rotating wheel of about four or five chi in diameter. And the wheel was painted with flowers, birds, people and many other objects. Seven bu away from the wheel stood a man with bow and arrows, shouting "this time I would shoot the leaves of the willow trees, the tentacles of fish, and the wings of swallows!" With these words he shot three arrows to the fast rotating wheel. And when the wheel stopped, all the three arrows precisely found their targets, which won the man a lot of acclamations from the crowd. When Zhou Mi was about to step forward to have a try himself, he was dragged away by Zeng Zhaoyang to the snake charmer's.

The appearance of the snake charmer was somewhat intimidating, for six of his fingers were gong and on his arms entwined seven to eight hissing poisonous snakes. Beside him lined dozens of baskets of different sizes which were probably filled with snakes.

"Brother Dai, please unleash the snake king and let this gentleman have a look". It seemed that Zeng had already acquainted with the snake charmer and they began to be on intimate terms.

The snake charmer simply took out a reed pipe and whistled, without even putting down the snakes on his arms. Soon the lid of the largest basket was popped open, from which raised a huge head of snake. When the flamboyant snake fully slipped out of the basket, the big boy which was about six to seven chi long really scared Zhou Mi who immediately steppe back. And this snake king was, in fact, a cobra.

"Don't be scared, it won't bite!" Zeng said.

The sound of the pipe was changed and the snake coiled up with its head pointing to the sky. Then it wiggled its body to the music, making all kinds of postures. Zhou Mi was no longer scared by that time. He walked up to have a closer look.

Suddenly the sky darkened and Zhou thought it was simply a few dark clouds blocking out the sun. But when he looked up to the sky, there was no cloud at all. What's the matter?

Then there came the cries "the sun was being swallowed by the Heavenly Hound!"

Indeed, half of the sun was gone at first, then a good half, and finally the whole of the sun vanished. All of a sudden, the world was flung into darkness and one could see nothing even within the distance of about a chi.

Everyone got panicked, stampeding and crying the names of relatives in the darkness. Zhou Mi and Zeng Zhaoyang started to rush blindly as well.

Suddenly Zhou Mi felt he had trod on something slippery. And when he promptly realized it was the very snake dancing before him, he let out a cry "Snake!", and hopped into the sky. He elbowed his way through the crowd and bolted for life.

"There was a snake, a snake!" People began to scream as well. In the chaos, the big rotating wheel was knocked down to the floor and smashed with a thump. A man fell into the sink with a splash. The fish thrown out of the sink were slopping against the grounds, while the monkeys were squawking beside.

When they at last retuned home, Zhou Mi was still badly shaken. Zeng then began to repeatedly blame himself for having hustled Zhou out. But Zhou Mi was totally absorbed in his thought that whether this solar eclipse betokened a catastrophe.

Fortunately, the sun gradually came out of the darkness after the midday and began to shine over the earth again. This solar eclipse, starting from around 9 o' clock lasted for a solid four hours.

It was indeed a bad omen. Soon, the Song army suffered a crushing defeat in Jiaoshan. At the end of the same year, the Yuan troops marched south, threatening to capture Lin' an. Faced with such powerful enemy, the Southern song Emperor as well as his courtiers decided to give up

元代城市
生活长卷

The Urban Life of the
Yuan Dynasty

resistance and relinquish the city by means of surrender. On Febuary 12, 1276 the Yuan army entered the Lin'an city and 14 days later Qubilai, Emperor of the Great Yuan Dynasty, issued "the Imperial Edict to Submitted Citizenry of Lin'an", demanding that the surrendered Song Emperor, Empress Dowager, other royal members and the courtiers of the Southern Song Dynasty should move to the north. He also ordered to make an inventory of the books in the Palace Library of Song, the ritual vessels, astronomical and geographical materials in the Court of Imperial Sacrifices of Song, and the Song census records, and to transport them back to Dadu.

During the ensuing months, a large number of vehicles and boats headed out to north in succession, and the Southern Song Emperor along with his courtiers were driven out of Lin'an under armed escort. Zeng Zhaoyang left Lin'an and retired into the mountains, while Zhou Mi was determined to stay in Lin'an to witness and record all the important affairs that were to take place in this old capital of the Song Dynasty.

4

Jiahui, Baiguan and Bazi Gate,

Spiral shells (Luoshi) clung to Gaoqiao Gate.

Agaist Houchao Gate clear waves (Qingbo) splashed,

Yongjin and Qiantang Gates safeguarding the city.

There were altogether eighteen city gates in Lin'an. Among them thirteen were overland gates and five Watergates. To memorize the names of all those city gates, people composed the above doggerel. The southern gate or the main entrance of the capital was Jiahui Gate. In the southeast of the city there were another seven gates, namely the Northern Watergate, Southern Watergate, Bian Gate, Houchao Gate, Bao'an Gate, Bao'an Watergate and Xinkai Gate or Caoqiao Gate. In the east there were

Chongxin Gate, Dongqing Gate, and Genshan Gate or Luoshi Gate, Caishi Gate and Bazi Gate. In the west there were Qiantang Gate, Fengyu Gate, Yongjin Gate, and Qingbo Gate. And in the north there were Tianzong Watergate, Yuhang Watergate and Yuhang Gate. Yuhang Gate was often referred to as "beiguan" because it was used to be called Beiguan Gate in the past, and the word "beiguan" was usually pronounced as "baiguan" after many repetitions.

Each city gate performed different functions, which could be mirrored by a ballad popular in Lin' an:

Fish were sold at Baiguan Gate,

Clothes were made at Bazi Gate,

Bridle paths meandered outside of Jia hui Gate,

Salt was available at Luoshi Gate,

Vegetables could be bought at Caoqiao Gate,

Taverns lined outside of Houchao Gate,

Bundles of firewood occupied Qingbo Gate,

Boats were paddled outside of Yongjin Gate,

Incense was burnt outside of Qiantang Gate,

Manure was transported outside Caishi Gate.

From food to clothing and from Buddha worshipping to spring outing or sightseeing, each city gate performed its own functions, and everything was in perfect order.

Though Lin' an was renamed Hangzhou during the Yuan Dynasty, its prosperity didn' t perish and its symbol—the West Lake still boasted of a grand view, continuing to attract tourists from all under heaven.

Not that the city remained intact under the rule of the Mongols, after the unification of China, Qubilai once decreed that "all the city walls except those of the capital in the country be removed", saying "now that the whole world had been unified, every walled city should remove their city walls to fully practise the spirit of 'the whole world

as one community' ". (ZSZJJ, Vol. 2) This move, however, was out of military considerations, for these city walls had caused great difficulty for the Mongol troops during their invasion to those cities. Thus in order to facilitate the suppression of the possible insurrections, the Mongols took the initiative to remove all the city walls. As a result, most of the city walls, saving those of the capital and the cities on the steppe, were torn down. And Hangzhou was no exception. The city became more open, whereas less table after being stripped of city walls. By the end of the Yuan Dynasty, there cropped up peasant uprisings, which forced the local officials and the gentry to raise money to rebuild the city walls out of their own interests. Soon it was prevalent in Jiangnan Region and the Central Plains to restore city walls and city moats. The city walls, therefore, didn' t get totally destroyed in the Yuan times. Instead, they survived to the Ming and Qing Dynasties.

Since the exile of the Southern Song Emperor and his courtiers, the imperial palace of the former Song capital grew more and more bleak and desolate. But such situation didn' t last for long. With the arrival of Yanglian Zhenjia, a "Tibetan Monk" sent from the Yuan capital to take charge of the Buddhist affairs as well as promoting Lamaism in Jiangnan Region, all the palaces in Hangzhou were transformed into Buddhist monasteries. In addition, another five monasteries (Zunsheng Monastery, Baoguo Monestery, Xingguan Monastery, Chuanruo Monastery and Xianlin Monastery) were successively built in Hangzhou and with them the Zensheng Pagoda rising 20 zhang high, in the shape of a kettle. Zunsheng Pagoda stored with hundreds of thousands of Buddhist scriptures used to be called as "the White Pagoda", "Bottle Pagoda", or "Tibetan Pagoda" by local people, because it was painted all white. During the construction of Zunsheng Pagoda, Yanglian Zhenjia was to use the stela carved with Jiu Jing (Nine Classics) the authentic work of calligraphy by the Emperor Gaozong of Song as the cornerstone of the pagoda, but was finally dissuaded by Shentu Zhiyuan, Administrative Assistant of Hangzhou Route Command. Yanglian Zhenjia, however, didn't let it go as that. He began to dig caves in the mountains surrounded the West Lake, especially Feilai Feng, and wherein he made sculptures of Buddha. All those sculptures, though seemed strange to the southerners, embodied the very deities worshiped by the Mongols and the Tibetans.

After the Song court was moved to the south, the imperial mausoleums of the Song Emperors were generally referred to as "Cuan Gong" because the mausoleums of their ancestors were located in Henan and these imperial mausoleums in Hangzhou only expedient ones. During Yanglian Zhenjia's stay in Hangzhou, two wicked monks, Monk Fu Wen of Tianyi Monastery and Monk Yun Ze of Yanfu Monastery, robbed the Mausoleum of Prince of Wei and stole a considerable amount of treasure in order to bribe Yanglian Zhenjia. The two then instigated Yanglian Zhenjia to rob the mausoleums of the Song Emperors and they were joined by two more accomplices, Monk Zongyun and Monk Zongcheng of the Taining Monastery in Kuaiji District, Shaoxing Route. In 1278, Yunze, with the support of Yanglian Zhenjia, raided the imperial mausoleum with his henchmen. Luo Xi, guard of the mausoleum, tried to stop them but was severely beaten and driven out of the mausoleum instead. The mobs first destroyed and sacked the mausoleums of Emperor Ningzong, Emperor Lizong, Emperor Duzong and Empress Yang, randomly scattering the skeletons of the dead. What's more outrages was that to get the mercury and the luminous pearl kept in Emperor Lizong's mouth, they even hung the body upside down on a tree for three days and then simply chopped the head off. Having reached their end, the mobs continued to sack the mausoleums of Emperor Huizong, Emperor Gaozong, Emperor Xiaozong, Emperor Guangzong, and those of their Empresses. In a few months, the number of the robbed Song imperial mausoleums and graves of the

Song courtiers totaled more than one hundred, and all the stolen treasure was shipped to the north. After the robbery of the mausoleums, Yanlian Zhenjia, asked his underlings to collect and piled the remains of the Song Emperors, upon which he built a stupa called "Zhennan Stupa". Lamaism attached special importance to "malediction"; and employing the power of Buddha to repress the ghosts via placing a stupa over the remains of the dead was the means of malediction.

Adherents of the overthrown Southern Song Dynasty, however, feared nothing of the so-called power of Buddha or malediction. Their only conviction was to protect the remains of their Emperors from further insults. It was said that Luo Xi, guard of the imperial mausoleum, collected encoffined and cremated all the remains of the Song Emperors. In the following several weeks, the surrounding mountains were all shrouded in cries of lamentation. But according to another version of the event it was Lin Jingxi who finally obtained the remains of Emperor Gaozong and Emperor Xiaozong through bribing the Tibetan monks and buried them in Dongjia. Yet there existed a third version that was somewhat mythical and more bizarre than the previous ones. In this version it was the Confucian scholar Tang Yu who had the remains of the Song Emperors buried in another place by secretly changing them with those buried in suburbs, with the help of the young people he hired in his district via selling off all his property and borrowing money from others. In addition, around the new graves of the Emperors, he especially planted several evergreens transplanted from Changchao Hall of the Song Imperial Palace. Tang Yu was there upon thrown into penury and remained unmarried. Before long, however, he was told by a deity from the heaven in his dream that he would be rewarded for what he had done and that the Lord of Heaven would bestow a wife and three children on him.

"Finally the imperial souls rested in peace among the lofty Tianmu Mountain," Sighed Zhou Mi in his records of the appalling crimes committed by Yanglian Zhenjia. Yet as a frail scholar that was all he could do at that moment.

5

Qubilai had once taken auspices for Hangzhou and the hexagram statement read "the place would be taken over by thistles and thorns after six or seven decades." (Hexagram Statement, Vol. 2, NCZGL) The prophecy did come true eventually!

The residents of the Hangzhou city didn't have their lifestyle changed in the new dynasty. And Hangzhou still remained "the land of extravagance". According to the record, "people of Hangzhou were extravagant. Only less than two out of ten men were honest and kind; Women were mostly gossipy, gluttonous, and seldom did needlework. As for food and daily necessities, they preferred only those new and expensive. They never bargained even if they wanted lest they be scorned by the others." Such kind of hedonistic urban lifestyle, however, was drastically in the late Yuan Times.

"Be cautious about fire every day and stay alert to burglars every night" was a saying once prevailed in the western part of Zhejiang Province. Since cities, especially a big city like Hangzhou abounded in timber structures which were prone to fire. Thus fire prevention was one of the top priorities of a city. However, even with a variety of preventive measure, disasters still cropped up. Between 1304 and 1327, Hangzhou was afflicted with four conflagrations and every time hundreds of houses were burnt down in fire. The year 1341 witnessed an extremely huge conflagration in Hangzhou. A total number of 15,755 houses including government offices, civilian residences, and monasteries were destroyed and 74 people were killed in the fire.

Fire, however, was not the most dreadful when compared with wars.

元代城市
生活长卷

The Urban Life of the
Yuan Dynasty

100

By 1357 Hangzhou had been besieged by the enemy troops for almost 3 months. "Every road for transportation of food had been blocked off and the rice price soared to 25 stringed coins a dou. In just a few days the rice were sold out and bran began to be sold at the price of rice in normal days. Even that could only be accessed by the rich. Then brain was also sold out in a few days and people began to eat chaff. Severe scarcity of food reduced people, men and women, young and old, to beggars in the streets. They begged in small groups with exquisite clothes still on their backs and make-up on their faces. But extreme hunger had stripped them of their sense of shame. The situation had deteriorated to such an extent that there even were families, fathers and sons, husbands and wives, brothers, committed suicide by drowning themselves, hand in hand, down the rivers. Alas, what a pathetic picture! Of the entire citizenry, six or seven out of ten were starved to death." (Misfortune befell on People in Hangzhou, Vol. 11, NCZGL)

The post-war Hangzhou went through a rather slack time. And it was not until the Ming Dynasty did it restore its former prosperity.

Chapter Five | The Nighttime Curfew and a Series of Other Prohibitions

To facilitate their control over the cities, the Yuan rulers issued a series of prohibitions to maintain order in cities, in addition to the massive garrisons already stationed there. The prohibitions, though proved effective in consolidating the public security, restricted the freedom of the citizenry and caused inconveniences to city life to a certain extent.

1

After the unification of China, the question of civic security became the top priority of the Yuan court's military concerns. The Yuan armies once excelled in "field operation" were therefore assigned a new mission of safeguarding the cities as well as the nearby areas as Territorial Armies.

Dadu and Shangdu, the political centers of the country, were naturally under special protection from the Imperial Armies which were purposefully organized by Qubilai to safeguard the two capitals. During the reign of the subsequent emperors after Qubilai, the Imperial Armies underwent a radical expansion, growing into a bulky organization of over 30 Guards and almost 300,000 soldiers.

Every imperial army was composed of soldiers of the same ethnic background, which gave rise to such designations as the Chinese Army, the Semuren Army, and the Mongolian Army.

元代城市
生活长卷

The Urban Life of the
Yuan Dynasty

The Chinese Army consisted of former Jin soldiers from North China and the surrendered Southern Song soldiers were assigned to the Five Guards (the Front Guard, the Rear Guard, the left Guard, the Right Guard, and the Center Guard), the Militant Guard, the Brave as Tigers Guard, the Loyal Guard, and the Coastal Guard. The encampments of the Five Guards and the Militant Guard "which was responsible for the construction, maintenance, and repair of the military installations," were located to the south of Dadu. The Brave as Tigers Guard was stationed in and out of Dadu, the Loyal Guard in Dadu and the Coastal Guard at the seaside of Zhigu (modern Tianjin).

In areas between Shangdu and Dadu there stationed the Semuren Army consisted of such ethnic guards as the Tangut Guard, the Left Qariua Guard, the Right Qariua Guard, the Guichi Guard, the Western Asian Guard (staffed with Qipchags), the Left Asut Guard, the Right Aust Guard, the Longzheng Guard, the Longyi Guard (staffed with Qariuas) and the Russian Guard. Among them the Longzheng Guard, drawn from soldiers of other ethnic guards such as the Tangut Guard, the Qariua Guard, the Guichi Guard, the Western Asian Guard, and the Asut Guard, was responsible for guarding the Juyong Pass.

The southern and northern parts of Dadu were stationed by the Mongolian Imperial Guard Left Wing, the Mongolian Imperial Guard Right wing, and the Zongren Guard, all of which were mainly staffed with Mongols.

Besides, there existed other guards in the Imperial Armies that were exclusively loyal to the Heir Apparent or even the Empress Dowager. Such troops were also stationed in the northern and southern Dadu.

To maintain social stability in areas of Shandong, Henan, Sichuan and Shanxi, the Yuan court assigned the so-called tammachi, or the Allied Army, to four Mongolian Military Brigades respectively stationed in areas of Shandong and Hubei, Henan and north of the Hui River, Sichuan and Shanxi, with Puzhou (located to the north of the modern Shandong Province), Luoyang, Chengdu and Fengxiang as their seats from which cities of the four regions were governed.

Major cities along Yangtze River were stationed by garrisons which were primarily Han and Newly Submitted troops (staffed with surrendered Southern Song soldiers) with only a few of Mongol and Semuren units. Military organization like Brigade and Battalion was established to ensure the security of the cities and the surrounding areas. The scale of protection, however, was in proportion to the rank of the city. Hangzhou, the former capital of the Southern Song Dynasty, for example, was installed with four Brigades to command the garrisons; Yangzhou, Jiankang (modern Nanjing in Jiangsu Province) and Zhenjiang, the three cities were installed with a total seven Brigades due to their strategic positions, other cities like Tanzhou, Guangzhou and Ezhou were also stationed by Brigades.

Nevertheless, military defense was very different from security patrol. Cities located to the north of the Yangtze River were policed by turns by archers who were dispatched by officials of the Administration Offices of the cities. Whereas cities located to the South of the Yangtze River were originally patrolled by the local garrisons. "Different from the inland cities, those newly submitted ones in Jiangnan Region were ruled by the stationed garrisons. Day and night, the street would be patrolled by military officers as well as their soldiers dispatched by the head of the Territorial Armies after the bell of curfew. The local Administration Offices, however, never took part in the patrol, nor did they send any archers." The situation wasn't changed until 1283 when new rules were issued, ordering the garrisons be joined by archers in their patrols and the officials of local Administration Offices work with the military officers to safeguard the cities.

元代城市
生活长卷

The Urban Life of the
Yuan Dynasty

2

The protection from the Territorial Armies alone proved far insufficient in maintaining peace and order in cities. There should be a series of regulations to maintain public order in cities.

The one came first was the arms control. The Yuan Dynasty was notorious in history for imposing a stiff restriction upon weapons, banning the production and possession of weapons including bows and arrows, knives and spears, even catapults and iron rods among the civilians. He who was found to produce and possess weapons against the law would be ruthlessly punished. The monarchs of the Yuan Dynasty did not have much confidence in other ethnic groups, especially the Han Chinese, decreeing that soldiers of the Chinese Army and the Newly Submitted Army could only get access to the weapons when fighting on the fields or performing duties, otherwise, they should hand in the weapons to the arsenals guarded by the Mongol or Semuren Soldiers. Anyway the policy of arms control adopted by the Yuan monarchs did enhance the public order of the city. As a result, all the weapons like knives, spears, swords, and halberds used in ceremonies honoring the ancestors were bogus ones—wooden articles coated with gold or silver foil.

What followed next was to restrict the urban residents' nocturnal activities. The Yuan court, like the previous dynasties in the history, imposed a curfew within the city walls that was draconically enforced. "It was decreed that all should get off the streets after curfew except those with urgent official business or faced with an emergency such as funeral, illness or childbirth. Anyone who broke the curfew should be sentenced to twenty-seven blows if he was a commoner and one if he was an official serving in the government." (Section nineteen, Curfew, Vol. 57, YDZ) Those who were to go out at night on official business were required to produce a pass issued by the government. In zhongtong period under

Emperor Shizu, an official related "now the curfew was so rigorously enforced that I had to ask my subordinate to prepare a liberty pass in case of nocturnal official business. I dare not go out at night without the pass. Even if I was to go out at night, I wouldn't go to any other places except the government offices." (Notes of the Grand Councilor, Vol. 80, QJJ) Those who were to send for a doctor or report a death had to carry a lantern as had been stipulated by the law.

The curfew highlighted the role of the Bell Tower and the Drum Tower in urban life. "They announced the time during the day, but stopped working at night." And they functioned as the official timepiece in the city. Temples and other institutions were not allowed to toll the hour of day. The function of the Bell Tower and Drum Tower was not only confined to giving the time signal. Being at the commanding height of the whole day, they turned themselves into the ideal watch posts and therefore were always guarded by soldiers. Besides the two towers, the public timekeeping system also included a night watchman who walked around the city at night and with a wooden clapper or a gong to announce the time. Night watchmen in southern cities of China were concurrent bridge guards as well. Every major bridge was installed with a post and was guarded by a group of ten people by turns. Every guard was assigned with a wooden clapper and a gong, and every post a water clock.

In addition, the Yuan court imposed a blackout during the curfew, especially in the southern cities. At night soldiers would patrol the city during the time of blackout to check if there were candles still burning inside houses. If one was found breaking the blackout, the door of his house would be marked and the next day he would be interrogated by the local authorities. If the transgressor could not justify himself, he would then be punished. The Blackout hadn't been officially lifted until 1292 for the reason that "it had been eighteen years since the submission of Jiangnan Region, and people there had already lived and worked in peace

元代城市
生活长卷

The Urban Life of the
Yuan Dynasty

and contentment. Thus it was advisable to lift the blackout."

3

The nighttime curfew and blackout undoubtedly affected the nightlife of the residents, while and a series of bans on public assemblies, to a certain extent, hindered people's daytime activities.

The Yuan authorities imposed rigorous restrictions on public assemblies. In cities, villages and residential areas, people were banned from inciting a crowd to a religious ceremony or organizing a gambling party. Monks and Taoists were also prohibited from gathering a crowd to conduct the Buddhist or Taoist rites to appease and pray for the dead. Only those "recorded in the Book of Sacrificial Rites, such as the rituals of worshipping the Five Sacred Mountains and Four Great Rivers, were allowed to be duly carried out by the relevant local officials." Other activities such as the ceremonies conducted by Shamans and witches in the streets, nocturnal small restaurants, and storytelling were all banned. In the mid-Yuan times, even storytelling practiced in the marketplace of countries, towns, and counties was banned. The transgressors would also be punished. "The prime culprit would be sentenced to 47 blows; the principal officials of the very district and the ordinary prefecture would both be sentenced to 17 blows, the head of the association as well as their neighbors 27 blows, and those who had connived at the transgressors were found doubly guilty." "As for the ignorant masses, including the traders in the market, traveling merchants and the audience, they could be spared." (Miscellaneous Rules, Vol. 27, TZTG, sic passim)

The marketplaces of cities were always haunted by gangs of local ruffians and rascals who "strolled along the streets dressing in inappropriate colors." They would make trouble whenever there was a chance, such as robbing pedestrians' hats, snatching women's jewelry, seducing and raping other's wives and daughters, fighting and even killing people when begging for food and drinks or money in brothels and restaurants. They would even openly swindle in the Tax Offices, state-owned wineries and storehouses, defraud the officials of a variety of goods, and impersonate the police to intercept and mug pedestrians. "Whenever there was a wedding they would flock to the bride's house with their henchmen and mingle with the bride's relatives to extort the groom's party of food and money, which would always result in a delay in the wedding ceremony and a fight with injury and casualty." Such activities as assembling a crowd to create a disturbance were banned by the Yuan court. All the transgressors would be punished, and the severity of the punishment was in proportion to the gravity of the crime, spanning from "having doors be marked with red earth" and "being paraded through the streets while chained up to a puppet" to flogging and exile, etc.

Every city would be plagued by such a group of people who consisted of the rich and the powerful as well as ruffians. They colluded with the local authorizes and thereby held sway over the region and were called "the well connected". "Whenever a new official took office, they would try every means to gain access to him, either by pleading with his relatives for a recommendation or through bribing his subordinates. Once acquainted with the official, they would manage to keep him under their control. They first invited him to dinners and next sent him gifts by way of congratulation. Then they simply wait to discover his hobbies and try to cater to his likes through different bribes —sending beauties were him a womanizer; bribing him with luxury items like jade and precious brocades were him greedy for money; enriching his collection were him interested in rare and exquisite objects. When the official started to be on intimate terms with them, he tended to turn a blind eye to their notorious reputation. They would eat at the same table or play chess together like

元代城市
生活长卷

The Urban Life of the
Yuan Dynasty

brothers. Their families were also in open and even close contact without any avoidance of suspicion. Seeing that, their neighbors all bribed them to seek refuge with them. Having accepted their bribes, the official would always as he was told." To deal with this problem, the Yuan Court issued a series of laws and regulations to prevent the officials from colluding with local tyrants, decreeing that all the lawbreakers should be severely punished.

4

To purify the social atmosphere, the Yuan Court crack down on whoring activities and gambling as well.

During the Yuan times there were many prostitutes in cities and towns. The number of the prostitutes in Dadu alone (excluding these unlicensed ones) was said to be 25,000. And whores could be found throughout the Hangzhou city. The government didn't ban the commoners from visiting whores but imposed strict laws to prevent officials from visiting prostitutes. Once discovered, "the whoremonger as well as the prostitute should all be punished." There were also restrictions on the brothels. "Local authorities should not connive at the purchase of girls by the brothels, issue vouchers to them and levy a stamp fax on the brothels without a record. Any transgressor should be punished." Abortion and infanticide were banned in brothels. All the newborn babies in brothels should be reported to the Secretariat every quarter.

Gambling was also banned by the Yuan Court and an imperial edict was once issued to "prohibit people from organizing a gambling party". If such gambling tools as gambling tables, money, gambling paraphernalia and chips were found on spot in a gambling house, all the money and property would be confiscated or given to the informer as a reward, and the gamblers would either be sentenced to 77 blows or "exiled to farm in fields in the far north". Gamblers who were not caught red handed or were given away by others would not be convicted. Any official engaging in gambling would be dismissed from office immediately.

With the influence of the Chinese moral principles the Yuan Court grouped the following ten offences into "The Ten Abominations" and were determined to punish the transgressors without leniency. "The Ten Abominations" are plotting rebellion, plotting great sedition, plotting treason, contumacy, depravity, great irreverence, lack of filial piety, discord, unrighteousness, and incest.

Of the Ten Abominations, plotting rebellion, plotting great sedition, plotting treason and great irreverence referred to treacherous behaviors that endangered the national security or irreverent attitude towards the Emperor, including reproaching the Emperor in front of the imperial sedan chair, irreverent to the Emperor, misleading the people though sedition, collecting and keeping banned books, rabble-rousing, etc. Any one who committed the above four offences would usually be executed.

The last four abominations—lack of filial piety, discord, unrighteousness and incest—were especially designed to maintain the traditional Chinese morality. The offences that fell into the category of lack of filial piety included "cursing one's grandparents and parents, immigrating while one's grandparents and parents were still alive and refusing to support them thereafter, getting married while still in mourning", deliberately concealing one's parent's death and refusing to observe period of mourning, falsely claiming the death of one's grandparents or parents, and visiting prostitutes while still in mourning. Such offences would be punished for "harming the publish morals". Discord referred to such behaviors as quarrel and even murder happened among relatives while splitting the family property. If a widow remarried without observing a period of mourning for her deceased husband, or

元代城市
生活长卷

The Urban Life of the
Yuan Dynasty

110

abused her stepchildren after remarriage, or a husband maltreated his parents-in-law, they would all be considered as unrighteous. While incest referred to such despicable behaviors as raping one's daughter-in-law, sister-in-law or biological daughter and taking liberties with one's daughter-in-law. Discord, unrighteousness and incest were considered "contaminating the public morals" as well, and the offenders would also be convicted.

As for contumacy and depravity, the two strictly prohibited abominations, designated slanderous actions and all kinds of cruel deeds, such as murder of one's master, one's superior, beating and killing one's own grandparents, parents and relatives and dismembering a corpse.

Except the above Ten Abominations, the Yuan Court also considered the following six behaviors unethical and illegal:

1. Bloodying oneself with a dagger piercing through the arm and then begging in the streets.

2. Displaying snakes, insects and wild animals in the streets to attract people to buy his home-made medicine.

3. Itinerant story-tellers in the cities.

4. Raising money by carrying statues of Buddha in the streets.

5. Rabble-rousing witchcraft in the form of books of superstitious prophecies, manslaughter by sorcery, arts of casting spells.

6. Writing anonymous letters and documents.

The Yuan court also prohibited non medical people from producing and selling poisons. Any transgressor, if found have caused deaths with poisons or bogus drugs, would be executed. The poisons listed in the ban spanned over 10 kinds, including arsenic, croton seed, rhizome of Chinese monkshood, setose thistle, and black henbane.

The Mongolian traditional customs had it that butchery and hunting should be prohibited on specified days. The Mongol Yuan court therefore imposed strict restrictions on butchery and hunting. First, it specified days when killing of the livestock were banned throughout the whole country. The first day, the eighth day, the fifteenth day and the twenty-third day of every lunar month were no-butchery days during the reign of Mongke Khan. After the accession of Qubilai, these dates were changed to the first day and the fifteenth day of every lunar month plus another respective ten days of the first and the fifth lunar months and the day of the "Imperial Birthday." After Emperor Renzong mounted the throne, he ordered the first fifteen days of the third lunar month to be the no-butchery days as the eighth day and the fifteenth day of the third lunar month, asserted by the Tibetan Lamas, were respectively the birthday and the date of death of Buddha, and, more importantly, the third day of the month was also the birthday of the Emperor himself. Besides, when there was a natural disaster, butchery and even the sales of pork and mutton would be prohibited by the court as well.

The Han Chinese had long been notorious for squandering money on feasting. "On occasions of marrying off daughters or taking a wife, they would throw a lavish banquet of about twenty to thirty tables and courses all night long without ever considering their own financial capacities." To strictly enforce the nighttime curfew and eliminate the practice of extravagant feasting, the Yuan court decreed that "all feasts be held during daytime or before the bell of curfew, and that except the imperially awarded ones, the number of courses in the feasts be decreased, with that of the upper and the middle households limited within three and that of the lower households two." The banquets held between the officials, "like the lavish ones openly held by those who sought higher positions in officialdom or extended gratitude after a promotion, though not serious enough to be identified as bribery" were banned as well. A breach on the part of the official as well as the one sought higher positions in officialdom would be punished. On the occasions of an official taking office or an envoy arriving at his destination, he was not supposed to feast

or attending the feasts held by other officials, except that the host or his guests were the relatives and old friends. The transgressors would also be punished.

The Yuan court had once imposed a ban on gold and silver which hadn't been lifted until the accession of the Emperor Renzong who permitted the gold and silver "be sold in the market", yet he still prohibited the merchants from collecting gold and silver and shipping them overseas.

The Yuan Court implemented a strict inspection on measuring instruments, prohibiting people from making unqualified bailing buckets, dippers, steelyards, and rulers. The local authorities were required to test the instruments regularly, stamp the qualified ones and distribute them to the service providers. In case of any violation, once discovered, the person would be sentenced to 57 blows. The principal officials of the local bureau and country would also be punished for remiss: the first offender would be deprived of one month's stipend, while a habitual offender would be sentenced to 27 blows.

The Yuan Court adopted a protective attitude towards monasteries and places of historic interest surviving the previous dynasties, prohibiting "monasteries and historical sites in famous mountains and by great rivers from being demolished", stationed, and occupied as government offices, places of entertainment or working place for artisans. Those famous monasteries, Taoist temples, Confucian temples, the memorial temples of the Five Sacred Mountains and temples of the God of Earth were given additional protection by the special imperial edict. And without the permission from the central government, local authorities were forbidden from changing Buddhist monasteries into Taoist temples and vice versa.

Every monarch desired his subjects to be meek and submissive, and the Yuan rulers were no exception. Although they ruled the cities with meticulous care, such harsh governance meant more like an immense mesh of prohibition to the citizens, for within which one had to abide by a variety of rules even when seeking recreation. Such kind of life, of course, was boring, but a majority of the citizenry reconciled themselves to it. Only a few, disillusioned of the vanity of urban life, chose to retire to the mountains to pursue freedom.

元代城市
生活长卷

The Urban Life of the
Yuan Dynasty

Part Three

Part
Three

Chapter One | **Clothing: the Identification Mark of the Citizens**

Clothing served as an ethnic marker in the city. With the arrival of the nomads at the cities, came the clothes of exotic flavor. As different occasions called for different dresses, it is necessary for the monarch to prepare a wardrobe of miscellaneous clothes and his subjects to correspondingly change their costumes.

1

The city was actually a magnified exhibition booth of textiles where such silk fabrics as duan (satin), sha (plain gauze), luo (gauze), ling (twill damask) and juan (silk tabby) as well as a wide variety of cotton cloth could be found.

A major part of the satin bolts used by the Emperor and Imperial Princes came from the state-owned workshops and the rest was made to order by the local governments and handed over as the so-called "silk levied as tax". Every procedure for the manufacture of satin bolts was specified by the court. The satin for the Emperor measured eight or six tuo in length (one tuo equals 4 chi) and one chi four cun and five fen in width; the satin for Imperial Princes and officials was eight or six tuo long and one chi and four cun wide; the "silk levied as tax" was six tuo or two zhang and four chi long and one chi and four cun wide. Each local government was supposed to finish weaving the allotted number of satin bolts before the end of the year and pack up on the first day of the first lunar month. And there was a strict acceptance inspection when the officials from the court taking delivery. If the bolts were considered of poor quality, then both the artisans and the supervising officials would be punished. It was noteworthy that a considerable amount of silk levied as tax was obtained through "fair purchase" (compulsory purchase by nature imposed by the court on the masses). For example, areas in Jiangnan Region were assigned to weave 70,000 bolts of "silk levied as tax" every year. The number later dropped to 10,000 with the other 60,000 bolts obtained by fair purchase.

Silk textiles in the Yuan Dynasty spanned a wide range of varieties, such as nas i j, green and red striped silk, satin, etc. Nas i j, a kind of brocade woven with gold filaments in silk fabrics, was the most popular silk fabric among the privileged. Originated in the Central Asia, it was brought to the Mongol Empire by a group of western weavers who were then lodged in areas of Hongzhou and Xunmalin, which later became home to Hongzhou Nas i j Bureau and Xunmalin Nas i j Bureau. In those places the western weavers "recruited local households and exiles and taught them to weave nas i j". Chengdu, in Sichuan, then boasted polychrome brocade, especially the Ten Patterns of Brocade, including Chang'an Bamboo, Great Happiness, Elephant Eyes, Lotus-leaf with Iron Stalk, etc. Silk fabrics, especially kesi product (silk fabric woven with fine silk and gold thread by the tapestry method) and satin, produced in Jiangnan Region enjoyed even greater and more widespread popularity.

"There were several types of kesi product. Those with a motif of a complete tree in pure blossom were of the top rank, while those with a snapped branch or flowers of miscellaneous colors were of the inferior rank. Some were multicolored and some were of two colors, but all were

元代城市
生活长卷

The Urban Life of the
Yuan Dynasty

116

amazingly beautiful. There was satin with faint flower design. Though fairly sumptuous and subtle, such satin appeared somewhat ordinary and couldn't parallel kesi product. But it could still entertain the owner a lot." (Song Kesi Product, Vol. 1, ZZZJ)

Strict specifications were also imposed by the Yuan court on the satin bolts sold in market: every bolt of satin should be over 5.5 tuo long and 1 chi and 6 cun wide. People were prohibited from producing the imperial satin bolts privately and from embroidering satin with dragon, Buddha and Swastika design, such as satin with a five-clawed and dual-horned coiling dragon, a robe with voluminous sleeves with dragon embroidery, gold brocade with dragon embroidery, robe of six flowers with a dragon motif, etc. Besides, manufacture and use of cloth dyed with such colors as willow green, cock's comb purple, brown, mast red, rouge-red were strictly banned among the commoners. And the Yuan court had also repeatedly ordered to forbid gold filaments from being interwoven into the satin sold in the market.

Ling (twill damask), luo (gauze), juan (silk tabby) and bo (fine silk) ranged a wide variety in the Yuan Dynasty. As for luo, there were imperial luo, luo with floral design, Tibetan luo, luo with triangular design, etc. As for sha (plain gauze), there were sha with moth design, sha interwoven with silver threads, sha with fish and water design, sha interwoven with gold filaments, sha with floral design, indigenous sha, etc. As for ling (twill damask), three were big ling and small ling. As for chou (crepe) three were chou made of waste silk, and chou with wave design, etc. As for juan, there were southern juan and northern juan.

Cotton planting prevailed in the Yuan Dynasty, which led to a considerable increase in the consumption of cotton cloth. Statistics in the report from Imperial Silk Vault in 1299 revealed that every year the court had collected over 500,000 bolts of kapok cotton cloth from all the

Branch Secretariats. And cotton cloth featured in a wide range of varieties as well, such as kapok cotton cloth, Korean ramie cloth, Tieli cloth, ko-hemp cloth, plantain-fibered cloth, bamboo-fibred cloth, green ramie cloth, mature ramie cloth, Tibetan cotton cloth, indigenous hemp cloth, cloth with chessboard design, grass cloth.

2

Fur and hide were widely used in Yuan cities, especial those northern ones. Fur of the big animals was usually obtained from silver foxes and lynxes, while that of the small animals was from stoats and sables.

Stoats, squirrels, yellow-throat marten, mountain rats, chestnut white-bellied rat, chipmunk, and fire rats were rodents whose fur could be used to make clothes. The finest stoats "were from areas to the north of Qara-qorum, with rocky cracks on mountains as their habitat. The newborn stoat had a grey coat which would turn white after the snow. Stoats, fully grown while still white in color, were fairly precious. And Sakhalin, east to Liaodong Peninsula, was rich in such stoats. Thus the inhabitants of Sakhalin used to hunt stoats in forests on islands so as to barter for things from China. But they never met the Chinese during the transactions, which was their custom. Stoats varied in size and length, but they all had yellowish fur under the belly. As fur of rodents went, ermine was of the top quality. It was therefore paid as tribute to the Marten and Rodent Bureau in southern Dadu for the imperial army tents, curtains, clothes and bedding". Squirrels "had a glossy and fluffy coat. Their tails had a greenish tinge and bellies were embellished with a layer of white fuzz. When made into tunics, only the grey part of the fur would be used. The remaining white fur would then be patched together to make a sash. And if trimmed by ermine, or fur of otter or sable, the clothes would appear more stunning". The yellow-throat marten "had a grayish

元代城市
生活长卷

The Urban Life of the
Yuan Dynasty

118

brown coat. Its fur, light and fluffy, was short and thick, but was inferior to ermine as a surface material. The fire rat "lived in northern great mountains. It could be made into clothes which were fire-proof". (XJZJY, p. 233)

Sable was very precious. "The finest sable was as black as it was thick and was usually used to trim the collars. Often the dignitaries would decorate their clothes whose front was usually made of nas i j with a tailed ermine, and some even embellish their clothes with sable trimmings. Sable, if mixed with white fur, was considered inferior." The fur of foxes such as red pandas and red foxes "could be used to make fur hats, curtains and the like." Fur of the felines like wild cats, leopard cats and masked palm civets was also widely used. Besides, fur and hide of such beasts as lions, tigers, leopards, bears, elks, deer, water deer, badgers, and wolves were used to make clothes and bedding as well.

Sable often served as a unit of fur. According to the original practice, a sheet of tiger hide equaled 50 sheets of sable, a sheet of leopard 40 sheets of sable, a sheet of bear 15, a sheet of Amur leopard 10, a sheet of deer 7, a sheet of North China leopard bejeweled with gold filament 6, a sheet of jackal 10, a sheet of goat 5, a sheet of pink water deer 3 , and a sheet of fox 2. Later the Directorate for Leather and Fur Manufactures renewed conversion principle. For example, a sheet of sable equaled a sheet of such small animals as mountain rat, tortoiseshell cat, cub of sika deer, tiger cub ,Siberian musk deer, wild fox, Marmota himalayana, Siberian weasel, small Indian civet, musk deer, bamboo rat, night monkey, large Indian Civet, bobak marmot, otter and badger .

3

In addition to gold and silver, people, especially nobles and families that had produced public officials for several generations, in the Yuan dynasty favored jade and precious stones as accessories. "Gold eclipsed all metals, and jade all stones. Like gold, the value of jade depended on its purity. Jade of one hundred percent purity was fair, delicate and free from any blemish, and was therefore of the top rank. Jade of ninety percent purity, however, was hard to detect, only an expert with meticulous insight was able to distinguish. Jade of eighty percent purity was inferior, while that of seventy or sixty percent purity was of even lower rank. But an antique jade was precious for its antiquity. Thus the jade tinged with the color of mercury or blood was considered a treasure regardless of its purity." (Agate & Jade and Gold, Vol. 3, ZZZJ)

The Central Plains and areas in Jiangnan Region produced jade and precious stones. And the gems from the Central Asia were called "Muslim Stones". Precious stones were considered every precious. In dade period under Emperor Chengzong, "a ruby weighed one liang and three qian and worth 140,000 ding paper money4 was sold by a local baron to the court. The ruby was then inlaid into the top of the royal coronet that was treasured and passed down to the succeeding Yuan Emperors who would only wear it on festive occasions celebrating the lunar New Year's Day and the Imperial Birthday."

There was a wide range of precious stones in the Yuan Dynasty. Ruby (the red stone) alone could be further classified into: ci (rose-pink ruby), bizheda (deep crimson ruby), xilani (dark red ruby), and kumulan (ruby of a mixed colors of red, yellow and black). There were three ranks of emeralds (the green stone): emeralds of dark green belonged to the top rank and were called zhubabi; those of bright green were of medium rank and were called zhumula; those of light green, called sabuni, were the worst. Sapphire (yagu) also had a wide range of varieties, including wupunilan, red yagu (pink sapphire), masigendi (padparascha), yellow yagu (yellow sapphire) and white yagu (opal). Among them, wupunilan

with a color of dark blue was of low value. Cat's-eye gemstone included the chatoyant cymophane and the inferior corundum cat's-eye without chatoyancy called zoushuishi. Turquoise (dianzi) has been known by many different names and has various sources. The Muslim diaazi from the Central Asia was called nishebudi; hexi dianzi from areas belonged to the former Western Xia Dynasty was called qilimani; xiargyary dianzi from areas in Xiangfan was called Jinzhou stone.

Because the commoners were dined the free access to jade and precious stones by the court, accessories made of agate prevailed in Jiangnan Region. Someone commented that "agates exhibiting a succession of parallel lines were of high value and those with one red band or two in between were of the top rank. There was a saying going like this 'agates without a red band were deprived of any value', which meant such agates were worthless. Another saying had it that 'agates covered with red bands were valueless', meaning excessive red would, on the contrary, spoil an agate. Only those agates with a tenuous red band running parallel to other yellow and white bands down the surface of the stone were the best. Some people in western Zhejiang Province were in a rush to collect agate wares, such as agate cups, agate-studded ashes and hilts. Each object was worth over 10 ding, much more expensive than jade. That was probably because jade wares were banned items. People then turned to agates as substitute material." Scholar-officials in the capital, however, took no fancy to agates. Different from people in Jiangnan Region, they considered them as "inferior and accessories associated only with prostitutes and entertainers."

Influenced by the customs of northern Chinese, people in Jiangnan Region began to wear accessories made of jiantie (a kind of ferroalloy). Someone commented that "jiantie items like accessories and hilts were on trend at the time, and became hot selling items in markets of Yugan,

Qiantang and Songjiang. They, however, were merely remnants of Jurchen practices and were not worth collecting, for the metal was heavy in weight and prone to rust. It was more a suitable maternal for hilts, saddles and reins than for accessories." (Jiantie Accessories, Vol. 4, ZZZJ)

4

In their "barbarian" garments and hats the nomadic Mongols entered the city.

The Mongols wore robes overlapping on their right, different from peoples in the Central Plains and Jiangnan Region.

There was only a slight difference between the Mongolian robes of two sexes. According to the western missionary John of Plano Carpini, "men and women would often be dressed identically. They were robes of buckram velvet or brocade, instead of cloaks, capes and hoods. Their clothes split open on the right side and fastened by knots, one on the left and three on the right, with the material folded back double over the chest. All the fur clothes were of the same style except that the outside garment whose fur expose outward opened at back with a tail extending to the knee. Married women wore long and loose robes opened at the front." Rubruck also mentioned that "the dress of the girls differs not from the costume of the men, except that it is somewhat longer. But on the day following her marriage, a woman shaves the front half of her head, and puts on a tunic as wide as a nun's gown, but everyway larger and longer." (CSMGJ, p. 8 & pp. 119-120, sic passim)

The color of a robe was determined by its material. "Materials like felt, down and leather were associated with the old, while those like silk and gold filament were reminiscent of the young. Either dyed red, purple, dark red or green, or embroidered with the motif of the sun, the moon, the drag or the phoenix, a robe carried no more significance than a loincloth." (HDSL) The major materials used by the Mongols for clothes originally confined to leather and fur which were later substituted by silk fabrics and cotton textiles. Fur clothes, however, were never discarded due to their excellent warm-keeping qualities. Just as Rubruck has said, "from Cataia and other regions of the east, and also from Persia and other regions of the south, are brought to them silken and golden stuffs and cloth of cotton, which they wear in summer. From Ruscia, Moxel, and from greater Bulgaria and Pascatir and Kerkis, all of which are countries to the north and obey them, are brought to them costly furs of many kinds, which they wear in winter. And they always make in winter at least two fur gowns, one with the fur against the body, the other with the fur faced out; the latter are usually made of the skins of wolves or foxes; and while they sit in the dwelling they have another lighter one. The poor make their outside gowns of dog and kid skins." The fur gown was what the Mongols called "Dahu", meaning "fur-lined gown". Dahu worn by the commoners were made of sheep or kid skins, only those aristocrats could get access to marten ermine Dahu.

Apart from robes, the Mongolian wardrobe also included a series of clothes called "Chancha", the Chinese transliteration of a Mongolian word meaning "upper garment". In addition to robes and a variety of upper garments, the Mongols wore trousers, especially the fur trousers to keep warm in winter.

Not all materials used by Mongols for clothes were reflective of their status. Just as Zheng Suonan, a scholar of the Southern Song Dynasty, has pointed out, "the formal wear of (the Mongol) people was the Haiqing Robe which allow the stretching of arms out of the robe. Through the two slots opened between the shoulder and the upper part of sleeves one could stretch the arms out of the robe. The remaining sleeves would then be fastened to the back of the robe, which gave people the illusion that the wearer seemed to have four arms. Toadies of the northern intruders flattered the wearers by comparing them to the legendary figure "Marshal of the Heavenly Canopy". The name of the costume "Haiqing" was derived from the bird Gyrfalcon for its lightning speed, which also account for the title "Haiqing emissary". There were no hierarchical differences in etiquette or clothes between the rulers, officials, commoners and monks of the northern intruders." (A Sketch of Cardinal Principles, XS) Xiong Mengxiang living in late Yuan times elaborated on the clothes worn by the Yuan noblewomen: "they usually wore red gowns of gold brocade with dragon and cloud design. Sometimes the gowns were embellished with jade and pearls and exquisite embroideries. And different gowns were made to fit the different seasons. Their ceremonial dress was a long and loose gown with wide sleeves and narrow cuffs of only five cun wide. It was usually embroidered with gold claws on purple background and had many folds in the armpits. The gown was fastened by a purple silk sash to the back with purple braids of silk girdling around the waist. When walking outside, they needed maidservants to hold the train of their gowns for them." (XJZJY, P. 206)

A colored ribbon, or sash, usually girdled the waist outside the gown. "Besides, braids of red and purple silk, or waistband, were also worn in parallel clusters around the waist. Such waistband was well suited to riding and hunting and meanwhile made the gown seem rather fancy." Women "tied their gowns with a piece of blue silk stuff at the waist and they wrap another band at the breasts, and tied a piece of white stuff below the eyes which hung down to the breast."

5

The Mongol men wore their hairstyle in a way different from those of other races. "From Chinggis Khan to the commoners, all men wore their hair in "Pojiao", resembling the "three-patch hairstyle" which was typically worn by a Chinese kid who would have his hair shaved leaving only three patches of hair on the lead—one on the fontanel and the others on both sides of the head. The Mongols would trim the hair on the crown regularly but leave that on the two sides to grow. They then plaited the hair on the two sides together and let them hang over the shoulders." (MDBL)

The so-called "Pojiao" simply referred to the hairstyle in which "men braided their hair in two plaits right up to the ears or wore a tiny mallet-like bun". To have such a hairstyle, one should first have his hair on the crown shaved, leaving only a semicircle of hair growing at the front rim of the head. They then had the hair over the forehead trimmed and made tresses with the hair on the sides which they plaited together and wore down over the shoulders. The two braids were referred to as 'Bulanger' (view-blocking hairstyle) because they would block one's view when one glancing back and prevent one from looking around freely. Therefore some people chose to have their long braids behind. Besides, every Mongol man wore earrings." (A Sketch of Cardinal Principles, XS) Such hairstyle obviously attracted attraction of Friar Rubruck. "They have a tonsure on their head like our clerics from which they shave a strip three fingers wide from ear to ear. On the forehead, however, they wear their hair in a crescent-shaped fringe reaching to the eyebrows, but gather up the remaining hair which they plaited into two braids to each ear like women." (CSMGJ, P7& P119)

Mongolian men wore hats in winter and special hats called "Li" in summer. Li was a large bamboo hat with a conical crown and broad brim. "Every man, officials and the commoners, wore hats whose brims were either circular or circular in the front while square at the back, or of a terraced shape, probably evolved from a helmet of old days. Their hair was either braided or coiled up in a ban, and the commoners usually wore a tiny mallet-like bun." It was said that the front brim was added to the hat by Qubilai's Empress Chabui. According to Yuan Shi (History of the Yuan), "the traditional hats worn by the Mongols had no front brim. It was later added to the hat by the Empress after hearing the Emperor complaining of the dazzling sunlight during hunting. When the Emperor was presented with the new hat, he was overjoyed and decreed the same improvement be made to all the hats in the country." The extant pictures show that there are two kinds of Li in the Yuan Dynasty: the broad-brimmed Li and the valanced Li. "The clothing of the northern people was lavishly ornamented. Their hats had gold finials; their coats were girdled with colored silk strands; and their boots had slightly upturned toes." (Section two, Miscellaneous Institutions, Vol. 3, CMZ; Section one, Biography of the Imperial Consorts and Concubines, Vol. 114, YS) The aristocrats in the Yuan Dynasty had their Li decorated with pearls or jade and their warm hats worn in winter made of different precious fur to go with the Jisun Robes (it will be introduced in the next chapter).

The commoners were banned from copying the style of the hats worn by the Emperor. In 1297, a craftsman of the Directorate for Leather and Fur Manufactures made a new black leather hat with delicate floral design for Emperor Chengzong who then asked the craftsman "never to make another similar hat for others, otherwise he would be executed". The Emperor also warned, "if a similar hat were found in the streets, not only the maker but also the wearer should be punished by law." In 1308, Emperor Wuzong issued an edict to punish the craftsman for copying the style of his hat, saying "how dare this leather hat maker give the style of my hat that I have worn in front of the Commandant-escort to others! From now on, never reveal my hat style to the commoners. Leave the hat maker to Regency and inform the masses that all those involved should be punished." He also decreed that "never teach others to make or wear crests in the shape of golden wings or the crusts of leather hats with golden wings design, or both the maker and the wearer should be

punished." (The Ministry of Works, Vol. 58, YDZ)

6

The Mongolian women's headgear was of more distinctive features. The headdress usually worn by noblewomen was called "guguguan", a transliteration of a Mongolian word with various written variants. It was also referred to as "botahei", the Chinese transliteration of the Persian word "bocca", meaning the headgear worn by married women.

People who had been to the steppes were all impressed by this distinctive headdress of the Mongolian women. According to the envoy sent to the steppes by the Southern Song Dynasty "women there wore gugu on the head"; "wives of every tribal chief wore guguguan, a three-chi iron wire frame adorned with red and blue brocade, pearls or gold on which they put a light cane decorated with red and blue woolen stuff"; "The guguguan was made of birch bark and covered with red or golden silk. Its top, resembling the capital of a column, was made of a willow branch or iron wire of four to five chi long. It was then covered with blue felt. The wealthy ladies would decorate their headdresses with our polychrome silk which blew in the mind, while others used pheasant feathers instead." (HDSL; MDBL)

Such Mongolian traditional headdress continued to enjoy high popularity in the imperial palace and among the Mongolian noblewomen in the Yuan Dynasty. "All the imperial consorts and concubines and the wives of the courtiers wore guguguan and loose gowns, while those of the lower ranks wore leather hats. The guguguan was about two chi high and covered with red silk." (Section two, Miscellaneous Institutions, Vol. 3, CMZ)

Zheng Suonan, the adherent of the former Southern song Dynasty, also mentioned that "barbarian (Mongolian) women with a noble title all wore guguguan which was about two chi high. It was made of thin bamboo strips and covered with gold-sprinkled red silk. Women in the north wore Muslim hats instead, to which a black silk veil was added in the front. However, a handkerchief was still needed to defilade the wind and sand." The description of the headgear could also be found in the Yuan poetry. Taking Luanjing Zayong (Poems on Luanjing) for example, in which the poet Yang Yunfu wrote:

> In luxurious chariot, with gem-studded guguguan,
> To the maidservant she entrusted the plume on her hat.

The poet then annotated that "when a lady traveled in a chariot with guguguan, she would took off the plume, of about one chi high, which would be held by the maidservant sitting opposite to her. Even the imperial consorts and concubines would do so when they travelled in an elephant-drawn carriage." According to the customs in Dadu, the fifteenth day of the second lunar month was the day for a grand Buddhist ceremony which would be celebrated by a parade around the imperial city with people carrying the statue of Buddha. "The procession started from Qingshou Monastery and headed for Longfu Palace. The Empress together with all the imperial consorts and concubines as well as wives of the imperial relatives waited in the imperial palace." "The route of the parade extended from Donghua Gate to Houzai Gate, passing the eleventh Ordo and Qingning Hall. In the imperial palace over three thousand imperial consorts and concubines in guguguan and leather hat watched the parade, but they themselves were already a spectacular picture attesting to the prosperity of the country after the unification!" (XJZJY, PP. 215-216)

However, the guguguan prevailed in the Yuan imperial palace and among the Yuan aristocrats was far more opulent than that of the Mongol

元代城市
生活长卷

The Urban Life of the
Yuan Dynasty

Empire period. Xiong Mengxiang had a detailed description of the guguguan worn in the Yuan Dynasty.

"The guguguan was a light bamboo frame wrapped in red silk. The bigger it was, the higher it became in both rank and quality. The guguguan itself was a luxury: it would first be decorated at both front and back by big pearls connected and formed into a variety of motifs like dragons, phoenixes, mansions and towers. Then strings of pearls would be employed to cover the seam in the hat. Besides, other adornments like flowers and gold were also added to the hat. The entire headdress resembled an upside-down pagoda with its top inlaid with a golden cross to hold the tails of pheasants. Such pheasants were only raised in Zhengding which was located beyond the Wutai Mountain, and they were therefore very expensive. Five-colored Plumes were inserted into the back of the headdress, making the hat look like a fan. Before putting on guguguan, women would first wrap the bun in a pearl-studded purple silk. A button was attached to either side of the hat near the ears from which dangled two patterned chains of pearls to the chin. The chains of pearls were used to conceal the ears. A red gauze or nas i j was used to cover the shaved forehead. It would be changed into thin silk with plum blossom design in summer and a patch of ermine lined with nas i j in winter. Then another handkerchief of fine silk was added to the forehead before putting on the lofty guguguan."

People in Jiangnan Region viewed guguguan with great curiosity, which could be seen from the following poem dedicated to the Mongolian women by Tao Zongyi.

In her drunken stupor, the beauty leaned over the horse,
Dangling were her two braids worn in an alien style.
No eyes in Jiangnan have ever laid on such a coiffure,

All rushed to draw up the curtains to see guguguan.

（Green Windows, Vol. 8, NCZGL）

The guguguan had also influenced the style of the headgear of other ethnical races. According to Shilin Guangji (Vast Record of Varied Matters) published in zhishun period, "Khitan and Muslim women also wore guguguan. Such guguguan was covered with red-lacquered leather or paper painted with gold pattern. But the female southerners were banned from wearing it."

7

The Mongol rulers were greatly influenced by Han Chinese clothing.

According to Yu Fu Zhi (Record of Vehicles and Garments) in Yuan Shi (History of the Yuan), Mongke Khan began to wear mianfu (religious court dress of emperor, officials or nobility) in 1252 when he worshiped the Heave in Riyue Mountain. But it was not until the accession of Qubilai did the Mongol rulers began to design their court dress following the Chinese code of dress. But it was not totally Chinese, since Qubilai and his successors all paid great attention to preserve their Mongolian heritage. He then demanded an incorporation of the element of traditional Mongolian clothing into the formal imperial dress. Just as a Yuan official has said: "The code of vehicles and dress of our mighty dynasty should take into consideration the element of convenience and meanwhile absorb all desirable features of the other countries. Ever since the establishment of the Yuan Dynasty by Emperor Shizu, the court has thrived, the entire bureaucracy has coordinated well, and the whole country booms. And it was high time that His Majesty decided to formulate a code of dress based on that of the previous dynasties." (Vehicles and Garments, JSDDXL)

The mianfu for the Mongol Emperor to attend sacrificial ceremonies,

元代城市
生活长卷

The Urban Life of the
Yuan Dynasty

130

have the coronation, and hold court assembly was almost identical with that of the Chinese emperors. The manfu consisted of a crown, a ceremonial robe, a cummerbund, a ribbon and shoes. The crown, with a jade hairpin inserted horizontally over, was made of satin. On top of the crown there was a lacquered board which measured one chi and six cun in length and eight cun in width, with twelve jade tassels respectively attached to both its front and back. The imperial robe was made of blue gauze embroidered with motifs of the stars, the moon, the sun, dragons, mountains, fire, pheasants, tigers and monkeys. The lower garment with rice embroidery was made of red gauze and decorated with jade tassels. An inner garment made of white plain gauze would be dressed inside the lower garment, and outside a red silk bixi5 would be added to the lower garment. The cummerbund was made with red and white gauze. The ribbon holding the jade pendants from the belt was made of nas i j. As for the shoes, some were high boots made of red gauze and some were shoes made of nas i j. And the socks were made of red twill damask.

The ceremonial dress for the Heir Apparent consisted of a nine-tasseled crown, a reddish-black ceremonial robe with mountain, dragon, pheasant, fire, tiger, and monkey design, a lower garment decorated with jade tassels and rice embroidery, white inner garments, bixi, leather sash, four-colored ribbons, red socks, and red shoes.

Since the Emperor began to wear mianfu, the design of coiled dragons has been reserved only for the royal family. In 1297, officials of the Secretariat reported to the court that "the silk sold in the market was decorated with the motif of the dragon similar to that worn by the Emperor with only the difference in the number of the dragon's claws". Emperor Chengzong then especially decreed: "allow them to make silk clothes with dragon design on both the front and back. It doesn't matter. But if they dare to duplicate our coiled dragon design, stop them. Wanze (the Grand Councilor of the Right of the Secretariat6) had issued a ban on it throughout the country." During the reign of Emperor Renzong, the Secretariat had dictated different clothing colors for people of different ranks and declared illegal the use of dragon, especially the five clawed and two horned type, and phoenix design among both the officials and the commoners. (Garments, Vol. 9, TZTG)

The Yuan court also dictated the type of jifu (ceremonial dress for state sacrificial ceremonies) for the courtiers to wear on occasion of "state ceremonies" like the sacrificial ceremonies. For instance, when sacrificing to the Heaven and to the spirits of the land and grain at altars, the participants were required to dress in accordance with their ranks in the court. They were to wear cyan gauze robe, red gauze skirt or purple gauze gongfu (formal court dress of a government official) and red leather shoes or black boots with white damask socks. And their hats, somewhat the mark of their ranks, spanned a wide range of variety, such as Longjin Diaochan Guan (gilded gauze guan7), Diaochan Guan (gauze guan), Xiezhi Guan8, Shuijiaozan Jinliang Guan (gilded ridged guan with a horn hairpin) (ranging from two ridges to seven9), Jiaojiao Futou (Twisted futou10) and Heiqi Futou (black-lacquered futou), etc. When conducting a sacrificial ceremony in the Confucian Temple, a ceremonial official were required to wear the Seven-Ridge Guan, a cyan robe, a red brocade sash, a red gauze skirt, white silk inner garments, the red gauze bixi, leather shoes and white silk socks. And his assistants were required to wear the Confucian Dress, the Unframed Tang Jin, and the black boots. To memorize the order of dressing, someone even invented a mnemonic rhyme which was also recorded by Tao Zongyi: "when Son of Heaven sacrificed to Heaven and Earth in the suburbs and the ancestors in the Ancestral Temple, all the entourage were required to wear ceremonial dress. All should dress according to the mnemonic rhyme lest there should be any unnecessary mistakes. The mnemonic rhyme was as follows:

Socks and shoes, inner garments and yellow Ribbon,

元代城市
生活长卷

The Urban Life of the
Yuan Dynasty

132

Skirt and bixi, girdled by the sash,

Round-collared robe with blue waistline,

Jade ornament and guan on head,

The ensemble is completed by the hu 11in the hand."

(Rhyme of Dress, Vol. 5, NCZGL)

8

The Keshikten, the imperial bodyguard, were lavished with political and financial privileges. Even their costumes reflected their extraordinary status, and, in addition, a tangible influence from the Han Chinese clothing. According to Yu Fu Zhi (Record of Vehicles and Garments) in Yuan Shi (History of the Yuan), the number of their headgear like jin12 and guan alone reached 13.

1. Jiaojiao Futou. Its wings were twisted up to the back of head cloth.

2. Fengchi Futou. It was similar to Tang Jin. Its wings were turned upward to form the shape of clouds and a pair of "phoenix wings" was attached to the side.

3. Scholar Hat. It was similar to Jiaojiao Futou, with its spoon-like wings draped to the back.

4. Tang Jin. Its wings were round at the end and were turned upwards to form the shape of the clouds.

5. Konghe Futou. It was similar to Jiaojiao Futou. Its front was interwoven with gold filaments.

6. Huajiao Futou. It was similar to Jiaojiao Futou. Its wings and front were decorated with different patterns of embroidery.

7. Pingjin Ze13. Made of black-lacquered leather, it was similar to the square gauze guan, a variant of Jinxian Guan.

8. Red Gauze Headband. It was embroidered with auspicious floral patterns.

9. Five-colored Silk Jin. It was painted with auspicious floral patterns.

10. Jin Hat. It was made of lacquered satin, with the back higher than the front, tilting slightly frontwards. Its back was made of brocade with the pattern of overlapping coins.

11. Wu Bian. It was made of leather.

12. Armored Riding Guan. It was made of leather and was painted with black lacquer. It was trimmed with bright yellow valance.

13. Jindou Helmet. It was made of leather. Its metal part was dyed with five different colors which were determined by those of the armor.

The ensemble of imperial guards consisted of the robe, lined jacket and leather armor with complementary items like cloud-shaped shawl, oversleeves, trousers, etc.

1. Cloud-shaped shawl. It looked like four clouds. It was made of five-colored gauze interwoven with gold filaments, and had blue trim.

2. Inner armor. It was similar to the cloud-shaped shawl. It was made of blue brocade and trimmed with white brocade.

3. Sleeveless Garment.

4. Inner robe. It was made of red brocade, and was worn by warriors under the sleeveless garment.

5. Soldier's Robe. It was made of silk and decorated with the auspicious pattern of flowers.

6. Narrow-sleeved Robe. It was made of gauze or coarse silk.

7. Braid-girdled jacket. It was similar to a narrow-sleeved upper garment, and was pleated at the waist and girdled with silk braids.

8. Konghe Jacket. It was made of blue and red brocade and

decorated with auspicious pattern of flowers.

9. Narrow-sleeved Jacket. It was dark red in color.

10. Musician's Jacket. It was made of red brocade with wide sleeves and narrow cuffs, and was pleated at the waist and girdled with silk braids.

11. Leather armor. It was painted with the motif of tiger or lion or golden chain mail.

12. Oversleeves. Each oversleeve was made of brocade and lined with green stain with a garter.

13. Silk Sash in the Shape of a Flying Snake. It was one zhang and one chi long and lined with red brocade.

14. Belt. It was a red leather waist belt, a litter smaller than a waist band, decorated with two otter tails. Its bronze belt buckle was gilded with gold.

15. Tassel Ring. It was made of bronze and encrusted with gold.

16. Trousers. They were made of blue brocade and were decorated with the motifs of ferocious beasts and clouds and trimmed with brown brocade interwoven with silver filaments.

The imperial guards usually wore tall leather boots, boots with cloud-shaped toes, ramie shoes and silk gaiters. The shafts of boots with cloud-shaped toes were also decorated cloud motif.

From the above introduction of the clothing of the Keshikten, it could be concluded that such traditional Mongolian clothes as the robes were still worn by the Keshikten, but some of the other clothes like the leather armor were almost Chinese, and that their traditional headdresses like the hat li were almost replaced by the Chinese ones, such as futou and Tang Jin.

During the era of the Mongol Empire, there lacked a clearly defined bureaucratic system which resulted in a confusion in officials' court dress. The situation was changed after the accession of Qubilai who gradually established the central and local bureaucracy with the help of his Han Chinese advisers. In 1271, advisers like Bingzhong, Wang Pan, and Tudan Gonglü proposed that all the officials should observe proper rituals in gongfu when attending the court assemblies and ceremonies celebrating festivals, receiving the imperial amnesty, and issuing the imperial edict. Qubilai adopted their proposal and dictated three different colors of garments for the officials: purple gauze garment for officials above the fifth rank, light red gauze garment for officials above the sixth rank, and green gauze garment for officials above the ninth rank. In 1287, at the suggestion of the Bureau of Military Affairs, the court dress of the military officials began to follow the same dress code of the civil officials.

According to the dress code of gongfu, gongfu had to be tied to the right, and officials were permitted to wear the gongfu of the subordinates but not of the superiors.

The dress code of gongfu was as follows:

1. Officials of the first rank were to wear a purple gauze garment decorated with a large medallion of five cun in diameter and a jade belt.

2. Officials of the second rank were to wear a purple gauze garment decorated with a small medallion of three cun in diameter and a belt studded with carved rhinoceros horns.

3. Officials of the third rank were to wear a purple gauze garment decorated with the motif of a leafless flower of two cun in diameter and a gold belt imprinted with the leech pattern.

元代城市
生活长卷

The Urban Life of the
Yuan Dynasty

136

4. Officials of the fourth rank were to wear a purple gauze garment decorated with the motif of small miscellaneous flowers of one cun and five fen in diameter and a gold belt imprinted with the leech pattern.

5. Officials of the fifth rank were to wear a purple gauze garment with the motif of small miscellaneous flowers of one cun and five fen in diameter and a belt studded with black rhinoceros horns.

6. Officials of both the sixth and the seventh ranks were to wear a light red gauze garment with the motif of small miscellanea flowers of one cun in diameter and a belt studded with black rhinoceros horns.

7. Officials of both the eighth and ninth ranks were to wear a light red gauze garment with no floral decoration and a belt studded with black rhinoceros horns.

The futou worn by the officials were made of lacquered gauze. Their belts were "made of red leather with eight buckles". And their boots were made of black leather. Someone had summarized the dress code of gongfu in the following words: "Officials of the first and the second ranks wore robes with a large medallion and the jade or leather belts decorated with rhinoceros horns. Officials from the fifth to the third ranks wore purple robes and the gold belts; officials of the sixth and the seventh ranks wore light red robes; official of the ninth and the eighth grades were green robes. All the robes were made of gauze. When receiving the appointment of the provincial level, officials of all the levels were to wear wingceltis-brown robes, the futou and black boots." (Section two, Miscellaneous Institutions, Vol. 3, CMZ)

The gongfu of the Subofficial Functionaries consisted of a tight wingceltis-brown upper garment, a leather belt decorated black horns and the futou with stretched wings.

As for the Court Ladys, those above the third rank were to wear garments with a floral pattern interwoven with gold filaments and accessories of gold beads and jade. Those above the fifth rank were to wear garments of gold brocade and accessories of gold, jade and pearls. Those below the sixth rank were only permitted to wear gold-sprinkled garments or those made of golden coarse silk and accessories of gold (but they were allowed to wear jade and pearl earrings).

10

In 1315, the Secretariat issued a regulation on the color of clothing on Emperor Renzong's orders to purify the extravagant social atmosphere and restore people's hierarchical awareness. The Mongols and the Keshikten, however, were not subject to the regulation, only that they were forbidden from wearing clothes with dragon and phoenix design.

It was dictated by the court that the commoners should only wear clothes of ramie cloth with faint patterns, silk, and fur, and that they were forbidden from dressing in the bright and vibrant colors, especially the color of reddish brown. They were not supposed to decorate their headdresses like li and other hats with gold or jade. Women were only allowed to wear silver accessories. But they could have a jade and a gold hairpins and a pair of earrings with gold beads and jade pendants. Thus a majority of the masses wore clothes of dark colors, which, however, inspired the dyers to develop over ten shades of dark colors which ranged from silver gray to pitch-dark.

The folk dress consisted of shanggai (outer garment), cotton robes, tuanshan (the ceremonial dress for women in the Yuan Dynasty), Tang Blouses, qunyao (skirt), beida (a sleeveless short garment), hanta (an unlined inner jacket), and guodu (bellyband), etc.

The Shanggai referred to a formal outer garment for men. Descriptions of shanggai could be found in Yuan zaju14. For example

in Shen Nu Er the protagonist Shen Nu' er sighted to himself: "all my classmates laughed at me for I had no beautiful cloths." On hearing that, his father said: "I would go and buy a piece of colored satin for my child to make the shanggai." In another drama Chen Zhou Tiao Mi (Selling Rice in Chenzhou), there way another line: "Old man, follow me to my home to get dressed up. I will give you a decent shanggai, a new hat, a tea-brown tasseled sash, a pail of clean leather sandals and a pair of boots. What I want from you is only a dutiful gatekeeper. Isn' t it a good deal?" From the above lines in zaju it could be inferred that shanggai was the formal dress for men in the society.

Shanggai was a term that could be used to designate either an upper garment like an unlined jacket or a robe. "Since the cotton unlined upper garment for man was usually called a cotton robe, shanggai could also be classified into robes." (Virtues and Filial Piety, Vol. 11, NCZGL)

The cotton robe was usually worn in summer and its quality varied according to the family financial situation. In winter it would be substituted by a lined robe or a kapok one. However not everyone could get access to decent clothes. For some students and scholars, a cotton robe was the only decent clothes they could afford all their lives. Taking Li Zhongqian from Zouxian District, Tengzhou, for example, when he served as a Scribe in Surveillance Commission in western Zhejiang Province, because of his scant stipend he was unable to support his parents and even his wife who was then compelled to work to make the ends meet by selling the cloth she wove. Zhongqian had only one cotton robe, so all the washing or sewing and mending work could only be done when he was off work. If a guest happened to pay a visit at that time, he would be gently declined with the words that "our master way unavailable, occupied with the washing." Another example came from Lü Sicheng, an impoverished student, who was forced to barter his only cotton robe for rice one day in the morning when he woke up to find that their home had run out of rice.

But his wife considered it a great pity and was reluctant to sell the robe. To console his wife, Sicheng improvised the following poem:

For the breakfast, I have to pawn off my robe,
But don't be so sorrowful my dear.
Without vinegar one can't even make dishes,
With scant money one should not aspire to fish.
Thanks to the book I have read,
Never would I do anything too absurd.
After all the hardships we've gone through,
Hope the good news will soon arrive in this small cottage.

In Jiangnan Region, there was a retired scholar who was "erudite and good at making poetry and articles". But be could not even afford a cotton robe and all be had is a short garment of buckram, a pair of cotton socks and a pair straw sandals. Kongqi, a scholar, had a well-to-do family for his father had served as a Scribe in jiankang period. However, his clothes and the household goods were very simple: "his most clothes were of coarse silk and kapok, and only a few were made of fine fur, ramie and fine silk. A white silk jacket, old but clean, had been used for 30 years." "His cotton clothes and plain shoes, porcelain and wooden chopsticks were no different from those used by the ordinary people." (Dress Simply, Vol. 3, ZZZJ)

Women's ceremonial dress was called tuanshan or dayi, and was usually worn by the bride on her wedding day. Description of tuanshan could also be found in Yuan zaja. In the drama Wang Jiang Ting (Watching the Pavilion beside the River), there was a line of a matchmaker: "She was made not the legal wife but only a concubine.

The Tang Blouse and qunyao were very popular among the women in the Yuan Dynasty. Vivid description of women wearing the Tang

元代城市
生活长卷

The Urban Life of the
Yuan Dynasty

Blouse could also be found in literary works in the Yuan Dynasty. For example "She was more slender than she was in the last spring, looking more beautiful than her Tang Blouse." (Zhao Xianhong, Whirling Wind, Other Thoughts, QYSQ, pp. 1701-1706) And "slowly she moved with her petite feet, her slender body swayed; her Tang Blouse swung tenderly, her sash blew in the wind, and her dancing sleeves drooped." (Guan Hanqing, Woman Commandant, QYSQ, p. 178) Different from the Mongolian robes, the Tang Blouse, the traditional clothes for women in the Han territory, attracted special attention from people at that time. Qunyao referred to the skirt worn by the women in the Yuan Dynasty.

Beida was a sleeves short garment popular among the commoners. Description of beida could also be found in Yuan zaju. In the drama Zhao Li Rang Fei (Saving Zhao Li), there was line "I just saw him wearing a short silk jacket inside-out, over which loosely covered a broken beida". In Yan Qing Bo Yu (Yan Qing Gambling on Fish), there was the line "My white felt hat could protect me from the wind and this shabby beida could also shelter me from the rain for the time being." From the above description we can infer that beida fell into the type of everyday suit instead of formal clothes.

Hanta or hanshan generally referred to the underwear worn by both men and women in the Yuan Dynasty. It was usually worn together with other pieces of underwear like the bellyband and corset. Hanta as well as bellyband could also be found in Yuan zaju and palace poetry. In the drama Dong Xi Xiang (Tunes of the Western Chamber), there was the line: "the hanshan and a bellyband were not worth mentioning, except that they were made by me." In Xi Xiang Ji (The Romance of the Western Chamber), there was the line: "my letter is written. How to express my feeling but send him a hanshan, a guodu, a pair of stockings, a lute, a jade hairpin and a pen of specked bamboo! Boy, pack up these with care! In Hou Ting Hua (Backyard Flowers) there were such lines as "from tomorrow on, you have to get me, your beloved husband, and our kid dressed up. Please buy me a black gauze head cloth and a big red bellyband and our kid a pair of silk trousers and a cotton coat." Zhang Yu also mentioned bellyband in one of his poems.

His jisun robe of blue and red brocade compelled obedience,
His bellyband studded with circles of pearls beckoned felicity.
(Songs under the Imperial Carriage)

From the above lines of dramas and Zhang Yu's poem, it could be inferred that bellyband was then widely used by all the people, rich and poor, with only a difference in quality.

As for the headgear, men usually wore a head cloth or futou, such as Tang Jin, headband, and kenao. The Headcloth for women was called baoji.

Women always took a fancy to accessories. In the Yuan Dynasty most women had such accessories as shoushi (head ornaments) and toumian (jewellery). Shoushi included hairpins, headbands, earrings and combs, while toumian mainly referred to bracelets including armlets and wristlets, and could be classified into several groups according to the material, such as gold, silver and jade. The difference between shoushi and toumian could be mirrored by the following Yuan Zaju. In Hou Ting Hua (Backyard Flower), a women was forced to relinquish all her shoushi and toumian to save her own life, while the recipient still needed to verify "whether the hairpins and the armlets were of gold or silver" before making any commitment. It showed that not only shoushi but also toumian was valuable. In Bai Hua Ting (Baihua Pavilion), the difference was made all the more clear by the line "Jie Yuan, I have only this set of gold toumian, complete with both armlets and wristlets. Please take them as your travelling expenses." In the Yuan Dynasty shoushi and toumian

were also part of women's make-up, which could be verified by the line in the drama Jiu Feng Chen (Saving the Dusty-windy) by Guan Hanqing: "Straighten the collars and smooth the sleeves; put on the accessories and comb the hair." Shoushi and toumian were a woman's personal belongings and were highly cherished. In the drama Lu Zhai Lang (Lu Zhailang), a woman confessed that "I had forced others to sell their silver toumian while I myself still wearing my gold toumian." Accessories like gold, silver, pearl, jade and jadeite were usually regarded as the symbol of status, and were, therefore, highly desired. But their value, in fact, was not worth the price. No wonder there was such a comment that "shoushi inlaid with jadeite were the most useless thing, because it cost people a lot but became worthless when it was locked away. Pearls, though much more expensive were also of no practical use··· There was a saying that 'silver was vital, gold ill and pearls dead' with no comment of jadeite. The saying probably meant that silver was desired by everyone, and gold was gradually fell out of use, while pearls where almost abandoned by people, just like a dead thing. Peace and prosperity would blind people to hidden dangers and drive them to an extremely extravagant and luxurious way of life. Besides the gold, sliver, pearls and jade, people also pursed jadeite and precious fur, not knowing that life was short and that all these things would be reduced to rubbish after the death of their owners." (Shoushi inlaid with jadeite, Vol. 3, ZZZJ) The commoners, however, couldn't afford gold, sliver, pearls, jade, or jadeite. Their shoushi and toumian were very simple, which could be proved by Hou Ting Hua (Backyard Flower). In the drama what a woman was asked to buy was only "a bronze hairpin and a jujube-wood comb."

The practice of foot binding dates back to the Five Dynasties. It started to gain popularity in the Southern Song Dynasty, though still not quite common in the Northern Song Dynasty, and continued to prevail in the Yuan Dynasty, especially among the woman in Jiangnan Region, to such a degree that "almost every woman followed the practice and those who refused to would be ridiculed." (Foot Binding, Vol. 10, NCZGL) Those "three-inch golden lotus", or "the half-folded golden lotus" — a term usually associated with the bound feet, fascinated the literati a lot.

> Under the silk blouse produced half of the golden lotus,
> From the green sleeves stretched the tender arms.

> The sleeves enveloped ten slender fingers,
> The swaying blouse revealed half bow-shaped shoes.
> (Shoes for women with bound feet were called bow-shaped shoes.)

> Small as the shoes were,
> They were decorated with flowers of four seasons,
> And wrapped to form a pointed front.

Women with bound feet usually had their shoes embroidered with binds and flowers; while those didn't bind feet wore saxie (shippers). "People in western Zhejiang Province wore flat straw shoes called saxie which were also worn by women who didn't bind feet. (Shoes, Vol. 18, NCZGL) In addition to the above shoes, people also wore boots, cloth shoes, hempen sandals, clogs, and straw sandals, etc.

People in different regions wore different clothes. In areas of Dadu, for example, it was popular to wear kapok shoes and hempen shoes and in winter leather clothes. "People (in Dadu) usually made and sold tea-brown kapok shoes to others and people of Xishan usually carried hempen shoes outside of the city for sale. Even women with bound feet wore hempen shoes which they tied to their feet for the convenience of mountain climbing." "The residents usually wore a single garment of sheep skin to keep warm in winter. They would sell it at a lower price in

元代城市
生活长卷

The Urban Life of the
Yuan Dynasty

the next March or April, and buy a new one, regardless of the style, in the next winter. In the same way, they bought and sold their leather trousers that were usually with fur and were tightly clinging to the skin." Besides, people in areas of extreme climate employed articles similar to today's goggles. "Desert areas of Youyan were prone to sand storms in windy weather. Dignitaries in possession of what was called "demon's eyes" would put them over their eyes. They were then fixed to the head through a dark blue silk ribbon." (XJZJY, p. 202)

In the late Yuan times, "Korean style clothes with a square collar, a high waist line and short sleeves prevailed in the imperial palace." "The dignitaries in the capital all regarded it a great honor to own a Korean girl, whose elegance, beauty and considerateness usually won her the favor from the master. Ever since zhizheng period, a major part of Palace Serving Women in the imperial palace had been Korean. Therefore, most of the clothing and utensils in the imperial palace were made in the Korean style." (GSWS) Even areas in Jiangnan Region were influenced by the trend, which could be proved by the anecdote recorded by Tao Zongyi. "When Master Du Qingbi stayed in Qiantang, many a Confucian scholar poured in his residence to pay a visit. A man name Yan Mengchu them made a poem to mock them. 'With wisteria hats and Korean boots, they contended to be the Keshikten before the door of the recluse.' In the poem wisteria hats and Korean boots were used to allude to a short-lived fashion." (Keshikten before the Door of Recluse, NCZGL, Vol. 28)

11

Confucian scholars, monks, entertainers and prostitutes dressed in a different way from the ordinary people.

Regulations issued in 1273 dictated that gongfu worn by the masters of ceremonies of every route should consist of a tight tea-brown gauze

garment, a belt decorated with black rhinoceros horns, and a futou with stretched wings. Confucian scholars who were to attend the sacrificial ceremony at the Confucian Temple "usually preferred to wear everyday court dress, because casual clothing reduced one to a commoner."
In the same year, the Secretariat especially ordered those Confucian scholars attending the sacrificial ceremony at the Confucian Temple to wear a leather waist belt and Tang Jin because "clothing reflected one's status as well as reverence for Confucius". In 1306 the Secretariat further ordered that Confucian officials wear the gongfu of the same style as that of the Subofficial Functionaries. Because Confucian officials, including instructors and provosts, "if dressed in the same way as the students would be considered lacking due regard for priority in rank."
However, Confucian Scholars in Jiangnan Region who were used to wearing shenyi15 when attending the sacrificial ceremonies, refused to wear the leather waist belt and Tang Jin, which forced a concession from the Secretariat. The Secretariat later decreed: "scholars could dress according to the local customs so long as the clothes conformed to the norm of etiquette." (Section two, the Ministry of Rites, Vol. 29, YDZ, sic passim)

Medical officials didn't wear gongfu until 1316 when the Imperial Academy of Medicine submitted a memorial to the throne, asking for the same gongfu as the Confucian scholars for the medical officials, on the grounds that "all the regularly selected Confucian scholars wore gongfu but not the regularly selected medical instructors, who were thereby reduced to the commoners and were therefore striped of their identity. And that seemed to run counter to the basic principles." Their proposal was finally approved by the Emperor.

In Baoning Temple of Youyu Couty, Shangxi Province, there is a wash painting of the Yuan Dynasty about a group of literati and Confucian scholars wearing robes and head cloths of the Tang and Song styles.

Among them, six wore round collared robes of Song style and Tang Jin of Yuan style, and one wore Confucian garbs with an overlapped collar and the Confucian head cloth. The major difference between the round collared robe of Song style and that of Tang style was that the former had a detachable collar. And the different between Tang Jin of Yang style and Jin of Tang and Song styles was that the former had its wings droop apart at the back.

Monastic habits were divided into three ranks by the court in 1286. Instructors wore red Kasaya and red habits; Elder Masters wore yellow Kasaya and yellow habits; and ordinary monks wore tea-brown Kasaya and tea-brown habits. Tibetan monks usually wore red habits which were banned among the monks in the Han Territory.

The entertainers were dressed in the same way as the commoners. But during the performance, they were free to wear all kinds of clothes according to their roles in the play. In the Water God's Hall of Guangsheng Temple in Zhaocheng Town, Hongdong District, Shanxi Province, there was a fresco entitled "The Late Sanyue16 Actress Zhong Duxiu Had Performed Here". The fresco presented a vivid picture of drama performance in the Yuan dynasty and revealed the entertainers' dressing style on the stage at that time.

Prostitutes had a low social status and were subject to the strictest restrictions on the clothes. In 1268 the Secretariat decreed that "prostitutes and their families, who used to dress in the same way as others, should dress according to their respective ranks. Prostitutes should, and always should wear dark purple garments with headgear. Their male relatives should wear the green head cloth and female relatives purple socks. None of them should wear the hat li, clothes of gold brocade, and ride horses. Once a transgressor was arrested, his horse should be given to the person who caught him as a reward." In 1315 the Secretariat further decreed that "the prostitutes and their families should wear black beida when going out, and should not ride on horses or in carts".

Clothing always bears the most distinctive mark of an era. When the nomads came to power, the clothing of the citizens did get changed but its traditional elements hadn't been totally eradicated. The secret of the longevity of the Chinese civilization lies in the fact that on the one hand it has inherited the agrarian culture, and on the other hand it keeps absorbing the essence of other cultures, such as the nomadic and even fishing and hunting cultures. And the Yuan clothing served as the very paradigm of that.

In the next chapter, we'll introduce another special costume in the Yuan Dynasty—Jisun Robes.

元代城市
生活长卷

The Urban Life of the
Yuan Dynasty

Chapter Two | **"Jamah Banquet" in the Imperial Palace**

In the Yuan Dynasty, all the attendants of an imperial banquet were to be dressed in the same color, which was probably unprecedented and unique in the Chinese history. Now let's have a close look at these sumptuous banquets in the Yuan imperial palace.

1

Regardless of extended journey, all the princes returned to the imperial palace,

Where wine was prepared and music played by judges.

All the officials dressed in the same-colored garments studded with pearls,

With gorgeous belts girdled around the waist.

Annotation: whenever a prince or a foreign emissary came to the court for a visit, the Emperor would throw a banquet called Jisun Banquet for them. "Jisun" in Chinese means the same color, referring to the fact that all the attendants were dressed in the same color.

The most distinctive costumes in the Yuan court were no doubt the Jisun Robes.

The Mongolian word "jisun" means color. Its Persian synonym "jamah", meaning garment, refers to the same colored clothes worn in the imperial banquets. "A banquet would be held on the occasion of an audience, a ceremony, the arrival of an imperial prince at the court, and the imperial inspection tour. In the banquet people are seated according to their intimacy to the emperor and their ranks in the court. The complicacy of the etiquette, the magnificence of the music, the dissemination of his Majesty's grace and the rigorousness of the law displayed by the banquet reflected the profound insight of the ancestors. Costumes for the banquet, including clothes and headdresses of the same color and quality, were called jisun and were all endowed by his Majesty" (Banquet, JSDDXL) " 'Jisun' in Chinese meant clothes of one color and were only worn during the imperial banquets. There were jisun for winter and summer, but there was no specific regulation on it. All the imperial relatives with meritorious records, courtiers and Court Attendants of the Emperor would be awarded jisun by the Emperor. Even people of no ranks like entertainers and imperial guards could receive jisun. Such costumes, though of different quality according to the owner's rank, were all called jisun." (Record of Vehicles and Garments, Vol. 78, YS)

The imperial banquet that required jisun was called "Jisun Banquet" or "Jamah Banquet". Because every day required a change of clothes, the Emperor, aristocrats and the courtiers were all in possession of many sets of jisun. Zhou Boqi had recorded the opulence of the Jamah Banquet, relating that the banquet would run for three days and "the Palace Guards, the courtiers and the Court Attendants all wore the jisun studded with pearls and jade, which they change every day." (On Jamah Banquet, Vol. 1, JGJ) Marco Polo had a more detailed account of jisun:

Now on his birthday, the Great Kaan dresses in the best of his robes, all wrought with beaten gold; and full 12,000 Barons and Knights on

that day came forth dressed in robes of the same color, and precisely like those of the Great Kaan, except that they are no so costly; but still they all of the same color as his, and are also of silk and gold. Every man so clothed has a girdle of gold; and this as well as the dress is given him by the Sovereign. And I will aver that there are some of these suits decked with so many pearls and precious stones that a single suit shall be worth full 10,000 golden bezants. And of such raiment there are several sets. For you must know that the Great Kaan, thirteen times in the year, presents to his Barons and Knights such suits of raiment as I am speaking of. And on such occasion they wear the same color that he does, a different color being assigned to each festival. Hence you may see what a huge business it is, and there is no prince in the world but he alone who could keep up such customs as these. When his Majesty assumes any particular dress, the nobles of his court wear corresponding, but less costly, dresses, which are always in readiness. They are not annually renewed, but on the contrary are made to last about ten years.

Now you must know that the Great Kaan hath set apart 12,000 of his men who are distinguished by the name of Keshican, as I have told you before; and on each of these 12,000 are Barons he bestows thirteen changes of raiment, which are all different from one another: I mean that in one set the 12,000 are all of one color; the next 12,000 of another color, and so on; so that they are of thirteen different colors. These robes are garnished with gems and pearls and other precious things in a very rich and costly manner. And along with each of those changes of raiment, ie., 13 times in the year, he bestows on each of those 12,000 Barons a fine golden girdle of great richness and value, and likewise a pair of boots of Camut, that is to say of Borgal, curiously wrought with silver thread.

According to Yu Fu Zhi (Record of Vehicles and Garments) in Yuan Shi (History of the Yuan), Jisun robes for the Yuan Emperor in winter had the following 11 different types:

1. Nas i j (golden brocade) robe with a gold brocade warm hat.

2. Khmael（plush velvet）robe with a gold brocade warm hat.

3. Crimson baoli17 garment (one-piece garment with a lapel at the knee) with a jewel-encrusted guan.

4. Peach-red baodi garment with a jewel-encrusted guan.

5. Purple baoli garment with a jewel-encrusted guan.

6. Blue baoli garment with a jewel-encrusted guan.

7. Green baoli garment with a jewel-encrusted guan.

8. Pink leather robe with a red gold-brocade warm hat.

9. Yellowish leather robe with a red gold-brocade warm hat.

10. White leather robe with a white gold-brocade warm hat.

11. Ermine robe with an ermine warm hat plus an ermine vest.

Jisun robes for the Emperor in summer fell into 15 categories:

1. Dana dorr nas i j robe (large pearls basted on gold brocade) with a jewel-encrusted baoli with golden phoenix design.

2. Sobhe dorr nas i j robe (small pearls basted on gold brocade) with Juanyun Guan18 decorated with pearl tassels.

3. Nas i j robe with Juanyun Guan decorated with pearl tassels.

4. Crimson baoli garment studded with big pearls and red gems, with a pearl-brimmed li.

5. White baoli garment of gold cloth studded with gems, with a white rattan warm hat.

6. Camel-brown robe studded with gems with a whit rattan hat.

7. Five-colored gauze robe embroidered with crimson dragons, with a red li decorated with golden phoenixes.

元代城市
生活长卷

The Urban Life of the
Yuan Dynasty

8. Five-colored gauze robe embroidered with green dragons, with a red li decorated with golden phoenixes.

9. Five-colored gauze robe embroidered with blue dragons, with a blue li decorated with golden phoenixes.

10. Five-colored gauze robe embroidered with silver brown dragons, with a silver brown li decorated with golden phoenixes.

11. Five-colored gauze robe embroidered with reddish brown dragons, with a reddish brown li decorated with golden phoenixes.

12. Five-colored gauze robe embroidered with golden dragons, with a li decorated with golden phoenixes.

13. Cyan gauze robe with golden dragon design, with a satin guan decorated with golden phoenixes.

14. Brown jewel-studded robe of gold brocade in the form of dragons playing with pearls, with a yellow jewel-encrusted hat with a flap at the back.

15. Cyan suf (Muslim woolen cloth) robe interwoven with gold filaments, with a gem-studded stain hat with a flap at the back.

Jisun robes for the officials in winter were of 9 types: Crimson nas i j robe, Crimson khamel robe, Crimson formal dress of plain gauze, peach-red formal dress of plain gauze, blue formal dress of plain gauze, green formal dress of plain gauze, purple formal dress of plain gauze, yellow robe of plain gauze, and dark blue robe of plain gauze. And in summer they wore the following 14 types of jisun robes: plain nas i j robe, Baoli garment of nas i j with converging pattern, reddish-brown robe of gold brocade studded with pearls, crimson plain baoli garment with a plain sash, crimson robe of gold brocade decorated with pearls, peach-red gauze robe, blue gauze robe, green gauze robe, silver brown gauze robe, Korean dark blue gauze robe with cloud-shaped sleeves, camel-brown gauze robe, alizarin-red gauze robe, white robe studded with gems, and dark blue plain baoli garment with a plain sash.

Jisun robes, the embodiment of the royal favor and great honor, had become a symbol of high standing of the dignitaries in the society. Quite a few literary sources of the Yuan Dynasty have mentioned "the Emperor's distribution of clothes, usually the jisun robes, among the officials". Taking the Alahan family of the Jalayir clan for example, as a reward for his meritorious service Alahan was granted nine garments that were made of "the most opulent fabric in Tibet". Later he was awarded another nine gold-brocade garments and a jade belt. And his son Yesudier was also awarded two gold-brocade garments by Emperor Renzong in the Gaiyuan year of huangqing period and by Emperor Yingzong in the Gaiyuan year of zhizhi period respectively. After the accession of Emperor Wenzong, he was awarded three gold-brocade garments and jisun robes.

"The so-called jisun referred to the clothes the courtiers worn during the imperial banquets, just like today's Jiangyi (crimson garment) granted by the emperor. Their shoulders and back were studded with big pearls and so were their hats. A complete set of jisun robes consisted of 9 nas ı j garments. And nas ı j referred to gold brocade." Nas ı j garment and the gold-brocade garment were both jisun robes by nature.

3

A group of servants in the imperial palace were specially assigned for preparing and serving the imperial banquets and the Emperor's diet.

Imperial kitchens, including a big one and a small one, were installed within the imperial cities of both Dadu and Shangdu where the Emperor's food was prepared. "The small kitchen was where the palace maids, prepared the "Eight Delicacies", and the big one was where people of the Palace Provisions Commission made the mutton broth. Dishes from the small kitchen were served first and all the officials who wanted to have an audience with the Emperor must wait outside until the

元代城市
生活长卷

The Urban Life of the
Yuan Dynasty

Emperor had finished the last course of dish sent from the big kitchen."
(LJZJ) The so-called "Eight Delicacies" referred to "cheese, young
river deer, wild camel hooves, moose lips, camel milk porridge, roasted
swan, grape wine, and koumiss. "All of them were made in the small
kitchen", while the big kitchen was where mutton, Mongolian gazelle,
and Citellus dauricus were prepared.

Twenty "Meal Servers" and Twenty "Koumiss Servers"
usually waited upon the Emperor during his mealtime in the hall. The
Meal Server, or Bagurqi in Mongolian, referred to "the cook of the
Emperor who was also required to present the dish to the Emperor in
person." And the "Koumiss Server", or Haraqi in Mongolian, was the
one in charge of pasturing the horses and presenting the Emperor with
the koumiss. Because the top koumiss was black, or in Mongolian qara,
those who served koumiss were then dubbed as Haraqi, and most Haraqi
were Kipchak. (Meritorious Record of Prince of Jurong District, Vol. 26,
DYXGL)

It was said that those who waited upon Emperor Shizu with his
dishes and drink had their mouth and nose muffled with a veil or a piece
of silk, so that no breath from those people should taint the food presented
to the Emperor. However, another version of the origin of this practice
was that it was initiated by Emperor Renzong. Once during a banquet
hosted by the Emperor Renzong in Changchun hall, one of the Eunuchs
waiting upon him steward for food kept coughing which irritated the
Emperor a lot. The Emperor then decreed that all the stewards for food
should cover their face except for the eyes with golden gauze. Later it
became an establish practice. And to ensure dietetic hygiene, even the
flour-milling machine in the imperial palace was especially made. "The
Food Service produced the imperial wheat flour on the milling machine
installed in a two-storey house with the millstone on the second floor and
the spinning axis extended to the first floor. Thus the flour would stay

free from the contaminants neither from the livestock pulling the mill nor from the people passing by. And this contraption was made by a brilliant craftsman surnamed Qu. (Flour in the Imperial Palace, Vol. 5, NCZGL)

According to Marco Polo, a special dining table measured eight cubits19 in height was installed in the center of the Imperial Kitchen of Qubilai. Near the table there was a cupboard for all the tableware of the Emperor. Its opulence could be discerned from the following poem.

> The peaches in the Imperial Garden mellowed in the late spring,
> Golden plates filled with food were sent into the imperial palace.
> Bowls brimming with tasty cheese,
> Were distributed among the officials on duty waiting before the hall.

The tableware of the Emperor included not only many valuable utensils of gold and silver, but also quite a few delicate porcelain and lacquer ware. Among others, there were some exquisite items sent from out of the imperial palace and even the country as tribute.

4

Big wine containers and exquisite drinking vessels were a necessity in a large-scale palace banquet.

The wine container was called jiuju, or tusurge in Mongolian, which was later used to refer to all the pitchers or leather bags for holding the wine. In the early days of the Mongol Empire, the Mongol nobles usually used leather bags or jugs to hold the wine. After Qubilai ascended to the throne, he ordered goldsmith to make wine containers with gold and silver in the shape of animals, such as the elephant, tiger and horse. And every such container had a silver bowl placed in front of it to hold the wine poured from the mouth of the animal-shaped container. Such pot

元代城市
生活长卷

The Urban Life of the
Yuan Dynasty

156

was probably the so-called jiucao or a butt and it was sometimes made of pure gold "weighing thousands of liang", and sometimes simply of iron. Ogedei was addicted to wine in his later years. To curb his drinking excess, his courtier Yelü Chucai presented himself before Ogedei with a golden jiucao one day, saying: "this butt was made of iron, but it was still corroded by the wine. How could our viscera be free from the erosion of the wine when they were no stronger than the iron?" Ogedei then told the Court Attendants not to provide him more than three cups of wine a day." (Song Zizhen, Record of the Secretariat Director Yelü Chucai, Vol. 57, YWL)

After the enthronement of Mongke Khan, he ordered the Parisian artisan William to make a large multifunctional container in his palace tent because he considered it unseemly to have the leather bags filled with milk and other drinks in the tent. This container was really a great silver tree. There were four lions of silver crouching at the foot of the tree, each with a conduit extending to the room outside the tent where the beverages were stored. From these four conduits belched forth the grape wine, the black koumiss, the honey mead, and the rice mead respectively. And for each liquor, there is a special silver bowl beneath the lion's mouth to receive it. On the top of the tree there was an angel holding a trumpet controlled by the man hidden in a vault underneath the tree. If there ran out of a particular drink, the angel would blow his trumpet and immediately the servants outside would pour the beverage into the proper conduit which lead it down into the bowl prepared for it. And then people in the tent could continue to enjoy the drink. This container, though elaborately made, was proved inconvenient because it was man-powered and it also required another smaller tent outside the Khakhan's to store the beverages.

In 1285, Qubilai had the craftsmen make a big wine vessel which "rising one zhang and seven chi high was made of wood, gilded with silver inside and carved with dragons and clouds outside". It was actually a "wooden lacquered pitcher gilded with silver", or Jiuhai "with a capacity of over 50 shi of wine". According to Marco Polo, this piece of furniture was in the form of a square chest, each side being three bu in length. The inside was hollow and contained a huge vessel of pure gold, and in each corner of the chest was a vessel of smaller size to hold beverages like mares' milk and camel's milk, etc. Although the story may sound fantastic, it was indisputably true because the Mongols who were given to drinking bouts did have a predilection for huge wine vessels. In Yuwen Pavilion which is located in front of Tuancheng Hall beside the Beihai Park in modern Beijing, there was a big jade vessel called "Dushan Dayuhai". It measured 70 cm in height, 135 cm in diameter and weighing about 3,500 kilograms. It was a solid huge wine vessel carved out of an entire black jade.

In his palace poem Nian Xia Qu (Songs under the Imperial Carriage), the poet Zhang Yu had a vivid description of the imperial banquet.

In the huge gold pitcher rippled thousands shi of wine,
In the clatter of imperial stoups and ladders the feast is on the way.
In their tipsy ecstasy the Emperor and his courtiers,
Celebrating the great peace and harmony in the hall.
All the officials over the hall rising and falling in turns,
Drinking a toast to the Emperor with sophisticated drinking etiquette.
The chieftain announced the imperial edict with a toasting cup,
Requiring all to empty the gold goblets at one smug.

From the poem, it could be inferred that not only the wine container jiuhai but also shao (stoup) as well as the jinzhong (gold goblet) were

元代城市
生活长卷

The Urban Life of the
Yuan Dynasty

158

indispensable in the banquet.

Marco Polo also mentioned a gold stoup in his description of the Imperial banquets, which was big enough to hold drink for eight or ten persons. And one gold stoup was put between every two men seated at the table. Thus the stoup must be a kind of container placed beside the guests to hold the wine drawn from the capacious pitcher—Jiuhai, and the guests then filled their gold goblets with the wine from the stoups and drank.

If such inference makes sense, then the so-called stoup must the long lost ritual vessel yi in the Chinese history. Because the sapphire-blue porcelain yi decorated with golden patterns unearthed in Baoding, Hebei Province just resembled a big stoup.

The Mongols used to drink with big bowls which were later replaced by huge cups with or without stem or bowl-like cups in the imperial banquets. Among the relics unearthed from the Yuan graves in Wujiadi Village, Wuguquan People's Commune, Xinghe District, Ulanqab City, Inner Mongolia Autonomous Region, there was a bowl-like cup with a mouth in the shape of a flower. It has a thumb piece, underneath which there was a ring. Its inner bottom and the thumb piece were engraved with peony and honeysuckle design. And its brim was decorated with a circumference of honeysuckle pattern. Apart from the gold cups, there were also bronze and porcelain ones of the similar style.

In Nian Xia Qu (Songs under the Imperial Carriage) there was another line:

With music played behind the white horses from the Music Office,
Carried away the wine made by the Court of Imperial Entertainments.

This poem demonstrated that the wine served in the imperial palace was provisioned by the Court of Imperial Entertainments. The Court of

Imperial Entertainments was a unit of the Palace Provisions Commission in charge of the transportation of foodstuffs, including "collecting the imperial beverages from the Wine Stewards Service and delivering wine to the taverns by the roadside." Thus the manufacture and delivery of wine fell naturally under its duty.

5

The large-scale palace banquet Jamah Banquet followed a strict procedure.

Zhou Boqi, who was lucky enough to have been invited to a Jamah Banquet, wrote the Poem Zha Ma Xing (On Jamah Banquet) (JGJ, Vol. 1) and in the prelude to the poem he introduced the sumptuous Jamah Banquet to the readers.

I traveled north to the capital by cart on official business. In the early morning of an auspicious day in the sixth lunar month, The Keshikten and Court Attendants, dressed in fine golden clothes garnished with pearls and jade the Emperor bestowed on them, proceed in lines from outside the city on their garishly decorated horses towards the imperial palace with decorated weapons on the Emperor's orders. His Majesty, dressed in his finest, watched the parade from the tower in the imperial palace. After the end of the parade, the banquet commenced. During the banquet, only the Imperial Princes, imperial relatives, the Keshikten and the courtiers were permitted to drink a toast to the Emperor, while the rest were to drink in their seats which were arranged in an order according to their ranks. Then the all musical instruments began to play and a number of players and jugglers performed before the Emperor. The banquet lasted for three days and all the attendants changed their clothes every day. In the hunting activity followed the banquet, every high-ranking official would be

元代城市
生活长卷

The Urban Life of the
Yuan Dynasty

160

allotted 2,000 sheep and 3 ponies. The banquet was called Jisun banquet. Jisun in Chinese meant clothing of one color and the banquet was also called Jamah Banquet

With Zhou Boyi's account and the complement from other sources, we can piece together the procedure of the Jamah Banquet:

1. Picking an auspicious day. The Jamah Banquet was usually held on the lunar New Year's Day after the court assembly or on the Imperial Birthday following a series of celebrations. Sometimes it would also be held on an auspicious day of a certain month. As the banquet would run for 3 days, once the specific date for the banquet was chosen, a rain-dispelling alter was set by Lamas to ensure the fine weather during the banquet.

Garnished horses and fine clothes, the feast is one the way,
Only a sunny day could match such a great occasion.
Dispelled was the lingering rain by the Tibetan monks,
Who were summoned in the dawn and rewarded with gold.
(Song Jiong, Jamah Banquet)

2. Entering the imperial palace in one's finest. To attend the banquet one should not only wear Jisun Robes of a designated color, but also dress their horses up. One of the trendy ways to do that was to decorate them with pheasant tails. When entering the imperial palace, all should carry a bamboo tally of credentials and proceed in order, as was accounted by the following poems:

Thousand of officials on horses arrived at the mountain top.
All were on horses decorated with gold saddles and pheasant tails.

161

They dismounted from the horses when summoned to the banquet,

Before the palace gate they changed into the jisun robes.

(Yang Yunfu, Poems on Luanjing)

In jisun robes of blue and real brocade,

And the bellyband studded with circles of pearls,

The Imperial Guards holding the gold ceremonial weapons,

Filed into the imperial palace with an awing roar.

(Zhang Yu, Songs under the Imperial Carriage)

3. Getting seated in order. Marco Polo has elaborated on the arrangement of seats in the palace banquets. "His table is elevates a good deal above the others, and he sits at the north end of the hall, looking towards the south, with his chief wife beside him on the left. On his right sit his sons and his nephews, and other kinsmen of the Blood Imperial, but lower, so that their heads are on a level with the Emperor's feet. And then the other Barons sit at other tables lower still. So also with the women; for all the wives of the Lord's sons, and of his nephews and other kinsmen, sit at the lower table at his right; and below them again the ladies of the other Barons and Knights, each in the place assigned by the Lord's orders. The tables are so disposed that the Emperor can see the whole of them from end to end, many as they are. Further, you are not to suppose that everybody sits at table; on the contrary, the greater part of the soldiers and their officers sit at their meal in the hall on the carpets."
In the hall there were Keshikten specially assigned for order maintenance and victuals provision and only they were free to move during the banquet.

4. Chanting the Great Yasa. The Great Yasa, meaning "order, decree", was a collection of laws issued by Chinggis Khan based on the Mongolian customary law and his "maxims and instructions".

It was later revered by the Mongols as the great code of the ancestors. "Whenever there was a banquet, all the erudite courtiers must chant the Great Yasa." (Ke Jiusi, GCYSWS) Chanting the Great Yasa before the banquet was to remind people of the hardships their ancestors had gong through when founding the empire.

On the court assembly celebrating the start of Zhiyuan Period,
His Majesty repeated the ancestral maxims before those of Imperial Blood.
So as to remind all the divine generations yet to come,
That the great cause was derived from arduous work.
(Songs under the Imperial Carriage)

5. Commencing the repast. Drinking bouts started after representatives of the imperial princes and aristocrats had made a toast to the Emperor. Then people in the banquet would drink around until they all got drunk. Because drunkenness indicated that one has drunk to his satisfaction.

6. Enjoying entertainments. "Whenever there was a banquet the Bureau of Musical Ritual, to which all the musicians and performers in the country affiliated, would present performances with actresses all dressed in the finest to entertain His Majesty as well as the guests." The content of performance during the banquet was somewhat miscellaneously rich, including singing, dancing, and acrobatics like wrestling and animal performance."

The music performed by musicians of the Bureau of Musical Ritual,
Was as if wafted down from heaven by a divine wind.
All actresses with floral hats clustered aside, the dancing was halted,
To give prominence to the fantastic music singing the great harmony.

(Poems on Luanjing)

The Buddhist music was drawing out in lengthened sounds.

To which danced beauties in glamorous clothing with ornamental strings.

Singing and dancing were staged in the hall of the banquet.

Chanting the Avatamsaka Sutra, a sea of eminent monks blessed the Emperor.

(Songs under the Imperial Carriage)

From throughout the country thousands of officials came to attend the banquet.

Where their eyes were feasted on animal performance and wrestling.

Actresses in purple danced lithely with their slim waists.

The fantastic symphony filled the banquet with an air of spring.

With ferocious animals performing in the banquet,

All cheered with mirth to the great reign of the emperor.

(On Jamah Banquet)

7. Leaving the banquet. The banquet didn't end until after the sunset when lights were all lit.

The well-served banquet indicated great imperial favor,

The conch blowing toward the Emperor signals the end of the feast.

Closed were the imperial canopies and summoned were the imperial guards,

All dispersed in a hubbub on horses in the sound of fireworks.

(Songs under the Imperial Carriage)

Steeds whinnied in the wind against the setting sun,

元代城市
生活长卷

The Urban Life of the
Yuan Dynasty

164

Performers started to dance to the soft music played by the lute.

Whips cracked and the palace doors closed, his Majesty retired to his quarters,

All prostrated themselves and shouted banzai in repeated chorus.

(Yuan Jue, Song of Jamah)

Then what kind of food and drinks would be served on such a mirthful banquet? The answer would be revealed together with the diet of the urban residents in the next chapter.

Chapter Three | **Three Meals a Day**

The Yuan Dynasty was a nation of many races and each race had its own distinctive dietary habit. But when people of different ethnic backgrounds came to live in a unified country, especially in the same city, their dietary habits were bound to be influenced by each other. The practice of having three meals a day instead of two was established in the Yuan Dynasty. And it was in the Yuan Dynasty that people started to transport foodstuffs from the south to the north by sea.

1

In the Yuan literature one could find such terms as the Han Foods, Muslim Foods, Jurchen Foods, Tibetan Foods and Uighur Foods, etc. In fact a coexistence of diverse dietary habits characterized the Yuan Dynasty. Throughout the country, especially in the cities, the Chinese Foods were the most popular while the Mongolian and Muslim Foods the second.

Since the majority of the Han Chinese engaged in agriculture, their food was mainly comprised of agricultural products. They mainly feed on rice and flour, with meat of livestock, mainly mutton and pork, vegetables, fruits as well as meat of wild animals as auxiliary food. And their daily

元代城市
生活长卷

The Urban Life of the
Yuan Dynasty

166

beverages included wine made of grains or fruits, tea and soup made of fruits and spices.

Small in number as they were, the Mongols dominated a special status in the Yuan Dynasty. They were mainly engaged in animal husbandry and led a nomadic life. Therefore meat of the livestock (mainly sheep and then cattle and horses) and dairy products comprised their staple food which was further complemented by meat of wild animals. And their beverage consisted of koumiss and milk of the livestock. With the expansion of their military forces, their contact with other peoples increased, their somewhat simple dietary habit was greatly influenced by others, and their lifestyle, especially the lifestyle of those migrated to the sewn, changed considerably. The Yin Shan Zheng Yao (Proper and Essential Things for the Emperor's Food and Drink), a cookbook on the imperial cuisine published in the early 1330s attested to this change. Taking the Yuan imperial palace for example, tea and rice had already been consumed during the reign of Qubilai. And when it came to the mid-Yuan times, the Mongols had already developed a composite taste.

The Muslims of the Yuan Dynasty referred to those Central Asian and Southwestern Asian Islamists. They mainly ate mutton and beef, but never touched pork. And their staple food consisted of rice, flour and beans, to which they usually added various nuts (like walnuts, pine nuts, peach pits and hazelnuts) and spices. Their daily beverage was mainly sherbet and it was they who introduced araq to China.

In addition to the differences in their culinary habits, they also used quite different eating tools during the meal: the Han Chinese mainly used chopsticks and spoons, the Mongols hands and knives, while the Muslims hand, and only the right hand.

In ancient times, the Chinese usually had two meals a day, namely the breakfast and the supper. In the Tang and Song dynasties, more and more people began to have three meals a day. And in the Yuan Dynasty,

"Three Meals a Day" had become a household idiom among the folks. For example in zaju Yu Shu Ji (Record of a Jade Comb), there was the line: "meat must be served in the three meals every day, and new clothes must be bought in different seasons." Still in another drama Ju An Qi Mei (Living in Conjugal Harmony), the line "send three meals a day to our young mistress" also attested to the popularity of the idiom. The establishment of three meals a day not only gave birth to such words as "breakfast", "lunch" and "supper", but also exerted a considerable influence on people's daily life and work.

2

A geographical impact has long been felt on the grain production in China, with the north characterized by the growth of wheat and the south rice. In the Song Dynasty, there were such terms as the Southern Foods and the Northern Foods with the former featured wheaten food and the latter rice products. This pattern didn't change in the Yuan Dynasty; people in the southern agriculture districts still lived on a diet of rice products and those in the northern agricultural districts barley or wheaten food.

This geographical division in the grain production, however, was not absolute, for since the Tang and Song dynasties, the growth of barley and wheat had prevailed in areas south of the Yangtze River and the Yellow River. Especially after the fall of the Northern Song Dynasty, a great number of northern residents moved south and with them their staple food—barley and wheaten food, which not only promoted the cultivation of barley and wheat in the south, but also enriched the varieties of the processed food of barley and wheat. Several extant local chronicles of areas in south China in the Yuan Dynasty revealed that it was popular to grow barley, wheat and buckwheat in the south. In the Yuan Dynasty, rice

元代城市
生活长卷

The Urban Life of the
Yuan Dynasty

had already been cultivated in the northern areas like Kaifeng, Taiyang, Huaizhou (present-day Qingyang, Henan) and Xingyuan (present-day Xingyuan, Shanxi) where, with the establishment of water conservancy facilities, the planting of rice developed and rice began to be consumed by the northern people.

Vast as the agrarian area in the north was, it had a low productivity and certainly could not meet the needs of the capital. The Yuan court therefore had to import large quantities of grain from Jiangnan Region to Dadu every year, with a maximum record of over 300,000 shi in one year. "All the government agencies as well as people in the capital depended on the provisions from Jiangnan Region." (Section One, Record of Foodstuffs, Vol. 93, YS) Since rice account for a major part in the foodstuffs transported from the south, it naturally became the most important staple food among the residents of Dadu.

Originally the grain other foodstuffs were transported from the south to the north mainly through the inland waterways, which were replaced by the canal constructed in the Sui Dynasty after the decline of the Southern Song Dynasty. Starting from Hangzhou the canal traversed Zhenjiang and wound its way to the north across the Yangtze River to join the Huai River, and then it wound westward across the Yellow River and finally out to enter Zhongluan (present-day Fengqiu County in Henan Province). The grain, after being moved along this waterway, would be transported to Qimen (located to the southeast of the modern Qi County, Henan Province) by land, from where it would be transported to Tongzhou (modern Tong County, Beijing) through the Yu River (present-day Wei River) and the Baihe Canal. And then the grain would be transported again by land to Dadu. This devious grain-transportation line, covering both land and water, was proved quite inconvenient. To tackle this problem, the Yuan court constructed the Huitong Canal in 1289 and the Tonghui Canal in 1291. Thus the modern Grand Canal, the North-South axis, came into being. It ran from Hangzhou in the south to Dadu in the North. Designed as a straight line linking the two cities, the new canal was 900 kilometers shorter than the one built in the Sui Dynasty, greatly facilitated the transportation between the south and the north. Since the completion of the (new) canal, "all the agricultural tribute, grain, caravans and traders from Yangtze-Huai Valley, Huguang Xingsheng, Sichuan Xingsheng and the overseas vassal states could reach the capital much more conveniently. (The Grand Councilor Bayan, the Prince of Huai'an, Vol. 2, YCMCSL)

While endeavoring to tap the potential of the shipping capacity of the inland waterways, the Yuan court, in the meanwhile, sought to transport grain by sea and set Zhu Qing, Zhang Xuan to work on it. Soon three south-north sea routes were opened up respectively. The first shipping line, opened up in 1282, measured 13,350 li in length. It led from the Liujia port (located in present-day Liuhe Town in Taicang County, Jiangsu Province) through the Chongming Island to the Wanli Beach (located in the east of the present-day Rudong County, Jiangsu Province). Then it twisted onward along the northern seashores to the Chengshan Mountain (located in east of the present-day Shangdong Peninsula), and then westward to the Bohai Sea through the Jie River (modern Hai River) to the Yangcun Dock (present-day Wuqing County in Hebei Province). However, it was notoriously dangerous to travel along this route, for it was as twisted as it was filled with shoals. And it usually took two months to finish the voyage. The second line, opened up in 1292, changed its course after the Wanli Beach, extending through the Qingshui Sea and the Heishui Sea to the Chengshan Mountain and then to the Jie River via the Bohai Sea. The voyage along this route was greatly reduced to half a month under favorable conditions or a month or even over 40 days under unfavorable conditions. It was because the section between the Wanli Beach and the Chengshan Mountain was almost a straight line on far seas and thereby avoided the coastal shoals. The third line, opened up in 1293,

led from the Chongming Island straight into the Heishui Sea, skipping the Wanli Beach. Since the entire route was set on far seas, the voyage was further reduced to 10 days under favorable conditions.

After the opening of the sea routes, the grains imported from the south increased year after year. "Grain shipped from south of the Yangtze River by sea amounted to millions of shi every year." (Record of the Transport Commissioners in the Capital, Vol. 8, DYXGL) This breakthrough in the state grain transportation greatly delighted the residents of Dadu.

Since Zhu and Zhang opened up sea routes,

Millions of ships had fared through the oceans.

But for rhymes reminding of the dangers on the voyage,

Rice would never be presented to his Majesty by the cook.

(Zhang Yu, Songs under the Imperial Carriage)

3

In his Nong Shu (Treaties on Agriculture), a noted book on agriculture, Wang Zhen, the agronomist of the Yuan Dynasty, pointed out that "rice has many names. It could roughly be divided into two types: low gluten (rice) and high gluten (rice). Low gluten rice, was served as meal; while the high gluten rice was used to make wine." Other agricultural works that further divided the low gluten rice into late ripening rice and early ripening rice. Thus the low gluten rice was also called late ripening rice.

Both the low gluten rice and the high gluten rice had different varieties, among which some were good enough to be paid as tribute to the Emperor, like the aromatic rice which was the best of all the low gluten rice. According to Wang Zhen, "there was a kind of rice called little aromatic rice whose husk was red and seed smooth and translucent as jade. When cooked, it was as fragrant as delicious. Whenever there was a sacrificial ceremony or banquet, it would be served among all the delicacies for its rareness."

Every year Wuzhou Route (present-day Jinhua, Zhejiang Province) of Jiangzhe Xingsheng would send 33 shi of aromatic rice to the court as tribute, which was recorded in the following poem:

> There was a fine strain of rice in Jinhua,
> With translucent seeds sending out fragrance.
> All the folks engaged in cultivating the rice,
> For annually they would be taxed on it.
> It was said that when the seeds were just sown,
> Pedestrians all took the route skirted the field.
> And all that harvested had to be handed in as tax,
> No one dared to have a taste of it.
> ...
> Plump and round in the middle,
> All the rice was packed in silk bags.
> ...
> When the required quantity was reached,
> It would be shipped north to the imperial granaries.
> (Wu Shidao, Sending the Low Gluten Rice to the Capital as Tribute, Vol. 2, WLBJ)

The best and most famous glutinous rice in the Yuan Dynasty was the Sumen glutinous rice. Sumen (the presented-day Hui County of Henan Province) was originally a county in the Jin Dynasty and it was later renamed Huizhou in the Yuan Dynasty.

When served at the dinner table, rice was usually either steamed or made into porridge. As for the steamed rice, there was a saying that "lovely and pure was the dehusked rice. It became all the more fragrant and delicious which after being cooked." Rice gruel or rice broth was usually consumed by the poor so as to scrimp on the grain. "Most of the peddlers and artisans in Dadu used to have rice gruel as breakfast and supper, and such dim sun as steamed cakes, baked sesame-seed cakes, and pastry as lunch. They would have their meal together by sitting on the ground with a black bowl and a wooden spoon instead of the chopsticks." (XJZJY, PP207-208) In zaju Dong Tang Lao Quan Po Jia Zi Di (Mr. Dongtang Exhorting the Bankrupt Prodigal), when Yang Zhounu, son of a wealthy family, went bankrupt, he and his family were reduced to huddling in a kiln, cold and starving. He was then forced to turn to his old acquaintances for "some rice to make gruel." Rice porridge when added with tonic, however, was served as the nutritious food for the old and wealthy families.

The Mongols like the Chinese were obsessed with the nutritional and medical aspects of food. Staple food in the imperial palace like minced mutton broth, and rice broth, all with the ingredients of rice and mutton, were consumed for their nutritional and medicinal value.

According to the Yin Shan Zheng Yao, a cookery-cum-health book written by Hu Sihui, there were broths with special curative property, such as sheep's bone broth, pig's kidney broth, Chinese wolfberry broth cooked with sheep's kidney, Chinese yam broth, wild jujube broth, Chinese Foxglove Root broth, Piper longum Linn broth, Lesser galangal broth, Tetradium ruticarpun broth, lotus seed broth, gordon euryale seed broth, walnut meat broth, radish broth, Portulaca oleracea L. broth, Herba Schizonepetae broth, etc. Some of these broths such as pig's kidney broth, Piper longum L. broth, lesser galangal broth, lotus seed broth, gordon euryale seed broth, walnut meat broth were also popular among the commoners. In addition, they also had many other broths, such as

173

Siberian Cocklour Fruit broth, Jasmine kernel broth, bamboo leaf broth, deer's kidney broth, black-boned chicken broth, carp's brain broth, hen broth, sparrow broth, and mutton broth, etc.

The steamed rice and gruel were usually made of low gluten rice, but sometimes of glutinous rice as well. And glutinous rice was used to make zongzi20, and rice balls, etc.

4

Another integral part the Mongol diet consisted of wheat, barley, and buckwheat.

"Bing21 made of wheat flour were plump and chewy. When made by professional cooks, it became all the more delicious." Wheaten food mainly included noodles, mantou (Chinese steamed bread), steamed cakes, sesame seed cakes, wonton (dumpling soup), jiaozi (Chinese dumplings), etc. Noodles spanned a wide range of varieties. They varied according to their region of production, ingredients, shape or width, and manner of preparation. Another the imperial cuisine of the Yuan Dynasty, there were chunpan noodles, sheep's kidney noodles, Chinese yam noodles, dried noodles, Jingdai noodles, sheep skin noodles, etc. Noodles consumed by the commoners with a record in history included Shuihua noodles, Jingdai noodles, Suo noodles, Tuozhang noodles, Shrimp noodles, Cuilü noodles, Chinese yam noodles, and carrot juice noodles, etc. Among these noodles the Suo noodles were probably dried noodles served in the imperial court, which are still consumed today. There were two ways to prepare noodles. One was to make dough of wheat flour, oil, salt, and water and roll it out into a flat sheet which would then be cut into strips. The noodles could be cooked either in water with a dipping sauce after been drained or in broth like Shuihua noodles and Jingdai noodles, etc. The other way to prepare noodles was to make dough from wheat flour and the juice or meat of other ingredients, process the dough into thin strips and then cook. Noodles like the Chinese yam noodles, shrimp noodles, carrot juice noodles were made in this way.

Both mantou and steamed buns in the Yuan times had fillings. In imperial cuisine, there were dome-shaped mantou, Deer's milk and fat mantou, eggplant mantou, elaborately cut mantou, and mushroom mantou. Their fillings were mainly made of mutton and sheep fat seasoned with other ingredients like the deer's milk and fat, eggplant, and mushrooms. Mantou consumed by the commoners mainly used mutton, pork and fish as their fillings and also enjoyed a wide range of varieties, such as big mantou with a low arch domed shape, small mantou with a low arch domed shape, mantou with a high arch domed shape and imprinted mantou, etc. All the mantou and steamed buns were made of leavened dough with fillings.

Steamed products without filling included steamed cakes (present-day mantou), and steamed twisted rolls.

Sesame seed cakes in the Yuan Dynasty were almost the same as the present ones. Black sesame seed cakes and milk sesame seed cakes were served in the palace, while plain sesame seed cakes, golden sesame seed cakes, crisp sesame seed cakes and crusty sesame seed cakes were for the commoners.

Wonton was very popular among the folks. It was a dumpling made of a thinly rolled piece of dough with a small amount of filling either of minced meat or of vegetable wrapped in the center. Besides, jiaozi, shaomai22, and pancake were all popular wheaten foods.

In the Yuan court, there was also some special wheaten food. One was called "tutumashi", a kind of handmade noodles, which were dough pressed into thin sheets by hand. "Boiled tutumashi could either be stir fried, or served with sauce." Another one was called "maqaliao", which was also a kind of handmade noodles. Both

175

maqiliao and tutumashi belonged to "Muslim food". The third one was called "shuoluotuoyin", a kind of "coin-like noodles". It belonged to the Uighur Diet. It was usually served with sauce made of mutton, mushroom, Chinese yam and carrot, etc. Of the above three kinds of wheaten food, tutumashi was the most popular one.

Although wheat was usually consumed in the form of flour, when dehusked it could also be steamed or made into porridge, just like rice. For instance, the wheat porridge or steamed wheat served as breakfast in the Yuan imperial palace. However, very few people today still consume wheat in this way.

Different from wheat, barley "was usually consumed as porridge or steamed barley." The barley broth in the imperial cuisine was a kind of barley porridge made of mutton and "two pints of barley washed in boiling water". In the Yuan times, the staple food of the impoverished peasants mainly consisted of "steamed barley and wild herb soup". Barley was sometimes milled to make flour. The barley flour served in the Yuan palace was made of barley, beans and other ingredients.

Buckwheat, chilly in nature, was a common plant in the countryside around both Dadu and Shangdu. Areas south of the Yangtze and Huai River also produced buckwheat but with a lower output. In north China, buckwheat, dehusked and milled, could be made into either pan cakes served with garlic or a kind of noodles called "helou", which were as smooth as rice noodles but inferior to wheat flour based ones and were consumed as a staple food due to the local customs. helou, still consumed today in the northern countryside, were strands of noodles made of buckwheat flour based dough extruded by wooden instruments. It could also be found in Yuan literary sources, such as "corn flour based noodles served with helou sprinkled with chives and leeks" in zaju and "buckwheat flour based helou" in sanqu. Judged from the variants of helou (like heluo), this word probably did not come from Chinese,

which partially explained why this food seemed to be only consumed in northern China. In areas south of the Yangtze and Huai River and some areas north of the two rivers, buckwheat was usually "milled and soaked to make bing as a complement to wheaten food." Since buckwheat was indigestible, "buckwheat flour based foods were very popular among peasants and people of lower classes and were usually consumed as daily meals by them in winter".

5

In addition to rice and wheat, other cereals like foxtail millet, proso millet, and beans were also popular among people in China.

The foxtail millet ranked first among the "Five Cereals" in the past, for "the flat and vast Central Plains was suited for the growth of the crop." In areas north of the Yangtze and Huai River, wheat was harvested in summer and foxtail millet in winter. Generally speaking, the foxtail millet was co-planted with both the wheat and barely. In the northern countryside in the Yuan times, foxtail millet was levied as tax grain by the court. A cluster of fifty neighboring families in the Yuan Dynasty was organized into a Community, a tax-collecting unit, by the government. There was a Charity Granary in every Community for storage of grain surpluses in anticipation of future bad harvests. On each man in the household an annual tax of one dou of foxtail millet was levied. (Agriculture and Sericulture, Vol. 16, TZTG) Although this rule was inherited form the previous dynasties, the principal reason lying behind this rule was that foxtail millet was a crop with high output. Quite a few mountainous and dry Yangtze and Huai River plant the foxtail millet as well, but only on a small scale.

Foxtail millet could be either steamed or made into porridge. The Herba Schizonepetae broth served in the imperial palace contained foxtail millet.

There were two types of proso millet: white millet and red millet. They were mainly produced in the north for "only they could thrive in the far north and could be harvested in the very summer when they were planted. The plant of proso millet was short and small; its grains could be used to make either wine or gruel. It could also improve the soil composition of the land." The red millet "has yellow and glutinous grains which could be steamed like rice". The white millet's grains were inferior to those of the red millet, and could only be used to make wine. "Sorghum, also belonged to proso millet, was sometimes called Sichuan millet. Its grains were edible, which could be either used an alterative to rice or used as forage for animals, and were a good famine relief." (Proso Millet, NS) The grains of sorghum were usually cooked to make porridge, such as the Sorghum porridge in the imperial cuisine. And they could be used as an alterative to rice in minced mutton broth and rice broth. Since proso millet and sorghum were cultivated on a much smaller scale than the foxtail millet, they accounted for a relatively small part of the cereal structure of Yuan people.

Bean plants, belonged to food crops, were also widely cultivated in the Yuan Dynasty, such as soybean, Azuki bean, pea and chickpea. There were three kinds of soybean in the Yuan Dynasty: white, black and yellow soybeans. "The black soybeans were edible and could be used as an alternative to rice. They provided relief during a famine year and forage in the harvest years. The yellow soybeans were the major ingredient of tofu and sauces, while the white soybeans could be served with rice. Different as the three soybeans were in color and function, they all acted an important role in people's life." "As for Azuki bean, there were mung bean, cowbean and red bean… The mung bean was widely consumed in northern China and was widely planted by peasants there. Almost every household used it to make porridge, cakes, flour or fish feed. With a sweet

元代城市
生活长卷

The Urban Life of the
Yuan Dynasty

178

taste and a cooling nature, mung bean had the function of expelling toxins and therefore was a healthy food for people. It was also planted in the south." "Pea was one of the most useful plants among the cereals and beans. It was convenient to prepare: either steamed or boiled. And it could be used as an alternative to rice… people in Shanxi made flour with peas and a little wheat. Such flour would then be used to make bing. Pea had the longest shelf life among all the Five Cereals and could be preserved to relieve famine. Therefore pea was a desirable hungry relief." (Soybean, Azuki bean and Pea, NS) Chickpea, "usually cultivated in Muslim areas and with a seedling resembling to that of pea, could be found easily in the fields." It was the most widely consumed bean in the imperial palace. (Rice and Cereal, YSZY) And according to Li Shizhen, the Ming eminent doctor and author of Ben Cao Gang Mu (Compendium of Materia Medica) the chickpea was a type of pea.

6

The diet of the nomads consisted mainly of meat and dairy products with a supplement of cereals. According to Meng Da Bei Lu (Record of the Mongols and Tatars), "they (the Mongols) also had a few patches of land that produced black millet which they also used to make gruel." After their migration to the cities, their lifestyle including their dietary habits was greatly affected by those of the agrarian Han Chinese and people of other ethnic groups. A majority of the Mongols, therefore, began to live on cereals.

Nevertheless many Mongols and semuren still attached a particular fondness to mutton.

Mutton was a major ingredient in the imperial cuisine, for according to the Mongolian customs it took five sheep to make a whole day's meals for the Emperor. Since the accession of Emperor Shundi, the last

Emperor of the Yuan Dynasty, the number of the sheep used in daily meals for the Emperor had dropped to four, which was considered a sagacious act of the Emperor. In a chapter especially contributed to "the exotic delicacies" of the imperial cookbook Yin Shan Zheng Yao, there were over 70 difference recipes containing mutton either as the major or supplementary ingredient, accounting for about 8/10 of the total number of the recipes recorded in the chapter. And among the recorded 61 recipes for diet therapy, 12 of them contained mutton. Beside, mutton also played an important role in the banquets held in the imperial palace.

Mutton was the main meat served in the government offices. After the collapse of the Southern Song Dynasty, the Song Grand Empress Dowager and the young emperor were brought to Dadu where they received munificent treatment with the allotment of a million shi of grain every month and six thousand jin of mutton every day. When a delegation of Korean nobles came to visit Dadu, every day they were allotted 5 jin of mutton in addition to certain amount of rice, flour, firewood and money. The principal officials working in the postal station were allotted one sheng of rice, one jin of flour, one jin of mutton and one liter of wine every day.

Mutton was also widely consumed among the folks in Dadu. "Usually the breakfast of those from wealthy families started with a bowel of hangover soup or snacks followed by some stewed mutton with noodle or boiled viscera of sheep." Whenever there was a banquet, "twenty fat rams, excluding those castrated" were always on the top of the shopping list. And a birthday present usually consisted of "a sheep removed of the head and viscera bought from the market". And cured hooves of sheep were usually served to go with the rice in the daily meals. (LQDYJ)

In the southern agricultural areas where pork was widely consumed, mutton was still an important meat for people, which could be verified by

Ju Jia Bi Yong Shi Lei Quan Ji (Collection of Necessary Matters Ordered for the Householder), an encyclopedia on the daily life of the southern residents. In the book, among over 50 recipes which fell respectively into the categories of "roasted meat", "stewed meat", "meat going with the wine", "viscera stuffed with meat and minced meat", "meat going with the rice" and "meat broth", more than half of which contained the ingredient of mutton, far outnumbered those with pork.

Apart from mutton, the second widely consumed meat in the Yuan times was pork, whose nutritional value, however, had been long underestimated by the Chinese medicine circle. Just as Hui Sihui had recorded in his Yin Shan Zheng Yao, pork, "though nonpoisonous, had a bitter taste, hindered blood circulation, undermined sinew and bones, and fattened people up. It shouldn't be consumed all the time, especially those with gout and metal-inflicted wound." (Meat, YSZY) Such a bias against pork would certainly affect the consumption of the meat. Beef, horse meat, and donkey meat, more expensive than either mutton or pork, were also commonly eaten and were usually reserved for banquets. "Both officials and commoners would slaughter horses and cattle for meat for the wedding banquet or any other banquet." (Livestock, YDZXJ) The imperial banquets like the Jamah Banquet would always entail slaughtering horses and cattle.

The Yuan court once issued a "ban on slaughter" of lambs and ewes, mainly out of reproduction reasons. In 1261, Qubilai decreed that "horses and oxen, basis of both military operation and civilian life either served as a tool of cultivation, a vehicle of transportation, or a weapon of war, were usually slaughtered and ended up in the kitchen, what a pity it was! From now on, no horse or cattle should be slaughtered by government officials for banquet or in slaughterhouse. Any transgressor should be sentenced to 100 beats." Only those horses or cattle that had died of disease or the dying ones were subject to slaughter with the approval of the local authorities. (Ban on Slaughter, Vol. 57, YDZ) In spite of the prohibition, illegal slaughter still lingered on. In his sanqu Niu Su Yuan (Grievance of the Ox) the Yuan poet Yao Shouzhong expressed his disappointment towards the reality:

> A multitude of thanks went to the Secretariat,
>
> For prohibiting the slaughter of us throughout the country.
>
> Local authorities of all levels precisely abide by the rule,
>
> Heads of each village and community propagated the decree.
>
> The oxen slaughterer should be arrested and reported to the Route.
>
> …
>
> The law enforcers winked at the butcher's savage act,
>
> The disciplinarians snatched my limbs and neck,
>
> And the archers robbed my chest
>
> …

Nevertheless, the repeated prohibition on slaughter issued by the government was no doubt a heavy blow to the open slaughter of oxen or horses. In spite of the illegal butchery, which was carried out on a limited scale, the proportion of beef and horse meat in people's diet stayed low throughout the country.

In 1279, an edict was issued by Qubilai. "Since the unification of the country by Chinggis Khan, each ethnic group has been able to retain their own customs owning to his great favor. Only the Muslims, however, spurned the offer by repeatedly rejecting our diet. With the celestial help, we defeated and enslaved them. And how dare they refuse to take our food? Ask them to eat as we do, and punish those performing Islamic slaughtering … They said they never eat animals slaughtered by other peoples. But, in the meanwhile, they never stopped harassing the poor of the other ethnic groups. From now on, Muslims as well as Jews should accept any meat given by others and stop their way of slaughtering the

元代城市
生活长卷

The Urban Life of the
Yuan Dynasty

sheep." The Muslims and Jews only ate the meat of the animals that were slaughtered by those of the same religions as theirs. And the animals should be slaughtered by a cut through the neck instead of stabbed directly at the chest. In Qubilai's view, Muslims, subjects of the Mongols, were not in a position to reject the Mongol diet. He then forced them to accept animals slaughtered by anybody and prohibited them from slaughtering the sheep in their traditional way, which was no doubt a violent inference in the Muslim customs, and an act of racism. If anyone dared to perform the Islamic-Jewish slaughtering during the prohibition, he would be killed in the same way. And his wife, children, house and property should all go to the informer as reward. Soon, there launched the movement of informing against others, and it finally resulted in "a majority of an ethnic minority's retreat from the Han territory", which seriously damaged the commerce and revenues in that place. Seven years later, Qubilai revoked this decree. (Vol. 2, pp 346-347, SJ; Ban on Slaughter, Vol. 57, YDZ)

7

Poultry consumed in Yuan times mainly included chicken, duck and goose. In the imperial cuisine, there were many a recipe consisted of poultry, such as lotus chicken, chicken cooked with glutinous rehmannia, black-boned chicken soup, green duck soup, black-boned chicken liquor, etc. And in the folk cuisine, there were roast goose, tender boiled chicken, chicken soup, stewed goose or duck, salted goose and duck, etc. Even eggs could be made into different dishes. Poultry, though not as widely consumed as meat of the livestock, was also a major meat in the Yuan Dynasty.

The Mongols had a particular fondness for hunting and the meat of wild animals as well. Since wild animals were obtained through hunting, their meat was considered more valuable than that of poultry and livestock and therefore was usually served in the banquets. In the imperial cuisine, there was deer's head soup, bear soup, soup with stir-fired deer, roasted wild goose, soup with deer's kidney, soup with deer's hooves, fox soup, broth, pheasant soup, wood pigeon soup, fox broth, bear broth, wild boar, broth with other's liver, etc.

When the Grand Empress Dowager and the young emperor of the Southern Song Dynasty arrived in Dadu, Qubilai had thrown altogether ten banquets which contained many wild animals for them by way of celebrating his victory.

Anyway, wild animals could only be accessed by royal families, aristocrats, officials and the wealthy. They hardly appeared on the tables of the commoners.

8

Aquatic products were also an integral part of people's diet in the Yuan Dynasty.

Aquatic products could be further classified into two major types: those from the freshwaters and those from the oceans. Sea fish caught by the fishermen in coastal areas mainly include yellow croaker, flatfish, perch, hilsa herring, butter fish, conger pike, puffer and ribbonfish, etc. Besides, there were crabs, shrimps, sea cucumbers, sea snake, squids, cuttlefish, and oysters, etc. A majority of sea fish was sold in the coastal areas; only those cured ones could be transported to inland areas for sale, such as salted and dried yellow croakers, dried flatfish, and dried eel. As for freshwater fish, there were carps, crucial craps, trout, silver carps, variegated carps, and mackerels, as well as such crustaceans as crabs, shrimps and soft-shelled turtles. Among them crucial carps, silver carps, variegated carps and mackerels, which could be bred, were the most

widely spread and commonly eaten ones.

The imperial cuisine only contained fresh water fish, such as soft-shelled turtle soup, carp soup, crucial carp broth, etc. And many of the imperial cuisine dishes contained carps.

In folk cuisine, fish could be made into different dishes, such as steamed fish, fish soup, steamed hilsa herring, crab broth, soft-shelled turtle broth, etc. Of all the fishes consumed by the commoners, hilsa herrings, puffers, soft-shelled turtles, and carps were the most precious ones.

In the Yuan Dynasty, rivers in northeastern Liaoyang (currently areas near Heilongjiang River and Songhua River) produced Chinese sturgeon and sturgeon, with the former measure one to two zhang in full length and the latter five to six zhang. (YSZY) Both fish belonged to the trout family and some Chinese strugeon may weigh up to thousands jin. Since they were only reserved for the royal families as tribute, they could only be appreciated by the commoners in literary works.

> The delicacy sent to the Imperial Kitchen was from Eastern Liao,
> The trout one zhang long in reserved vehicle.
> It would be sent to the court every spring,
> Where it was cooked with beans and dried pheasant.
> (Zhang Yu, Songs under the Imperial Carriage)

9

Vegetables were an integral part of food for the citizens in Dadu, for "to maintain health, one must eat cereal, and cereal should be served with vegetables. This is the principle of daily life that people, rich and poor, should follow." (NS) The most commonly consumed vegetables in the Yuan Dynasty included radish, eggplant, cucumber, pepo, white gourd, mustard cabbage, spinach, lettuce, amaranth, taro, chive, ginger, green onion, garlic, Chinese onion, Chinese cabbage, malva crispa, mushroom, etc.

Chinese cabbage was a widely planted vegetable in China. In a poem depicting the winter life in Dadu, there was the line— "frosted Chinese cabbage, snow smothered chives and sugar-coated haws on a stick", from which it could be inferred that the Chinese cabbage was an important vegetable in Dadu. Besides Dadu, Zhenjiang in Jiangnan Region and the coastal city Guangzhou also planted Chinese cabbage.

There were several varieties of eggplants. According to Nong Shu (Treaties on Agriculture) the purple eggplant could be found everywhere, while the green and white eggplants mainly grew in the Central Plains. The eggplant vegetable could be preserved for a long time and could cook in many different ways such as fragrant eggplant, eggplant pickled with distillers' grains, eggplant with mashed garlic, mustard eggplant, eggplant with pickled cucumber, etc.

Spinach, or red root, was brought to China from Nepal at the Tang Dynasty. It was planted all over China and was an all-season vegetable.

Widely planted and growing fast, turnip was somewhat multifunctional. It could be eaten raw, looked or cured and was also a good famine relief. A well travelled poet in Dadu once devoted a poem to the turnip:

Sweet as taro when ripe,

And crisp as pear when half-grown.

Cured me of my chronic disease,

Miraculous was the turnip.

Back in my old garden, already a feet long,

Their green leaves appeared all the more lovely.

(Xu Youren, Spinach, Vol. 13, ZZJ)

White gourd was a vegetable widely planted and ripened only after being frosted. It could be preserved for a very long time. In the Yuan Dynasty, it was also taken as a fruit, its pulp could be made into candied fruit and its seeds could be served with tea. Cucumbers could either be eaten raw or cooked in many different ways. They were best to be consumed in summer and autumn. Pepos could be divided into two types: sweet and bitter. Only sweet ones were edible. As a high-yield crop, pepos were available all year round and could be made into different dishes.

The leaves of chives could grow to two or three cun long in spring. People in the city usually invited friends and relatives to enjoy the fresh chives in each other's houses. Even cut, the chives would grow again; therefore they were also called "Ever Growing". They were one of the vegetables that were not only easy to cultivate but also nutritious. So they were favored by all the families, wealthy and poor, in the city. In winter, if removed the roots of chives to cellar and covered then with horse waste, they would sprout when it turned warm. The leaves could grow to one chi high and were yellowish due to the lack of sunshine. Such chives were then called hotbed chives, which were much more nutritious than the ordinary chives and were liked by people in North China. Ginger, pungent in taste but not in smell, could be used to get rid of gamy odor. It was therefore a necessary seasoning in looking. Unlike other vegetables that must be eaten while fresh. Garlic could be preserved for a long time without any change in the flavor. It has the function of detoxification, which has long been realized by people in the past. Besides, it could also relieve summer heat, thus it was especially useful during a long trip and was suitable to be eaten in the summer days. In north China, it was also a necessary seasoning for the pasty.

The green onions were straight outside but hollow inside, with a long stem and spicy leaves. They were a necessary seasoning to other delicacies. Chinese onion, similar to ginger, garlic and green onion, had a pungent flavor. Originally produced in Pingze of the Lu Mountain, it could be found everywhere.

Mushrooms were another commonly eaten food. There were both wild mushrooms and bred ones. They could either be cured or cooked.

In addition to the above mentioned vegetables that were produced in both the south and the north, there were turnips, mainly produced in areas north of the Yangtze and the Huai River, and bamboo shoots and water-oat shoots, both of which were mainly produced in areas south of the two rivers. Beside, two other vegetables were especially worth mentioning: one was the carrot, the other Muslim onion. According to Ben Cao Gang Mu written by Li Shizheng, "carrots were brought to China from the western region which was indicated as "hu" in Chinese in the Yuan Dynasty. And since they had a similar flavor with the radish, they were thus named "hu luobo" or carrot." But the vegetable had already been mentioned in the local gazetteers of the Southern Song Dynasty, which then disproved Li Shenzhen's supposition. However, one thing was certain that it was not until Yuan Dynasty did the carrots get widely spread all over China and became an integral part of the vegetables consumed by the Chinese. The easiest record of the Muslim onion appeared in the Yuan Dynasty where it was described as "having the shape of a flat garlic, many layers and a flavor similar to the green onion, a vegetable that could be eaten either raw or cured," and usually grew in the nettle woods in the vicinity of Dadu. Judged from the picture in the Yuan literary source, the Muslim onion was probably today's onion. Nettle woods outside of Dadu used to be the settlements of the Muslim artisans from the Central Asia. Obviously the Muslim onions were one of the favorite vegetables among those Muslim artisans who were probably the ones that introduced the plant to Dadu and promoted it to the whole China.

The Mongols living in the steppes seldom ate vegetables. After their

元代城市
生活长卷

The Urban Life of the
Yuan Dynasty

migration to the Central Asia, their dietary habit changed considerably and vegetable became an integral part of their food. Vegetables employed in the imperial cuisine included radish, carrot, mushroom, Malva crispa, yam, chive, hotbed chive, stem of cattails, cucumber, turnip, and pepo, etc. Among them the radish, mushroom and carrot were the most frequently used ingredients. Generally speaking, vegetables served only as the supplementary ingredients to meat in the imperial cuisine. But there were still some recipes which were mainly composed of vegetables, such as pepo soup, Malva crispa soup, turnip soup, etc. Vegetable's entry into the imperial cuisine was mainly due to two influences. One was from the Han Chinese Foods and the other was from the Muslim Foods and those of other ethnic groups. For example, the "Baerbu Soup" contained mutton, the Muslim bean and radish belonged to the Western Foods or the Hindu Foods. "the Shaqimouer Soup" mainly consisted of mutton and turnip, was obviously Islamic Muslin food. And "Shuoluotuoyin" with yam, carrot and mushroom in it, belonged to Uighur Foods. A similar change in the diet could also be detected on the part of the Mongols migrated to the inland agricultural areas.

On the whole, meat could only be accessed be the royal family, aristocrats, officials and the rich. As for the commoners, they could only eat vegetables, and some even can't afford them. Taking Dadu, the capital, for instance, on the one hand, there were "delicate table piled with meat and fish," and lavish meals full of wine and meat; on the other hand, in sharp contrast to the rich of the capital, local artisans and vendors could only afford green onions, chives, garlic, sauces, salt and the like to go with their meals.

10

Condiments played an essential role in cooking either meat or vegetables, and the condiments of the Yuan Dynasty mainly consisted of the salt, sauces, vinegar and sugar, etc.

Slat could be divided into three types: sea salt, lake salt and well salt. Sea salt was obtained by boiling or from the evaporation of sea water by the heat of the sun. A Yuan literary source had it that "since there were many other substances like alumina, nitre, and calcium carbonate dissolved along with the salt in the brine, it must be reboiled for severed times. Only those natural salt or salt obtained by solar evaporation in areas east of the Yangtze River was edible, while that obtain by boiling was poisonous". (Jia Ming, Condiments, Vol. 5, YSXZ). It indicated that people in the Yuan Dynasty began to differentiate different types of salt and salt products.

Sauce was mainly made of beans and flour and could be divided into soy sauce and fermented flour paste. Among different varieties of vinegars, such as wine vinegar, peach vinegar, grape vinegar, jujube vinegar and rice vinegar, etc, the rice vinegar was the best. And the top rice vinegar was produced in Jintan, Zhengjiang. Such rice vinegar, once the tribute to the Emperor, had a strong but pleasant flavor and has been a famous product of Zhengjiang.

In ancient China, the sugar consumed by people was the rock sugar composed of sugar crystals obtained from sugarcane. It was not until the Yuan Dynasty did the sucrose with two varieties of brown and white began to be produced, a technique introduced by Egyptians. Other condiments with a sweet flavor included honey and maltose. The Sugar Office in the Yuan Dynasty was "in charge of the production of sugar and honey and the orchards in the country." Sugar and honey, however, were also allowed to be produced by the folks. Other condiments used in the Yuan Dynasty included pepper, fermented and seasoned soybeans, fennel, and cinnamon bark, etc. In the Muslim Foods, other foreign spices like frankincense, saffron, and Ferula teterrima were usually added to

improve the flavor.

Cooking oil included the animal fat and vegetable oil. Sheep fat when melted over fire could be used as cooking oil and was widely consumed both in the imperial palace and among the commoners. Another kind of cooking oil commonly used in the imperial palace of the Yuan Dynasty was the yak butter which was a kind of butter made from milk and is a traditional food for the Mongols. Although lard was another important animal fat due to the dominant position of the pork in meat, there was no detailed record of it. Vegetable oil mainly included the sesame oil, soybean oil and rapeseed oil.

11

Melons and fruits were also loved by people in Dadu. Some were planted all over the country, such as pear, peach plum, cherry, Chinese pear-leaved crab-apple, apricot, jujube, chestnut, persimmon, water melon, grape, and muskmelon, etc. Some grew only in the south, such as the red bayberry, sugarcane, tangerine, mandarin orange, grapefruit, lemon, olive, banana, orange, lychee, and longan, etc. Lychee was mainly produced in Fujian and Guangdong, and longan in Fujian. Longan, when first dried in the sun and then baked over a low fire until they got hard, could be preserved for a long time. The dried longans were then sent to the imperial palace as tribute in bamboo baskets lined with bamboo leaves.

Peanut, which could be classified into small-seed peanut and big-seed peanut, was a foreign species. Small-seed peanut had been introduced to China by the time of the Yuan Dynasty and was eaten as fruit by the Yuan people.

Fruits were mainly eaten raw, but they could also be processed in many ways. One of the most common ways was to add sucrose, honey and other ingredients into the fruits to make different beverages (which would be introduced in the next chapter). Fruits could also be made into candied fruits by being cooked with sucrose or honey. Some fruits like crab-apple, jujube, and persimmon could be sun basked into candied fruits that could be preserved for a long time.

In the palace, "seasonal fruits" parties would be held all around the year. The following two palace poems introduced such parties:

The peaches in the Imperial Garden mellowed in the late spring,

Golden plates filled with food were sent into the imperial palace.

Bowls brimming with tasty cheese,

Were distributed among the officials on duty waiting before the hall.

(Nai Xian, Eight Palace Poems)

Crimson cherries overed with yellow veils,

The imperial favor bestowed on consorts and servants.

Taking over the award on knees with gratitude,

Back in quarters, all eager to taste the scasonal fruit.

(Zhang Yu, Palace Poems)

元代城市
生活长卷

The Urban Life of the
Yuan Dynasty

Chapter Four | **Black Koumiss, Araki and Sherbet**

People in the Yuan Dynasty drank a miscellaneous assortment of beverages, including koumiss brought by the herding nomads, liquor from the Central Asia, the traditional fruit wine and grain wine produced in the agricultural areas, and milk and fruit juice.

1

Mare's milk and koumiss, an alcoholic concoction fermented from the mare's milk, were the favorite beverages of the Mongols due to their nomadic lifestyle. According to the Franciscan Friar Rubruck who traveled to the Mongol Empire in 13th century, the collected milk, sweet as cow's milk, would be poured into a bag or large skin and then churned with a specially made club as thick at the lower end as a man's head and hollowed out until the mix began to bubble like new wine and to turn sour and ferment. Churning would continue until butter could be extracted. It was considered ready for drinking when it was moderately pungent······. Qara kumis, or black koumiss, was made in the same way and presented to the Mongol lords for their consumption. (CSMGJ, pp 116-117) After settled in the agricultural areas, the Mongols retained their predilection for koumiss. The Emperor as well as the aristocrats all had their own herds of cows for milk. "When His Majesty started the imperial inspection tour to Shangdu, all the Chamberlains for the Imperial Stud and their subordinate officials should join the escort. The Chamberlains for the Imperial Stud would first go to the Jiande Gate to pick strong mares for milk during the drip. And the Emperor as well as his accompanying courtiers would set up their own tents as the milking parlour. When the Emperor returned to the capital, the Chamberlains for the Imperial stud had to prepare fifty koumiss carts with mares and brought them to the capital before hand. When the horses arrived in the capital, "Hachi" and "Halachi" who served as minister in the court were to breed them in person and make black koumiss, which were also called "refined milk", for the Emperor everyday. It would take forty mares to produce a cart of koumiss. After being milked, every mare would be given a sheaf of forage and eight sheng of beans, and every pony that accompanied the mare, a sheaf of forage and five sheng of beans. Since beans were expensive, millet was mixed into the beans to make up the amount. All the princes and officials were provided with mare's milk as well, only that the number of mares allotted to every koumiss cart dropped by twenty-five percent. Such koumiss was called "coarse milk". Every Imperial Mausoleum was installed with koumiss carts for sacrificial koumiss. (Horse, Vol. 100, YS)

"Hachi" and "Halachi" mean herdsman in Mongolian and were also used as the title for hereditary officials as well. When the Qipchaq Ban Ducha submitted to the authority of Mongke Khan, "the Qipchaq were dubbed as 'Qaracu', because they, famous for their bravery, served as herdsmen and koumiss server for the Emperor and the top koumiss was black or 'qara' in Mongolian." (Yu Ji, Meritorious Record of Prince of Jurong County, Vol. 26, YWL)

The reason why good koumiss should be black was answered by a Southern Song emissary who had been sent to the steppes in the middle of the 13th century. "When I first arrived in the golden tent, I saw the king

元代城市
生活长卷

The Urban Life of the
Yuan Dynasty

194

of the Tatars drinking a particular kind of koumiss, which was clear and sweet, contrary to the ordinary koumiss that was white, opaque, sour and pungent. Such koumiss was called black koumiss probably because clear liquid seemed dark to the eyes. When I asked how to make the beverage, the answer was that this koumiss had been churned for seven to eight days and the longer the churning was, the clearer the liquid got and less pungent it would be. Such koumiss I never saw it again elsewhere outside of the golden tent." (HDSL)

Koumiss was an integral beverage in the imperial palace and banquets held by the officials. When the Mongol aristocrats went out for hunting, they would bring koumiss with them. Koumiss also served as a reminder of the Mongolian traditions when the Emperor offered sacrifice to Heaven and the ancestors.

With the influence of the Mongolian customs, many Han Chinese and members of other ethnic groups began to show great interest in koumiss. A good example was the Khitan Yelü Chucai, who had written one poem to beg for koumiss and another two poems to express his gratitude after getting the beverage from others.

Xu Youren, a poet in the late Yuan times, had served in the Yuan court for a long time. During that time he often traveled between Dadu and Shangdu. One of his Shang Jing Shi Yong (Ten Poems on Shangjing) was dedicated to koumiss.

Sweet as the sugary dew,
Fragrant as if made of fresh spring.
The fresh wine still with white dregs,
Is the nectar in the secular world.
(ZZJ, Vol. 16)

In another poem depicting his tour between the two capitals, he applauded the koumiss again in admiration.

The koumiss attached to the saddled in the leather bag,

Went down the throat just like the sweet spring.

(ZZJ, Vol. 16)

2

Among many fruit wines, the most prominent one was the grape wine. When Chinggis Khan established the Mongol Empire, Yi Duhu, the Uighur chieftain, was the first one to pay homage to Chinggis Khan. The Uighurs, ancestors of today's Uyghur people, once lived in areas centering around Halahe Prefecture (present-day Turpan in Xinjiang), and Bieshibali (present-day Jimsar County in Xinjiang). And Halahe Prefecture was the provenance of grape wine. Later in the military expeditions to the Western Asia, the Mongols conquered many areas of the Central Asia and brought back to their imperial palace the Central Asian grape wine which was very popular among the Mongol nobles. When the Southern Song envoy went to the Mongolian steppe, he found "the grape wine in the glass bottle, enough to fill over ten small wine utensils, was very sweet and as clear as the southern persimmon phloem. It was said that excessive drinking led to drunkenness, but I had no opportunity to verify that myself. The wine was sent from the Muslim country as tribute and it wasn't the first time I had seen it in the golden tent." (HDSL) The reason why the Southern Song envy would especially mention the grape wine lay in that there was no such wine in areas south of the Yangtze and Huai River. And the "Muslim country" in the above statement referred to an ancient country in Transoxiana, which had been conquered by the Mongols in their western military expedition.

Shanxi began to produce grape wine during the time between the Jin Dynasty and the Yuan Dynasty. Anyi in Shanxi "yielded abundant

grapes but no one used them to make wine." It was not until in the tinzhen period did the grape wine was "discovered" by "a man who had taken refuge in the mountains from the bandits. When he returned home he found that the grapes stored in the bamboo utensil had all turned into juice leaving only the dried grape skin floating on the surface. The liquid, sending out the aroma of wine proved to be wine of the top class. It was probably naturally fermented from decayed grapes, and the secret was soon learned by all the people living around." (Yuan Haowen, On Grape Wine, Vol. 1, YHWQJ) Ever since then, Anyi had been famous for its grape wine, which became the tribute to the Mongol rulers after their conquest of the northern agricultural areas. In the second year of zhongtong period (1261) Emperor Shizu decreed that "Anyi District of Pingyang Route stop sending the grape wine as tribute to the court". (Section one, Annals of Emperor Shizu, Vol. 4, YS) This indicated that the grape wine had long been a tribute to the court. The edict of Emperor Shizu, however, was never really carried out. In the third lunar month in the second year of yuanzhen period (1296), another edict was issued by Emperor Chengzong, which "Taiyuan and Pingyang Rout should stop sending the grape wine to the court and the vineyards appropriated by the court should all be returned to the people there. (Section two, Record of Emperor Chengzong, Vol. 19, YS) It could be inferred from this edict that the grape wine continued to be sent to the court as tribute even after the second year of zhongtong period, and that other places like Shanxi began to join Pingyang District to produce the wine. It remained unknown whether the grape wine was really crossed off the list of tribute by the Mongols after the edict of Emperor Chengzong. According to the imperial culinary work Yin Shan Zheng Yao, "grape wine, benefiting qi23 and improving digestion and memory, ranged from several varieties, such as the grape wine from the western regions, Halahuo grape wine, Pingyang and Taiyuan grape wine, with that produced in Halahuo of the superior taste." It could be assumed that Halahe Prefecture, Pingyang and Taiyuan in Shanxi were the major producing areas of the grape wine in the Yuan Dynasty.

The grape wine of the Yuan Dynasty was made in a way different from the past. In the past the grape wine was brewed by mixing the grain with grapes in the Central Plains, while in the Yuan Dynasty it was made by fermenting crusted grapes in a big jug using the natural yeast in the grape skin. For example, in Halahe Prefecture "three to five huge room-like containers with the capacity of several shi were built with bricks on the clean ground. Their bottoms were covered with broken tiles inlaid deep into the ground for convergent purpose. Then mountainous piles of green grapes were poured into the containers, trodden crushed, and pressed on top with large logs which were then covered with woolen or felt carpets to add weight on the wood. The grapes were then left to ferment, without any use of yeast. Only when the pressing logs sank down after a period of about fortnight, could people reenter the room-like container, remove the carpets and logs, and test the mellow wine in the container." (Tribute from Foreign Land, XJZJY) This method was later widely adopted in areas of the Central Plains.

Together with koumiss, grape wine was ranked as one of the major alcoholic drinks served in the imperial palace and it was frequently mentioned in many poems, such as "All the princes and officials jubilantly holding the grape wine, by way of wishing His and Her Majesty longevity." (Sa Dula, Poems on Shangjing, Vol. 6, YMJ) And "All the princes and Commandants-escort wished longevity to the Emperor, emptying their jade cups filled with grape wine." (Zhu Youdun, Yuan Palace Poems, LJYGC, pp 19-26) The Emperor also frequently accorded the grape wine to his officials as the imperial awards. In the eleventh year of the zhiyuan period (1274), Aju was awarded with two bottles of grape wine by Qubilai for his meritorious service in the conquest of the Song

元代城市
生活长卷

The Urban Life of the
Yuan Dynasty

198

Dynasty. Shi Tianze, Assistant Director of the Left, fell ill when leading the Mongol troops attacking the Song. He was then consoled with the grape wine sent by Qubilai. And when the young emperor of the Southern Song Dynasty along with his entourage arrived in Dadu, "the Imperial cooks prepared them with the grape wine," so that "they could take it for the chrysanthemum wine on their first Double Ninth Festival in the alien land. (Wang Yuanliang, Ninety-eight Songs on Huzhou, Vol. 2, ZDHSLG) The grape wine therefore was in great demand in the Yuan imperial palace. Yang Yu who had served in the court in the late Yuan times noted that "the Wine Stewards Service still kept the grape wine sent to the court as tribute during the zhiyuan and dade periods." (SJXH) Zhiyuan and Dade were the regnal years of Emperor Shizhou and Emperor Chengzong respectively, roughly equivalent to the period between the late 13th century and the early 14th century. The Wine Stewards Service was a unit of the Palace Provisions Commission "responsible for preparing and serving the Emperor's wine." Its parallel agency in Dadu was the Imperial Winery that "produced wine for the Emperor's table." (Section three, Monograph on Offices, Vol. 87, YS) And Shangdu were also installed with the two same agencies. From Yang Yu's statement, it could be inferred that the Wine Stewards Service as well as the Imperial Winery had reserved large quantities of the grape wine sent from the local places as tribute for half a century or even longer time.

The grape wine could also be bought in the market. In Dadu area, "from the wuwu year to the fifth year of zhiyuan, for every ten jin of the grape wine, one jin was to be collected as tax"; "when it came to the sixth and seventh years of zhiyuan, quotas were established, for every thirty jin of the grape wine, one jin was to be collected." (Liquor Tax, Vol. 22, YDZ) The wuwu year referred to the 8th year of during the reign of Mongke Khan (1258); the fifth year of zhiyuan was the year 1268. That means the grape wine had already been sold in Yanjing (the later Dadu) by the time no later than the wuwu year. Since the Dadu area produced grape wine, the wine sold in the market was probably a local product.

In addition to the grape wine, people also drank fruit wine in the Yuan Dynasty. The recorded fruit wine included jujube wine and mulberry wine. "Jujube wine was produced in Zhengding, in the Southern part of the capital with the use of a little yeast." " Mulberry wine, common in areas of Zhengding in the southern part of the capital, greatly boosted heat in the body and was poisonous, causing a full stomach after drinking." (Product, XJZJY) Other places may also have different kinds of fruit wine.

3

Despite their popularity in the Yuan Dynasty, the koumiss and grape wine had to give their prominence to the grain wine in the vast agricultural land mainly inhabited by the Han Chinese. The major ingredients of grain wine included glutinous rice and proso millet. And the top glutinous rice for wine was respectively the fragrant glutinous rice produced in Jiangnan Region and Sumeng glutinous rice yield by Huizhou Prefecture (present-day Nanhui County in Henan) of Weihui Route. The Liyuan Storehouse installed in the central government of the Yuan Dynasty "was responsible for the ingredients of wine and yeast of the country, such as sedges and Sumen glutinous rice which were to be reserved for the imperial winery or distributed among the officials as awards at the end of year".

It took large quantities of grain to make the wine. Taking Dadu for example, "one tavern in Dadu was capable of yielding up to three hundred dan of wine a day, and consuming about ten thousand shi of grain a month. Since there were hundreds of such taverns in Dadu, the amount of the grain used in the wine production was far beyond calculation". (Yao Sui, Tomb Passage of Yao Wenxian, Vol. 15, MAJ) To scrimp on

元代城市
生活长卷

The Urban Life of the
Yuan Dynasty

the grain Qubilai issued an interdict on liquor in Dadu during the famine years, decreeing that "all the property of the violator be confiscated and given out to the impoverished." (Section six, Annals of Emperor Shizu, Vol. 9, YS) But the interdict was soon lifted. In the eighth year of Dade during the reign of Emperor Chengzong (1304), the Wine Tax Supervisorate for Dadu established 100 wineries. In the next year these wineries were amalgamated into 30. The daily amount of grain to be consumed per winery was controlled within 25 dan. Then all the 30 wineries could consume up to 750 dan of grain every day and 270,000 dan every year. In the third year of Zhida under Emperor Wuzong (1310), the wineries increased to 54. If still following the original quotas set by the government, then every year, these wineries would consume about 50,000 dan of grain, which roughly accounted for 1/6 of one year's grain imported from Jiangnan Region to Dadu by sea, and equaled amount of the rice (mainly sold to the commoners) in all the rice markets in Dadu. The wine produced in the wineries in Dadu was mainly sold to the commoners. It was the foresaid Imperial Winery and the Wine Stewards Service in Dadu under the Court of Imperial Entertainments that produced and reserved the wine, in addition to the grape wine, for the imperial palace. And all the imperial princes and officials were allowed to fetch wine from the Court of Imperial Entertainments through certain procedure. There was an anecdote about this. "Once a group of officials decided to hold a banquet, they then decided to send people to the Court of Imperial Entertainments to fetch wine with the official document, because they considered the wine sold in all the countless taverns unpalatable. (PTSYJ) The wine produced in the Court of Imperial Entertainments was obviously superior to that made by the local wineries, but the wine from the Court of Imperial Entertainments required certain official document. Some imperial princes as well as officials, therefore, used to get wine from the Court of Imperial Entertainments by taking advantage of their power and post.

Various medical herbs and items could be steeped in the grain wine to make different tinctures, such as the tiger bone wine, wolfberry wine, Chinese Foxglove wine, lamb wine, acanthopanax bark wine, olnul "naval" (penis and testes of the seal) wine, and millet wine in the imperial cuisine. Such tinctures, especially the lamb wine, were very popular among the Yuan people for their nutritional properties. Lamb wine was made of rice wine added with steamed "top lamb meat". And its prominent status among alcoholic beverages could be proved by a zaju in which a country tavern was scorned as "a humble hut crammed with only inferior local wine but devoid of lamb wine served in gold cups." (Book four, Vol. 1727, YQX) Other prevailing tonics included Chrysanthemum wine, lucid asparagus wine, calamus wine, and purple perilla wine.

Apart from koumiss and grape wine, grain wine had also been consumed in the Mongol imperial palace by the time of mid 13th century. However, the grain wine, designated as "darasun" in Mongolian, hadn't become familiar to and liked by the Mongols until they entered the agricultural areas. Darasun was later widely used in the Yuan Dynasty to refer to the grain wine and therefore was frequently mentioned in zaju, such as "go and buy a bottle of darasun to kill time"; "(Let's go) and buy five bottles of darasun." (Book two, YQX, p. 517; YQXWB, p. 1021)

4

When distilled, fruit wine and grain wine could be made into another kind of liquor called araq (Arabian, meaning sweating) to allude to the liquid condensed on the surface of the utensils during distillation. It had already been served at the imperial tables by no late than the middle Yuan times. In Yin Shan Zheng Yao, it was described as "sweet,

元代城市
生活长卷

The Urban Life of the
Yuan Dynasty

piquant and potent with the main function of removing coldness from the body; and distilled from good wine." In the imperial palace, araq was made of good wine, while in the late Yuan times, ordinary wine based araq was also frequently consumed by the commoners who then referred to it as "jiulu" (condensed wine vapor) due to its unique method of manufacture.

Distilled liquor represented a big revolution in the history of Chinese liquor and brought about fundamental changes in both the manufacture and consumption of wine. "Araq was the best of all wine. It was as fresh as water in the well and clearer than the dew in the morning." (Huang Jie, Araq, Vol. 2, BSXYYL) Thus araq was very popular among the commoners in the Yuan Dynasty.

5

As nomadic herders, the Mongols' daily beverage consisted of the milk of their livestock. "They drank mare's milk in very large quantities if they have it; they also drank the milk of ewes, cows, goats and even camels." For the milk of animals could not only quench thirst, but relieve hunger. "Thus they consumed a lot of mare's milk but little meat in summer," which was all the more true for the impoverished herders. Animal milk was also used to treat guests. When the European missionaries travelled in the steppes, they were treated by the Mongols with milk and were even provided with severed additional leather bags of milk to drink during the rest of their journey. (CSMGJ) When the Mongols entered the cities, they also brought their habit of drinking milk, especially the milk of camels, which was called "airag" by the Mongols. Airag was "mild and sweet;" it benefited qi, improved digestion, strengthened the physique and relieved hunger." (Beasts, Vol. 3, YSZY) Whereas the Han Chinese preferred milk of cows, in that "it maintained people's health by improving the blood circulation and strengthening the heart and muscles, and was thus very suitable for the old…Far more nutritious than the meat." (Nutritional Recipes for the Old, Vol. 1, SQYLXS)

Milk of cows and sheep could also be made into cheese and butter. Cheese was also called "vrum" by the Mongols. And butter was a kind of cream obtained from boiled milk. Cheese, sheep butter, and cow butter belong to the Mongolian diet, but the Han Chinese also showed a great interest in cheese.

Cow or sheep butter could the processed to curds, which were also very popular. In the Yuan imperial palace, "curds could be cooked with noodles in dices. It could nourish the stomach and spleen, and accelerate excretion when taken before the breakfast." Other court recipes, like the pearl powder and Taimiao soup also had the ingredient of curds. (YSZY, Vol. 1 & Vol. 2)

All these dairy products were popular in Jiangnan Region, which could be verified by Jiu Ming, a native of Haining (modern Haining in Zhajiang), who kept a record of the cheese, butter and curds in his book Yin Shi Xu Zhi (Must Know for Diet).

6

Another important beverage in the Yuan Dynasty was soup. The major ingredient of soup was medicinal herbs or sometimes candied fruit, which were either ground into powder or stewed into syrup and then taken with boiled water. There was a splendid array of soups in the Yuan times. Such as longan soup, lychee soup, fruit of Chinese magnoliavine soup, Chinese yam soup, red date an ginger soup, Four-substance soup, fennel soup, white plum soup, papaya soup, hangover soup with orange peel, butter soup, jasmine soup, orange soup, olive soup, and bean soup, etc.

In fact soup had already been widely consumed as a beverage in the

Song Dynasty. According to the Song literally sources, "somehow tea was served to welcome guests while soup represented a farewell, which was observed by both the officials and the commons. However, there was a military officer named Wu Chengyang, who insisted: 'what my guests were greeted with were medicinal tonics instead of the farewell soups.' His guests then were usually served with candied fruit soup or papaya soup on arrival. (NCJT) Medicinal soups as well as candied fruit soups were popular among the people in the Song Dynasty as a welcome or a farewell treat like tea. And this custom perpetuated into the Yuan Dynasty. In the Yuan zaju Dong Su Qin (Su Qin), there was a plot that when the impoverished Su Qin went to visit Zhang Yi, the Grand Councilor, he was received by Zhang's servant, Zhang Qianyi, who ordered a soup for him. Su then responded that "soup was a euphemism for farewell and I would take my leave." (Book three, YQX, p. 449)

Among the above listed soups, many were served at the imperial tables. Soup was also a popular beverage among the folks. And it was so popular that it was even served in teahouses, which could be verified by zaju, like Lü Dong Bin San Zui Yue Yang Lou (Lü Dongbin Getting Drunk in Yueyang Tower for Three Times). In the play when the protagonist Lü Dongbin came to the teahouse of Yueyang Tower, he ordered, among other things, a papaya soup and an almond soup. (Book two, YQX, pp. 620-621)

7

Sherbet was a foreign drink that was introduced to China in the Yuan Dynasty. The word "sherbet" came from Persian. In Mongolian, it means "water that quenches thirsty". (Product, Vol. 7, DDNHZ) Sherbet could be made from all kinds of fruit, by stewing them with sugar or honey into syrups, such as papaya sherbet, kumquat sherbet, cherry sherbet, peach sherbet, pomegranate sherbet, red bayberry sherbet, grape sherbet, mulberry sherbet, apricot sherbet and Cherokee rose sherbet, etc. Sometimes, aromatic spice could also substitute fruit in making the sherbet, for example the imperial sherbet, five-flavor thirsty-quenching water, and Lemon thirsty-quenching water, etc.

The Mongols encountered sherbet during their conquest of the Central Asia. According to Zhi Shun Zhen Jiang Zhi (Record of Zhenjiang of the Zhishun Period), "Samarqand, lying over a hundred thousand li northwester to the Central Plains, was a land ruled by Nestorianism······ When Emperor Taizu just took the land, the Heir Apparent Tolui fell ill and didn't recover until Mar Sargis (annotated by the writer) brought him sherbet with Marhasia leading a crowd praying for the Heir Apparent at the same time. Later the office of sherbetchi was established in the court, and Mar Sargis was appointed Nestorian Tarkhan. In the fifth year of Zhiyuan, summoned by Emperor Shizu, Mar Sargis came with the tribute of sherbet and the Emperor accorded many awards to him. Sherbet was a concoction composed of fruit and honey. And sherbetchi was the official title of the sherbet maker. Mar Sargis was then given a gold pedal by the Emperor to especially responsible for the manufacture of sherbet. In the ninth year, he was transferred to Yunnan with Sayyid Ajjal Shams al-Din Omar. In the twelth year, he went on to make sherbet in Fujian and Zhejiang." (SS, Vol. 9) Samarqand is now a city of the Central Asian country Uzbekistan. Nestorianism was a sect of Christian in ancient Asia. Tolui was the fourth son of Chinggis Khan and farther of Emperor Xianzong Mongke and Emperor Shizu Qubilai. And Marhasia referred to the bishop of Nestorianism. From this historical record, it could be inferred that since the Mongols' western military expedition. Tolui had already asked the local Christians to make sherbet for him and installed sherbetchi in his own Keshig. Later Qubilai, son of Tolui, summoned Mar Sargis from Samarqand and made him responsible for the manufacture

元代城市
生活长卷

The Urban Life of the
Yuan Dynasty

of sherbet. Mar Sargis had made sherbet which was sent to the court as tribute in areas of Yunnan, Fujian and Zhejiang, and he was later appointed darughachi of Zhengjiang Route, turning the place a supplier of sherbet for the court. Ever since then sherbetchi had become a permanent unit of the Yuan Keshig.

Apart from Zhenjiang, Quanzhou and Guangzhou were also suppliers of sherbet for the court. Sherbet from Quanzhou in the Yuan times was made of Cherokee rose. (Local Tribute, Vol. 20, BMTZ) And sherbet from Guangzhou was made of lemon. "Lemon, resembling orange, gave a sour taste. In the 3rd year of dade, the sherbet maker of Quanzhou Rout began to use lemon juice to make sherbet. Now two imperial lemon orchards, totaling 800 lemon trees, were respectively established in our route, namely Liantang in the east of Fanyu District and Lychee Bay of Nanhai District. The provision of sherbet stopped in the seventh year of Dade." (Product, Vol. 7, DDNHZ)

A good refreshment as it was, sherbet, in the eyes of Zhu Zhenheng, the prominent doctor of the Yuan Dynasty, "was not beneficial to the health despite its sweet taste. For instance, the Cherokee rose sherbet decreased urine; sherbet of apricot, red bayberry, rose apple and cherry caused excessive internal heat, thus could cause fever during humid seasons. Only mulberry sherbet was nonpoisonous and could be used to quench thirsty." (GZYL) Such negative view towards sherbet from the Traditional Chinese Medicine, to some extent, explained why sherbet was popular in the Yuan Dynasty and soon sank into oblivion in the later dynasties.

8

In the Yuan Dynasty, there was another unique beverage called "tree milk". According to the gazetteer of Dadu, "Mountains lying north of the desert abounded with white birches of seven to eight chi high. Their branches, when properly cut, could form burls, from which, if inserted with bronze or iron tubes during the first or second lunar month of the next year, seeped juice of the tree. The juice had a strong and pleasant taste and could be kept for a long time in the underground. It was consumed as wine and also as the hunger-relief by the local residents. The trees after being extracted of the juice would usually wither away." (Tribute from Foreign Land, XJZJY) The so-called "tree milk" was, in fact, the juice of white birches and is still a favorite drink among the Russians. And "the mountains lying north of the desert" in the historical record obvious denotes the land of Russia. Dadu had once housed many Russians. For example, in 3rd year of zhishun during the reign of Emperor Wenzong (1330), there was a unit in the Imperial Armies, which consisted of about ten thousand Russians. Since Dadu did not produce white birth juice, the beverage in Dadu was obvious imported from the faraway land of Russia mainly to meet the needs of the Russians there. And the appearance of the white birch juice attested to the prosperity of cultural exchange in the Yuan Dynasty.

Chapter Five | **Custom of Drinking Tea**

Tea, the Chinese traditional beverage, was already a common drink during the Tang Dynasty and became enormously popular in the Song Dynasty. In the Yuan Dynasty, it was also favored by people of all levels and ethnic backgrounds in the city.

1

Wang Zhen, one of the most esteemed scholars in the Yuan Dynasty, noted that "tea was indeed a valuable plant. It was lucrative as crop and refreshing as beverage. It was a daily necessity to either dignitaries or commoners, and a profitable source of revenue for the government" (Tea, NS, sic passim) In many Yuan zaju, one could frequently encounter the popular saying "firewood, rice, oil, salt, soy sauce, vinegar and tea, the seven priorities to start the day", which in turn attested to the indispensable status of tea in people's daily life. (Book two & four, YQX, p. 474 & 1335)

Tea was mainly produced in areas south of the Yangtze River and Huai River. The famous tea in the Yuan Dynasty included Beiyuan Tea and Wuyi Tea, both from Jianning in Fujian, Guzhu Tea from Huzhou, Yangxian Tea from Changzhou, Rizhu Tea from Shaoxing, and Fandianshuai Tea from Cixi in Qingyuan, etc. In fact all above tea, except Wuyi Tea and Fangdianshuai Tea, was already famous in the previous dynasties. Guzhu Tea, an article of tribute in the Tang Dynasty, once ceased to be produced in the Song Dynasty when its feeding spring dried up. When the Mongols pacified Jiangnan Region, the spring ran again, bringing back the tea as well. Beiyuan Tea, once served in the Song imperial palace, had its fame extended to the Yuan Dynasty. It was revered as superior to all the other tea. It was also called "the imperial tea" because it was only reserved for the royal family in the Yuan Dynasty. Yangxian Tea was also especially reserved for the imperial palace, hence the saying "the fame of Yuanxian Tea spread afar." Rizhu Tea from Rizhu Hill in Shaoxing, Zhejiang had been highly regarded as "unexcelled" in the Song Dynasty. It was also served in the Yuan imperial palace, which could be proved by the Yuan poet Ke Jiusi who had once served in the Hall of Literature in the palace.

The yellow seal was torn open, revealing Rizhu Tea,

Its fragrance wafted afar when brewed in fresh spring.

Not summoned in the Hall,

I may as well roll up the curtain and appreciate the willow catkins.

(Two Poems Made in the Hall of Literature in Spring, Vol. 1, CTYJ)

Both Wuyi Tea and Fandianshuai Tea gained their popularity in the Yuan Dynasty. Wuyi Tea was produced in the Wuyi Mountain under the jurisdiction of Chong' an District of Jianning Rout. In 16th year of zhiyuan, when Gao Xing, the Manager of Governmental Affairs of Zhejiang Xingsheng passed the Wuyi Mountain, he picked up some local tea call "Shi Ru" and then sent several jin of the tea to the court. From then on, Wuyi Tea started its history as tribute to the Yuan court. Later Gao Jiu, the son of Gao Xing, was appointed Route Commander of Shaowu Route in Fujian. He then established a Tea Office called the Imperial Tea

Garden in the Wuyi Mountain to make tea for the court. The Yuan court "installed the Superintendency of Wuyi Tea headed by a Superintendent in Beiyuan of Jianning. The Superintendency of Wuyi Tea was responsible for the annual provision of tea for the court and was under the direct jurisdiction of the Palace Provisions Commission." (Section two, The Imperial Tea Garden, Vol. 9, WYSZ; Section three, Monograph on Offices, Vol. 87, YS). The Palace Provisions Commission was the agency in charge of the Emperor's diet. Thus Wuyi Tea was mainly reserved for the imperial palace, just like Beiyuan Tea. As for Fandianshuai Tea, "it was produced in Qingyuan Route in Zhejiang and had a flavor and color superior to those of other tea." It was named after the former Southern Song Vice Commander-in-chief of the Palace Command Fan Wenhu, who surrendered to the Yuan court and was later addressed by his official title "Dianshuai" (Commander-in-chief of the Palace Command). The local gazetteer of Qingyuan (present-day Ningbo, Zhejiang) of the Yuan Dynasty had it that "the tea was produced in mountains of Cixi District, with that from the Gangshan Hill where Ziguo Monastery was located of the top class and that beside Kaishou Monastery the second. The tea leaves were processed with water from Hua'an Monastery and only the finest tea could be sent to the court as tribute." (Grass and Trees, Vol. 5, ZZSMXZ). This tea was designated as Fandianshuai Tea in the Ming local gazetteer of Cixi. "Fan Wenhu, the Song Commander-in-chief of the Palace Command, established the Tea Office to produce tea for the Emperor. The Yuan Court retained the office and installed it in the Kaishou Monastery." (TQCXXZ, Vol. 1). Fandianshuai Tea continued to be sent to the court as tribute in the Ming Dynasty.

2

According to Wang Zheng, "tea could be divided into Ming Cha (loose-leaf tea), Mo Cha (powered tea), and La Cha (waxy tea)". Ming cha referred to the roasted loose-leaf green tea, which is still popular today. Mo cha was prepared by "roasting and pulverizing the tea". During Tang, Song and Yuan dynasties, Mo Cha was usually further compressed into tea bricks which should be ground into fine powder before consumption. And La Cha was the refined form of Mo Cha. "La Cha was the most expensive (tea), and was processed in a sophisticated way with the powdered top-class tea buds mixed with spicy oil and then compressed into various shapes with auspicious design like dragon. The tea bricks would then be smeared with spicy oil again. La Cha was only reserved for the Emperor, and was seldom accessed to the commoners." The reason why La Cha was called waxy tea was that it was usually coated with a layer of spicy oil which gave it a shiny quality like wax.

The Yuan court levied tax on the two major tea sold in the market, namely Mo Cha and Cao Cha (grass tea), at different tax rate. Cao Cha, a term already appeared in the Song Dynasty, was what Wang Zheng called Ming Cha, or loose-leaf tea.

3

Loose tea and compressed teas were brewed in quite different ways. According to Wang Zheng, "Ming Cha should be rinsed in boiling water to purify its flavor before decoction, as was widely practiced in the south." The Yin Shan Zheng Yao also mentioned the following words— "steep the tea, drain the infusion, and decocted it with water." Thus it could be inferred that loose tea (Ming Cha or Cao Cha) was prepared by decocting the rinsed tea with water, instead of directly steeping it in boiling water as is practiced today.

As for Mo Cha, Wang Zheng noted that "it was prepared in a more

元代城市
生活长卷

The Urban Life of the
Yuan Dynasty

subtle way. The compressed tea would first be briefly roasted to remove the moisture and then be finely ground. Next certain amount of boiling water would be added to the powdered tea, and the thickness of the infusion depended on the quantity of water. To brew a cup of sweet and smooth tea, one needs one qian seveb fen of powered tea. First infuse a modicum of boiling water to dissolve the tea powder, then whisked, with more boiling water, the mixture to a uniform consistency. There must be no lumps left in the liquid, and no ground tea should remain on the sides of the bowl. This method, however, was known to very few people in the tea-producing areas of Southern China." Another way to prepare Mo Cha was to decoct it with water, which were mainly adopted by the Tang people. During the Song Dynasty, this decocting method gradually gave its prominence to the brewing method as described by Wang Zheng. The decocting method, however, didn't extinct after the Song Dynasty; instead it was still practiced in the Yuan Dynasty.

Therefore in the Yuan Dynasty tea could either be decocted with water or brewed. Usually Ming Cha or Cao Cha was prepared with the former method, while Mo Cha in both ways. As for the current way of brewing tea (usually loose-leaf tea), it didn't appear until the Ming Dynasty.

The brewing method was very popular in the Yuan Dynasty, which could be verified by the frescos discovered in two Yuan tombs in the Yuanbao Mountain in Inner Mongolia. The No. 1 fresco is about grinding tea cakes into fine powder, and the No. 2 is about brewing tea with hot water. Many tea wares were also depicted in the frescos, such as stone mortar, pestle, tea bowls, tea caddy, water vessel, tea holder, and tea whisk. Nevertheless, decocting tea powder with water began to gain popularity among the Yuan people, especially among the literati and artists. "When a friend comes, fetch spring to decoct tea sprouts; boiling tea in the stone cauldron and filling the ceramic bottle with fresh water" (QYSQ, p. 114; Ma Zhiyuan, Ma Danyang Preaching Ren Fengzi for Three Times, Book four, YQX, p.1677) It could been inferred that "decocting tea sprouts" had become an integral part of the life of literati and it prevailed in south China of the Yuan Dynasty, thus the reason for Wang Zheng's claim that "the (brewing) method was known to very few people". The change in the tea preparation method led to the change in the drinking utensils. In the Song Dynasty, black ceramic tea bowls were used to hold brewed tea, while blue and white ones was preferred in the Yuan Dynasty. In fact, Yuan Dynasty acted as an important turning point of preparing tea in China. Although it was still popular to brew tea and decoct powdered tea, as was widely practice in the previous dynasties, the method to "boil tea sprouts" began to gain popularity in the Yuan Dynasty.

4

During the Tang and Song dynasties, salt, ginger and aromatic spices were usually added to the tea to create different flavors. The practice continued to be observed in the Yuan Dynasty. The "aromatic tea" served in the Yuan imperial palace was s kind of compressed tea consisted of pulverized mixture of white tea, borneol, Chinese gall leaven and musk with stewed aromatic rice added as pasting agent. Such "aromatic tea" was very much like the waxy tea and should be finely ground before consumption. Different types of "aromatic tea" were found in Yuan encyclopedic works such as Collection of Necessary Matters Ordered for the Householder and Vast Record of Varied Matters, but all contained the basic ingredients of borneol and musk. Apart from the aromatic tea, there was another tea-based beverage called "Chinese wolfberry tea" in the Yuan imperial palace, which was made of pulverized Chinese wolfberry and Queshe Tea.

元代城市
生活长卷

The Urban Life of the
Yuan Dynasty

Lei Cha was a kind of tea-based beverage favored by the commoners in the Yuan Dynasty. It consisted of a mix of tea leaves and herbs that are ground together with various roasted nuts, seeds and grains. And it is still consumed in areas in southern Jiangxi Province. The flowering tea which was popular in north China imparted tea the fragrant flavor of flowers. As for the origin of the flowering tea, there existed many different explanations. In the Yuan Dynasty, it was said that the flowering tea was obtained by placing flowers such as sweet-scented osmanthus, jasmine, chrysanthemum, and jasminum grandiflorum around the tea caddy to scent the tea. (SLGJ, Vol. 7)

As the national drink of China, tea was not only prepared in the family, but also served in myriad teahouses that dotted the whole country. Taking Dadu for example, "As soon as the sky turned light, all the teahouses in the capital were besieged with numerous carts." (Ma Zhen, Early Spring in Dadu, Vol. 4, XWSJ) Beside, other beverages like soup were served in teahouse. In a teahouse, the owner and the waiters were generally designated as "tea masters". For example, in zaju Qian Da Yin Zhi Kan Fei Yi Meng (Governor Qian Solving the Case by Stratagem) written by the famous playwright Guan Hanqing, there was an character who had the line, "I'm tea master, the owner of this teahouse."

5

While tea played a critical role in modern Mongolian diet, back in the early 13th century the major beverage of the Mongols still consisted of koumiss and milk of the livestock. Only during their pacification of the agricultural areas ruled by the Jin Dynasty, did they began to know about tea, which was mainly produced in areas south of the Yangtze River and Huai River, but was "sought after by the Jin people throughout the country, especially by the peasants." (Tea, Vol. 9, JS) The tea drinking habit of the Jin people obviously had an impact on the Mongols. And when they seized tea-producing areas in Jiangnan Region after their unification of the country, they had more convenient access to tea. To cater to the new rulers, officials would send their local famous tea to the court as tribute, just like the aforementioned Gao Xing and Fan Wenhu. With the revival of the Jinsha Spring, Guzhu Tea experienced its resurrection in the Yuan Dynasty. In the first lunar month of 15th year of zhiyuan (1278), the spring was renamed Ruiying Spring by Qubilai (Section seven, Annals of Emperor Shizu, Vol. 10, YS). Qubilai's interest in the spring was obvious derived from his interest in the famous Guzhu Tea, which in turn indicated that the Mongol aristocracy headed by Qubilai began to take an interest in drinking tea.

An entry of Yin Shan Zheng Yao recorded that "in early zhida period (1308-1311), Emperor Wuzong invited the Empress Dowager to go hunting in the willow woods. When they passed Zoudian, His Majesty wanted to quench his thirst with tea." The officials then decocted tea with the local well water and the infusion was praised by the Emperor for its superb color and its distinctive flavor different from that provided by the Directorate of the Imperial Treasury… From then on, the water was fetched every day for the Emperor. It imparted tea a far more pleasant flavor than the other water". This record indicated that tea had been one of the major beverages in the imperial palace by the time of Emperor Wuzong, and that what the Emperor drank was obviously pure tea without condiments, or he wouldn't have detected the tender change in the flavor of tea. In fact, the Yuan Emperors used to drink tea to aid digestion after the meal which usually consisted of fatty mutton. This could be proved by a poem of Ma Zuchang who was a famous poet of the mid-Yuan times.

Tired of the greasy meal of mutton brought by Provisioners,

His Majesty was served with the fresh tea from Jiangnan in jade

元代城市
生活长卷

The Urban Life of the
Yuan Dynasty

216

cups."

(Ten Poems in Reply to Minister of the Left Wang, STXSJ, Vol. 5)

This line also mirrored the statement of Emperor Wuzong recorded in Yin Shan Zheng Yao that "(tea was) usually provided by the Directorate of the Imperial Treasury." The last emperor of the Yuan Dynasty, Toghun Temür was an aficionado of tea. His Korean wife, the later Qi Empress, was once his tea server who thus had the opportunity to get access to Emperor Shundi and thereby won his favor. However, not all the tea servers of the Emperor had her luck and most of them ended up old women living lonely in the imperial palace.

Tea-based beverages with special ingredients were also served in the imperial palace. One was Chao Cha (stir-fried tea), which was made by "stir-frying a mix of Masige Oil, milk of cow and tea sprouts on a hot iron wok". The Masige Oil was in fact the cream extracted from milk of cow. The second was called Lan Gao, a kind of fragrant concoction made of "three spoons of Jade-Mortar Mo Cha mixed with flour and yak butter, which should be brewed with boiling water before consumption." The so-called "Jade-Mortar Mo Cha" could be obtained by "pulverizing the mixture of top-class Zisun Tea and Sumeng Stir-fired Tea in a jade mortar." The third was called Su Qian, "a concoction of two spoons of Golden-letter Mo Cha and yak butter, and should also be brewed with boiling water before consumption." The Golden letter Mo Cha, sent as an article of tribute from Huzhou in Jiangnan Region, was Guzhu Tea by nature. (Tea and Soup, Vol. 2, YSZY) All the three types of tea, though processed in different ways, had one thing in common, that is they all had yak butter, which was very different from the tea consumed in the Central Plains. Beside, in the imperial palace there was another tea-based beverage called "Tibetan Tea", which also included yak butter and had a bitter taste. It is probably today's butter tea by nature. The Tibetans had already drunk tea in the Tang Dynasty and they changed it to suit their way of life. And the aforesaid three types of tea consumed in the Mongol palace were probably an inspiration of the Tibetan Tea, or simply an invention of the Mongols themselves.

The funny thing was that this special way of drinking tea—with the condiment of yak butter—was later practiced by the Han Chinese and other ethnic minorities. For instance, Xu Youren who served in the Yuan court in Dadu in the late Yuan times pointed out that "the masses took tea with yak butter as the Lan Gao". And he especially made a poem on it. (On Lan Gao, Vol. 16, ZZJ) In zaju Lü Dongbin Getting Drunk in Yueyang Tower for Three Times, when a customer tasted the beverage contained Su Qian served by the teahouse, he immediately pointed out that "the Su Qian was not authentic". (Book two, YQX, p. 621) In another zaju Yue Ming He Shang Du Liu Cui (Monk Yueming Preaching Liu Cui) of an anonymous author, when Liu Cui and Monk Yueming entered the teahouse, Monk Yueming ordered a cup of Su Qian. (Book four, YQX, p. 1342) The Yuan encyclopedia Collection of Necessary Matters Ordered for the Householder also introduced the preparation methods of "Lan Gao Tea" and "Su Qian Tea", which attested to the popularity of the yak butter-based tea in the Yuan Dynasty.

元代城市
生活长卷

The Urban Life of the
Yuan Dynasty

Part Four

Chapter One | **Diverse Marriage Customs**

In the Yuan dynasty, different communities, ethnic groups, and classes were allowed to maintain their respective marriage customs, a policy reflective of the Mongol ruler's respect for ethnic diversity. But when all these distinctive marriage customs were bound together with the same yoke of unification, especially when they were hustled into the same patch of land called city, they inevitably fell under the influence of each other.

1

The Mongols in the Yuan dynasty practiced polygamy. "They have as many wives as they can afford"; "no one among them has a wife unless he buys her. So it sometimes happens that girls are well past marriageable age before they marry, for their parents always keep them until they sell them." Economics was the determining factor in the number of wives a man might have. Thus some may own more than ten or even tens of wives, while some could only afford several, or one, or, even worse, none. (CSMGJ, pp.8-121) After their migration to the Central Plains or Jiangnan Region, a majority of them still retained polygamy. The number of wives averaged out at five to ten for ordinary officials and nobles, and two to three for the commoners, among whom quite a few actually led a monogamous family. Theoretically, a Mongol man could have as many wives as he wished in terms of law. (Marriage, Vol. 4, TTGZ)

Endogamy was remorselessly banned by the Mongols. But there were no restrictions on marrying two or several sisters from other tribes in succession or at the same time.

Some Mongol tribes usually maintained constant marital relationships with one anther, such as the marriage of the family of Chinggis Khan.

For the male Chinggisids, who were the Khakhan or Emperor in particular, "they were supposed to marry only the girls from certain tribes." (Chronicle of Imperial Concubines, Vol. 106, YS) For the Mongol princesses and noblewomen, they were only to marry "families" of great merit and princes of vassal states, so as to consolidate the Emperor's rule over the border areas via forging an alliance by marriage." (Chronicle of the Imperial Princesses, Vol. 109, YS) Tribes that maintained stable marriage relationships with the Golden Family included the Onggirat tribe, Ikires tribe and ?ngüt tribe. The Onggirat tribe was the most favorable marriage partner of the Mongol royal family. Ogedei Khan once declared, "The girls born in the Onggirat tribe shall become the Empresses (of Mongol rules) for generations; the boys born in the Onggirat shall marry Princesses (of the Mongols) for generations. This should never be ceased." It turned out that most of the Empresses of the Mongol Empire or the Yuan Dynasty were of the Onggirat origin, and that all the Onggirat noblemen had the title of Commandant-escort. (Biography of Dei Seichen, Vol. 118, YS)

After the expansion of the Mongol Empire, Mongol men began to marry Han and Western Asian women through formal agreement or sometimes abduction. But to "preserve the Mongolian heritage", most

Mongols would marry at least one Mongol woman and such practice was perpetuated until the late Yuan times.

Among the many wives a Mongol man may keep, normally there would be only one chief wife or official wife who had a higher status than all the other wives in the family and only her sons would continue the blood line. When she died, she could be replaced by a lesser wife, normally the one with a status only inferior to her in the family. Except the chief wife, the other wives, usually labeled with the ordinal number for distinguishing purpose, were ranked in chronological order of their wedding time: the sooner one entered the family, the higher one's status was. In the imperial harem, the Emperor could have several Empresses simultaneously. The Mongol Khakhan usually built four major ordos to house his four Empresses, but the first ordo always belonged to the chief wife, or the official Empress. Besides, in each ordo there lived other imperial consorts and concubines who were all subservient to the Empress of the ordo. "Every wife of a Mongol man on the steppe had her own tent and retinue"; and her status in the family was demonstrated by the position and quality of her tent. The first wife placed her tent on the extreme west side. After hers were the tents of the other wives according to their rank, so that the tent of the last wife would be placed in the extreme east.

Although the Mongols suffered heavy casualties in their decades long military efforts to establish the Yuan Dynasty, the population on the steppes didn't drop, but increased instead. Except for the fact that many slaves of different ethnic groups were brought to the steppes during that time, it was mainly because of the polygyny the Mongols observed for the purpose of reproduction: as a "Mongol man may have more than one wife, and a wife would usually give birth to several children." And "Chinggis Khan even legalized the practice by decreeing that there should be no feelings of jealousy (among the wives) as long as their great cause could be inherited by more and more Mongols." When a soldier died in battle, his family would be well looked after. "When a soldier died in service, if his slaves could carry him back home, they would be rewarded by their master's livestock and property; if it was done by a stranger, he shall have all the property of the deceased, including his wives, slaves and livestock." (HDSL) After the unification of China, there was a chaotic period when several Mongol chieftains of the eastern and western Empire rebelled in succession and the steppes were inflicted with a series of droughts and storms, leaving many people destitute and forcing them to sell their daughters as slaves. (Biography of Baiju, Vol. 136, YS) In this way, the normal pattern of marriage on the steppes was changed, but the custom of polygyny was retained.

2

Like other nomadic tribes in the north, the Mongols also practiced levirate marriage, a type of marriage in which a widowed woman could be taken by one of her husband's relatives. According to the seniority of the successor and the succeeded (the widow) in a family or clan, levirate marriage can be classified into two major categories: the two parties in a levirate marriage were in the same generation, such as a younger brother who by succession married his elder brother's wife, or an elder brother who took the wife of his deceased younger brother. The other is that the two parties in a levirate marriage were in different generations, or cross-generation levirate marriage, such as the case where a son inherited his father's widowed concubine, a nephew married the widowed wife or concubine of his uncle, a grandson married his successive paternal grandmother and so on. One important reason for such practice was that it could protect the family's property from being brought to a third family with the remarriage of the widow.

According to some western missionaries who had been to the Mongol steppe, a levirate marriage was considered legal by the Mongols; a widow will not remarry even if she was left alone. It had become deeply rooted in the Mongol traditions and got survived to the Yuan Dynasty despite the condemnation from some elite of the society.

Some Mongol women, influenced by the Han Chinese notion of chastity, remained unattached after the death of their husbands, as was the example of Shanga Lagyi, the Great Princess of the Lu state in the Yuan Dynasty. She "preserved her chastity by choosing to raise her child alone after her husband's death." (Section two, Record of Emperor Wenzong, Vol. 33, YS) Another famous woman in the Yuan history was from the Onggirat tribe. She also refused to be taken by her stepson and denounced his act as that of beats. (Section one, Biography of Famous Women, Vol. 200, YS) However, their efforts were just a drop in a bucket in eradicating this form of marriage from the society.

Another type of marriage, the ghost marriage, was also popular among the Mongols. "When one man has had a son, and another man a daughter, although both may have been dead for some years, they have a practice of contracting a marriage between their deceased children, and of bestowing the girl upon the youth. They at the same time paint upon pieces of paper human figures to represent attendants with horses and other animals, dresses of all kinds, money, and every article of furniture; and all these, together with the marriage contract, which is regularly drawn up, they commit to the flames, in order that though the medium of the smoke, those things may be conveyed to their children in the other world, and that they may become husband and wife in due form. After this ceremony, the fathers and mothers consider themselves as mutually related, in the same manner as if a real connection had taken place between their living children. (Travels of Marco Polo, pp. 67-68)

In a Mongolian family, women were supposed to do most of the housework and engage in the production activity. "A Mongol preferred to travel with his families in that they could help him take care of luggage, clothing and property. And women, especially, were expected to erect the tents and dwellings, saddle the horses and apportion the packs and loads to the camels and horses." (MDBL) In the daily life on the steppes, it was also the duty of women to prepare food for the family, control the servants, look after the kids, and make daily necessities like the leather coats. In addition, they were supposed to raise the livestock and participate in the animal husbandry work. As for the Mongol men, they did nothing but make bows and arrows, practice shooting with bows, and go hunting; sometimes they also do some animal husbandry work. Since the Mongol women participated in almost all the aspects of life, they enjoyed a relatively higher status in the family than the Han women. They engaged in most social activities and had a say in many family issues. And in a polygamous family, all the wives could get along with each other harmoniously, even if there were ten or more of them.

The Mongols were also reputed for their way of supporting both the old and the young. In a Mongol family, children were supposed to move out after marriage, except the youngest son of the chief wife, who could stay at home even after marriage. The youngest son was called "the master" or "the kitchen guardian", for "the family fire in the kitchen represented the center of the family life and the youngest son who usually stayed at home was left to take care of the fire as well as the house." Usually he would inherit most of the property of his father and continue to live with the parents after his marriage, thus it was him who was obliged to support his old parents. His elder brothers would also get a piece of property from their father and the elder he was, the bigger his

元代城市
生活长卷

The Urban Life of the
Yuan Dynasty

portion would be. Anyway, the children of the chief wife had an obvious advantage in inheriting their father's property. If a husband died leaving a group of underage children, the widow who stayed to raise them would inherit all his property until the children were old enough to establish a family of their own.

In a traditional Mongol family, the husband was supposed to allot his time to all his wives by living with a different wife every day, but he usually stayed in the tent of his chief wife. If the husband chose to spend the night with a particular wife, she was allowed to sit next to him the next day in her tent, to which all the other wives would assemble to have meals or important family meetings. And she was also entitled to all the gifts sent to the master on that day. After the Mongols' migration to the city and the agricultural land, although the whole family still ate together, the men no longer slept in a different tent every night. But this practice was preserved in the Yuan imperial palace.

"His majesty spent the night with a different concubine every three days. Each chosen concubine would be informed in advance with the imperial edict. If she got pregnant thereafter, verification should be done following the old institution of the former Jin Dynasty." (Section two, Miscellaneous Institutions, Vol. 3, CMZ) This system later evolved into a more elaborate one. For example, when Emperor Shundi wanted to spend the night with Empress Bayan Khutugh, he was declined for a successive three times due to the reason that "it was already late at night, no longer a suitable time for Your Majesty." (Empress Bayan Khutugh, Vol. 114, YS)

All the imperial consorts and concubines aspired to the arrival of the Emperor's goat cart at their courtyards and win his favor, which became one of the major topics of the Yuan palace poems.

225

4

The matrimonial customs of the Han Chinese, which allowed a husband to have one legal wife and several concubines, were also influenced by those of the Mongols and Semuren.

A housewife adopted a pivotal status in a Chinese family; therefore marriage was attached with great importance. And a desirable marriage, however, was determined by regional, social, familial, and ethnic factors.

When picking a spouse, most Han Chinese were inclined to choose one from the same region, usually in the same or nearby countryside, or even the same neighborhood. Sometimes they would marry a bride from a neighboring prefecture, town or district, but they seldom marry one from a distant prefecture or district. A cross-regional marriage often happened under fortuitous circumstances. For example, when a northerner came to the south to work as a government official or run a business, he would probably marry a local girl, and vice versa. Although the unification achieved in the Yuan Dynasty greatly facilitated the communication between the south and the north, most regions were still held in isolation by localism. While it seldom occurred in the country side, cross-regional marriage was common in big cities like Dadu, Shangdu and Hangzhou.

People of different social standing had different expectations for their future spouses in terms of family status, financial resources, and moral conduct. Some sought wealth, status or seductive beauty in a marriage, while some insisted on finding a well educated bride of dignified grace and a good sense of judgment. Generally speaking, the quality of a marriage was determined by one's social status, family backgrounds as well as education. During the Yuan times, endogamy among different classes were practiced, Chinese families of bureaucrats, merchants and plutocrats from the upper class usually formed matrimonial alliances with one another. In 7th year of zhiyuan (1270), a memorial to

元代城市
生活长卷

The Urban Life of the
Yuan Dynasty

226

the throne from the Department of State Affairs reported: "a majority of officials transferred from route-level agencies formed alliances with the wealthy and powerful families of our department by marriage, so as to take advantage of the power and position of their relatives by marriage to bully the others." (Matrimonial Alliances with the Officials, Vol. 18, YDZ) In the south, rich merchants and landlords all attached to local authorities through marriage with the aim to expand their influence. In this way, the social hierarchy was reinforced, making it difficult for people of different social, familial or even professional backgrounds to tie the knot. Therefore marriage between families of similar backgrounds became the major pattern of marriage in the society, such as the marriage between two Confucian families, peasants, handicraftsmen, and small retailers. While there did exist cross-professional marriages, they were usually confined to small retailers, handicraftsmen and peasants.

The instability of the society would change the pattern of marriage and threaten its stability. The Mongol-Jin War and the Mongol-Song War (the former lasted for over two decades, and the latter three decades) split numerous families and hustled those stranded in a foreign land by war into mismatched marriages. With the establishment of the Yuan Dynasty, the social stability was restored and marriage of different places returned to normal. But the peace was upset in the late Yuan times, and during that time, many people in the Central Plains and Jiangnan Region were involved in a wave of hasty marriage by a rumor. In the sixth month of third year of zhiyuan during the reign of Emperor Shundi, "rumor had it that the court would choose some minors of both sex to send them to the Tatars as slaves. And their parents should escort them to the northern border. Hearing that, all the families with children aged above twelve in the Central Plains and Jiangnan Region hurriedly married off their children even without the six rituals required in a traditional marriage. Some wealthy and powerful families even walked their daughters to

227

the groom's house before the arrival of the sedan from the groom's family, lest anything untoward happen. Even those officials and Tartars and semuren were no exception, and this chaos lasted for over ten days. After the rumor was over, regret filled these mismatched couples, resulting in a lot of tragedies: either the husband abandoned the wife, or the wife resented the husband. Some were able to settle the mistake in the government office, while some died in the wedlock." (Tao Zongyi, Rumor, Vol. 9, NCZGL) After a decade, China was plunged into war again, which greatly damaged people's marriage for another time.

With the unification of the Yuan Dynasty, people of different ethnic groups came to live together, which brought the question of transracial marriage to some Han Chinese, especially those lived in Jiangnan Region. According to the southerner Kong Qi who strongly opposed transracial marriage, "the traditional marriage institution should be observed all the time as Sima Guang had expounded. Some scholar-officials, however, were seduced by wealth and breached the tradition by forming matrimonial alliance with those alien races. Consequently, their family traditions declined and descendents became unworthy." He continued to argue, "in the past, people never marry their daughters to alien races on the grounds that it was already inappropriate to marry their women, how could we embarrass our ancestors by marry our daughters to them? This was because the alien peoples lacked morality. When they were in a privileged position, they tend to marry another woman of the same ethnic origin, thereby humiliate our girls. If they were decreased to poverty, they would constantly bother you for help······Therefore we should always be on our guard by reminding ourselves of the saying that a man of different race always had an alien heart. (Earnest Advice on Marriage: Never Marry Alien People, Vol. 1 &3, ZZZJ) Although Kong Qi's view had a tinge of nationalism, he, nevertheless, revealed an undeniable truth, that is it was hard to restrain some wealth and privilege seeking Han Chinese

from forming matrimonial alliances with the Mongols and semuren, for most of the Mongols and semuren were officials, merchants and soldiers with either high status, wealth or power. Since the Mongol ruler didn' t oppose transracial marriage, some Han Chinese chose to marry people of different ethnic background.

5

According to the Mongols, their marriage institution was different from that of the Han Chinese, and they tried every means to perpetuate the difference. The Mongolian marriage allowed a man to have several wives, while a Chinese man could only have one legal wife but several concubines. The Yuan court decreed that the Han Chinese "if married more than one wife should divorce all of them other than the legal one. Only thus could he be pardoned." If both parties agreed, his other wives could be converted to concubines who henceforth would be striped of the title of lesser wife and the status of a wife. (Marriage, Vol. 4, TZTG) To preserve the stability of marriage and protect women from being divorced by an unfaithful husband or sold by a wicked spouse, the Yuan government issued a series of laws by referring to the Chinese traditions. "A husband could initiate a divorce on any of the following seven grounds: (1) failing to have a son, (2) adultery, (3) disobedience to parents-in-law, (4) gossiping, (5) theft, (6) jealousy and ill-will, (7) incurable disease. However there are three clearly defined exceptions: she has no place to return to; she had observed a three-year period of mourning for a deceased parent-in-law; she married the husband before he got rich. If a man was found selling his wife for money, all the money he obtained should be confiscated and their marriage dissolved. If a wife was found committing adultery, she should be divorced. (Divorce, Vol. 18, YDZ; Xu Yuanrui, LXZN, p72 Another similar version of "seven grounds" or "seven outs" could be found in p.148)

Betrothal in the Yuan Dynasty was based on a betrothal letter instead of verbal promise, such as the prenatal betrothal and matchmaker's remarks. Other traditional matrimonial customs of the Han Chinese, such as baimen, meaning the couple should pay a visit to the bride's family usually three days after the wedding, and chi ganyang were also banned. "Chi ganyang, usually practiced in Shanxi, was a custom in which neighbors of a bridegroom's family would come uninvited to the family's home for free meals." According to the laws of the Yuan Dynasty, "a betrothal letter should be signed in a betrothal. The practice of chi ganyang, though a custom in Shangxi, should be abandoned just like the practice of baimen." The betrothal letter should include the personal information of the couple and the amount of the bride price. In the case of an uxorilocal marriage, the obligation of the groom and the time he was to stay and serve for the bride's family should also be stipulated in the betrothal letter. Both the master of the wedding ceremony and the matchmaker should sign on the betrothal letter. "The betrothal letter should be clear and unambiguous in meaning. The amount of bride price should be put in black and white with the groom's and matchmaker's signatures. The bride's family should send a receipt to the groom's family, which should also contain the specific amount of the bride price they had received and the signatures of the bride and the matchmaker. The two families would add the character "contract" to the back of the two letters and exchange them as certificate. If a betrothal letter or a receipt from the bride's family didn't contain complete signatures and the mark of the character 'contract', it would be announced as illegal in the case of a lawsuit caused by ambiguity in either letter." Besides, the Yuan government, drawing on the Chinese notions of ethics and chastity, banned brides from breaking off an engagement, unless the groom died or committed treason, because there was such a case happened between two affluent

families. In the case the groom's family failed to provide the original amount of bride price due to bankruptcy. The bride's family then broke off the engagement and remarried their daughter to others. (Marriage, Vol. 4, TZTG; Marriage, Vol. 18, YDZ) In the Yuan Dynasty people refused to marry orphaned girls, and the girls from "families committing Anantarika-karma, adultery and homicide, and families afflicted with serious disease. (LXZN, p.148)

As for the aforementioned "endogamy among the wealthy and powerful families of the Department of State Affairs", the Yuan government didn't object such marriages, for "the transferred officials were Western Asians who usually found it necessary and urgent to marry their children at a suitable age to a suitable family because they were sometimes far away from hometown and constantly shifting between different posts." An official could remarry or take a concubine on condition that his wife had died or he had no descendant. The new marriage should be witnessed by an official matchmaker with a betrothal letter. (Matrimonial Alliances with the Officials, Vol. 18, YDZ)

A concubine was originally taken to bear children for a man when he and his wife had no heir. However, some wealthy Chinese with wife and children still took many beautiful concubines via purchase, abduction and matchmakers simply to satisfy their lust. Sometimes they even took prostitutes as concubines. Concubinage was approved by the government, but a man should sign a betrothal letter when taking a concubine and produce a divorce announcement when divorcing the concubine.

Influenced by the Jurchens, Mongols, semuren and the Han Chinese began to practice levirate marriage as well. Such marriage was especially popular in north China and could also be classified into two categories: levirate marriage within the same generation and that between different generations. At first, the Yuan government didn't recognize the legitimacy of the levirate marriage among the Han Chinese. In between

231

the seventh lunar month and the eighth lunar month in the seventh year of zhiyuan (1270), the Department of State Affairs issued an edict which banned levirate marriage among the Han Chinese and the Bohai people. In the second lunar month of the next year, another imperial edict ordered that "a widow should keep chastity for her deceased husband and should not marry her brother-in-law." In the twelfth lunar month, when the Department of State Affairs asked the Emperor for a ban on a son's marrying his father's widowed concubine or step-mother and a brother's marrying his widowed sister-in-law, the reply they got was just the other way round, which marked the legitimacy of the levirate marriage among the Han Chinese. But soon the government issued a series of laws to restrict the levirate marriage among the Han Chinese, prohibiting not only the cross-generation levirate marriage between a son and his father's widowed concubine, and between a nephew and his uncle's widowed wife, but also the levirate marriage between an elder brother and his widowed sister-in-law. These laws made the levirate marriage between a younger brother and his widowed sister-in-law the only legitimate form of levirate marriage among the Han Chinese in the Yuan Dynasty.

To protect those widows who preferred to keep chastity for their deceased husbands, the government permitted them not to marry their deceased husbands' younger brothers, and decreed that "the successors should not object, unless their widowed sisters-in-law intended to remarry others." If the widowed sister-in-law was much too older than her deceased husband's younger brother, the levirate marriage would also be banned. (Levirate Marriage, Vol. 3, TZTG; Illegal Levirate Marriage, Vol. 18, YDZ)

However it has to be noted that levirate marriage was only confined to the impoverished Han Chinese, because it was considered incest and therefore condemned by the Chinese scholar-officials. Levirate marriage rarely occurred in Jiangnan Region where women were deeply influenced

元代城市
生活长卷

The Urban Life of the
Yuan Dynasty

by the notions of chastity and ethics advocated by Neo-Confucianism.

As "many widows remarried instead of observing chastity for their deceased husbands, and some even remarried within the period of mourning for the deceased," the Yuan court especially decreed that Court Ladies should not remarry. "Women with a title because of their husbands or sons were different from the commoners. They should not remarry after the death of their husbands or sons. Anyone who breaches the law should be stripped of the title and punished, and the marriage should be nullified." (Matrimonial Alliances with the Officials, Vol. 18, YDZ)

6

As for the other ethic groups in the Yuan Dynasty, some had practiced polygamy, while some were converted to polygyny or concubinage with the influence of the Mongols and the Han Chinese.

Most ethnic groups that were grouped into semuren by the Mongols had long practiced polygyny. Taking the Tanguts for example, "a man could marry as many wives as he pleased as long as he could afford. Beauty was the most important attribute of a young girl. It can conceal her humble origin and bring her to a healthy man who would be glad to pay a fortune to her parents as the bride price." "The laity take to themselves as many thirty wives, some more, some fewer, according to their ability to maintain them; for they do not receive any dowry with them, but, on the contrary, settle dowers upon their wives, in cattle, slaves, and money. The wife who is first married always maintains the superior rank in the family; but if the husband observes that any one of them does not conduct herself well, or if she becomes otherwise disagreeable to him, he can send her away." (Travels of Marco Polo, pp.54-55)

In Tibet, polygyny was also widely practiced and even monks of different Buddhist sects were allowed to get married and have children. The head of the religious sects, deacons and Brigade Commanders usually had more than one wife, and some had five to six wives. This custom was later introduced to the Central Plains by Tibetans and was adopted by some Buddhist monasteries there.

Most ethic groups of semuren in the Yuan Dynasty practiced levirate marriage. Just as the Mongols, the Tangut, Qipchaq, Naiman and Uighur practiced all types of levirate marriage. Different from people of the above tribes, the Muslims prohibited cross-generation levirate marriage, and acknowledged only the levirate marriage within the same generation. In the seventh lunar month of the sixth year of zhiyuan (1340), Emperor Shundi issued a "ban on the levirate marriage between a semuren and the widowed wife of his deceased uncle," imposing more restrictions on the cross-generation levirate marriage among semuren. (Record of Emperor Shundi, Vol. 40, YS)

7

The Mongol rulers adopted a lenient and protective policy towards the different matrimonial customs. In the second lunar month of the eighth year of zhiyuan (1271), Qubilai decreed that "an endogamy follow its own matrimonial institution; an exogamy observe the matrimonial custom of the groom, Mongol women excluded." (Matrimonial Rituals, Vol. 3, TZTG) According to the edict, people of the same ethnic origin could hold the wedding in their traditional way, while an transracial marriage should follow the groom's tradition, but a Mongol woman in an intermarriage may not necessarily follow the tradition of the groom. In the ninth lunar month of the eighth year of zhiyuan, a series of matrimonial rituals based on those recorded by Zhu Xi in his Jia Li (The Family Rituals) were issued by the Ministry of Rites under the Secretariat:

元代城市
生活长卷

The Urban Life of the
Yuan Dynasty

1. Proposal: Only when both parties had no mourning duty to observe could they were suited to marry. A matchmaker should be sent for and bride price should be arranged after the agreement of the bride's family.

2. Engagement: The two families should inform their ancestors by way of a letter drafted by the groom's father. The letter should then be sent to the ancestral temples of both families.

3. Bride price: The groom's family should send the matchmaker to present the bride price to the bride's family.

4. Wedding ceremony: The groom should go to fetch the bribe to his home where the wedding ceremony would be held and wedding banquet be thrown.

5. Visiting the groom's family: In the next day after the wedding ceremony, the bride should serve food to the groom's family, starting from the groom's parents and then the oldest family members.

6. Visiting the ancestral temple: Two days after the wedding ceremony, the groom's parents should take the bride to their ancestral temple.

7. Visiting the bride's parents: The couple should pay a visit to the bride's family in the next day.

Certain rituals in a wedding ceremony could be simplified depending on the economics of the groom's family. The bride price given to the bride's family usually include cloth, jewelry and lamb wine.

In Dadu it was customary for a bride to take a bath before the wedding day. Another matrimonial custom was "mat relay", a custom already practiced in the Tang Dynasty, in which a bride should walk on bare feet on relayed mats that led to the wedding hall when she arrived at the groom's house in sedan.

Since the wedding ceremonies of semuren were quite different from those of Han Chinese, their weddings usually attracted lots of attention from their neighboring Han Chinese. One extreme example could be found in a Muslim wedding in Hangzhou. In the case the wedding hall collapsed due to overcrowded spectators, causing many deaths. (Tao Zongyi, Mocking the Muslims, Vol. 28, NCZGL)

8

Since marriage played a pivotal role in people's life, great importance was attached to the wedding ceremony. In the Yuan Dynasty, an ideal wedding ceremony was as this. "The basic form of the moral relationship was marriage; and a marriage started with a wedding ceremony. Before the wedding circumspection should be employed, but afterwards trust must always be maintained in a marriage. When picking a spouse, it was necessary to consider his or her temperament and the family tradition before signing the betrothal letter. The amount of bride price should be in proportion to the economics of groom's family, but the betrothal presents should be of good quality. Once the wedding date was settled, it should be duly carried out by both parties. A wedding banquet, simple or lavish, should be held by way of meeting the relatives and old friends. Only in this way, could the moral relationship be properly realized and marriage completed." (Wang Jie, Significance of Good Customs, Vol. 6 WZJ)

In reality, however, everyone aspired to an extravagant life and they usually dump a considerable sum of money on wedding. "Because there was no restriction on the amount of bride price, it kept increasing everyday. The ever increasing bride price either spoiled or delayed the wedding by bringing bankruptcy to the groom's family or even causing one family to sue the other." Often the matchmaker would take advantage of the occasion to charge for her service. In some places, a matchmaker was usually paid with 1/10 of the bride price. Thus someone sigh, "Nowadays people tried every means to waste money on all kinds of ceremonies, like weddings and funerals with no consideration for the economics of their family. Many people sold their family property or even borrow an enormous sum of money only to buy luxury items." (Hu Zhiyu, On Agriculture, Sericulture and Water Conservancy, Vol. 22, ZSDQJ)

To deal with this social problem, the Yuan court issued the following policy to curb the increase in the bribe price in the second lunar month of the eighth year of zhiyuan (1271). "The standard of the bride price was as follows:

(Nonmonetary items such as cloth, jewelry and livestock should be converted to Zhongtong Yanbao Jiaochao24; while a settled bride price was not subject to this rule.)

The officials with a rank:

> 500 guan for officials above the second rank;
>
> 400 guan for officials above the third rank;
>
> 300 guan for officials above the fifth rank;
>
> 200 guan for officials above the seventh rank;
>
> 20 guan for officials above the ninth rank.

The comments:

> 100 guan for upper households;
>
> 500 guan for medium househholds;
>
> 20 guan for lower househholds.

As for the scale of the wedding banquet held by the groom's family, that of the officials with a rank should contain no more than four courses, that of the upper and medium households no more than three courses, and that of the lower households no more than two courses." In the seventh lunar month of the same year, another edict from the court specified the amount of the bride price of an uxorilocal marriage. "If the groom would stay in the bride's family to support her parents all his life, he may only pay half normal amount of the bride price; if the groom would move out some time in the future, he should pay 2/3 of the normal amount of the bride price." (Wedding, Vol. 18, YDZ) In the fourth lunar month of the nineteenth year of zhiyuan (1282), the Yuan court further stipulated the qualifications and obligations of a matchmaker. "The matchmakers, preferably old and honest, should not overcharge their clients, and should not take 1/10 of the bride price as their own. Any transgressor would be punished in public." (Marriage, Vol. 4, TZTG)

These regulations on the bride price from the Yuan court, however, were just like water off a duck's back. According to Hu Zhiyu, "although the specific amount of the bride price had been stipulated in the law, people were still unsatisfied, partially due to the sentence "all were up to the parties concerned", and partially due to the soaring prices. For example, in the year when the law was issued, a single blot of cloth was worth one guan, but today it cost eight guan." He then advised to the court, "the bride price should be further divided into three ranks and every detail of which be specified. Prohibit the commoners from wearing clothes of gold brocade and reduce the standard of the bride price for the medium and lower households to a lower lever." (ZSDQJ, Vol. 22) His advice was finally adopted by the Yuan ruler. In the first lunar month of the eighth year of dade (1340), an imperial edict advocating "frugal wedding" was issued. It also stipulated that the expenses of a wedding for upper households should not exceed one liang of gold, five liang of silver, six pieces of polychrome satin and forty bolts of silk tabby; that of the medium households should not exceed five qian of gold, four liang of silver, four sheets of polychrome stain; thirty bolts of silk tabby; and that of the lower households should not exceed three liang of silver, two sheets of polychrome stain, fifteen bolts of silk tabby. The wedding banquet of the upper and medium households should contain no more than three courses, and that of the lower households no more than two courses. All

元代城市
生活长卷

The Urban Life of the
Yuan Dynasty

the wedding banquets should be held in the daytime and end before the bell of curfew." (Matrimonial Rituals, Vol. 3, TZTG; Marriage, Vol. 18, YDZ) However, the new edict still proved ineffective to the extravagant society.

Besides, it was quite popular for officials to take gift of money from colleagues and subordinates. Some even directly deducted it from their subordinates' stipends. A memorial to the throne in the sixth lunar month of the seventh year of yanyou under Emperor Renzong revealed, "during the recent years, many officials were invited to attend the wedding banquets held by their superiors, who either took their gift of money in private or directly deducted it from their subordinates' stipends"; "now all the gift of money an official received was deducted from his subordinates' stipends. The gift of money was originally intended to show our concern for the relatives and friends, but when it accounted for a majority of an official's stipend, it was no different from a bride." The court therefore especially issued an edict, prohibiting all the officials from deducting money from their subordinates' stipends as the gift of money. (Penalties and Prohibitions, YDZXJ) The officials, however, were not really deterred by these laws. They continued to extort money from their subordinates, only in a more private way.

Chapter Two | **The Mongol Funerary Customs**

The imperial funerals of the Yuan Dynasty were generally carried out in accordance with the Mongol customs. But their sacrificial rites, influenced by the Chinese customs, were based on a dual-track ceremonial system.

1

The Mongols usually buried the dead in the ground without leaving any sign on the burial spots, though they still held a memorial service called "shaofan" (incineration) for the deceased. Through various historical sources we could catch a glimpse of the traditional Mongol funerary customs.

According to the customs on the steppes, those who had touched a dead body were not allowed to enter the ordo of the Khakhan or the tents of the nobles. "The funeral and memorial rites of the Mongols were rather simple. They were buried in a coffin made of a single large log without a tombstone. Their relatives didn't wear mourning or abstain from wine and meat during the mourning period which however lasted no longer than a month." (Huang Jin, Inscriptions on the Tombstone of Dalu, Vol. 28, JHHXSWJ). The dignitaries were usually buried with such funerary objects as gold and silver. The gravesites of the Mongols were kept a secret and there were no sign left on the ground to mark the location. According to the Southern Song envoy sent to the Mongol Empire, "their graves were stamped over by horses to erase the sign of the burial sites on the ground." (HDSL) A more elaborate description of the burial rites of the Mongols could be found in the work of John of Plano Carpini.

When one of them dies, if he is a noble, he is buried secretly in a field that pleases them. What is more, he is buried sitting in the middle of one of his tents, and they place a table before him and put a tray of meat and a bowl of mare's milk on it. Furthermore, there is buried with him a mare with a foal and a horse with a saddle and bridle, and they eat another horse and fill the skin with straw and mount it on two or four poles up high, so that in the next world he may have a tent where he may stay, and a mare from which he may have milk and by which he may increase the number of his horses and the horses he may ride⋯ The Tartars bury gold and silver with him; the cart in which he was drawn is broken, and no one dares name anyone with his name until the third generation.

There is another way the Tartars bury some great men. They go secretly into a field and dig up a plant with its roots and they make a large hole in the side of this pit underground, and they put a slave they have chosen beneath him; he lies there long enough that he begins to die, then they take him out so that he can breathe, and they do this three times, and if he survives he is thenceforward free and does whatever he wishes and is important in the camp and among his relatives. The dead man, however, is buried in the hole in the side of the pit with the things described above. The Tartars fill in the pit which is before his hole and put the shrub above it as it was before so that it may not be told from any other place. They do

241

otherwise as described above, but leave his tent outside in a field.

In the Tartar country there are two cemeteries, one in which emperors, princes and all the nobles are buried, and no matter where they die, if possible, they are brought there. There is in fact a great deal of gold and sliver buried with them. The other cemetery is the one in which the men who were killed in Hungary are buried, for many were killed there…

Relatives and anyone else who remained in the hut must be purified through fire. The purification is done this way: they build two fires and they place two spears near the fires and a line between the tips of the spears and they tie onto the line strips of buckram beneath which and between the two fires the people, animals and tents pass. There are two women, one here and the other there who throw water and recite certain songs, and if somehow the cart is broken there, or something should fall the sorcerers keep it. And if someone is killed by lightning all the people who lived in the household must pass between the fires in the aforesaid way; tent, bed, cart, felt and clothes and whatever things of that kind he possessed are not touched by anyone, but are treated by everyone as if they were defiled.

The traditional way for the northern nomadic tribes to offer sacrifices to their ancestors was to burn them in fire. And the Mongols were no exception. It was said that "in the Yuan Dynasty a dinner would usually be offered to the deceased through incineration, while in a large sacrificial ceremony, horses would be burned as sacrifice." And more information on this sacrificial rite would be revealed in the following chapters.

If a Mongol died on a foreign land he would be brought back to be buried on the steppes. "If a man was killed in battle, his fellows should either bring him back, or bury him with all the money they had." The Southern Song envoy Xu Ting also related, "If a servant could bring his deceased master back from the battle field, he would be rewarded with

元代城市
生活长卷

The Urban Life of the
Yuan Dynasty

242

all his master's livestock and property; if a stranger did this, he should have all the property of the deceased, including his wives, slaved and livestock." (HDSL) During the reign of Emperor Chengzong, an ?ngüd was appointed Prince of Gaotang and he was then sent to the northwest to arrest a rebel prince, unfortunately he was killed and buried there. After the accession of Emperor Wuzong, his son confided to his retainers one day, saying "I would die without regret if I could get the permission from His Majesty to bring my father's remains back." His retainers then sent an appeal to the Emperor with the help of an official of the Bureau of Military Affairs. Emperor Wuzong agreed. Soon people were sent to the Northwest to find Prince of Gaotang and he was finally brought back by an escort of 500 soldiers and buried in the cemetery of the ?ngüd tribe. (YS, Vol. 118) Therefore it was a common practice for the Mongols, especially the nobles, to be buried back on the steppes.

2

Ever since the Chinggis khan, an imperial cemetery had been selected for the Mongol Khakhan. It was called kilengu in the Chinese historical sources of the Yuan Dynasty and it was where most of the royal members were buried.

According to the Persian historian Rashīd al-Dīn, Chinggis Khan had already chosen a grave site for himself. "When Chinggis Khan was hunting outside, he ran into a lone tree growing on an open ground. He dismounted and felt very happy under the tree. He then ordered, 'make this place my burial site and mark it!' So at his funeral his retainer repeated his words, and his relatives and officials to decide to follow his will and bury him there." According to Rashīd al-Dīn, Chinggis Khan was buried at the foot of Mount Burkhan Khaldun. (Section two, Vol. 1, SJ, pp. 322-323) The Southern Song envoy Xu Ting also stated, "legend has it that Chinggis Khan was buried in a place near the Lugou River, probably because it was where he was born. But it was not verified." (HDSL) And according to the History of the Yuan, Chinggis Khan was buried in kilengu. All these historical sources, however, were proved consistent by the modern historical studies, for kilengu was found to be a Chinese transliteration of a Mongolian word in Yuan Chao Mi Shi (The Secret of History of the Mongols), and it was a place lying south to the Mount Burkhan Khaldun, probably located in T?v and Khentii Provinces in northern Mongolia.

Chinggis Khan died on the territory of the Xixia Dynasty. His men didn't release the news of his death as had been ordered by him before his death and started the long journey back to the steppes with his body. For fear that the death of their Khakhan should be discovered before their arrival at the Khankhan's final resting place, the soldiers killed every person encountered by the funeral cortege on its journey to the steppes where a grand funeral was waiting for Chinggis Khan. According to the Mongol customs, the Khakhan was buried with a fabulous treasure, horses, and, according to the Persian historian Juvaixli, 40 beauties bedecked with finery. (Book one, SJZFZS, p. 220)

The tomb of Chinggis Khan had no sign on the ground, just as those of the other Mongol Khakhans. It was said that trees were planted on top of it, and eventually the burial site of Chinggis Khan was swallowed in an impenetrable forest, even the forest guards couldn't find it. This forest or "great qoruq" in Mongolian later became a forbidden place on the steppes and was henceforth guarded by a battalion of the Uriyangkhan clan.

The descendants of Chinggis Khan including Ogedei Khan, Mongke Khan and Tolui were all buried in kilengu, following the same burial rites as Chinggis Khan.

元代城市
生活长卷

The Urban Life of the
Yuan Dynasty

Qubilai and other emperors of the Yuan Dynasty were also buried in kilengu according to the Mongol funerary customs. "On night of the twenty-second day of the first lunar month of the thirty-first year of zhiyuan (1249), His Majesty expired in Zitan Hall in the Imperial Palace. His coffin was later transferred into the palace tent placed by the palace wall according to state rites. In the early morning of the third day, the imperial bier was carried to the northern imperial garden in the suburb through the Jiande Gate. After the sacrificial ceremony for the ancestors was done, all the officials wailed and retreated." (Wang Hui, Eight Memorial Speeches for the Late Emperor, Vol. 13, QJXSDQWJ) Because the bureaucrats of Han Chinese were not allowed to attend the Mongol Emperor's funeral, they could only escort the imperial bier to as far as outside the Jiande Gate.

The coffin, burial rites and memorial rites of the Yuan royal family were of the same style as those in the Mongol Empire, "every imperial coffin was made of a single log of fragrant cedar which was longitudinally cut into two and hollowed out. The empty space in the log, resembling the shape of a man, was only big enough to contain the body. The Emperor would be dressed in a sable coat, a fur hat, socks and shoes, a girdle, and a pouch, and the latter three were all made of ermine. In addition, two gold pots, a drinking vessel, a bowl, a plate, a spoon and a pair of chopsticks were loaded into the coffin as sacrificial objects. After the Emperor was encoffined, the coffin would be closed and bound with four gold wires. The hearse was roofed with nas i j and brimmed with white felt. The coffin was also covered with nas i j. The funeral procession was headed by a female Mongol Shaman riding a horse and dressed in new clothes. She was followed by another horse called "the golden funeral horse" which was decorated with gold saddle and rein and was also covered with nas i j. Every three days during the journey, sheep would be sacrificed to the deceased Emperor. When the funeral procession arrived at the burial spot, a crypt would be dug in which the coffin was buried; the left clods would be transferred to a faraway place. The grave would then be protected by three officials who had escorted the coffin. During the three-year mourning period, they were to offer sacrifices to the deceased Emperor everyday from their dwelling which was five li away from the grave." "If an Emperor or Empress was inflicted with an incurable disease, he or she would be transferred to the felt tent. If they died, they should be encoffined there. After the funeral, sheep would be sacrificed to them through incineration twice a day for 49 days." (Section six, Record of Sacrificial Rites, Vol. 77, YS; Tao Zongyi, The Golden Funeral Horse, Vol. 30, NCZGL) "In the Yuan imperial palace, the coffin was made of pieces of rare wood, which were then hollowed out to form a man-shaped space. When the deceased was encoffined, the coffin would be coated with lacquer and bound with three coils of gold. Then the coffin would the transported to the imperial cemetery on the steppes. The burial site would be stamped by thousands of horses and protected until it disappeared in the meadow. (Section two, Miscellaneous Institutions, Vol. 3, CMZ) According to Zheng Suonan living in the Southern Song Dynasty, all those encountered the funeral procession of the Yuan Emperor would be killed by the convoy accompanying the coffin. "The Tatar king and his wife would be shrouded in horsehide after death and encoffined into a hollowed-out log. The coffin would then be bound in gold wires and transferred back to their homeland to be buried, their burial site was kept a secret and all the living creatures along the funeral procession's route to the royal cemetery were put to the sword." (ZSXJ, pp.182-183)

元代城市
生活长卷

The Urban Life of the
Yuan Dynasty

246

4

Chinese elements were incorporated into the memorial rites observed in the Yuan imperial palace.

The state sacrificial rites included the Sacrifice to Heaven, Sacrifice to Ancestral Spirits and the incineration of sacrifices to the Mongol deceased emperors.

The Mongol held the Heaven in great awe and attached great significance to the ceremony of Sacrifice to Heaven. "Every year, His Majesty arrived in Shangdu on the twenty-fourth day of the sixth lunar month to "make aspersions of the milk of mare".

During the ceremony, Mongol Shamans, four Mongol and Chinese courtiers and their subordinates were sent by the Emperor to worship the Heaven. The sacrifices offered to the Heaven included one horse, eight gelding rams, nine bolts of polychrome satin and plain silk, nine tassels made of white wool and three sheets of sable. Then all would shout the name of Chinggis Khan and say the following words "thanks for Your Majesty's blessing; we'll offer sacrifices to you every year." After the ceremony, all the sacrificial money and other sacrificial objects were distributed among the attendants." (Section six, Record of Sacrificial Rites, Vol. 77, YS) The Sacrifice to Ancestral Spirits was held not long after the Sacrifice to Heaven ceremony. "Every year, on the seventh or ninth day of the seventh lunar month, the Emperor and the Empress would honor their ancestors with the libation of koumiss in plain clothes, facing the direction of the imperial cemetery on the northern steppes. They would be accompanied by other members of the royal family and the Mongol aristocrats." (Zhou Boqi, Five Poems Written on the Beginning of Autumn, Vol. 1, JGJ) This ceremony was usually carried out in the "western imperial harem" or the Shira Ordo in Shangdu.

The royal family of the Yuan Dynasty still kept the practice of incinerating sacrifices to their ancestors. "Every year in the ninth lunar month or after the sixteenth day of the twelfth month, the Emperor would send a high-ranking Mongol official to burn sacrifices in the palace yard with the help of a Mongol Shaman. The sacrifices offered to the ancestors included one horse, three sheep, koumiss, wine, three bolts of red gold cloth with coin pattern and three bolts of plain silk. While burning the sacrifices, the Shaman would pray and say in Mongolian the names of all the late Mongol Emperors." (Section six, Record of Sacrificial Rites, Vol. 77, YS)

An ancestral shrine of the Mongol Emperors was established in the vicinity of Shangdu. In 1276, the thirteenth year of zhiyuan, the young Emperor and the Empress Dowager of the Southern Song Dynasty as well as their entourage were brought to Shangdu for an audience with Qubilai. On the third day of their arrival," they were arranged to worship in the Mongol ancestral shrine which was 5 li north of the Western Gate in the morning. They were divided into two groups with the Empress Dowager, the young Emperor, Prince of Fu, Madam Luoguo and Imperial Commissioners travelling before and their retinue such as Wu Jian, Xie Tang and Liu Jie following behind. On arrival at the ancestral shrine, all of them prostrated themselves twice in front of the hall with the Empress Dowager and other noblewomen prostrating in the Mongolian way and Price of Fu and the State Councilor still in the traditional Chinese way. Another one prayed and kowtowed twice to the ancestral shrine." (Yan Guangda, Journey of the Peace Mission, Vol. 9, QTYS)

After mounting the throne, Qubilai immediately set about building the Ancestral Temple in Yanjing in the third lunar month of 1263, the fourth year of zhongtong, with the help of his Chinese advisors. However, the new temple which was finished in the tenth lunar month of 1266, the third year of zhiyuan was soon relegated to a temporary ancestral shrine by the completion of the new capital—Dadu. In the eighth lunar month of 1277, fourteenth year of zhiyuan, Qubilai ordered to build a new Ancestral Temple in Dadu. In the twelfth lunar month of 1280, the seventh year of zhiyuan, the new temple was completed. Qubilai then ordered the memorial tablets of his ancestors to be moved there and had the old one torn down. According to the traditional layout of a Chinese capital, "the Altars of Soil and Grain should be on the right (west), and the Ancestral Temple should be on the left (east)". The new Ancestral Temple was located in the east of the imperial city of Dadu and to the north of Qihua Gate. The Temple was built in such a way that its "main hall was situated in front of the sleeping quarters". The Ancestral Temple mainly consisted of a T-shaped main hall with thirteen chambers, seven consecutive ones of which faced the south and the T-shaped sleeping quarters with 8 chambers, five consecutive ones of which faced the south. The two parts together formed the letter I. The compound was flanked on both sides by a row of side halls of over 60 chambers, which were concurrently the outbuildings of other structures. During the reign of Emperor Yingzong, the imperial Ancestral Temple was expanded. Another hall covering 15 rooms was built in front of the temple, relegating the original main hall to the sleeping quarters; and over 50 outbuildings were added to the new Ancestral Temple. (Section three, Record of Sacrificial Rites, Vol. 74, YS; The Ancestral Temple, XJZJY)

The ancestral memorial tablets placed in the Ancestral Temple could be grouped into two types: wooden one and gilded ones. The wooden ones were designed by Liu Binzhong in the third year of zhiyuan based on the traditional Chinese style and all were made of chestnuts. The gilded ancestral memorial tablets, though wooden in nature, were made by Phags-pa Lama on the Emperor's orders in the sixth year of zhiyuan. From then on, most of the ancestral memorial tablets in the Ancestral Temple were gilded ones.

During the reign of Qubilai, the Mongol ancestors worshipped

249

in the Ancestral Temple included Yisügei (Emperor Liezu), Chinggis Khan (Emperor Taizong), Ogedei (Emperor Taizong), Güyük (Emperor Dingzong), Mongke (Emperor Xianzong), J?chi, Chagatai and Tolui. After the decease of Qubilai, his successors revered Chinggis Khan as their ancestor and highlighted the Tolui-Qubilai lineage by continually setting up sacrificial memorial tablets for the descendants of Qubilai in the Ancestral temple, so as to clarify the genealogical relationships.

The sacrificial ceremonies held at the Ancestral Temple were more Chinese than Mongolian. "The Sacrifice to Ancestral Spirits of the Mongols was part of the state rites. It Included sacrifices of animals, aspersions of the milk of mare, and prayers in Mongolian offered by Shamans." "Every year four cyclic rites would be performed by the official from the Directorate of Sacrifices with eminent Mongol Shamans chanting prayers at the Ancestral Temple. During the stage of sacrifice inspection, the official, dressed in ceremonial clothes, would go to imperial palace with three deacons to assure the royal family of the quality of the animals picked as sacrifice. Then they returned to the barn to beckon the spirits of the deceased Mongol Emperors and Empresses by calling their names. In the next day, after offering sacrifices to the ancestral spirits for three times, the deacons, Censors, Chamberlains for Ceremonials and Erudites returned to the imperial palace for an audience with the royal family. Then the Mongol butchers killed the sacrificial animals on their knees. The chamberlain for the Imperial Stud sprinkled mare's milk with a red-lacquered vessel. The Shamans chanted prayers to celestial deities. And the Great Supplicator brought spirit money to the burning site. At the end of the ceremony the beacons and their subordinates would perform prostrations before the ancestral memorial tablets of the Mongol ancestors." "Every spring, food in season would be offered to the Ancestral Temple. At the beginning of each season a large-scale sacrificial ceremony would be held at the Temple. During the

元代城市
生活长卷

The Urban Life of the
Yuan Dynasty

250

ceremony, music was performed, first the court music and then the state music. In every month a new type of food in season would be offered to the Ancestral Temple according to the state rites." "The first sacrificial offering was performed by high-ranking officials or the Keshikten; the second offering was carried out by Grand Academicians of the Hall of Scholarly Worthies or Libationers; the final offering was executed by Commissioners of the Commission for Ritual Observances. And all the above officials involved in the ceremony should wear ceremonial dress." Although the sacrificial ceremonies of the Yuan Dynasty were modeled on the Chinese ones, a tangible Mongolian influence could also be found in the sacrifices offered in the ceremonies, such as "swans, wild horses, badger-like animals, pheasants, Mongolian gazelles, turtledove-like birds, mare's milk, and grape wine. All the sacrifices were offered to the Mongol ancestors according to the state rites." (Section three & six, Record of Sacrificial Rites, Vol. 74 &77, YS; Annals, XJZJY)

Not only the sacrificial memorial tablets of the Mongol ancestors were placed in the Ancestral Temple, but their portraits were preserved in a portrait chamber called Shenyu Hall in the Buddhist monasteries in Dadu. "All these portraits were made of brocade by Adornment Service." For instance, the brocade portraits of Qubilai and the Heir Apparent Jingim were placed in Wan'an Monastery where sacrificial objects like Jade Books and Jade Seals were also kept. The portrait chamber of Emperor Chengzong was in Wanning Monastery, that of Emperor Wuzhong in Fuyuan Monastery; and the portraits of Emperor Renzong, Emperor Yingzong and Emperor Mingzong were respectively placed in Puqing Monastery, Yongfu Monastery and Yangsheng Monastery. "Memorial ceremonies would be held for them on the first day, the eighth day, the fifteenth day and the twenty-third day of every month; cyclic rites were also observed on the lunar New Year's Day, Tomb Sweeping Day, Dragon Boat Festival, Double Ninth Festival,

Winter Solstice, and the anniversary of the deceased Emperors." The brocade portraits of Emperor Taizu, Emperor Taizong and Emperor Ruizong (Tolui) were placed in the Hanlin and Historiography Academy "where sacrifices were offered to the deceased Emperors in every spring and autumn." (Section four, Record of Sacrificial Rites, Vol. 75, YS; Ancestral Temple, XJZJY)

5

The Yuan court highly prized "the traditional customs and the fundamental values like filial piety and loyalty." Therefore efforts had been made by the Yuan rulers to maintain the traditional Chinese funerary customs through a series of rules and regulations.

The Yuan court adopted a protective attitude towards the funerary customs of each ethnic group and had recognized and codified the traditional Chinese funerary customs which were represented by the "five-rank mourning" system and memorial rituals. "No dress code was issued during the early days of the dynasty. In 1304, the eighth year of dade, all the officials of the court, native and foreign, began to observe a three-year period of mourning for their deceased parents on the Emperor's orders. By the time of zhizhi period, Da Yuan Tong Zhi (The Comprehensive Institutions of the Great Yuan) was finished and since then the 'five-rank mourning' system had come into effect." (Preface to Great Institutions of Statecraft, Vol. 42, YWL) The Comprehensive Institutions of the Great Yuan was a code of rules compiled by the Yuan court and was issued in 1323, the third year of zhizhi by Emperor Yingzong. It stipulated the five-rank mourning system in which the mourning was divided into five ranks according to the closeness between the wearer and the deceased. "In areas between the Yangtze River and the Huai River, it was customary for people to wear cloth futou and cotton

robes at funerals." In 1315, the second year of yanyou, the Secretariat standardized the style of the mourning in the country, demanding all the subjects in the country, except Mongols and semuren who were allowed to be dressed according to their own customs, wear mourning made of hemp. Meanwhile, the Secretariat also prohibited the people from making the mourning in the style of gongfu. (Funerary Rites, Vol. 30, YDZ)

In the Yuan Dynasty, the Han Chinese mainly practiced inhumation in which the deceased would usually be buried in the family cemetery or sometimes, the public cemetery. Since the early days of the Yuan Dynasty, it had been stipulated in law that those who died in penury could be buried in a deserted land owned by the government and that local officials should be responsible for burying stray bones. This regulation resulted in the appearance of public cemeteries throughout the country. And it was still observed until the final days of the dynasty. In 1358, the eighteenth year of zhizheng, a large-scale famine hit the capital and Qi Empress sent her favorite eunuch Bak Bulhwa to built cemeteries around the eleven city gates. Over 100,000 corpses were buried and she also asked monks to perform Buddhist ceremonies to console the deceased. (Section one, Biography of the Imperial Consorts and Concubines, Vol. 114, YS). The location of the cemetery in cities was specified by the government. For example, in 1269, the sixth year of zhiyuan, it was decreed that the northern and eastern parts of the capital were banned from burying the dead, which was clearly out of the consideration of the expansion of Dadu, for the prohibition was lifted after the completion of Dadu. But restrictions were still imposed on the use of suburbs as graveyards.

The Yuan court also prescribed the size of the grave for the officials and the commoners. The grave for officials of the first rank measured 90 paces, that for the officials of the second rank 80 paces, that for the officials of the third rank 70 paces, that for the officials of the fourth rank 60 paces, that for the officials of the fifth rank 50 paces, that for the officials of the sixth rank 40 paces, and that for the officials below the seventh rank 20 paces. And the grave for the commoners measured 9 paces. Later a revision of this regulation further specified that the gave for the officials of the first rank was 300×300 paces, that for the officials of the second rank 250×250, that for the officials of the third rank 200×200 paces, that for the officials above the fifth rank 150×150, and that for the officials below the sixth rank 100×100. And the grave for the commoners or that in the monasteries 30×30 paces. The standard of the stone ornaments of the grave was also prescribed by the court. "The grave for officials of the first rank could have four stone figures, two stone pillars, two stone tigers and two stone sheep; that for the officials above the third rank could have two stone figures, two stone pillars, two stone tigers, and two stone sheep; that for the officials above the fifth rank could have two stone figures, two stone tigers and two stone sheep." (DYTZ; Huang Shijian, YDFLZLJC, p. 74) Thus the number of the stone ornaments of a grave reflected the status of the deceased.

In the Central Plains and Jiangnan Region, funerals of officials and wealthy families were usually conducted with great pomp and circumstances. And it was popular to burn paper houses or other paper objects as sacrifices to the deceased. "The cost of these paper objects averaged out to one or two ding for every household". In 1270, the seventh year of zhiyuan, the Yuan court banned "the incineration of such paper objects as paper houses, paper money (except the spirit money), paper figures and horses as well as other offerings such as silk, clothes and tents." (Funerary Rites, Vol. 30, YDZ, sic, passim) In 1308, the first year of zhiyuan during the reign of Emperor Wuzong, a memorial from Jiangxi Xinsheng to the Secretariat read, "nowadays, in Jiangnan Region the fundamental value—filial piety has been identified with ostentatious funerals with ornate coffins, elaborate burial suits, large graves, fancy offerings like jewelry, figurines, horses and carts. Such practices, though

元代城市
生活长卷

The Urban Life of the
Yuan Dynasty

254

tolerable, should not be advocated. Those elaborate graves, more often than not, ended up being disinterred by either ungrateful descendants or grave robbers, which was really a shame. Thus I ventured to suggest a ban on the use of extravagant funerary objects in a funeral apart from the burial suits and coffin as was stated in the funerary rites, such as silver and gold, precious jade and jewelry. Any transgressor should be considered unfilial and punished, so as to restore filial piety and reduce grave robberies as well." The Secretariat then imposed another ban on the extravagant funerals by drawing on the relevant rules issued in the seventh year of zhiyuan, but the prohibition bore no fruit. And ostentatious funerals still prevailed in the Yuan Dynasty.

Although inhumation was popular in the Han territory, some Chinese, influenced by Buddhism, Khitans and Jurchens, adopted cremation. "Some citizens in Dadu didn't place the corpse in the ceremonial room, though monks were still invited to pray for the deceased and music was played by a brass band all night long. When the coffin was bought from the market, it was placed at the doorstep where the deceased would encoffined after a wait of one or two days. The coffin was then loaded on a hearse, and the funeral procession headed by the son would slowly make for the nearby monastery. In the monastery the coffin would be cremated and a dinner would be held in the monastery by the family of the deceased. The relatives dispersed after the dinner. After cremation, the bones would be collected and buried just beside the burning spot. The son only needed to cry once back at home after the funeral and no memorial tablet would be set up in the house. When it was the time to burn sacrifices to the east, he simply placed a bowl of rice and sprinkle wine to the east; the same procedure would be repeated when it was the time to burn sacrifices to the west. And when it was the first day or the fifteenth day of a month, rice and wine would also be offered to the deceased after dusk." (Customs, XJZJY) Although the Yuan court didn't impose a blanket ban on cremation out of respect for the customs of different ethnic groups, it required indigenous Han Chinese to stick to their funerary rites and be properly buried instead of being cremated.

6

Han Chinese attached great significance to funeral and they usually held a fancy funeral procession which involved throwing spirit money and putting up roadside altars. Wealthy families often took this opportunity to flaunt their wealth. They richly decorated the hearse and the stage for opera, established many roadside altars, and sent for the brass band and troupe. To exhibit their power and wealth to more people, the funeral cortege would even detour to take the major street of the place. An extravagant funeral could not only be used to exhibit the family's financial power, it could also be served as a way to receive gifts and even bribes. People would hold an elaborate funeral for their relatives not because they really cared for the deceased, but because they were expecting consolatory gifts from others, whether related or not. Sometimes a gift that seemed not so consolatory to the eyes of the receiver would give rise to a bitter quarrel before the coffin. In some places, a "decent" funeral would even involve an escort from the local government. Just as an official of the Provincial Surveillance Commission in Handong Circuit of Shangxi had pointed out, "local Subofficial Functionaries would usually be dispatched to run errands in a wedding or convoy a funeral procession. Those powerful families sent for them with privilege while the commoners with money." All these practices forced the Yuan court to impose a ban on lavish funerals. "No fancy hearse, roadside altars or gigantic stages. Mourning was only for relatives, not acquaintances, who were only obliged to send consolatory money. The funeral procession should take the most convenient route to the burial site." In addition, the

元代城市
生活长卷

The Urban Life of the
Yuan Dynasty

256

size of escort dispatched from the government in the funeral procession of officials depended on the rank of the deceased. The commoners were prohibited from hiring Subofficial Functionaries in either funeral or wedding. (The Remaining Institutions of Dade Period, YDFLZLJC, pp. 50-51; Funerary Rites, Vol. 30, YDZ)

It was also popular for people to hold feasts during the mourning period. An official of the Jiangnan Branch Censorate stated, "Recently it was popular, especially in Jiangnan Region, for the mourners to hold funerary feasts even before their deceased parent was dressed in burial suit. They started to dine on meat and wine. They sent for funeral band and performers during the funeral procession and they held a feast which always involved drunkenness right after the burial." It was also true of the people in the Central Plains, especially when they were "doing the sevens" for the deceased. "Filial piety was measured with the number of courses served in the feasts held on every seventh day"; "On every seventh day, anniversaries and the occasion of fetching the bones of a relative died afield, lavish feasts would be held for the relatives and friends. They would ornate the memorial hall, set up an elaborate stage, and then marched towards the Buddhist monastery or Taoist temple with monks and Taoist priests walking in front and brass bands playing around to perform religious service for the dead. And their meal in the temple was also quite lavish." In order to curb such practices, the court decree that "no feast should be held in funeral or during the mourning period. Any transgressor, once verified, would be punished in public. If the local authorities connived at the infringement, they would be punished as well." (The Remaining Institutions of Dade Period; Section three, Funerary Rites Vol. 30, YDZ)

Semuren, designating all peoples who immigrated from the west of China, were also demanded to be buried in their respective funerary customs, such as inhumation, cremation, sky burial and water burial, etc. And people of different ethnic groups had different burial rites. Taking inhumation for example, a man from what is now Kumul Prefecture of Xinjiang Province ordered, before his death, to be buried according to the traditions of his own land, which is "to be buried in paper clothes in a pottery coffin." (YS, Vol.124) And a traditional Uighur funeral must include the following elements: "coffin ornaments that were required by their funerary rites, gold to be placed on the head, chest, and navel of the corpse, people holding a plate of barley before camels and horses, an armored funeral horse, a funeral cortege, roadside altars, people responsible for burying the coffin". Although a Uighur funeral also had funerary objects, a funeral procession and roadside alters, it was conducted in a different ritual system from Chinese. During their mourning period, the daughters and daughters-in-law would be dressed in white mourning with their hair unbound, and the males in the family would either hang a white piece of silk on one's shoulder if he was a monk, or have his hair hang loosely. And they would all go on a vegetarian diet during the mourning period. However, those Uighur people who had migrated inland were influenced by the customs of the Han Chinese. "They disgraced themselves by abandoning their own customs and following the Han Chinese to hold lavish funerals by slaughtering many animals." Therefore, to protect the Uighur traditional customs, the Yuan court ordered all the Uighur people, no matter where they lived, to be strictly buried according to their own traditional funerary customs. The court also decreed that "no horse, cow or sheep should be slaughtered on the pretext of the funeral feast and that all those came to express their

元代城市
生活长卷

The Urban Life of the
Yuan Dynasty

condolence should only be provided with vegetarian food." The Uighur people also practiced cremation which would be conducted by Monks.

The sacrificial customs of semuren were different from those of the Han Chinese and Mongols as well. For example, El-Temür of the Qipchaq "had built a vault 70 li northwest of Shangdu to house the marble statues of his ancestors. When holding a memorial service for his ancestors, he would sprinkle wine over the statues and then smear them with minced meat." (Xu Youren, Accompanying Prince of Taiping to Offer Sacrifices to the Stone Statue of Grand Preceptor, Vol. 16, ZZJ) Thus it was the Qipchaq tradition to offer sacrifices to their ancestors by pouring wine on the statues and smearing them with meat.

Chapter Three | **The Impact of Chinese Traditional Ethics on Mongols**

People's social behavior was usually guided by some canons of conduct that were supported by certain ethics. Thus in our study of the social life of the Yuan cities, it was necessary to take into consideration the impact of the prevailing ethics at that time. After the establishment of the Mongol Empire, the Emperor ordered all his subjects to abide by the Mongolian traditional ethics and even incorporated it into the empire's legal code. But when the Mongol ruler determined to change the empire's formal title into a Chinese dynastic name "Da Yuan", he was also ready to accept the Chinese traditional ethics which soon became the fundamental moral standards for all his subjects.

1

Chinggis Khan once said that a nation would become weak and go to ruins if Yūsūn (convention) and Yasa were not strictly observed, such as a son disobeyed his father; a younger brother refused to listen to his elder siblings; a husband distrusted his wife; a father-in-law disliked his daughter-in-law, a daughter-in-law didn't respect her father-in-law; the elder didn't protect the young; the young didn't accept the teachings of the elder; people of high standing believed only in his body servants; and

元代城市
生活长卷

The Urban Life of the
Yuan Dynasty

the rich didn't help his poor fellows. (Section two, Book one, Vol.1, SJ, pp. 354-355) Chinggis Khan summarized and further developed the core of the traditional Mongol ethics in the above words, and he also codified it as the basic moral norms for his subjects after the establishment of the Mongol Empire. Thus people on the steppes were demanded to strictly abide by Yūsūn and Yasa, respect the elder, treat others with sincerity, and abstain from alcohol, adultery and robbery.

Chinggis Khan demanded all the Mongols to observe Yūsūn and Yasa. Yūsūn mainly referred to the convention or traditional prohibitions, while Yasa was mainly comprised of Chinggis khan's words and teachings. Thus a man should not only respect traditional customs, but also obey the Emperor, which became the basic code of ethics for the Mongols including the royal family of the Yuan Dynasty. In the Yuan Dynasty, "the Yasa would always be read at the royal assembly of imperial princes before a coronation" (Huang Qian, Tomb Passage of the Grand Councilor of the Right Baiju, Vol. 24, JHHXSWJ). Besides, "it would also be read out by a most erudite official before the imperial banquet." (Ke Jiusi, Palace Poems, Vol. 1, CYTJ). And all the Chinggisid princes of the Yuan Dynasty were required to memorize the Yasa and to recite it fluently. Thus by preserving and constantly observing the Yasa, the Mongols traditional moral concepts were passed down form one generation to another.

2

Neo-Confucianism, taking shape in the Northern Song Dynasty, was promoted to its culmination as orthodoxy of Confucianism by Zhu Xi in the Southern Song Dynasty. During the period of late Jin Dynasty and early Yuan Dynasty, it began to prevail in north China where it was further developed. And by the time of mid-Yuan period, there already emerged various schools of Neo-Confucianism, such as the Luzhai School, Jingxiu School, Caolu School, Beishan School, and Huizhou School, etc. All these schools, though different in the perspective to approach Neo-Confucianism, shared the same concepts like reverence for the sages, loyalty, filial piety, chastity, moral conduct, and benevolence for the people. Under the Mongol rule, some Chinese Neo-Confucian officials and other Confucian scholars endeavored to expose the Mongol monarchs to Neo-Confucianism so as to enable the Mongols and people of other ethnic groups to accept the Chinese traditional ethics. In the meanwhile, they tried to maintain the dominant role of Neo-Confucianism in the Central Plains and Jiangnan Region, where Han Chinese mainly inhabited, to preserve their traditional values.

In fact, the ethics of Han Chinese did not contradict those of the Mongols, though they were observed in a more sophisticated way. After the Mongols entered the Central Plains, the Chinese Confucian scholars tried every means to expose the Mongol rulers to the Chinese ethics, especially to the "ways of the sages to achieve self-cultivation and submission from others" and "the ruling methods leading to a peaceful world." (Biography of Zhaobi, Vol. 159, YS) But all their efforts didn't bear fruit until the era of Emperor Chengzong, Emperor Wuzong and Emperor Renzong who began to officially recognize the Chinese traditional ethics and set them as the code of ethics and conduct for the whole nation through the imperial edicts, because Qubilai, the founder of the Yuan Dynasty, wan inclined to adhere to his own traditional ethics stipulated by Yasa after coronation, despite the fact that he had already learnt about the Chinese ethics from his Chinese advisors before his accession. And such moral concepts advocated by the Mongol rulers were standardized or "sinicized" through a series of revisions and interpretations by the Chinese Confucian scholars. And the code of ethics and conduct advocated by the Confucian scholars and accepted by the

元代城市
生活长卷

The Urban Life of the
Yuan Dynasty

Mongol rulers mainly included such aspects as virtues of the Emperor, duties of officials, loyalty, filial piety and chastity, etc.

3

During the period of Mongol Empire, the Mongol Khakhans were required to abide by the Mongol traditional code of conduct. After Qubilai came to power, his Confucian councilors advised him to adopt the "virtues required in a legitimate Chinese Emperor". Qubilai agreed and declared that "necessary changes should be made to the ancestral rules, for I would submit myself to the institutions laid down by the sages of the previous dynasties." (Imperial Edict Issued upon Coronation, Imperial Edict Issued in the First Year of Zhongtong, Vol. 9, YWL) In order to project the image of a "legitimate" Emperor of China, Qubilai also agreed to "remove Mongolian misgovernment, establish new government, and restore law and order, etc. (Hao Jing, Suggestions on Governance, Vol. 32, HWZGJ) However, it was not an easy job to be a legitimate Chinese Emperor, for his Chinese underlings continued to pile more standards of an ideal Chinese Emperor on him. Some suggested him to act on "six principles", which included "living up to one's promise, staying alert to deceit, and employing people of virtue and talent. Some advocated "Three Foundations", namely the Heir Apparent as the foundation of the country, the Secretariat as the foundation of government and Talent as the foundation of governance. Some presented him the classic quotations and good policies of previous virtuous emperors. And still some recommended "Four Doctrines", namely ren (benevolence), yi (justice), li (rites) and xin (credibility) to be the foundations of the country. Of course, Qubilai didn't adopt all of their suggestions, but he accepted such suggestions as respecting the Heaven and Earth and holding memorial service for the ancestors, for they conformed to the Mongol traditional values.

After the decease of Qubilai, in order to refrain the Mongol Emperors from indulging in hunting, banquets and Buddhist activities, some Chinese officials advised them to worship the Heaven, respect the ancestors, purify heart, reduce desires and carry out reforms. And some suggested "holding court assemblies every three or two days". But all these suggestions proved ineffective, for "state affairs, in the eyes of the Mongol emperors, meant only three things: military expeditions, hunting and lavish banquets." (Wang Hui, Tomb Passage of Sir Lü, Vol. 57, QJXSDQWJ) While "virtues of emperor" displayed by them were only confined to their recognition of their "heavenly mandated" responsibilities as the Chinese monarchs and their occasional fear of the "warnings from the Heaven".

4

The core of Qubilai's Chinese-styled legal system mainly consisted of two parts. One was "the incorporation of Tang and Song codes into the Mongol customary law". And the other was "the establishment of a legal administration modeled on that of the former Liao and Jin dynasties to ensure the implementation of the laws". And the basic hierarchy of this legal administration was head by the Department of State Affairs of the central government, under which many judicial agencies were installed to handle the local affairs. (Suggestions on Governance; Imperial Edict Issued in the First Year of Zhongtong) Because it was the officials that enforced the laws, it was necessary for the Yuan court to device a system to evaluate the performance of the officials.

In 1260, the first year of zhongtong, two evaluation criteria were set for the local officials, i.e. "increasing population and collecting taxes". In 1264, the fifth year of zhiyuan, these two criteria were expanded to

five, i.e. "increasing population, exploring farmland, reducing lawsuits, eliminating crimes and balancing taxes and corvée". They were referred to as "Five Criteria", and they served as the basic evaluation criteria of the official's performance in the youyuan period. (Consolidating Officialdom, Vol. 1, YDZ; Five Criteria, Vol. 6, TZTG) The "Five Criteria" was also the prototype of the later "Regulation and Rule for Officials" and "Code of Official Conduct".

In addition to the "Five Criteria", the Yuan officials were also required to abide by the law, recruit people of virtue and talent, be out spoken and dare to make remonstrance, develop education, improve the welfare of the populace, observe local customs, advocate virtues like filial piety, refrain from scrambling for fame and official positions, relieve the people in stricken areas, loan people the money to pay taxes, care for the widowed and hold sacrificial ceremonies, etc. Besides, officials were not allowed to entertain themselves in teahouses, taverns and brothels. "He who went to a teahouse or a tavern should be questioned by Surveillance Officials." "Civil servants such as Scribes, Clerks and Agents were banned from visiting prostitutes and indulging in excessive drinking. Any transgressor should be punished." (Court Disciplines, Vol. 5; Evaluation of the Officials, Vol. 6, YDZ)

However, with all these evaluation criteria which were basically the same as those employed by the previous dynasties, there still existed a large gap between ideal and reality, for officials of different ethnic backgrounds have different interpretations of the "Five Criteria", which was simply because they were brought up to different moral concepts and to different political treatment.

The competences that the Yuan court required in the officials were almost the same as that of the previous dynasties. They simply included "appropriate conduct, articulateness, familiarity with codes and documents, erudition and calligraphy." (Competences, LXZN)

However, most Yuan officials lacked cultural cultivation and basic political qualities because a majority of them were either Keshikten or elevated from Subofficial Functionaries. As was pointed out by someone, "nowadays, most Mongol and semuren officials cannot sign their autographs with a writing brush. They, instead, used the ivory or wooden seals. Whenever the Steward-bulwark of State or the Court Attendant of the first rank received an imperial edict, they would sign with the jade seal specially granted by the Emperor." (Tao Zongyi, Making Seals, Vol. 2, NCZGL) Therefore the Yuan court would not place great demands on the competence of the officials.

5

People in the Central Plains and Jiangnan Region tended to observe the traditional Chinese ethics, such as loyalty and justice, filial piety and fraternal duty, chastity, discretion about words and deeds and prudence in social activates, and they also wanted the Mongols to accept their code of ethics. Since the establishment of the Yuan Dynasty, many had advised the Emperor to reward those loyal, righteous or chaste people with the purpose of prompting the Emperor to accept the traditional Chinese moral concepts. The result, however, was not that satisfactory. "Such practices as Recall and Restore25, honoring a chaste wife with a banner, signing a betrothal letter, respecting teachers, recompensing criminal informants and rewarding loyal officials and righteous people were not known to every household, and they were not observed by people in the least. Therefore they were nothing but empty words." (Wang Hui, The Memorial to Emperor Shizu on Political Affairs, Vol.35, QJXSDQWJ) Taking the Prestige Titles for example, "only some officials of merit were honored with posthumous titles in zhiyuan period. Valuable progress as it was, it wasn't codified as a rule." (Prestige Titles, Vol. 40, YWL) And it was

元代城市
生活长卷

The Urban Life of the
Yuan Dynasty

266

not until the ninth lunar month of 1309, the 2nd year of zhida during the reign of Emperor Wuzong, did the court began to "consider the code of Prestige Titles" so as to honor loyalty and advocate filial piety. In the eighth lunar month of 1316, the third year of yanyou during the reign of Emperor Renzong, the code of Prestige Titles was finally formulated. However, the practice of using posthumous name to reflect a person's life accomplishment, "originally an ideal system to deter wrong doings and encouraging good deeds, was now abused, greatly deviated from its original purpose." (Ma Zuchang, Fifteen Suggestions, Vol. 15, YWL) After Emperor Chengzong came to power, he began to praise "righteous husbands, virtuous wife, filial sons and worthy progeny" and condemn such immoral deeds as "sons betraying their father, slaves accusing their master and incest" in the imperial edicts. As for such "filial behaviors" as cutting a piece of one's liver or flesh to save one's parent, they were denounced as "irrational" by Qubilai soon after his accession. Thus it could be inferred that it was not until the mid-Yuan times did the Yuan rules began to accept the traditional Chinese moral concepts. And it was from then on, did such codes of conduct as "filial piety and fraternal duty, industry and scrupulousness, integrity, modesty, being law-abiding, sincerity, discretion and uprightness" began to be observed as the national codes of ethics and conduct.

6

It was also during the mid-Yuan times were the officials officially permitted to observe a period of mourning for one's parent or grandparent, as was required by the traditional Chinese ethics.

At the very beginning of the Yuan Dynasty, although the Chinese officials were tacitly permitted by the court to observe a three-year period of mourning for parents, there were no definite rules about it. In 1291, the twenty-eighth year of zhiyuan, officials were officially permitted to "hasten home for the funeral of a parent or grandparent". If a parent or grandparent died, one (official) could apply for a solid 30 days of paid leave, excluding the time spent on the route. In the case of relocating the grave of a parent or grandparent, a leave of 20 days would be granted. In 1304, the eighth year of dade during the reign of Emperor Chengzong, this practice was further legitimized by law. "The convention of three-year mourning period had been observed since time immemorial. From now on, all Chinese officials, except the Keshikten and those serving in territorial armies, were to observe a period of mourning for their deceased parents and were not allowed to return to office until the end of the mourning period. Recall and Restore was not subject to this rule. The Mongol and Semuren officials could either observe their own customs or follow the above rule." (Section one, Regulation and Rule for Officials, Vol. 10, YDZ) The so-called three-year mourning period, in fact, lasted only for 27 months, which was stipulated in law by Emperor Renzong after he came to power. "The mourning period for the Chinese officials should be 27 months, though the practice had been stipulated in law, so as to honor the Chinese customs. Those who were recall and restore to previously occupied post, Mongol and semuren officials, and military commanders were not subject to this rule." Later more details were added to this rule. For example, a memorial ceremony should be held at the thirteenth and the twenty-fifth months of the mourning period which started from the day when the official learnt the news of his parent's death. Officials converted from military officers, like the Administrative Clerk, were also allowed to observe a period of mourning for their parents. Officials who were found guilty of misconduct were allowed to be tried after the mourning period, but not the officials guilty of corruption. While the commoners who were found guilty of crimes should be tried and punished even during the mourning period. During the reign

元代城市
生活长卷

The Urban Life of the
Yuan Dynasty

of Emperor Yingzong, someone reported, "in the past officials who were recalled and restored were usually Confucian advisers or grand officials of merit. However this policy has been abused by some powerful officials so that even those children of wealthy families, incompetent Subofficial Functionaries, and ordinary officials could find ways to avoid observing the mourning period." Therefore, to prevent this policy from being abused by people with an ulterior motive, the court especially decreed that "Recall and Restore should only be confined to Confucian advisers and grand officials of merit." (Regulation and Rule for Officials, YDZXJ)

7

Although the Mongol rulers were somewhat reluctant to accept the traditional Chinese moral concepts, some Mongols, Tanguts, Uighurs, and Muslims who had migrated to the Central Plains during the era of Mongol Empire or in the early days of the Yuan Dynasty gradually adopted the Chinese moral concepts and began to follow the Chinese code of conduct.

Some of them had a keen interest in sinology, such as Xiang Wei, the descendant of Muqali the Mongol official of merit. He "didn't drink and seldom smiled but was fond of inviting scholar-officials for dinners, listening to their reading of the Confucian classics and history, and joining in their discussion of the historical events. Whenever he heard a righteous official defeat his enemy, he would burst into applause." (Biography of Xiang Wei, Vol. 128, YS) There was a Qarluq who "loved study and traveling with Scholar-officials, and he styled himself Hanging." (YS, Vol.122) Lian Xixian, a Uighur, was "addicted" to Confucian classics and history and was dubbed "Mencius Lian" by Qubilai.

Some actively engaged in the propagating Chinese ethics among the Mongols. There was another Uighur who was appointed to teach the sons of the younger brother of Chinggis Khan. "He always emphasized such moral concepts as filial piety, fraternal duty and amity, benevolence and generosity in his classes." (Ouyang Xuan, Biography of Gaochangxie Family, Vol. 24, GZWJ) A Tanghat called Gao Zhiyao had once advised Mongke and Qubilai to "govern the country with the Three Cardinal Guides and Five Constant Virtues". "He strongly advocated Confucianism and repeatedly expounded on its political significance." (Biography of Gao Zhiyao, Vol. 125, YS)

Some carefully observed such moral norms as filial piety and fraternal duty. There was a Uighur "who was a good son and brother. He had gone all the way back to his homeland to invite his mother to live in his mansion in Yanjing. He served his mother whole heartedly and always gave his stipend to her. When he was a young boy, his uncle cheated him of all his property. But after he rose to prominence, he still invited his uncle to live in the extension of his house, which his younger brother who had harbored strong resentment towards his uncle couldn't understand. He thus kept reasoned with his brother and finally talked his brother into accepting his uncle." (YS, Vol. 125) Qubilai once was intended to reward a man from Kashmir for his meritorious service by marrying a girl of blue blood to him. He politely declined Qubilai's offer, saying "my mother, a Han Chinese, always expected me to marry a Chinese woman and I couldn't afford to break her heart." (YS, Vol. 125)

Some chose to follow the traditional Chinese funerary customs. Taking "Mencius Lian" (Lian Xixian) for example, after the death of his mother, he "strictly practiced the funerary rituals by refusing to drink water for three consecutive days and keeping wailing until spitting the blood. After his mother was buried, he was determined to stay at the grave to observe mourning for her." As the court hadn't adopted the mourning policy by that time, officials of the Secretariat were sent to his dwelling to invite him back to office. But all their efforts were dissolved by the bitter cries wafted from Lian Xixian's house. Qubilai then had

to issue an edict to get him back to office. Soon Xixian's father also died. He "earnestly appealed the emperor for a mourning leave, but was refused and had to return to his post after observing a short period of mourning for his father." (Yuan Mingshan, Tomb Passage of the Manager of Governmental Affairs Lian Wenzheng, Vol. 15, YWL)

Some even propagate the Chinese ethics in the residential areas of the ethnic minorities in Jiangnan Region. For instance, Sayyid Ajjal Shams al-Din Omar and his son had both served as officials in Yannan. "People in Yunnan observed no matrimonial or funerary rites"; they neither cultivate such crops as rice, mulberry trees and hemp, nor did they send their children to school. Sayyid then taught them social etiquette and matrimonial, mourning, and burial rites. He taught them to sow seeds and build up water-conservancy systems. He encouraged the local education by establishing Confucius Temples, buying Confucian classics and history books, and starting public schools." When Sayyid's son inherited his father's post, he "continued to support local education by establishing more public schools and sending men of letter as teachers." (Biography of Sayyid Ajjal Shams al-Din Omar, Vol. 125, YS)

In mid Yuan Dynasty, there was an increasing number of Mongols studying Confucianism and they actively advocated it to the Emperor. Among them many were descendants of officials of merit and dignitaries. It was under their efforts, plus the help from the Qangli, Uighur, Tangut, and Muslim Confucians, that the traditional Chinese ethics were finally accepted by the Mongol rulers. In other words, but for the assistance from people of other ethnic groups, the Chinese officials would never have succeed in making the Mongol rulers accept their moral concepts.

271

Chapter Four │ From Simple Ritualistic Behavior to Sophisticated Court Etiquette

People had to observe certain etiquette which was either conventional or imposed by the rulers in their social activities. Although the court and folk etiquette of the Yuan Dynasty was fundamentally derived from the traditional Chinese etiquette and customs, it also incorporated quite a few elements of the Mongol and other ethnic groups.

1

In the early days of the Mongol Empire, there was no specific etiquette for the officials to follow when they were summoned for an audience with the Emperor. But people on the steppes were required to strictly abide by the traditional customs and never to breach the conventional prohibitions, or they would be sentenced to death. The Mongol court etiquette at that time was mainly employed in such aspects as honorific titles for the Emperor and the officials, Quriltai and court assemblies.

The Mongol Empire, "lying to the north of the Gobi Desert, was a nation of simple etiquette—even officials and their sovereign could share the same name." (Section two, Miscellaneous Institutions, Vol. 3, CMZ) It is true that the name of the Khakhan was not a taboo among his subjects

until he had an imperial title. For example, after Temüjin was granted the imperial title "Chinggis Khan" in the Quriltai in 1206, he began to be addressed as such instead of his name Temüjin. His son Ogedei was granted the imperial title "Khakhan" after his accession. And from then on Ogedei was addressed as Khakhan, Ogedei Khan or Ogedei Khakhan, and so was the case with Güyük and Mongke.

The honorific title for the wife of the Khakhan was "Khatun" which means "empress" in Chinese. And they could be called by the appellation consisted of her name and the title Khatun. But in most cases, the chief Empress was addressed as the First Khatun or Yeke Khatun ("Yeke" in Mongolian means "great"), while the other lesser wives of the Khakhan were called by the appellation with an ordinal number to indicate their seniority. For example, Toregene who later became regent of the Mongol Empire after the death of her husband Ogedei continued to be addressed as "the Sixth Empress" even after the change in her political status.

The male Chinggisids or members of the "Golden Family" used to address each other by name. But if an outsider were to address them, he should add a title behind their names, such as "prince" or "Khan". With the passage of time and under the influence of the Chinese culture, some Mongol chieftains no longer wanted themselves to be addressed by name and some Mongol imperial princes and empresses required complete avoidance of their names after their death. An outrageous example of the former was that Batu once killed a man who had mentioned his name in drunkenness. And the most famous example of the latter was that Tolui was addressed as Yeke Noyan after his death.

The Khakhan usually called his subordinates by name regardless of their ethnic backgrounds. But sometimes, in order to show his favor, he would confer such titles as "Tarkhan" and "Baturu" (warrior) on some officials. And such officials would be called by his name plus the corresponding title. A few Han Chinese were also granted a title by the Emperor. For example, Shi Tianze, a native of Zhengding, had the title "Baturu" and he was addressed as "Shi Baturu". Since it was difficult for the Mongols to memorize and pronounce the names of Han Chinese and some semuren, they usually renamed them in Mongolian according to their respective characteristics. A typical example was Yelü Chucai of the Khitan. He was addressed by Chinggis Khan as "Urtu Saqal" which "probably meant a man with long beard in Mongolian", because he "was eight chi tall with a long beard and a loud voice." (Biography of Yelü Chucai, Vol. 146, YS)

There was little appellative etiquette for the officials in the Mongol court. A Superior usually called his subordinates by name, while the subordinate has to call his superior by his official title or honorific title by way of respect. For example, the Scribes were addressed as bichigchi; the governors were addressed as darughachi, and the archers qoichi. (HDSL) The judges were addressed as jarliqchi. While Chinese tended to translate these Mongol official titles into corresponding Chinese ones.

Quriltai was a grand assembly, at which the Mongol ruling class elected their Khakhan, planned campaigns, and promulgated laws and edicts. And the Quriltai was usually held in the great ordo. The paramount significance of Quriltai soon gave birth to a set of relatively complete rituals that were carefully observed by the Mongol rulers as important court etiquette.

When the time of a Quriltai was fixed, all the Mongol imperial princes and aristocrats must arrive on time, or they would be severely punished. When they had arrived, they had to pitch their tents and settle their retinue, horses and livestock in areas stipulated by the law.

The Khakhan, imperial princes and the empresses were to seat in strict order in the great ordo where Quriltai was held. The Khakhan and his chief wife sat in the middle, and the imperial princes sat in descending

seniority on the right, while the ladies sat on the left. No change should be made to this order of seat, because it was already fixed by Chinggis Khan. Among the imperial princes, the brothers and sons of the Khakhan were seated in front of other imperial princes. During the Quriltai, all the attending officials were also required to sit or stand in descending seniority and no one, except those designated servants, was allowed to roam around in the ordo.

During the reign of Chinggis Khan, there was no rule for the royal members to perform prostrations before the Khakhan. When Ogedei was about to mount the throne, Yelü Chucai began to draft the court rituals, one of which was to require all the "royal members to prostrate themselves before the Emperor in order". To ensure all the Mongol imperial princes would conform to this ritual, Yelü Chucai turned to Chagatai for help. He persuaded Chagatai to lead other royal members and all the officials to perform prostrations before the Emperor during the Quriltai of coronation. He said, "Although Your Highness was older than His Majesty, you are still one of his subordinates in the court. So it is not inappropriate for you to kowtow to him. And if Your Highness would do it, all would follow." (Biography of Yelü Chucai, Vol. 146, YS) Thereafter, the ritual of kowtowing to the Emperor was codified. The Mongols usually genuflected by getting down on the left knee, but they were later demanded to kowtow on both knees after the accession of Ogedei. And a picture of the coronation of Ogedei in the book History of the World Conqueror written by the Persian Historian Juvaixli clearly revealed that all the Mongol imperial princes prostrated on both knees at the coronation. When performing prostrations before the Khakhan, one had to kowtow for nine times with hat removed and belt slung around the neck. (SJZFZS, p. 295, pp. 673-674) But other historical sources held that they only kowtowed for six times, with three to the Khakhan and another three to the sun. (SJ, Vol. 2, p. 30 & 175)

Quriltai was always accompanied by feasts and all those invited to the banquet were required to wear the same colored jisun robes and take prescribed seat without mistake.

All the sovereigns and chieftains of the subjugated countries or regions by the Mongols had to present themselves before the Mongol Khakhan and constantly send envoys to the Mongol court with tribute and news of the recent situation. Rulers of other countries or regions that hadn't been invaded by the Mongols would also send envoys regularly to the Mongol court to measure its military strength. Those envoys sent to the Mongol court had to prepare a good many gifts, which were not only for the Khakhan, but also have to be distributed among the Mongol imperial princes, officials and even their servants. Otherwise they would be given the cold shoulder on the Mongol steppes. The envoys from those countries that hadn't submitted to the Mongols wouldn't be arranged for an audience with the Khakhan before they purpose in coming was made clear through strict interrogations and the information of their identity, country and sovereign was registered by the clerks or bichigchi. Usually only very few of them could get access to the great ordo.

For those few lucky ones who were summoned by the Khakhan for an audience, they first had to walk through two fires with gifts, some of which were to be thrown in the fire. Next they had to bow to the nearby bushes, the statues of all the deceased Mongol Khakhans and the fires so as to remove bad luck from them. He who refused to perform these rituals would be punished with death and a Russian duke was thus killed because he refused to bow to the statue of Chinggis Khan. Then the envoys had to be searched thoroughly for weapons, and would be warned against some taboos in the great ordo, such as never to touch the threshold and ropes. Any transgressor would be punished.

When they finally entered the ordo, they had to wait until the clerk finished introducing them to the Emperor and the Mongol aristocrats in

high pitched voice. Then they were to kowtow to, all seeming to genuflect on the left knee, the Khakhan and tell him their purpose in coming in order. During this process, they were supposed to keep kneeling just as all the Mongol subjects did, unless they were allowed to get up by the Khakhan. Those who came for an audience with the Khakhan usually had no seat in the tent. Thus it would be considered a great honor to be awarded a seat by the Khakhan.

Besides, these envoys were not supposed to speak without the permission of the Khakhan. When they were allowed to speak, they were required to speak in a concise but comprehensive way. A western missionary had recorded, "the Tatar emperor never speak directly to a foreigner, no matter how significant his identity was; he only listened and then had a liaison to pass his message." If the envoy was a Chinese, the Khakhan would probably did the same, because he needed an interpreter to overcome the linguistic obstacles. "When the Emperor had announced his decision, no one was supposed to air any dissent, for it was not approved by their customs." (CSMGJ, p.66)

2

The Mongol court etiquette formed during the era of the Mongol Empire appeared primitive and unsystematic and therefore unsuitable for a mighty power in the eyes of those Chinese Confucians served in the Mongol court. Even after many years of the accession of Qubilai, "the royal members still dwelled in tents and no appropriate court ritual was established. On occasion of a celebration, a crowd of people, regardless of their status, would pour to the Khakhan' s ordo to congratulate him. When the guards were annoyed by their noises, they would beat the crowd with the stick until they completely dispersed." (Biographical Sketch of Wang Pan, Vol. 12, YCMCSL) They then repeatedly appealed to Qubilai for a draft of court etiquette on the grounds that "a set of elaborate and standardized court etiquette was necessary for a unified country with miscellaneous ethnic groups." (Biographical Sketch of Xu Shilong, Vol. 12, YCMCSL) In the first lunar month of 1269, the sixth year of zhiyuan, Qubilai finally agreed to their request and asked Liu Binzhong and Bei Luo to send "Zhao Binwen and Shi Kang to learn from the experts on court etiquette of the previous dynasties." This group, considered too small by Liu Binzhong, was soon joined by another eight Confucians to "finish codifying the court etiquette in a hundred days by combining the etiquette stated in the classics of rituals with the Yuan reality with the help of some former Jin official, such as Wangyan Fuzhao, Wangyan Congyu, Ge Congliang, Yu Boyi, the Chancellor of the Directorate of Education Xu Heng, and the Chamberlain for Ceremonials Xu Shilong." Meanwhile, Liu Binzhong started to recruit musicians and collect musical instruments for the court rituals with the approval of Qubilai. (The Entire Process of Drafting the Court Etiquette, Vol. 67, YS)

In the tenth lunar month of the sixth year of zhiyuan, Qubilai ordered to "regulate the color of the court dress". In the second lunar month of the next year, he "rehearsed the court etiquette drafted by Liu Binzhong, Bei Luo, Xu Heng and Xu Shilong" in the temporary imperial palace away from the capital.

In the second lunar month of the eighth year, the Palace Ceremonial Office was established. From the fourth lunar month onto the seventh lunar month of the same year, guards of honor, both interior and exterior, were recruited. The court rituals was put into action in the eighth lunar month, in which Qubilai's birthday fell, after the Office of Ancient Music was established and the guards of honor were trained. From then on, the court etiquette was to be observed on such formal occasions as the coronation, the lunar New Year's Day, the Imperial Birthday, the reception of imperial princes and foreign dignitaries, crowning

元代城市
生活长卷

The Urban Life of the
Yuan Dynasty

278

the Empress, declaring the Heir Apparent, presenting honorific title to the Emperor, crowning the Grand Empress Dowager and the Empress Dowager, sacrificial ceremonies in the suburbs or at the Ancestral Temple, and court assemblies. But when the Emperor feasted the royal members and the courtiers, he would still adopt the traditional Mongol court etiquette." (Section three & four, Annals of Emperor Shizu, Vol. 6 &7; Section one, Vol. 67, Record of Rites and Music, YS) The Mongols never totally abandoned their own court etiquette. Taking the coronation for example, the Emperor must first be led to the throne by the Mongol imperial prince according to the "state rites" and then could he hold the court assembly in the Chinese way. And Chinese were usually excluded from the "state rites".

Since the establishment of the court etiquette, it had undergone many revisions, which made the Yuan court etiquette appear quite different from that of the Mongol Empire in such aspects as the title of the dynasty, the era name, the title of the Emperor and rules of the court.

3

The Mongols originally employed a primitive dating system based on the life cycle of grass on the steppes and the movement of the moon. This system was later replaced by the calendrical system of "Earthly Branches" with the influence of the Han Chinese, Khitan and Jurchen. In 1220, they began to adopt the "Sexagenary Cycle", according to which the year 1220 was gengchen year, and 1221 xinsi year. The "Sexagenary Cycle" continued to be used until the accession of Qubilai who began to adopt the imperial reign years. In the fifth lunar month of gengsheng year (1260), Qubilai proclaimed Year One of Central Unification (zhongtong) to mark his coronation. "The reign year symbolized the imperial power, and the standardized calendar embodied unification." (Wang E, Imperial

Edict Issued in the First Year of Zhongtong, Vol. 9, YWL) From then on, the reign year proclaimed by the Mongol Emperor was used in all the formal occasions. After the unification of China, the former Southern Song subjects were all required to use the new reign year of the Yuan Dynasty. Those who continued to use the Song reign year would be considered rebellions against the court.

The title of the Mongol Empire was "Great Mongol Empire", which was usually addressed as "Great Dynasty" by the Chinese in books. In the eleventh lunar month of the eighth year of zhiyuan, Qubilai changed the title of the country into "Da Yuan" and decreed that these two characters should never be separated in referring to the dynasty.

In the tenth lunar mouth of 1266, the third year of zhiyuan, the Ancestral Temple was completed. Qubilai began to use the temple name to address the deceased Mongol Emperors. Thus Yisügei was revered as Emperor Liezu, and Chinggis Khan was revered as Emperor Taizu, Ogedei Khan Emperor Taizong, Tolui Emperor Ruizong, Güyük Khan Emperor Dingzong, and Mongke Khan Emperor Xianzong. Among them Tolui was later specifically honored as Yeke Noyan, the Grand Emperor. Since Qubilai, every Mongol Emperor had been granted with two temple names, one in Mongolian, and the other in Chinese. For example, the Chinese temple name of Qubilai was Emperor Shizu, and his Mongolian temple name was Secen Qayan. Emperor Chengzong was honored as Oljaitu Qayan in Mongolian; Emperor Wuzong was honored as Külü Qayan, and Emperor Renzong Buyantu Qayan, etc.

After the temple names of the deceased Mongol Emperors were established, the Yuan court decreed that the names of the deceased Mongol Emperors should be avoided. "The name of the deceased Emperor should be held as a taboo in daily life and other activities. Any transgressor should be punished by having his mouth filled with mud. And the provincial authorities must see to it that the law was learnt by

元代城市
生活长卷

The Urban Life of the
Yuan Dynasty

everyone." In the first lunar month of 1308, the first year of zhida, the court further decreed that all the past memorials to the throne as well as the government documents should be revised to remove all the characters contained in the names of the deceased Emperors. (Taboos for the Officials, Vol. 8, TZTG) And all the memorials to the throne and documents of the government, from then on, must avoid the name of the deceased Emperors. In drafting the imperial edicts, reports to the Emperor, government documents and tablet inscriptions, one should refer to the decreased Emperor by his temple name and the reigning Emperor should be addressed as "His Majesty". In the Mongolian and Tibetan versions of the imperial edicts, the deceased Emperors were referred to by their Mongolian temple names or their imperial titles during the Mongol Empire, or sometimes their Chinese temple names. In an audience with the Emperor, officials must call the Emperor by "Your Majesty". While the appellation for the Empress and Mongol imperial princes remained almost the same as that of the Mongol Empire.

Nevertheless, the naming taboo was not very strictly observed in the Yuan Dynasty. "People, even those scholar-officials, abide by it after a fashion, since they didn' t consider it improper to call the Emperor by name." (Section two, Miscellaneous Institutions, Vol. 3, CMZ)

4

Another two important aspects of the Yuan court etiquette were the gongfu institution and the prohibition of trespass.

Since the court etiquette was established and the color of court dress was regulated in the sixth year of zhiyuan, it had been officially demanded that "all officials should attend the court assembly celebrating the lunar New Year' s Day in gongfu." In the second lunar month of 1313, the second year of huangqing under Emperor Renzong, the Yuan court further decreed, "as gongfu symbolized an official's reverence for His Majesty, those who had attended the grand ceremony held for celebrating the lunar New Year's Day in the imperial palace should remove gongfu before receiving the guests." Officials were thereafter prohibited from receiving guests in gongfu. (Gongfu and Receiving Guests, Vol. 8, TZTG)

In the eighth year, Wang Pan, the Vice Chamberlain for Ceremonials, proposed to the Emperor, "According to the old practice, trespass on the imperial palace should be punished according to the severity of the transgression. It was advisable to establish the Palace Provisions Commission to list and group, according to the rank, the officials of the two major departments, who were not allowed to enter the palace unless summoned by the Secretarial Receptionist. Those who dare to skip the rank to enter the palace would be fined by the Palace Bureau; and those who dare to trespass would be convicted." This proposal was finally incorporated into the court etiquette. (Biographical Sketch of Wang Pan, Vol. 12, YCMCSL) Besides, the Yuan court also decreed that "those (court officials) who were absent from a court assembly should be fined for ten guan of Zhongtong yuanbao jiaochao, and those who breached the etiquette should be fined for eight guan of Zhongtong yuanbao jiaochao." (Section one, Regulation and Rule for Officials, Vol. 105, YS)

When a Mongol Emperor held a court assembly, he would be accompanied by guards of honor and officials like Manager of Seals and Imperial Diarist, just as emperors of the previous dynasties. But what distinguished him from his Chinese predecessors was that he had a group of imperial bodyguards called Keshig waiting on him in the court. "The Keshig was divided into four companies, each of which served three-day shifts. Commanders in the Keshig not only oversaw the Emperor's daily life, but also helped him sign the edicts. There was a special squad called ulduchi in the Keshig. It was the Emperor's most immediate attendants. Although they held posts in the court, they still served three-day shifts in

元代城市
生活长卷

The Urban Life of the
Yuan Dynasty

282

the imperial place. Armed with stick-like weapons and big knives, they constantly accompanied the Emperor by either escorting the imperial court cart or waiting outside the palace hall, to protect him from all dangers. Even the Steward-bulwark of State, who was to report to the Emperor every day, dared not get access to the Emperor without the presence of ulduchi." (Tao Zongyi, Ulduchi, Vol. 1, NCZGL; Guards of Honor, Vol. 79, YS) Besides these new rules, the old Mongol court etiquette especially that regulating the banquets and assemblies held in the ordo should be observed as well.

5

While most court rituals demanded absolute observance, some especially those involved in the interaction between the Emperor and the Tibetan religious leaders were not that easy to follow. The Yuan Emperors used to appoint the Tibetan religious leaders as their Imperial Preceptors. Naturally, an Imperial Preceptor was not supposed to prostrate himself before the Emperor like his subjects, yet it was also impossible for the Emperor, the sovereign of the country, to genuflect to the Imperial Preceptor. Qubilai who had sought knowledge and advice from Phags-pa Lama, the Sakya school of Tibetan Buddhism, when he was still a Mongol prince, skillfully tackled this problem with the help of his wife Chabui. He followed her advice to "let Phags-pa Lama take the seat of honor when there were only a few companions; consult the preceptor about all the Tibetan affairs before issuing an imperial edict, while leave all the other state affairs to Qubilai's own decision lest the preceptor's benevolence be taken advantage of by some mean minds." (SJSXS, pp. 88-90) This principle was continued to be followed by Qubilai after he ascended to the throne, and Phags-pa Lama had by then be appointed Imperial Preceptor of the Yuan Dynasty.

"In Tibet, the Imperial Preceptor's decree had the same effect as an imperial edict. And during the era of the Yuan Dynasty, the Imperial Preceptor was highly honored and respected in the court. Even the Emperor and Empress had to prostrate themselves before the Imperial Preceptor on occasion of a Buddhist ceremony. Besides, the Imperial Preceptor would be granted a seat in the audience hall when the Emperor held a court assembly." (Biography of Buddhist Monks and Taoist Priests, Vol. 202, YS) "All the emperors had to attend nine Buddhist ceremonies with the company of nine or seven attendants before being recognized as a legitimate sovereign." This practice was later incorporated into the "state institutions" of the Yuan Dynasty. (Tao Zongyi, Receiving Monastic Disciplines, Vol. 2, NCZGL)

Confucian scholars who lectured the Emperor and other royal members on the Confucian classics and history were also respected in the court. In the mid Yuan Dynasty, a special place was set up for the Emperor to listen to lectures on Confucianism. During the reign of Emperor Shundi, a palace hall called Duanben Tang was especially installed for the Heir Apparent to receive lectures on Confucianism. "The central seat of Duanben Tang were deliberating left vacant in case the Emperor should arrive. The Heir Apparent and the instructor seated respectively in the east and the west, while other officials seated facing them in order." (Record of Emperor Shundi, Vol.42, YS; Tao Zongyi, Virtues of Empress, Vol. 2, NCZGL) When the Emperor or the Heir Apparent was receiving the lecture, no disturbance should be made by the attendants. The Heir Apparent Ayurshiridar had an intense interest in Buddhism but little in Confucianism. One day when he was receiving a lecture in Duanben Tang, "his body servants tended to entice him into falconry by bringing a falcon with them and teasing it in the corridor outside the classroom. When he finished the class, he walked out and reprimanded them, saying, 'this place was for study only and how dare you desecrate it in front

元代城市
生活长卷

The Urban Life of the
Yuan Dynasty

284

of the master. Out, or you would be punished.' All his servants then hurriedly retreated with fear." (Tao Zongyi, Duanben Tang, Vol. 2, NCZGL) Although Confucianism adopted an inferior status to Buddhism in the Yuan Court, Confucian teachers were still held in great respect in the Yuan Court.

6

The imperial edict of the Yuan Dynasty was written in either Mongolian or Chinese. All the Mongolian imperial edicts would be translated "word for word" into Chinese. The Chinese imperial edict adopted a format similar to that of the Tang and Song Dynasties, but different from that of the word-for-word translated one. Those imperial edicts for Tibet, however, followed another different style.

"Every enthroned Emperor would have the Directorate for the Imperial Accessories make an imperial edict with all the characters composed of pearls. He would then confer it onto the Imperial Preceptor in Tibet".

"The edict was originally written with powder on a blue silk. Next all the characters on the edict would be embroidered with white silk thread and then studded with pearls. Coral was also used to decorate the imperial seal on the edict. When finished, the imperial edict was sent to the Imperial Preceptor in Tibet who would hang it in his residence." (Biography of Buddhist Monks and Taoist Priests, Vol. 202, YS; Tao Zongyi, Imperial Edict for Tibet, Vol. 2, NCZGL)

The appointment letter for officials was also subject to certain regulations in the Yuan Dynasty. "All the appoint letters in the Yuan Dynasty were made of paper. Appointment letters for officials above the fifth rank, called xuan, were white; while those for officials above the ninth rank, called chi, were red. Although they were not made of silk as those of the previous dynasties, they were still very exquisite." (Section two, Nine Rank System, Vol. 3, CMZ) Sometimes, special honor would be conferred on a retired official who was summoned back to the court by "the appointment letter made of court silk in the Emperor's own handwriting". (Kong Qi, Proposal for Establishing the Eastern Palace, Vol. 1, ZZZJ)

In the seventh lunar month of 1264, the first year of zhiyuan under Qubilai, "the imperial seal system was established. It was stipulated that appointment letters for officials above the second rank should be affixed with imperial jade seal; while those for officials above the fifth rank should be affixed with imperial gold seal. The seal with the inscription "Huang Di Xing Bao" (Treasure of the Emperor) was made when the Emperor was enthroned and it was only used for imperial edicts; another imperial gold seal was made for appointing the court officials." In the fourth lunar month of the sixth year, "a set of ten imperial seals of different sizes" was made. (Section two & three, Annals of Emperor Shizu, Vol. 5 & 6, YS) Official seals were also conferred on the imperial princes and the court officials. The material of the official seals signified the status of the bearers. "Officials of the first rank were granted three gold seals, and officials above the third rank were granted two silver seals. All the other officials, regardless of their ranks, could only use copper seals. Inscription on the official seals was usually written in Mongolian which was invented by the Imperial Preceptor Phags-pa Lama, while the inscription on the imperial jade seal for appointing court officials employed the Yuzhu Script whose characters were round and thick." (Section two, Miscellaneous Institutions, Vol. 3, CMZ)

"Court etiquette has to be established to proclaim the legitimacy of the sovereign and protect the harmony of the imperial court." (Preface to Code of Rituals, Vol. 40, YWL) This principle was somewhat achieved by the Yuan rulers via a combination of the old Mongol court etiquette with the new Chinese-styled one.

元代城市
生活长卷

The Urban Life of the
Yuan Dynasty

An official was also supposed to abide by a set of officialdom etiquette in his work and interaction with the other officials. Part of the officialdom etiquette was stipulated by the Yuan court. For example, the court had regulated the number, title, rank, and stipend of the officials and had specified an official's right and duty and the basic officialdom etiquette in the "Regulation and Rule for Officials". While part of the officialdom etiquette was either inherited from the previous dynasties or conventional.

Apart from the official title, an official could also be called by some generic appellations, such as zhengguan or zhangguan (a generic term referring to the head of a government agency), zhangli (a generic term for Prefectural Governor or Governor), zhang'er (a generic term for the top two executive posts in an agency), zuo'er (a collective reference to the second and lower tiers of executive officials in an agency), etc. Such generic appellations for officials usually appeared in the imperial edicts, official appointment letters, government documents, and other literary works. But on such formal occasions as a trial, the court celebrative ceremony, and reporting to the Emperor, officials of all levels should use the official titles and sometimes have to write or read out their names when necessary. In writing a biography of an official the writer had to introduce his name, official title and rank by way of respect; usually the prefixes "former" and "late" had to be added before the title if the official was no longer in that post or decease. But on the informal occasions, familiar officials could call each other by the courtesy name or pseudonym. An official usually use the term "benguan" (I) to address himself, but he had to use the appellation "daren" (Your Excellency) when addressing his superior.

There were over 30 different Suboffical Functionaries in the

Yuan bureaucracy and there were also generic appellations for them, such as gongli (a generic term for Clerks, Ushers, Agents and guards of all agencies), renli (a generic term for the assistants of Scribes with no stipend), and shouling guan (a generic term for the head of the Subofficial Functionaries), etc. (LXZN)

With the establishment of the Secretariat, the "Code of Official Conduct" and a set of officialdom etiquette were formed, and officials of both the central and the local governments were faced with increasingly strict demands.

An official was supposed to work in the government office. In the Yuan Dynasty, officials and Subofficial Functionaries were required to work together in the same office. "The Senior Official took the central seat; the Associates took the first row of the seats lined on both sides of the room, and the Ancillaries the second row. If the Senior Official was an Imperial Prince or the former State Councilor, a third row of seats would be added for the Subofficial Functionaries of a lower rank than the Axillaries. "If two officials happened to be of the same rank, the one who took the position earlier should take the better seat. (Code of Official Conduct, Vol. 13, YDZ)

When dealing with the government affairs, officials of all levels had to follow certain procedures and rules. Taking the Secretariat for example, every day the two Ground Councilors had to go through two procedures: one was holding a discussion of the state affairs, including making relevant policies or corresponding measures; the other was reporting the results of their discussion to the Emperor. In 1261, the second year of zhongtong, the Secretariat issued ten rules to further regulate the discussion and report systems.

1. Report to the throne every three days; urgent military affaires were not subject to this rule.

2. Keep a record of all the results of discussion in a special minute

book with precise translation.

3. The Staff Supervisor has to arrange regular meetings to discuss state affairs and report to the Emperor whenever there was a conflict over important issues.

4. Such discussion requires no avoidance from irreverent Subofficial Functionaries unless it was about a top secret.

5. All the stuff has to arrive at the government office by the sunrise and leave at the noon; unless there was an emergency, one leave could be taken every ten days. And one should apply for a sick leave in advance lest the regular discussion of the state affairs should be affected.

6. Families of an official should not take the indictment.

7. In case of a vacancy in the group discussion, it should be substituted by an elected candidate.

8. The number of interpreters in the Secretariat was subject to specific regulation.

9. One must be accompanied by an interpreter when reporting to the Emperor.

10. He who had a close connection with the matter under discussion should be avoided.

In addition to the above ten rules, the procedures of singing and submitting government documents were also subject to specific rules. State Councilors were entitled to participate in the discussions of the state affairs but it was usually the Grand Councilor who had the final say in all the decisions. "Since the first year of zhongtong, it has been a common practice for a group of secretary officials, numbered from five to eight, to sit together to discuss the state affairs. Whenever there was a divergence, the issue would be submitted to the Grand Councilor who would make the final decision." (Biographical Sketch of Shi Tianze, Vol. 17, YCMCSL) Although the State Councilors were entitled to report all the different views to the Emperor when a consensus could not be reached on a particular issue, they seldom used this right. Once an issue was settled, the Staff Supervisor would draft an official document which needed the signatures of all the State Councilors and, more importantly, the signature of the Grand Councilor to become effective.

The Grand Councilor also had to follow a series of strict procedures when reporting to the Emperor in the imperial palace. He had to be accompanied by the Palace Censor of the Censorate when he entered the imperial palace and had to report to the Emperor in the presence of ulduchi and the Supervising Secretary who assisted in keeping the Imperial Diary. And when he was having an audience with the Emperor, all irrelevant people should be avoided for fear of the divulgence of secret.

Local officials were also required to hold regular meetings to discuss such issues of taxation, law enforcement, public security and agriculture. According to the relevant rule, "officials should diligently serve their duties, and were not permitted to leave the meeting until the matter was properly settled." But the reality was that this rule was properly observed by the local officials, which forced the Secretariat to resort to punishment. He who was deliberately absent from the meeting would be punished with a fine of money for the first time, seven blows for the second time, seventeen blows for the third time, and a dismiss from the office for the fourth time.

Officials had to follow a series of regulation and procedures in drafting a memorial to the throne as well as a government document. Officials above the fifth rank had to write the memorial in Mongolian, and had to prepare a duplicate of Chinese in regular script. Every provincial government and Pacification Commission should submit a congratulatory missive to the Emperor on his birthday as well as at other festivals. When writing the congratulating missive, one should avoid the name of the Emperor, and the use of over 160 inauspicious characters such as ji (end), hua (die) and wang (death). The latter was abolished during the reign of

元代城市
生活长卷

The Urban Life of the
Yuan Dynasty

Emperor Renzong. Date, signatures of the officials and official seals must be contained in the memorial to the throne. If an official of the Secretariat was transferred to a provincial government agency, when he report to the Secretariat he only need to sign his family name on the official document. The first page of the memorial to the throne should be pasted with a piece of yellow paper and a seal should be affixed on the yellow paper, the date and the ridge of the memorial. The cover of the memorial to the throne should contain the title "Shang Jin Jin Feng" (To Your Majesty) and it should also be pasted with a piece of yellow paper with a seal. The memorial to the throne should be wrapped in a sheet of double-layered red silk, while a letter in a sheet of single-layered light red silk. And the memorial to the throne from the local officials should be put in a box. (Section two, Code of Official Conduct, Vol. 14, YDZ; Section one, Record of Penal Law, Vol. 102, YS)

8

Besides, the officials had to follow a series of rituals and etiquette on occasions of celebrating a festival and receiving an imperial decree.

Whenever there was a festival, especially the lunar New Year's Day and the Imperial Birthday, officials of all levels were required to attend the celebration in gongfu, which was an important ritual in the officialdom and a custom as well. Officials serving in the capital only had to attend the celebration held by the court, while the local authorities were to hold a celebration on their own. A local celebration was usually organized by "banshou", a post usually reserved for the governor of the local government. Even those military officers with a higher rank who temporarily stationed in the place were subordinate to banshou. At the dawn of the ceremony, an incense altar would be placed in the Audience Hall of the local government office with its front facing the direction of

Dadu. And the seats for the official had also been arranged in the hall. The banshou would "arrange his subordinates, Confucian scholars, fellow countrymen, Buddhist monks and Taoist priests, and military officers" in lines and lead them to perform the prostration before the altar. Next he would step forward to prostrate, burn the incense, pray, and retreat to his place. Then he led the others to do the prostration again, dance, kowtow, and shout "Banzai" for three times. All the others would immediately shout the same words and kowtow twice, which also brought the entire ceremony to the end. "All would return home after having the banquet that followed the ceremony." On the Imperial Birthday all the local authorities would go to the local Buddhist and Taoist temples to invite the Waisui Pai, a tablet enshrined in the temples to pray for the longevity of His Majesty. They would either place it in the government office, or in a public place for people to pray and appreciate. And during the ceremony, the Waisui Pai would be carried by the local officials on a parade along the streets followed by a group of Buddhist monks and Taoist priests, a band, and a troupe. A ceremony would always be accompanied by a banquet. Although the local officials claimed to fund the banquet with their own stipends, it was, in fact, the populace that paid for the bill. Considering that parading with the Taisui Pai was a somewhat blasphemy to the Emperor, and that the banquet after the ceremony would burden the people, the Yuan court later banned these two activities and decreed that "all the local officials only need to go to the temples to pray for the longevity for His Majesty on the Imperial Birthday." But the ban didn't take effect.

(Norm of Rites, Vol. 8, TZTG; Section one, Norm of Etiquette, Vol. 28, YDZ)

Receiving and sending off the envoys delivering the imperial edicts also required strict and appropriate etiquette on the part of the officials. When receiving and sending off the envoys or listening to the edict,

元代城市
生活长卷

The Urban Life of the
Yuan Dynasty

292

all the officials were required to wear gongfu and hold Hu26. Even the Subofficial Functionaries should be formally dressed. According to Tong Zhi Tiao Ge (Legislative Articles from the Comprehensive Regulations) and Yuan Dian Zhang (Institutions of the Yuan Dynasty), the rituals involved in receiving the imperial amnesties were slightly different from those in receiving the imperial appointment letters.

The rituals in receiving the imperial amnesties were as follows. "The envoy delivering the imperial edicts would inform the local authorities of his arrival in advance. The banshou then should ride to the suburb outside the city to wait for the envoy with his subordinates, guards of honor, a band playing the music, a ceremonial cart, and an incense cart. When the envoy came into view, the banshou would dismount from the horse and go over to receive the imperial edict and then deferentially put it onto the ceremonial cart. After the banshou burnt incense before the incense cart, the procession would head for the local government office with the band playing music walking at the front and the ceremonial cart, the envoy and banshou followed after. They entered the government office via the main entrance." In the government office two tables, one for placing the imperial edict and the other for incense, and seats were properly laid, with the front the two tables facing the direction of Dadu and the seat for the envoy placed to the west of the tables. The envoy then put the imperial edict on the table, and dismissed the two carts. When he announced the opening of the ceremony, the banshou would lead his subordinates to prostrate, burn incense, and prostrate again. The Administrating Clerk then took over the imperial edict from the envoy on knees, and handed it over to two Stall Foremen to read, with all the other officials listening on knees. After that the imperial edict would be put back to the table, and the banshou should then lead the others to prostrate, dance and kowtow and shout "Banzai" for three times, just as they did on the celebrations of the festivals. At the end of the ceremony, the banshou and his subordinate would have a short meeting with the envoy and his entourage before seeing them off at the outside of the city with music.

When receiving the imperial appointment, different recipients were to follow different etiquette. If the recipient was, and usually was an official in active service, he needed go outside the city with his subordinates, guards of honor, a band playing music, the ceremonial cart and the incense cart to greet the envoy in advance. When the envoy came into view, he should dismount from the horse, and so did the envoy who would then put the imperial edict onto the ceremonial cart. Next the recipient should burn incense before the incense cart and tell the envoy that he dare not pay respects to him before the official appointment. After that they would head for the local government office following the same rituals involved in receiving the imperial amnesties. If the recipient was an official who had left office, he could just stay at home waiting for the notification of the date of the official appointment from the envoy. And the envoy would be lodged in the government-owned hotel in the city. When the date finally arrived, the recipient would go to the envoy's hotel with a band playing music and a group of guards of honor to greet him and then they would go to the local government office together. In the Audience Hall, a table for placing the imperial edict, the incense stand, and the seats (with the seat for the envoy placed to the west of the table) had already set for them. The envoy then would go to his seat and put the imperial edict on the table. The recipient should also go to his seat, standing towards the direction of Dadu, prostrate, and burn incense. Next the envoy would read the imperial appointment letter and pass the appointment letter to the kneeling recipient who would take it over and hold it tightly to his chest and then dance and kowtow. After the recipient would go to kneel in front of the envoy and enquire after His Majesty's health. The envoy would then bow and answer yes. Finally the recipient would lead the envoy to

元代城市
生活长卷

The Urban Life of the
Yuan Dynasty

294

meet the local officials.

The rituals involved in receiving the imperial rescript were much simpler. The procedure for receiving the rescript was the same as that for the imperial appointment, except that the recipient only needed to go to the Audience Hall of the local government office in gongfu to receive the rescript if he was an official in active service, or simply wait at home in his main hall in formal dress if he had left office.

Although such etiquette was designated to improve the integrity of officialdom, it would, however, get the local government in trouble and even seriously interfere with the official business. For example, an early notification from the envoy would always resulted in several days of futile wait on the part of the receiving officials; and it was also not uncommon for the military officers to be occupied with such business as receiving and sending off the passing envoys, Mongol Imperial Princes, Imperial Princesses and Commandants-escort, instead of attending to his own duty. All these finally forced the Yuan court to decree that officials and envoys delivering the imperial edicts should clearly notify the local government of the time of arrival, and that the local government only need greet the envoys delivering the relevant imperial edicts. Besides, provincial officials only had to receive the envoys delivering the imperial edicts and the Imperial Princes; other local government only need to send one official to receive the passing Imperial Princes, Imperial Princesses and Commandants-escort.

Every newly appointed official had to pay respects to his supervisors when he took office. And the Yuan court decreed that "one only need to pay respects to those supervisors who lived within one hundred li, and that a supervisor should not interfere with the official business by assembling the subordinates without a sound reason."

When officials of the supervisory agencies went on an inspection tour, the local government should receive them with proper etiquette.

"Every year the Investigatory Officials on the inspection tour would be received and sent off by a squad of archers of the local Police Office with banners and military drums and copper gongs. And the gong should be played after every two beats of drums." Coincidentally enough, the military drums and the copper gongs were also to be played when escorting criminals. The only difference between the two was that in the latter case the drums and gongs would be played alternately. Someone then especially made a poem to mock the officials.

One beat of drum and gong marked a criminal,
Two beats of drum and gong an official.
Since the drums and gongs were the same,
The officials were not different from criminals.

Part Five

Chapter One │ **Festivals of Each Season**

Every year grand celebrations, some in traditional Chinese style, while some in the northern nomadic way, would be held in the Yuan cities to observe the festivals of every season. Besides, there were many spectacular religious ceremonies that usually filled the spectators with great awe and joy.

1

In 1264, the first year of zhiyuan, Emperor Shizu ordered that "officials could take two days' leave on the Imperial Birthday and the Winter Solstice, three days' leave on the lunar New Year's Day and the Pure Brightness Festival, and one day's leave on the fifteenth day of the seventh lunar month, the first day of the tenth lunar month, the Beginning of Spring, the Dragon Boat Festival, the Beginning of Autumn, Double Ninth Festival and every ten days." In 1277, the fourteenth year of zhiyuan, modifications were made to the original holiday system, switching the holidays from the tenth, twentieth and thirtieth days of each lunar month to the first, eighth, fifteenth, twenty-third days and the Yihai Day of each month. During these holidays no animals should be slaughtered. (Holidays, Vol. 22, TZTG) From this holiday arrangement, it could be inferred that the Yuan ruler had almost adopted the traditional Chinese holiday system. But some special arrangement had been made to the seasonal celebrations (especially those of the spring, summer and autumn) by the Yuan court, because every year the Emperor would spend his summer in Shangdu with a large entourage. And he would stay there for nearly six months. (More details about the imperial inspection tour to Shangdu would be revealed in the next chapter) Under the long rule of the Liao and Jin dynasties, the Northern Han Chinese still observed their traditional festivals just as the people in Jiangnan Region did and they continued to do so in the Yuan Dynasty.

Different seasons had with different sceneries which in turn gave people different feelings and led them to different activities.

2

People celebrated the lunar New Year's Day, the Lantern Festival, and the Beginning of Spring in the first lunar month.

The lunar New Year's Day was considered the most important festival by the Han Chinese. But the Mongols had also celebrated for a long time. Someone from the Central Plains had witnessed the celebration of the lunar New Year's Day held by the Mongol court when it was ruled by Güyük Khan. "The palace tent was removed on the day before the lunar New Year's Day to make room for the celebration in the next day. All the officials were invited by the Emperor to a three-day feast before the tent. And during the feast all, including the Emperor, were dressed in white furs. After the feast, all the officials would go to the palace tent to greet the Emperor with presents." (Zhang Dehui, Travel Notes, QJXSDQWJ) The celebrations of the lunar New Year's Day on the steppes were originally carried out in a traditional Mongolian way. After Qubilai moved the capital to Dadu, Chinese elements were incorporated

into these celebrations making them become more elaborate and colorful.

On the first day of the first lunar month, a grand court assembly was held in the imperial palace to celebrate the lunar New Year's Day.

In the early morning of that day, all the officials would congregate at Chongtian Gate, waiting for the Emperor to hold the court assembly. When the Emperor and the Empress arrived they would seat themselves on the throne in Daming Hall. After the Time Keeper announced the opening of the court assembly, two groups of the imperial guards would respectively enter the hall via Rijing Gate and Yuehua Gate. Next, they would prostrate themselves before the Emperor, shout "Banzai", and stand in line at the two sides of the hall or wait outside according to the court etiquette. After the imperial consorts and concubines, imperial princes and Commandants-escorts presented presents to the Emperor in order, two groups of officials would file in the hall from Rijing Gate and Yuehua Gate, prostrate themselves before the Emperor, and shout "Banzai". The Grand Councilor of the Secretariat then would propose a toast to the Emperor for three times and read out a list of congratulatory missives and presents sent by the central and local governments. After that, Buddhist monks, Taoist priests and foreign guests would enter the hall to extend their congratulations.

During the court assembly held on the lunar New Year's Day, all the attendants, including the Emperor, were required to be dressed in white and all the presents sent from the central and local governments had to be covered with white cloth. According to Marco Polo, the number of the tribute should be the multiple number of nine. For example, the number of the horses paid as tribute which were usually white one on that day should be eighty one and the number of other articles of tribute like gold and sick should also be eighty one.

A large Jamah Banquet would be held after the court assembly. All the imperial princes, Commandants-escort, and courtiers were invited to the banquet. Officials above the fourth rank were allowed to drink in the hall, while those below the fifth rank had to drink at Rijing Gate and Yuehua Gate. (Etiquette in the Court Assembly on the Lunar New Year's Day, Vol. 67, YS)

After the court assembly on the lunar New Year's Day, people began to go to the each other's home to wish each other a happy New Year, and Dadu at the time would be filled with a festival air. "Although the officials had already celebrated the festival together at the government office, they still go to congratulate each other with presents as was required by the traditional customs. If one was invited for a dinner, then a bottle of wine was usually a preferable present. Thus until the thirteenth day of the month, horses and carts kept bustling along the streets and before the teahouses and taverns. As usual, people would make rice cakes with millet and distribute them among the relatives. In the market, merchants would set up reed huts at each corner to sell paintings, pastry, soup, and millet cakes, as well as all kinds of lanterns and fireworks. These small shops, opened from morning to night, would keep standing there until the fifteenth or sixteenth day of the month." (Customs, XJZJY, sic passim)

3

After the grand celebration of the lunar New Year's Day, people began to prepare the celebration of the Beginning of Spring. Influenced by the traditional Chinese customs, the Yuan court also began to hold such ceremonies as "Worship of the Sacred Ox of Spring". Every year the Astrological Commission was to determine and report the date of the Beginning of Spring to the imperial court. Then it had to order the local authorities of Wanping District or Daxing District to prepare the ceremonial instruments, such as the sculptures of the Scared Ox and

元代城市
生活长卷

The Urban Life of the
Yuan Dynasty

the statue of God of Spring. Three days before the Beginning of Spring, officials of Astrological Commission and Court of the National Granaries would invited the Grand Councilors of the Secretariat to congregate before the southern side of Qizheng Tower in Dadu to greet the Sacred Ox. In the early morning of the Beginning of Spring, "having led all the officials of Chi District to perform prostrations, in gongfu, before the Senior Officials, the Chief Minister of the Court of the National Granaries beat the model of Scared Ox with a decorated rod for three times and retreated. Then the envoys of the Aboriginal Official escorted the status of God of Spring to its temple." After that, the Ministry for Revenue would present the ornate sculptures of Scared Ox of Spring to the Emperor, the Heir Apparent, the Imperial Consorts and Concubines, the Imperial Princes, the Grand Councilors and the central government agencies.

The fifteenth day of the first lunar month was the Lantern Festival, when such palace agencies as the Palace Provisions Commission, the Household Service for the Empress, and the Household Administration of the Heir Apparent would purchase festival candles, pastry and desserts as was stipulated by the court etiquette. Outside Lizheng Gate of Dadu, there stood a big tree called the General Tree, a title granted by Qubilai, when it was the lunar New Year's Day or the Lantern Festival, the tree would be hung with many exquisite lanterns, reminiscent of a fire dragon when watch up from afar. "Near the tree there was a market selling a wide range of delicate snacks, such as different rice desserts, cakes, steamed cakes with dates, wine, tea and soup, etc. Many tourists there were unable to tear themselves away from the market." The tree had been a scenic spot during the Lantern Festival in Dadu until the mid Yuan Dynasty. It withered away in the late Yuan Dynasty and was replaced by another one planted beside it by people of Dadu.

Emperor Yingzong once "intended to build a turtle-like hill of lanterns in the imperial palace." But this plan met strong opposition. One of the dissenters said, "During the thirty-year region of Emperor Shizu, it was prohibited to use lanterns in civilian houses on the lunar New Year's Eve. Thus it was even more advisable to be cautious about the use of lanterns in the imperial palace." (Biography of Zhang Yanghao, Vol. 175, YS) Thus it could be inferred that the use of lanterns in Dadu was treated with great caution.

The sixteenth day of the first lunar month was the Lantern Burning Festival when people would string a kind of steamed cakes together with a willow twig and sell them in Dadu.

The nineteenth day of the first lunar month was made the Yanjiu Festival or Festival of Qiu Chuji by people in honor of Qiu Chuji, the Taoist master of the Compete Realization Sect because he was born on the nineteenth day of the first lunar month. Every year on that day, young men and young women with bamboo sticks would pack into the Changchun Palace and the Baiyun Taoist Temple in southern Dadu. They burnt incense, prayed, and went on a binge all day long. This assembly at the Baiyun Taoist Temple later evolved into a distinctive temple fair in Dadu.

4

The second lunar month, with gentle breeze and warm sunshine, was the best time for a spring outing. Officials and women living in northern Dadu usually thronged the southern city in their finery to enjoy the beautiful scenery of Dadu. Packed with people and carts, the Haizi Lake was at its most vibrant during this time of the year. This trend reached its culmination during the reign of Emperor Chengzong, Emperor Wuzong and Emperor Renzong.

The second day of the second lunar month was the Longtaitou Festival or Dragon Head Raising Festival. At the day break of that day, lime lines would be drawn to connect each residence with the nearby well.

元代城市
生活长卷

The Urban Life of the
Yuan Dynasty

On that day, one was not supposed to sweep the floor, lest they should hurt the dragon's eyes. Peddlers would string the small glass bowels with golden fish together with fine bamboo strips and peddle then along the streets. Just like the Yanjiu Festival, people of Dadu would throng to the Lushi Mountain to enjoy themselves.

Every year on the eighth day of the second lunar month there would be a grand Buddhist ceremony—the holy circumambulation of the imperial city in Dadu.

In 1270, the seventh year of zhiyuan, Qubilai, following the advice of the Imperial Preceptor Phags-pa Lama, installed a white canopy over his throne in Daming Hall. The canopy, "with golden Sanskrit script written on its white silk cover, was used to subjugate evil spirits and protect the country." From then on, a grand Buddhist ceremony would be held in Dadu in the second lunar month. That was highlighted by a spectacular parade with the canopy around the imperial city for the purpose of "warding off the misfortunes and praying for the welfare of all living creatures."

The guards of honor escorting the canopy in the procession consisted of a vast array of groups, including 8 guards of a total 120 drummers, 500 armed cavalrymen, 500 sedan-carries, 360 carts of Buddhist articles (each being carried by 26 men and accompanied by 12 monks), and a total of 1,024 musicians and entertainers. The parade stretched for over 30 li with its participants dressed in uniform and fabulous clothes provided by the imperial court. Officials from different central government agencies were sent to supervise the parade. Officials from the Ministry of Rites, the Ministry of Justice and Bureau of Military Affairs were respectively responsible for superintending the parade, patrolling the streets and guarding the city gates. They were in turn supervised by an official from the Secretariat. Every Steward-bulwark of State was to prepare a festooned vehicle to display all his treasures and collection of rare birds and animals so as to show the prosperity of Dadu and the imperial favor. The Ministry of Revenue would allocate money and grain to the local government. And the local government would spend the money and grain on troupes and lavish jisun banquets. All those who were invited to such banquets, even a Houseman, would be dressed in their finery so as to show off their wealth. In order to follow the imperial edict and to show the affluence of their country, all the wealthy and powerful families in the two capitals would try to flaunt their wealth by displaying their best treasures. Therefore every year the imperial court would spend twenty or even thirty thousand money on the holy circumambulation of the imperial city.

After assembled at the West Zhenguo Monastery, the guards of honor would follow the Heir Apparent to tour the four city gates and then they would head for the imperial city. The West Zhenguo Monastery which was located three li outside of Pingze Gate of Dadu was built by Qubilai's Empress Chabui. On the eve of the holy circumambulation, the Imperial Preceptor would hold a Buddhist ceremony with a group 500 monks in Daming Hall. In the next day, he would return to Daming Hall to take the canopy over the throne and place it onto the imperial cart with reverence. All the guards of honor would wait in lines outside the Daming Hall during this process. And a variety of alters were set up outside Chongtian Gate to welcome the canopy. The holy circumambulation would officially start after the guards of honor had had a vegetarian meal in Qingshou Monastery inside Shuncheng Gate.

The parade started from Qingshou Monastery and entered the palace city through Houzai Gate after a tour along the southern bank of the Hanzi Lake outside of the western gate of the palace city. Next it made for Longfu Palace where the Empress and all the other imperial consorts and concubines had already waited behind the bead curtains. After leaving Longfu Palace it went on to Xingsheng Palace where troupes performed

元代城市
生活长卷

The Urban Life of the
Yuan Dynasty

304

all kinds of drama. Then the parade would turn east to the Taiye Pond via the Tiao Bridge. The Emperor had already set up sumptuous tents decorated with gold brocade by the Taiye Pond. After the Emperor seated himself on the throne, all the Palace Attendants lined up beside him, and the Minister of State, courtiers, the imperial princes, and Commandants-escort were all seated according to the state rites, the parade was ushered in. Soon the Taiye Pond was turned into a large stage, with pennants flying in the wind, music played and all kinds of drama performed. After the guards of honor returned the canopy to Haming Hall, they would either be dismissed at Donghua Gate or outside Houzai Gate. While in Daming Hall, the Imperial Preceptor, with the assistance of other monks, had to hold another Buddhist ceremony which wouldn't stop until the next day. (Section six, Record of Sacrificial Ceremonies, Vol. 77, YS; Music, XJZJY)

In fact, similar activities would be held by the folks on the eighth day of the second lunar month as well. Some rich merchants in Jiangnan Region would call together all the troupes of the two capitals at the West Zhenguo Monastery in Dadu to "welcome the imperial golden tablet and the statue of Buddha of the monastery for a parade outside the city." In the meanwhile, shops selling all kinds of rarities and taverns like those in Jiangnan Region were set up beside the monastery, which really livened up the place.

5

In the third lunar month, people mainly engaged themselves in such activities as tomb-sweeping which was usually carried out around the Pure Brightness Festival and spring outing.

According to the customs of Dadu, the third day of the third lunar month was the Poverty Discarding Day when people would make rings, headgear and fetters with bean and millet stalks as the token of poverty and then throw them away in the water to show their wish and determination to get rid of poverty in this year.

The most important festival in the third lunar month was the Pure Brightness Festival, which fell on the 105th day after the Winter Solstice. It was the day for people to go to the tombs to offer sacrifices to their ancestors. There was such a line in zaju— "all went to the tombs to offer sacrifices to the ancestors at the Pure Brightness Festival and Cold Food Day", since the Pure Brightness Festival and the Cold Food Day were observed in the same day in the Yuan Dynasty. (Wu Hanchen, A Late-born Son, Book one, YQX, p. 377) It was also the most exhilarating time in the imperial palace, for elaborate swings would be erected and extraordinarily sumptuous feasts would be held. From the imperial palace to the ordinary household, from the dignitaries to the commoners, the entire Dadu city was immersed in the great joy of playing on the swings. From the second lunar month to around the Cold Food Day, activities as swinging and cuju began to be increasingly played throughout the county. In Hangzhou, swings were set up the around the West Lake, attracting throngs of tourists from nearby areas. Banquets would be held by the folks at the Pure Brightness Festival with "people drinking and singing, indulging themselves in the drunken delight in taverns".

The twenty-eighth day of the third lunar month was said to be the birthday of the God of Mountain. People would bring the womenfolk of the family to pray in the Temple of the God of Mount Tai and the streets leading to the temple would be packed with peddlers selling all kinds of food and sacrificial articles.

The Yuan Emperor usually started his annual trip to Shangdu in the second or third lunar month. The whole imperial court would travel with him, leaving only the merchants, Regents and some Keshikten behind in Dadu to guard the imperial palace and greet the Emperor when he

returned from Shangdu. Therefore all the important court celebrations would be held in Shangdu after the third lunar month.

6

Many religions ceremonies would be held in the fourth lunar month.

On the fourth day of the month, the steamed bread competition would be held throughout the country in honor of God of Mount Heng in Shanxi. Four days later, it was the Buddha's Birthday when all the Buddhist monasteries would hold Buddhist ceremonies and cook syrup with aromatic herbs called "sacred water". In Dadu, the Imperial Preceptor and eminent monks would also hold ceremonies to observe the festival. "The White Stupa Temple, Blue Stupa Temple and Yellow Stupa Temple under the Imperial Preceptor, and all the Buddhist monasteries in the two capitals held ceremonies to observe the Buddha's birthday; designed sacrifices would be offered in the Buddhist sanctuary in the imperial palace." "There was a hall for worshipping Buddha in the palace, called the Lama Hall. Sacrifices like the sacred water and the black cakes were offered and Buddhist sutras were chanted before the Buddha. The Tibetan Tantric Buddhism was promoted to ascendancy over all other Buddhist sects by the state rules, which resulted in a hierarchy of monasteries in the capital." The ninth day of the fourth lunar month and the ninth day of the ninth lunar month were originally the days for the Mongols to offer sacrifices especially the Koumiss to their ancestors. During the reign of Güyük Khan, "the Khakhan would assemble his entourage to the palace-tent to offer sacrifices to the ancestors with the libation of koumiss on the Double Ninth Day. All the sacrificial instruments were made of birch wood with no embellishment of gold or silver for sumptuary purposes." "The same sacrificial ceremony would be repeated on the ninth day of the fourth lunar month. Only in

these two days would sacrificial offerings be made to the ancestors."
(Zhang Dehui, Travel Notes) This sacrificial rite was still held in the Yuan
Dynasty only that its time was switched to the twenty-fourth day of the
sixth lunar month.

7

The most important festival in the fifth lunar month was the Dragon
Boat Festival. People in the Central Plains and Jiangnan Region followed
the traditional customs to "hang Chinese mugwort leaves over the gate,
drink Sweet Flag wine, take herbal baths, tied colored silk threads around
the arm and wear sachets." (Anonymous, Tune: Welcome to Spring,
Four Seasons, QYSQ, p. 1701) This festival was celebrated in many
different ways, such as hanging Chinese mugwort leaves, eating the rice
dumplings—zongzi, tying colored threads around the children's arms
or waists, wearing sachets, drawing the portrait of the Heavenly Master
Zhang Daoling to ward off evil spirits, holding grass competition, and
playing wrestling games.

The Yuan court also observed the Dragon Boat Festival under
the influence of the Chinese traditional customs. The Ministry of Rites
and the imperial household would provide the imperial court with fans
and food like glutinous rice cakes, zongzi, date cakes, peaches, lotus
roots, muskmelons and water melons, etc. "The Palace Provisions
Commission supplied the imperial court with fans, colored silk threads,
pearl headgear, golden gongs, wine, glutinous rice cakes, zongzi, etc. The
Household Service for the Empress and the Ministry of Rites provided
the imperial palace with gifts stipulated by the state rituals, which was
probably because it was an important festival in the imperial palace."
"On that day high-ranking officials such as the Three Dukes and the
Steward-bulwark of State and the mid-ranking ones were also allotted

元代城市
生活长卷

The Urban Life of the
Yuan Dynasty

308

such presents as painted fans, colored silk threads, dusters and glutinous rice cakes, only that the presents they received were of lower quality than those sent to the imperial palace. " Outside the imperial palace, the commoners could only get access to these things through purchase. Thus many reed sheds were set up in Dadu to sell glutinous rice cakes, zongzi, the Chinese mugwort leaves, statues of the Heavenly Master, colored silk threads and sachets, etc.

Government offices would make the portrait of Guan Yu27 at the Dragon Boat Festival and a competition would be held among them to select the most magnificent one. Bureau of Sable and Ermine had impressed all with a five colored ermine portrait of Guan Yu.

In Jiangnan Region, dragon boat races were traditionally held as part of the Dragon Boat Festival celebrations. But it was later prohibited by the Yuan court, which was triggered by an accident in a dragon boat race in which several people got drowned in the river in Fuzhou Route in 1294, the thirtieth year of zhiyuan under Emperor Shizu. This accident was then used by an official as the reason to stop the dragon boat race. In his memorial to the throne, the official stated, "it was customary for people of the fallen Song Dynasty to eat, drink and waste money on the dragon boat races at the Dragon Boat Festival. After the submission of the Song Dynasty, the dragon boat race still attracted a multitude of people to crowd along the river to watch the competition in areas of Jiangnan Region, and Jiangxi, Fujian, Guangdong and Guangxi. This situation should be changed lest more tragedies should be caused. And there even loomed the danger of people gathering a mod to undermine the stability of the area. Therefore I am here to propose a ban on the dragon boat race in all the routes under the supervision of each branch secretariat." This proposal was adopted by the imperial court that later issued a prohibition on the dragon boat race. But the prohibition was not seriously observed. In 1301, the fifth year of dade under Emperor Chengzong, the branch secretariat of Jiangnan Region reported another accident involving several deaths in a dragon boat race. "Last year, about seven people were drowned in the dragon boat festival instigated by someone called Ji Jicha." This accident caused the imperial court to issue another prohibition on the dragon boat race, which however was of little effect, either. (Miscellaneous Prohibitions, Vol. 57, YDZ) In fact, such large-scale entertainments as jiju and shooting willow (both would be introduced later in this book) would also be held in the imperial palace on the Double Fifth Day in the Yuan Dynasty.

8

People's life in the sixth lunar month mainly consisted of preventing sunstroke and consuming seasonal fruits. In this month, a large variety of fruits and vegetables would be sent to the imperial palace in Dadu. "Peaches, plums, melons, and lotus roots would be sent to the imperial palace in red-lacquered wooden boxes. Vegetables like eggplants and gourds and fruits like cucumbers, water melons, musk melons, grapes and walnuts were sent to the imperial palace once they were ripe." On the Double Sixth day, people in Dadu would go to fetch water in the early morning for the medical purposes, and the water fetched at that time on that day was called "lieshui" (hunted water). And it was customary for people to make cured meat on that day.

In the middle of the sixth lunar month, the Imperial Preceptor would perform a Buddhist ceremony in Shangdu which would also be followed with a grand parade in the imperial city. "On every fifteenth day of the sixth lunar month, a procession of troupes would be sent to the imperial city via Xihua Gate by Imperial Preceptor who would then throw a banquet in the city after the parade." (LJZY)

元代城市
生活长卷

The Urban Life of the
Yuan Dynasty

9

The seventh day of the seventh lunar month was the Festival to Plead for Skills or the Qixi Festival, which was a big festival in summer. The commoners would celebrated the Qixi Festival by hanging pictures of Niulang (the cowherd) and Zhinü (the weaver girl), holding weaving and needlework competitions, worshipping Mahoraga, God of Childbirth, and feasting. In the imperial palace and official residences, a shed would be erected in which pictures of Niulang and Zhinü would be hung up and food such as melons, fruits, wine, cakes, vegetables and meat would be prepared. Then all the womanfolk of the family would be invited to celebrate the festival in the shed where they would eat, drink and practice divination all day long. Therefore, this day was also called the Girls' Day. In addition, people in Dadu would welcome Erlang Shen, the powerful deity with a third truth-seeing eye in the middle of his forehead, in ceremonial procession. And merchants would put up reed shed to sell different clay idols which were quite popular among the citizens.

The fifteenth day of the seventh lunar month was the Ghost Festival when one should offer sacrifices to one's ancestors and deceased families. In Dadu, "the rich would hold a memorial service for the ancestors by sprinkling wine on the dried sesame stalks and burning the hell money and paper clothes before the tomb."

"The Emperor would hold the Sacrifice to Heaven and Sacrifice to Ancestral Spirits ceremonies in the sixth and seventh lunar months in Shangdu. Imperial wine and dried mutton would also be sent by the Emperor to Dadu to be offered as sacrifices in the memorial halls of the monasteries."

10

As an important traditional Chinese festival, the Mid-autumn Festival, which fell on the fifteenth day of the eighth lunar month, was celebrated by the Han Chinese in the Yuan Dynasty. The Beginning of Autumn and the Mid-autumn Festival were also celebrated in the Yuan imperial palace.

On the day marked the Beginning of Autumn the Emperor who was then in Shangdu would host a banquet and wear an autumn leaf on the head as the Han Chinese would customarily do on that day. Before the Beginning of Autumn, the Astrological Commission had to determine the date of the Beginning of Autumn, pick an auspicious day for the banquet and prepare the red autumn leaves which would be presented to the Emperor by Court Attendants. When it was the very day of the Beginning of Autumn, the Emperor would dine with the Heir Apparent, his wives and the imperial princes and go out to appreciate the red autumn leaves with an autumn leaf pinned to his hat.

After the Beginning of Autumn, the Astrological Commission had to pick another auspicious day around the Mid-autumn Festival for the Emperor to make aspersions of koumiss to his ancestors. "Great importance was attached to this ceremony which had to be carried out specific strict state rituals." By that time purple chrysanthemum and nasturtium had been in full blossom and it was the time for the Emperor and his entourage to return to Dadu. Thus feasts would frequently be held in the imperial palace and all the imperial princes and officials would go on a binge of eating and drinking. The Muqing Pavilion on the north city wall was the highest structure in Shangdu. "Emperor Shundi would go there to appreciate the sound of nature over dinner at the Mid-autumn Festival. The intangible sound, as if celestial music played in Heaven, was the most marvelous thing in the world."

元代城市
生活长卷

The Urban Life of the
Yuan Dynasty

312

When the sacrificial ceremony of sprinkling koumiss was held in Shangdu, the officials stayed in Dadu would go to inspect the mountains. Officials of the Secretariat, the Bureau of Military Affairs and the Censorate would go to the West Mountain on that day and dine in Zhenguo Monastery on their way home. After the Emperor had departed Shangdu, officials in Dadu had to inspect the storehouses in Tongzhou. The Keshikten in the imperial palace of Dadu had to spread bedding on the imperial bed, cover the floor with felt rugs and decorate the wall of the auxiliary halls with ermine and that of the main audience hall with tiger fur. And Officials of the Palace Provisions Commission had to "provide the imperial palace with seasonal fruits and vegetables like water melons to welcome the Emperor."

Outside of the imperial palace, the marketplace in Dadu "was packed with fruiterers selling such fruits as pears, dates, chestnuts, apples, haws, pine nuts and hazel." "People thronged to outside the southern and northern city gates every day, looking forward to the arrival of the Emperor. The increase in the population at those places boosted the local business; therefore the peddlers were also filled with joy. "

11

The ninth day of the ninth lunar month was the Double Ninth Festival or the "Chrysanthemum Festival", which was celebrated by the Han Chinese by climbing the mountains, appreciating the chrysanthemum and red autumn leaves, drinking the chrysanthemum wine, and sending each other the pastry. In Dadu people would also invite relatives and friends over for dinner and make a present of rice cakes on that day. Peddlers would erect sheds to sell food or peddle the rice cakes down the streets. In the imperia palace, the festival was celebrated according to certain rituals and such entertainments as polo would be held.

313

In the north another important event in the ninth lunar month was to welcome the Emperor back to Dadu. On the day of the Emperor's departure from Shangdu, officials stayed in Dadu would inspect the city by respectively assembling at Jiande and Lizheng Gates and dining together. From then on they would start count down the arrival of the Emperor.

The first day of the tenth lunar month was the Winter Clothing Festival. On that day people would offer sacrifices and pay respects to their deceased families at their tombs. "Since the first day of this month, or the Winter Clothing Festival, people in the capital had been to pay tribute to their ancestors at their tombs. The sacrifices they offered in this month were relatively lavish, for every household, rich and poor, would sacrifice animals to their ancestors." And according to the traditional Chinese customs, people should get together for a drink at the Winter Clothing Festival in preparation for the winter days.

In the tenth lunar month, a grand archery competition would be held by the Yuan court, which would be introduced in the next chapter.

The eleventh lunar month was called the winter month. At the Winter Solstice, Astrological Commission and the Muslim Grand Astrologers would present the new calendars to the Emperor, the Heir Apparent, the imperial consorts and concubines, the imperial princes, and the court officials. The Grand Councilor would lead all the other court officials to congratulate the Emperor during the court assembly, present the Emperor with the handkerchiefs and local products. The new calendars could also be bought in the cities, and people would go to each other's house to celebrate the Winter Solstice.

12

People prepared to welcome the lunar New Year in the twelfth lunar month.

The eighth day of the twelfth lunar month was the Laba Festival, a religious festival when the "red congee would be offered to the Buddha and monks". By the time of the Yuan Dynasty, it had become a civilian festival. "People in Dadu made the red congee on that day. The well-to-do families would present each other with the congee, which had been an old practice among the people." The imperial palace would celebrate the festival in a similar way. "On the eighth day of the twelfth lunar month, the Day of Buddha's enlightenment, laba congee was cooked in the imperial palace. The Imperial Preceptor would also be presented with the congee."

After the Laba Festival, people began to prepare the celebrations of the lunar New Year. "Government offices of all levels as well as the subordinate agencies of the Bureau of Musical Ritual would recruit entertainers to prepare for the celebrations of the lunar New Year in the imperial palace. The Bureau of Musical Ritual, Music Office, and Office of Ancient Music trained the court entertainers including the musicians and jugglers every day, preparing for the inspecton of the court officials on the Lunar New Year's Day."

At the end of the year the Yuan court would hold a series of activities to get rid of bad luck, ward off evil spirits and usher in the good fortunes for the next year." "The rituals of getting rid of bad luck and ushering in the good fortunes would be conducted annually on a specific day after the sixteenth day of the twelfth lunar month. On that day the Emperor, Empress and Heir Apparent would be seated in their bedchambers with their bodies bound with strings made of black and white wool. A Mongol Shaman stood by would hold a silver brazier burning with rice bran and yak butter inside and chant prayers. He would then puff the smoke from the brazier to the Emperor, cut the woolen strings for him and throw the strings into the brazier. Next he would give a red piece of silk measured several cun in length to the Emperor who would tear it up, spit to it for three times and throw it into the fire. At the end of the ritual, the Emperor would took off his clothes and hat and hand them to the Shaman." (Section six, Record of Sacrificial Rites, Vol. 77, YS) "The rite of warding off the evil spirits was held by Tibetan sorcerers near the end of the year in Daming Hall. They would first set an altar before the hall, put such sacrifices as mutton, horse meat, beef, and wine on it and hit the fan-like drums written with incantations. Next they would chant the incantations. In the meanwhile, another two sorcerers would hold a towel and one of them would sprinkle water on the towel to cleanse the place of evil spirits. After that they two had to carry a bucket of meat around each palace with one walk in front holding a black banner. After they walked out of Longfu Palace and Xingsheng Palace, they would load a horse-cart with the bucket, and drive out of the palace city via Shuncheng Gate. They beat the drum and cymbals and distributed the meat among the impoverished to get rid of the bad luck." In addition, the Emperor would also confer material for clothing called the silk of the New Year onto the members of the Imperial Coterie.

According to the traditional customs of the Han Chinese, people should offer sacrifices to the Kitchen God and cook bean congee on the twenty-fourth day of the last lunar month. And they also made a "Dispel the Cold" Picture after the Winter Solstice. On the lunar New Year's Eve, people would send presents to each other, stay up all night, play the game of maimeng28, set off firecrackers, and paste the portraits of the doorkeeper Zhong Kui to the doors, etc. All these activities still prevail in the Central Plains and Jiangnan Region.

13

Beside the above festivals, another important one in the Yuan Dynasty was the Tianshou Festival or the Imperial Birthday. Since

Qubilai, grand ceremonies had been held throughout the country to celebrate the birthday of the Emperor. And here is the list of the birthday of each Yuan Emperor:

Qubilai, Emperor Shizu (r. 1260-1295) of Yuan, August 23;

Temür, Emperor Chengzong (r. 1295-1307) of Yuan, September 5;

Khayisan, Emperor Wuzong (r. 1307-1311) of Yuan, July 19;

Ayurbarwada, Emperor Renzong (r. 1311-1320) of Yuan, March 4;

Sudibala, Emperor Yingzong (r. 1320-1323) of Yuan, February 6;

Yesün Temür, Emperor Taiding (r. 1323-1328) of Yuan, October 29;

Togh Temür, Emperor Wenzong (r. 1328-1332) of Yuan, January 11;

Toghun Temür, Emperor Shundi (r. 1333-1370) of Yuan, April 17.

On the Imperial Birthday people would congratulate the Emperor on his birthday. "One month before the Imperial Birthday, all the court officials would go to burn incense in temples and hold one month's Buddhist ceremony to pray for the longevity of the Emperor." (Paying Respects to the Sovereign, Vol. 28, YDZ) The court officials had to go to the imperial palace to congratulate the Emperor on his birthday, while the local officials had to hold celebrations in their own jurisdiction. According to the historical record, "since Emperor Shizu, every county had celebrated the Imperial Birthday by setting up large sheds to house banquets and various entertainments. This practice was brought to a halt by Emperor Shundi who banned slaughtering and feasting on his birthday so as to ease the burden for the people." (Section two, Miscellaneous Institutions, Vol. 3, CMZ) The religious communities would also hold ceremonies to celebrate the Imperial Birthday.

Chapter Two | **Ball Game, Shooting Willow and Race Walking**

The Mongols didn't abandon their recreations after their migration to the city; instead they popularized these recreations in the new domain. Thus hunting grounds were opened up around the cities and every year the whole city thrilled at such sports as shooting willow and race walking.

1

The Mongols would launch a battue hunt annually. Such large-scale hunting was designed not only to obtain game, but to temper their will power and to enhance their horsemanship and archery. The battue hunt, therefore, become a special way to train the troops. And since the days of Chinggis Khan, battue hunt been an integral part of a Mongol's life.

A battue hunt was usually organized by the Emperor or an Imperial Prince and all the Mongol nobles were required to bring their followers to participate in the hunting. The hunting ground was already set up before the hunting. "Hunting with arrows had already been incorporated into their customs. Whenever their ruler was about to hunt, they would throne to the hunting ground, digging holes and erecting stakes around it. These stakes then would be bound together with ropes, to which fur and feathers were attached, forming an enclosure just like the net for hunting hare in the Han Dynasty. The enclosure extended for about 200 li, with its fur

元代城市
生活长卷

The Urban Life of the
Yuan Dynasty

and feathers blowing in the wind. The beast, frightened by the moving feathers, dare not move, and was easy to shoot." (HDSL) Back to the era of Mongol Empire, their hunting ground was located on the northern steppes. "Heading south from Qara-qorum across the desert, one arrived at the forbidden place, the hunting ground. It was a moated place fenced with ropes. Before hunting, the hunting ground would be first cleared of furious beasts such as wolves and tigers." (Yelü Zhu, Battue Hunt, Vol. SXZYJ) During the reign of Ogedei Khan, the hunting ground in Wangji, the winter campsite, was once fenced with a wall, which was made of stakes and mud, with the circumference of about two days' walk. After the accession of Qubilai, with the center of the country moved to Dadu and Shangdu, the hunting ground was moved southward as well. "The Emperor and the royal members would go hawking or falconry as an interlude between the spring and autumn imperial inspection tour in the suburbs when winter was turning into spring. (Section four, Record of Warcraft, YS)

In spring, the Emperor would hunt in the willow woods in southeastern Dadu; while in summer they would went to live in Shangdu, where several hunting grounds were also opened up, such as the Northern Pavilion, the Eastern Pavilion, the Western Pavilion and Changanor. The Northern Pavilion was located 700 li northwest of Shangdu. "A summer palace was built in both the Eastern Pavilion which was 50 li east of Shangdu, and the Western Pavilion which was 450 li west of Shangdu, because both places were rich in water and grass, fish and animals. When the Emperor came to Shangdu, he would always hunt in the two places." (Zhou Boqi, Five Poems Written on the Beginning of Autumn, Vol. 1, JGJ) Changanor, meaning "white lake" in Mongolian, is located several li north of the modern Guyuan County. It was also installed with a summer palace and imperial aviaries where hawks were raise, for the Emperor would always go on a large-scale hunting whenever he passed here in his inspection tour.

As one of the pastimes of Emperor, the battue hunt followed a strict procedure. First, a squad of cavalrymen was dispatched to track the animals. Next all those taking part in the hunting set out in groups to serve as beaters. They would form a vast circle and gradually pull the circle tighter until the animals were all driven into the hunting ground. Then they assembled beside the hunting ground, waiting for the Emperor to hunt in the enclosure. After hunting, the Emperor would retreat to an elevation in the center of the hunting ground to watch the others hunt. Only then could the nobles, official and soldiers enter the hunting ground in order. The animals obtained in the hunt, apart from those preserved for the Emperor, would be distributed evenly among the imperial princes, aristocrats, soldiers, and all those engaged in the hunt. The Battue hunt ended with such rituals as kissing the dirt and presenting the gifts. And it would always be followed by a banquet. Such large-scale hunting activities must have left a deep impression on the people, for quite a few poets had devoted their poems to the Battue hunt.

2

The Mongols also played jiju (ball hitting) or polo, a sport game of great popularity in the Tang and Song dynasties. Zhao Gong who was sent as the envoy by the Southern Song court to the Mongol Empire had recorded that "they played polo in such a way that only 20 horses were engaged in the game, for they disliked the noises caused the horses. When the game ended, we were invited over to dinner. At the table, we were asked why we hadn't turned up in the polo game, and we answered that because we were not invited. Then Muqali, the Prince of State, said: 'now that you are in our country, you are no strangers. From now on, whenever there is a banquet, ball game or hunting, just come and join us, for families

元代城市
生活长卷

The Urban Life of the
Yuan Dynasty

320

need no invitation.' On hearing those words I laughed and emptied six cups of wine as a forfeit." (MDBL) Some Han Chinese commanders who had submitted to the rule of the Mongols were also fond of playing polo. For example, Zhang Hongfan, the "Scholar Commander", was "good at both polo and poems".

In the Yuan Dynasty, polo was an annual sport game in the imperial palace. It was usually held on the Dragon Boat Festival and the Double Ninth Festival. According to Xiang Mengxiang who lived in the late Yuan times, "the ball hitting game was inherited from the Jin Dynasty. The Emperor would pick players from the 10,000-man Brigades, 1,000-man Battalions and the Keshikten to play polo with the Heir Apparent and the Imperial Princes at the playground within Xihua Gate on every Double Fifth Day and the Double Ninth Day. Their steeds were all excellent ones which were equipped with saddle and mudguard and decorated with tails of pheasant, ornamental fringes, bells, tails of wolf, and wild camel fur. When the game started, a rider would move forward to cast the ball and soon all the other played would surge forward to get the ball with their wooden long-handled mallets. The skilled players could hold the ball with the mallet all the time while galloping on the field and the team that could first drive the ball into the opposing team's goal won. The spectators would always thrill at the final critical moment when the rotating ball flashed through the sky and hit the goal." (Customs, XJZJY)

Apart from Dadu, jiju was also play in other places throughout the country. For example, "a jiju game was held by Zhennan Prince on the Dragon Boat Festival in his palace in Yangzhou. The Prince and his wife were seated in front of the playground with the other imperial princes sitting beside them. The players followed the same rules as those in other places. The winners would be rewarded while the losers would be fined with such things as satin and fans. Such was the national game—ball hitting." (Customs, XJZJY) The popularity of polo extended even to the Ming Dynasty and it remained a custom to play polo in the imperial palace on the Dragon Boat Festival in the early days of the Ming Dynasty.

3

In addition to polo, people played what was called "chuiwan" (hit ball) by travelling on foot and hitting the ball with a similar stick. The major difference between chuiwan and polo was that the point of the former was to hit the ball into a hole in the ground rather than to a goal. Like polo, chuiwan already prevailed in the Tang Dynasty and its popularity continued through the Song, Liao, Jin and Yuan dynasties.

In the Yuan Dynasty Wan Jing (Classic of Chui Wan), a book on chuiwen, was published by Ning Zhi. The book attested the popularity of chuiwan, and it elaborated on the rules of chuiwen, the apparatus required in the field and the speculations of the instrument. And it is worth mentioning that chuiwen was, in many aspects, similar to the modern golf now so popular in the west.

Cuju, or football, was also played by people in the Yuan cities. "Cu" means kicking with feet, while "ju" refers to a kind of leather ball. Cuju dates back to as early as the Warring States Period, and achieved great development in the Han Dynasty when a research work on cuju appeared. The heyday of cuju was in the Tang and Song dynasties. During that time, it became a sport loved by all in the country. And its popularity continues in the Yuan Dynasty. In Shi Lin Guang Ji (Vast Record of Varied Matters), there was a Picture of Playing Cuju about the dignitaries playing cuju with a band playing music at side. The book also recorded, in detail, the rules and techniques of playing cuju. In the third scene of the zaju Monk Yueming Preaching Liu Cui, the protagonist Liu Cui had such a line, "Mother, hand me the ball please. I'd like to play it with my master." Here the "ball" refers to cuju. The eminent

playwright Guan Hanqing also played cuju, according to his own words. And his sanqu Woman Commandant to the tune of Fight of Quails was a masterpiece in depicting cuju played by women.

In the mid Yuan Dynasty some people, especially the young, were so heavily into these entertainments that they even neglected their academic studies, which naturally attracted a lot of criticism from the society. Wang Jie, the Route Commander of Shunde Route, commented, "I often heard the stories about children idling about doing nothing but playing cuju, hitting the ball, shooting the slingshot and capturing the birds." (SSYY) Among three ball games in the Yuan Dynasty (jiju, chuiwan and cuju), cuju was probably the most popular one.

Shooting willow was a common sport in the imperial palace in the Jin Dynasty and it was usually held together with polo. In the Jin Dynasty, "after the Sacrifice to Heaven ceremony at the Dragon Boat Festival, the shooting willow competition would be held. The target comprised two rows of peeled willow twigs stuck in the ground and tied at the top with a handkerchief belonged to each archer whose shooting order was determined by his status in the court. Each contestant aimed a flightless arrow at one of the twigs as they rode past. The point was to split it and catch the topmost half before it hit the ground. Archers that accomplished both feats scored the highest, followed by those who hit their twig but failed to catch the severed half. Those who hit the unpeeled part, or hit the twig but failed to sever it or even miss the target lost the game. Every time drums would be beaten to bolster the archers' morale." (Section eight, Record of Rituals, Vol. 35, JS) The shooting willow competitions held in the Yuan imperial palace were almost the sane as that of the Jin Dynasty.

The shooting willow competition was also held at the Dragon Boat

Part Five

Festival, and it would be carried out in the following procedure. "First all the imperial princes toasted the longevity of the Emperor. Then the Three Armies marched in the competition field and all the military officers were required to participate in the competition. The target was also a peeled willow twig stuck in the ground with its top tied with a handkerchief. When the archer hit the peeled part and served the twig, the sound of gongs and drums could be heard to elaborate his victory. Winners would be rewarded and losers should be punished. All the horses of the archers were decorated in the same way and it was a moment for the military officers to show off their skills. (Customs, XJZJY)

In addition to shooting willow, the Mongols also play the game— shooting dummy, which was a traditional activity for the nomads to get rid of bad luck. "Shooting dummy would be held at the West Zhenguo Monastery on an auspicious day in the late twelfth lunar month. On that day a scarecrow and a dog of straw decorated with colorful ribbons as their entrails would be placed near the inner wall of the temple for the dignitaries to shoot. The money used for making the two dummies were provided by the Directorate of the Imperial Treasury; the material was provided by the Directorate for Felt Manufactures and all the bows and knives were provided by the Court of Imperial Armament. When the dummies were completely destroyed, a sacrificial ceremony involving the sprinkling of sheep wine would be held. After the ceremony, the Emperor, Empress, the Heir Apparent and the imperial consorts and concubines participated in shooting dummy would take off their clothes to have them consecrated by the Shamans to get rid of the bad luck. People from certain clans, however, were prohibited from taking part in the activity, such as Jalayir and Naiman." (Section six, Record of Sacrificial Rites, YS)

By the late Yuan Dynasty, change had been made to this activity. According to Xiong Mengxiang, "it was a state ritual for the military officers to shoot dummy outside of Donghua Gate in the imperial city in the tenth lunar month every year." "After the Astrological Commission picked the auspicious date, the Military Commissioner would build three successive north-facing reed shacks, which extended for about three hundred bu, for the princes and officials to rest during their wait for the imperial edict. The left shack was for the Heir Apparent and the imperial princes, the middle one for the Steward-bulwark of State, and the right one for the military officers." "The Emperor was seated in the western palace; after a brief assembly of the Grand Councilors, the imperial princes began to enter the shooting range. When the imperial edict was issued the bows and arrows used in the shooting range would be adjusted and all the arrows used were small wind-chancing ones. Then the ceremony began: first the State Councilor would present the Heir Apparent with a bow and arrows on knees. The Heir Apparent then shot the scarecrow for three times. Next the State Councilor would return, bow to the Heir Apparent and shoot. Then it was the other imperial princes' turn to shoot the scarecrow. A lavish banquet would be held at the end of the ceremony." (Annals, XJZJY)

5

Wrestling and race walking were another two recreations frequently held in the Yuan imperial palace.

As a traditional sport for the northern nomads, it was loved by the Mongols and the famous wrestlers on the stepped were called B?kh (Men of Great Strength). Back to the Mongol Empire, wrestling had been used by Chinggis Khan as a way of getting rid of his dissident. Birin B?kh, according to the Secret History of the Mongols, was a famous wrestler in the Urkin Tribe. "One day Emperor Taizu asked Birin to wrestle with Belgütei who was no match for him in wrestling. But this time Birin fell to the ground and pretended to be defeated by Belgütei. Belgütei then took the opportunity to ride on him, with his hand holding Birin's head and his knee pressing against Birin's back. At this moment Belgütei turned to look at Emperor Taizu who simply bit his bottom lip. Having interpreted this signal, Belgütei immediately killed Birin by breaking his back with all his strength. In the last minute, Birin said, "I wouldn't have lost the game and had myself killed, if I hadn't feigned weakness out of fear of Emperor Taizu." "Thus even so mighty a wrestler as Birin with the strength unmatched in the entire country could not escape the fate of being killed." Later, Teb Tenggeri of the Qongqotan, who was in conflict with Chinggis Khan's brother over guiding power, was also killed in a wrestling match contrived by Chinggis Khan's brother. From the Mongol Empire to the Yuan Dynasty, wrestling matches were frequently held in the imperial palace and those eminent wrestles would be lavishly awarded. Ogedei even sent for the Central Asian wrestlers to wrestle in the imperial palace.

After the establishment of the Yuan Dynasty, wrestling matches were usually held in the two capitals. Emperor Renzong (Ayurbarwada) had a special passion for wrestling. When he was still a prince, he was very fond of this sport. He was once about to confer some bolts of satin on the wrestlers for their excellent performance in the West Garden, but was finally prevented by Wang Yue, an official in the Household Administration of the Heir Apparent. A Chief Military Commissioner named Ma Mousha was a skilled wrestler and always won in the wrestling matches. He was therefore greatly favored by Ayurbarwada and was promoted to the position of Manager of Government Affairs. After Ayurbarwada ascended to the throne, he especially installed an agency in the government to train the wrestlers. Under his influence, his Heir Apparent Sudibala had a special passion to wrestling. For example, he once conferred 1,000 guan of paper money to each of the 120 wrestlers after his coronation.

Such generous awards given by the Emperor to the wrestlers soon aroused great discontent among some Han Chinese officials. For instance when Emperor Shundi was to conferred thousands of money on wrestlers, the Assistant Administrator of the Secretariat Gai Miao immediately objected, saying "what have they done to deserve so much money when the whole nation suffered from the famine was still gasping for the relief from the court. (Biography of Gai Miao, Vol. 185, YS) But obviously the Mongols' enthusiasm for wrestling would not be extinguished by only a few people's exhortation.

Race walking was also a sport that was often held in Dadu and Shangdu. "Every year guyoqi (race walking) would be held in the country. It was simultaneously held in Dadu and Shangdu. The participants had to assemble before the starting lined in Hexiwu in Dadu or in Nihe'er in Shangdu, and would head to the imperial palace after the starting signal. To finish the race, they had to cover a distance of 180 li until they reached the imperial palace and performed prostrations before the Emperor. The champion was awarded with one ding of silver, the one came in the second place was awarded with four bolts of cloth, and the one came in the third place 2 bolts, and all the other participants one bolt." (SJXY) The race walking match started at the dawn and covered a distance of about 200 li. The match attracted great interest from people and many poems were devoted to it.

Music, dances and drama blossomed in the new circumstances of unification, leaving a large number of masterpieces of sanqu29 and zaju to the world. And it is a great joy to relive the urban life that had been the fountain of inspiration for those great playwrights and poets.

1

The Mongols were especially fond of music and dance which had been an indispensable part of the large ceremonies and banquets. Even a group of musicians and entertainers would be attached to the troops on a military expedition. For example when Muqali who was appointed "Prince of State" by Chinggis Khan "went on a military expedition, he was accompanied by a band consisted of about18 beauties, all of whom excelled in playing music and dancing. "Once when a Mongol official was to escort the Southern Song envoy back to his country, he was advised by Muqali to "spend more days in the good cities, eat and play the musical instruments to his content." (MDBL) Muqali's words also attested to the significance of music and dance in Mongol nobles' life. In the Yuan Dynasty, the Bureau of Musical Ritual and the Music Office were established under the Ministry of Rites to take charge of the musicians and the musical instruments. The Bureau of Musical Ritual supervised a

元代城市
生活长卷

The Urban Life of the
Yuan Dynasty

328

group of agencies that provided music for state ceremonies—Office of Ancient Music, Office of Contented Music, Office of Muslim Music and Office of Western Music. The Music Office was responsible for training court entertainers like clowns and jugglers. It had two subordinate units of its own, namely the Bureau of Joyful Music and the Bureau of Sacrificial Music. Under the Bureau of Musical Ritual and the Music Office there was the Office of Musical Supplies which was responsible for storing and repairing court musical instruments. (Section one, Monograph on Offices, Vol. 85, YS; Section two, Miscellaneous Institutions, Vol. 3, CMZ) Besides, there was the Imperial Music Office which was responsible for providing musical services for the sacrificial ceremonies. It was directly subordinate to the Commission for Ritual Observances.

A miscellaneous variety of music and musical instruments with no restriction of race and boundary could be found in the Yuan Dynasty. Generally speaking, the court music, dances and musical instruments of the Yuan Dynasty could be divided into three groups—Mongolian, Chinese and those of those northwestern ethnic groups.

The traditional Mongolian music and dances, which were usually referred to as hu (barbarian) music and hu dance by the Han Chinese, were very different from the traditional Chinese ones. "The musical instruments of Tatars, such as zheng (a Chinese plucked zither), qin pipa (moon guitar), and huqin (a spike fiddle), and the music produced by them were quite different from those of Han Chinese." (Tao Zongyi, Music, Vol. 28, NCZGL)

Hu music and traditional Chinese court music were usually used alternately, though they were of with different functions. For example "the court music composed by Emperor Huizong of Song was used in the court assembly, while the orchestral music and the hu music were played during the banquet. In the case of an imperial inspection tour, the Buddhist music was employed to announce the opening of the tour, while the hu music was played during the first half of the journey". (Miscellaneous Institutions, Vol. 3, CMZ)

According to the historical sources of that time, the Mongolian music could be largely divided into two types—long songs and short songs. Long songs were melismatic and richly ornamented, with a slow rhythm, while the short songs were strophic, syllabic, rhythmically tied, and were sung without ornaments. However, both long songs and short songs had incorporated elements of the music of other ethnic groups.

The Mongolian songs were usually strong and powerful. The most representative one was probably the song of "A-la-la". Even the Southern Song loyalist Wen Tianxiang was awed by the song sung by the Yuan soldiers when he was brought to Dadu after being captured. Greatly shocked, he asked about the song. And when he was told by the soldier escorting him that it was a Mongolian song, he sighed, "it's the very song of victory, we southerners are doomed." (Kong Qi, Wenshan Inquiring About the Song, Vol. 1, ZZZJ)

The traditional Chinese music, on the one hand, was employed to preserve the traditional Chinese rites and music in the Mongol court at the insistence of the Chinese Confucians. Thus it was usually played on such important occasions as the court assemblies and the sacrificial ceremonies. On the other hand, it was an indispensable entertainment in the imperial palace. For example, every year the Emperor would return to Shangdu. "When the imperial procession arrived at Yutian Gate in Shangdu, all except the Emperor should dismount from the horse and walk. Then the Emperor would proceed to the imperial palace on the horseback with a group of court entertainers singing and dancing in front. And when they finally reached the imperial palace the court entertainers would form the four characters "Tian Xia Tai Ping" (Peace reigns under heaven) in front of the steps of the imperial palace." "Whenever there was a banquet, the court entertainers would perform the traditional Chinese dances in finery." (Section one, LJZY)

The Tangut, Tibetan and Muslim music and dances were also very popular in the Yuan court. During the reign of Qubilai, a new musical instrument was sent as tribute from the Central Asia to the court. It was later modified by the Han Chinese Musicians and made into the xinglongsheng, a large organ-like instrument. "The xinglongsheng was placed in Darning Palace. It was a wind organ with many pipes played with a bellows. Two wooden peacocks stood on the top of it. They waved their peacock feathers when it was played. On occasion of a banquet, it served as the king of all the instruments, for when it played, all the other instruments played with it; when it stopped all the music stopped." "It took three people to play the xinglongsheng. One controlled the bellows, another played the music and the third one set the wooden peacock in motion." (Section five, Record of Rites and Music, Vol. 71, YS; Tao Zongyi, Xinglongsheng, Vol. 5, NCZGL)

The Tibetan music and dances were usually tinted with a religious color. Among them the most famous one was "the Dance of Sixteen Deities". It was a court dance choreographed in the late Yuan period under the influence of Tantric Buddhism. "The Mongols had a dance called "the Dance of Sixteen Deities" in which sixteen beauties danced by dressing themselves up as the Buddha." (Section two, Miscellaneous Institutions, Vol. 3, CMZ)

2

Play writing and drama performing played a significant role in the cultural life of the Yuan cities. The Yuan drama fell into three types: zaju, southern plays (nanxi) and various local plays (which were generally referred to as yuanben). As for the actors of the Yuan drama, some belonged to the Music Office and they usually performed in the imperial palace. But many belonged to the commercial theatrical troupes that traveling between cities and countries to entertain the commoners. In the Yuan Dynasty, theatres were mainly installed in goulan and washe, both of which were the pleasure quarters in cities.

Drama enjoyed a great popularity among the populace. Even a rehearsal of drama performance would attract many spectators. In 1362, the twenty-second year of zhiyuan, in a goulan near the Songjiang Superior Prefecture, a house collapsed during a drama rehearsal, killing a total of 42 people, among whom many were spectators. (Tao Zongyi, Collapse of Goulan, Vol. 24, NCZGL) In the Water God's Hall of Guangsheng Temple in Zhaocheng Town, Hongdong County, Shanxi Province, there was a fresco vividly depicting the scene of drama performance in the Yuan Dynasty. On the top of the fresco there was a line of words, read "The Late Sanyue Actress Zhong Duxiu Had Performed Here". And Zhong Duxiu was the stage name of a famous actress in the Yuan Dynasty.

The prominent zaju actresses in the Yuan Dynasty included Zhu lianxiu, Shun shixiu, Tian Ranxiu, Sai lianxiu, Yan shanxiu. (All were known by their stage names) Among them Zhu Lianxiu was the most famous and she was on intimate terms with many scholars of the time, such as Hu Zhiyu, Lu Zhi and Guan Hanqing. And many of these scholars had dedicated poems to her. Hu Zhiyu once expressed his admiration towards her by comparing her to the bead curtains in a poem. Guan Hanqing who had admired Zhu Lianxiu for a long time also wrote a poem for her when he finally met her in his travel to the south. Lu Zhi was a more passionate admirer of Zhu Lianxiu, and his love for her could be mirrored by his poems. For example, when he had to bid farewell to Zhu he sighed.

The erotic merriment a moment ago

Is followed by an early separation of woe,

How hard for me to part with you, oh no!

By the painted boat I am of my spring bereft

With only the moonlight over the river left.

(Lu Zhi, Parting from Zhu Lianxiu)

And Zhu also composed a poem to express her sorrow at his departure.

Mountains are countless,

Mist is boundless.

How miserable is my scholarly man!

Holding on to the windowsill that is tan,

I, though being alive, suffer a lot, too,

Wishing I could go to him following the eastbound river in view.

(Zhu Lianxiu, Reply to Lu Songzhai)

The later famous actresses such as Sai Lianxiu and Yan shanxiu were the disciples of Zhu Lianxiu. In the mid Yuan Dynasty, Shun Shixiu, whose original name was Guo Shunqing, was the most prominent actress, and Zhang Yu had praised her in his poem Nian Xia Qu (Songs under the Imperial Carriage)

Shun Shixiu, the actress of the Music Office,

Was not only famous for her sweet voice.

One never got tired of watching her performance,

Even veil could not conceal her unmatched beauty.

As for the famous actors in the Yuan Dynasty, according to Tao Zongyi, there were "Wei, Wu and Liu, the three officials of the Music Office." "Wei was good at singing, Wu turning somersaults and Liu performing. The three of them have been revered as masters by all the entertainers today." (Names of Yuanben, Vol. 25, NCZGL)

3

Of all the dramatic art forms in the Yuan Dynasty, only zaju was of the highest achievement. There were about 200 playwrights, and over 600 zaju scripts, of which only 150 are still extant. The playwrights at that time were called cairen and their association shuhui. Some outstanding playwrights like Guan Hanqing and Bai Pu were once the members of "Yujing Shuhui" in Dadu while others like Ma Zhiyuan belonged to the "Yuanzhen Shuhui" in Dadu.

Guan Hanqing was born in Dadu in 1320s and died in around 1297. According to Lu Gui Bu (A Record of Ghosts) he created 63 plays, of which only 12 complete works still survive, 3 partially extant and 2 extant with only single melodies.

He was an erudite, humorous, resourceful and romantic talent. According to the social standards of that time, a truly refined and cultured person should be "well versed in all activities, such as chess, pitch-pot game, pielan (raising money by drawing lots), betting with bamboos, calligraphy, poetry, cuju, jest, painting, tea drinking, horticulture, and music." (Baihua Pavilion) And Guan Hanqing was such a versatile person who called himself "the leading gallant under the sky, and the most dissolute lover on earth," and who, according to himself, would drink tea, bet with bamboos, gamble on horse-race and in lottery, and play all kinds of music— "I'm good at poetry, and at calligraphy; I can play on the string. And draw a picture of bamboo. I can also sing the songs of partridge too. With hands hanging down I can dance, in hunting I can advance, I know how to play cuju and chess. And! Gamble by chance." (Don't Say I'm Old) Now let's have a look at all these activities that

元代城市
生活长卷

The Urban Life of the
Yuan Dynasty

334

Guan were familiar with.

Among Go, Chinese chess and backgammon, the first two were the traditional Chinese board games, while the last one originated in India. The backgammon reached its great popularity in the Tang Dynasty, while fell into oblivion in areas south of the Yangtze and Huai River, though it was still popular in the northern areas in Liao and Jin dynasties. After the unification of China in the Yuan Dynasty, it was widely played throughout the country and was loved by men and women, commoners and dignitaries. The Backgammon was a game played by two people who each race 15 checkers which were all in the shape of the head of a horse around a prescribed track of 24 pips, framed within a rectangular board. In the game, the movement of the checkers was determined by throws of dice. "The players moved their checkers in opposing directions and one won by removing all of his pieces from the board." (Literature and Art, Vol. 6, continuation of SLGJ)

In the last chapter we have introduced hunting and cuju and now we'll make a brief introduction of pitch-pot game, pielan, beating with bamboos, the art of making tea, anadiplosis and character-dissection, all of which were entertainments used to add fun to a feast in the Han territory. Pitch-pot game was a traditional entertainment played by the Han Chinese during a feast, and betting with bamboos was also a game played at a feast in which the winner was decided by the number of tokens thrown into a distinct pot. Pielan or xielan was a way of raising money for a drinking party by drawing lots. In the game a picture of orchid would be painted with the number of its leaves equivalent to that of the participants. Except for one leaf, all the other leaves would be marked with a certain sum of money at the root. When drawing the lots, the roots of the orchid would be covered with a piece of a paper and every participant had to choose one leaf and signed their names on the top of the leaf. After the roots were revealed, all except one lucky guy had to pay the sum of money marked at the root. The art of making tea was a skill of forming a picture with the tea powder in the cup by controlling the angle and speed of the water poured into the cup. Anadiplosis and character-dissection were the word games played at a feast. The former demanded that the last word of a preceding clause be repeated in the next sentence, while the later required one to dissect a character into two words or to form a sentence. Besides, lottery and finger-guessing game were also played at a feast. All these games, usually played in brothels and by the literati, were familiar to Guan Hanqing. They provided him the opportunity to get access to people of all walks in the society as well as lots of material for his artistic creation. His strong sense of justice, deep love for the toiling masses and his hatred towards the corrupt tyrants prompted him to speak out on behalf of the broad masses in his plays. The zaju Gan Tian Dong Di Dou E Yuan (The Injustice to Dou E) is one of Guan's representative works. It tells a tragic story of a girl named Dou E.

Dou E became motherless at the age of three and was sold as a future bride to the Cai Family by her father when she was seven. Ten years later her husband died, and she and her mother-in-law were left all alone. A couple of local hoodlums, Zhang Lür and his father tried to force the two women to marry them. Angered that Dou E rejected his advances, Zhang lür plotted to kill Mrs. Cai. By mistake, however, he poisoned his own father and then accused Dou E of the murder when she refused to marry him. During the trial conducted by the cruel and corrupt official Tao Wu, Dou E was tortured and found guilty of murder. When she was carried to the execution ground, she cried out to Heaven and Earth of the injustice: "Heaven and Earth should distinguish the pure from the foul. But how they have mix up Bandit Zhi and Yan Yuan! The good suffer poverty and short life; the wicked enjoy wealth, nobility, and long life. Even Heaven and Earth have come to fear the strong and oppress the weak. They, after all, only push the boats following the current." Before

元代城市
生活长卷

The Urban Life of the
Yuan Dynasty

her execution, Dou E swore that her innocence would be proven by the upcoming abnormalities: dripping blood that never drops on the ground, snow in the midst of summer, and a three-year long drought in Chuzhou. All of these phenomena occurred exactly as she foretells. Three years later, her father returned to the region as a judge. Prompted by the ghost of his daughter, he reviewed the case, uncovered the injustice, and ordered the execution of Zheng Lür and the beating of Tao Wu.

In addition to the Injustice to Dou E, Guan Hanqing also created many other plays to expose and criticize the dark side of the society. His sympathy for the weak in the society and the realism displayed by his works promoted him to a new height in zaju creation.

4

Along with Guan Hanqing, Ma Zhiyuan, Zheng Guangzu, and Bai Pu were honored as the Four Great Yuan Playwrights.

Ma Zhiyuan, styled Dongli and a native of Dadu, had once served in the government as a supervisor in Zhejiang Province during the early Yuan Dynasty. But he later switched to zaju creation and performance with a group of playwrights and actors during the reign of Emperor Chengzong. His early aspiration for success in officialdom never came true after two decades' of efforts, which caused him to live in seclusion after seeing through fame and position and devote the rest of his life to zaju and sanqu creation.

Sixteen zaju scripts have been credited to Ma Zhiyuan but only seven are extent, such as Han Gong Qiu (Autumn in Han Palace), Qing Shan Lei (Tears on the Blue Gown), Jian Fu Bei (Jianfu Stele), Yue Yang Lou (Yueyang Tower) and Ren Fengzi (Ren Fengzi). The Jianfu Stele depicted a scholar who underwent a series of frustrations in his search for fame and position to criticize the dark side of officialdom and reveal the internal bitterness of the literati. In the Autumn in Han Palace, Ma told the stony of Wang Zhaojun to express his regrets of an unrecognized talent. Dramas like the Yueyang Tower and Ren Fengzi were of immortal theme, telling the stories about cultivated persons living in retirement. And such dramas reflected the author's longing for an undetermined recluse.

Bai Pu styled himself Renfu or Taisu, with alias Mr. Langu. Born in 1226, he died during the reign of Emperor Chengzong. He had studied with the literary giant Yuan Haowen in youth and grew up to an erudite and prominent scholar who was interested in anything but serving as an official in the government. In 1280, the seventeenth year of zhiyuan, Bai Du moved to live in Jiankang (modern Nanjing in Jiangsu Province) where he abandoned himself to nature and give himself to a life of wine and poetry with the company of the local celebrities and refined scholars, such as the dramatist Li Wenwei, Yang Xian, and Aodun Zhouqing.

Bai Pu wrote 16 plays, most of which were historical and romance ones, and only 3 survived, such as Wu Tong Yu (Rain on the Paulownia Tree) and Qiang Tou Ma Shang (Over the Wall). Rain on the Paulownia Tree tells the story of the tragic love between Emperor Xuanzong of Tang and Yang Guifei. Over the Wall tells the story between Pei Shaojun and Li Qianjin, who secretly get married and had children without parental approval. When the secret was discovered, the family was split. But the couple was finally able to reunite in spite of all difficulties. This play reflected the author's disapproval of arranged marriage in the feudalistic society.

Zheng Guangzu, styled Dehui, once served as a Subofficial Functionary in Hang Zhou Route. As a prominent playwright in the mid Yuan Dynasty, he was honored as "Master Zheng" by people in the drama circle. When he died, he was cremated and buried in the lingzhi Monastery by the West Lake where he was mourned by many scholars with poems and prose.

Zheng Guangzu wrote 18 plays, of which 8 are extant. Qian Nü Li Hun (The Disembodied Soul of Miss Qian) was considered the masterpiece of Zheng due to its ornate diction, subtle description and beautiful tunes. Although it was based on a Tang dynasty story, it surpassed the original story in artistic achievement and was a gem of zaju in the Yuan Dynasty. The play was a myth-like comedy. It told a story about a young girl name Zhang Qiannü who was in deep love with the young scholar Wang Wenju. When Wang left for the capital, Qiannü missed him a lot and was sick on bed. Her soul, however, left her body and pursued Wang along the riverbank and finally met Wang on his boat. She then accompanied Wang to the capital and returned home to reunite with her original sick body after Wang won honor in the civil service examination.

5

Wang Shifu, alias Dexin, was also a renowned dramatist though he was not included in the Four Great Yuan Playwrights. A native of Dadu, Wang was born before 1260 and died at around 1335. He had served in the Yuan government first as a district Magistrate and then promoted to the position of Investigating Censor of Shanxi Branch Censorate. He retired from office in his forties due to his incompatibility with his colleagues, and it was during that time that he began to write drama.

There are 14 plays attributed to Wang and only 3 are extant, namely Xi Xiang Ji (The Romance of the Western Chamber), Li Chun Tang (Lichun Hall) and Po Yao Ji (A tale of Broken Kiln)

As a light and humorous comedy, The Romance of the Western Chamber told the love story between Cui Yingying and Zhang Gong, the young scholar, in the late Tang Dynasty, and praised true love between the lovers. In the play, Wang successfully created the following characters.

Madame Cui, mother of Yingying, was the representative of the ruling feudal ethics. Though she projected the image of a kind and loving mother, she went against the wishes of her daughter and interfered in her love with Zhang, which, in turn, revealed the true colors of this hypocritical, vicious and dishonest woman.

Yingying was a rebel against feudal ethics. She was willing to abandon her shyness and gentleness and fight for her love. But she had a mixed character, for she was as strong-willed and sincere as she was weak and indecisive.

Zhang was a poor and resourceless young scholar who was in deep love with Yingying. They overcame all the obstacles and finally lived in happiness.

Hong Niang, the maid of Yingying, was originally sent by Madame Cui to spy on Yingying. Her sympathy for Yingying and Zhang as well as her disapproval of Madame Cui's perfidy led her to help the lovers to fight for their happiness. When she was interrogated by Madame Cui, her eloquence and resourcefulness forced Madame Cui to accept the relationship between Cui and Zhang.

Hong Niang's wit, courage, sincerity, honesty and sense of justice won her great favor from the audiences and readers. She even became the embodiment of the matchmaker in real life, which in turn attested to the great success of The Romance of the Western Chamber.

Part Six

Chapter One | **Escaping Summer Heat: The Imperial Inspection Tour of Shangdu**

To announce his legitimacy as the Emperor,

He built the capital in the north.

Every year, he went to Luanjing,

To pay respects to his ancestors.

Since the youyuan period, the historical city Yanjing (Dadu) and Kaiping (Shangdu), a new city on the steppes, had been closely connected by the imperial inspection tour.

1

Since the establishment of Dadu at Yanjing, the Yuan Emperor had started their annual trip to Shangdu, which gave rise to a sophisticated system of imperial inspection tour between the two capitals.

In Dadu, there are four routes leading to Shangdu. "Four routes connected the two capitals which were less than 1000 li apart. They were the Postal Route, two East Routes, and the West Route. As for the two East Routes, one passed Heigu while the other Gubeikou." (Zhou Boqi, Preface, HCJ, sic passim)

The Postal Route from Dadu to Shangdu extended for about 800 li with a total 11 postal stations strewn along the road, such as Changping,

341

Yulin, Hongzan, Pengwo, Longmen, Chicheng, Dushikou, Niuquntou, Ming'an, Lilingtai, Huanzhou. It first proceeded westward to Huailai via the Juyong Pass and then headed north through the Qianggan Mountain and the Pianling Mountain to Shangdu. The Postal Route was mainly used by officials and merchants.

The East Route passing Heigu was also called the "Imperial Road". It extended for 750 li with 18 nabo installed along the route. As the Emperor's exclusive route, only those courtiers of the Mongol origin and some military officers serving as the imperial bodyguards could get access to this route. Other officials, even having served the imperial court all their life, may never be able to set foot on the route. This route began to twist its way to the north via what is today's Yanqing District after it reached the Juyong Pass and finally entered the steppes through mountains and woods. It then joined the Postal Route at the Niuquntou Postal Station.

Nabo is the Chinese transliteration of what means field headquarters or seasonal camps in Khitan. It originally referred to the imperial tent the Liao Emperor stayed during his imperial inspection tour. It was then borrowed by the Yuan Mongols to designate the temporary dwelling place for the Emperor in the imperial inspection tour, such as the nabo in Longhutai and Bangchuidian at the southern and northern ends of the Juyong Pass. (Counties, XJZJY) The nabo for the Emperor and his entourage to stay during the imperial inspection tour usually consisted of a fixed tent and some houses. It was usually of a smaller scale than the ordo.

The other East Route to Shangdu which passed Gubeikou extended for over 870 li. It was a "forbidden route" because it was only available to the Investigating Censors and the military troops.

The West Route extended for 1,095 li. It first reached Zhangjiakou along the route of today's Beijing-Baotou Railway, and then headed

north to Shangdu. It was also called the "Beilao Postal Route" because it had been the postal route during the era of the Mongol Empire until 1262, the third year of zhongtong under Emperor Shizu, when the route of the postal relay system was changed and the Beilao Route became the route for freight transport of silk and fur.

The Yuan Emperors usually took the "Imperial Road" to Shangdu and returned to Dadu through the West Route every year. Therefore there were 24 nabo installed along the West Route.

2

Some Yuan scholars recorded the time of the imperial inspection tour in their works. According to Ye Ziqi, "after Emperor Shizu established Dadu in Daxing Superior Prefecture and Shangdu in Kaiping Superior Prefecture, he would leave for Shangdu where he escaped summer heat, accorded his relatives and fed his horses with water and grass in every the fourth lunar month when the grass turned green on the northern steppes. And he would return to Dadu in the eighth lunar month when the grass began to wither." (Section two, Miscellaneous Institutions, Vol. 3, CMZ) Kong Qi also stated that "it was customary for the Mongol Emperor to go to Shangdu in the fourth lunar month to escape summer heat and return to Dadu at the Double Ninth Festival." (JZZZZJ, Vol. 1) Most of these scholars, however, had never personally experienced the imperial inspection tour; therefore, their records were mostly hearsay in nature, and lack credibility.

In fact, it was in 1263, the fourth year of zhongtong, that Emperor Shizu started to spend his summer in Shangdu. He left for Shangdu on the thirteenth day of the second lunar month in that year and returned to Dadu on the twenty-fifth day of the eighth lunar month. From then on, he usually started his inspection tour of Shangdu in the second lunar month or sometimes in the third lunar month, but never in the fourth lunar month, and he often retuned to Dadu in the ninth lunar month.

This time schedule of the imperial inspection tour was inherited by Temür, Emperor Chengzong, while Khayisan, Emperor Wuzong changed it to from the third lunar month to the ninth lunar month. As for the other succeeding Yuan Emperors, those who were accustomed to the steppe life, such as Sudibala, Emperor Yingzong, and Yesün Temür, Emperor Taiding, chose to follow the time schedule of Emperor Wuzong, while Emperors who were more accustomed to the life in the Central Plains and could not stand the chilly weather on the steppes, such as Ayurbarwada, Emperor Renzong, Tugh Temür, Emperor Wenzong, and Toghun Temür, Emperor Shundi, tried to diminish their sojourn in Shangdu—they usually postponed their starting time of the imperial inspection tour to the fourth or ever fifth lunar month, left Shangdu in the seventh lunar month and returned to Dadu in the eighth lunar month.

It took twenty to twenty-five days to travel from Dadu to Shangdu, which means that the Emperor and his entourage would spend almost two months' time on the route between the two capitals.

3

During the imperial inspection tour, the Emperor had an enormous escort of over one hundred thousand people.

All the imperial consorts and concubines, the Heir Apparent and the Mongol imperial princes had to accompany the Emperor to the north to escape summer heat. Besides, all the major officials in the central government should also follow the Emperor to Shangdu. For example, the Secretariat with overall responsibility for administering the Yuan state was nominally headed by a Director which, in fact, was reserved for the Heir Apparent. Under the Director there were two Grand Councilors

元代城市
生活长卷

The Urban Life of the
Yuan Dynasty

(the Grand Councilor of the Right, and the Grand Councilor of the Left), Managers of Governmental Affairs, the Assistant Director of the Left, the Assistant Director of the Right and Assistant Administrators, etc. Every year, all of those officials would follow the Emperor to Shangdu except Managers of Governmental Affairs and one Assistant Director. The Bureau of Military Affairs primarily concerned with administering forces of the state was headed by the Military Affairs Commissioner which was also reserved for the Heir Apparent. Under the Military Affairs Commissioner there were Bureau Managers, Associated Administrators, Vice Military Affairs Commissioners, and Assistant Commissioners, etc.

"In accordance with the conventional practice, all the officials of the Bureau of Military Affairs should accompany the Emperor to Shangdu except one who was to attend to the affairs of the bureau in Dadu." (Biography of Zheng Zhiyi, Vol. 154, YS) And usually the official that had to stay in Dadu was either a Vice Commissioner or an Assistant Commissioner. The Censorate responsible for maintaining disciplinary surveillance over the whole officialdom was directed by Censors-in-chief with the assistance of the Vice Censors-in-chief, Attendant Censors, and Secretarial Censors, etc. All of them should go to Shangdu with the Emperor, leaving only the Vice Censors-in-chief and Attendant Censors in Dadu. Apart from the above three major central government agencies, all the principal officials of many other agencies were also on the list of the entourage, such as the Judges (jarliqchi) of the High Court of Justice that had judicial jurisdiction over the royal family and all the Mongol tribes, the Chamberlain for the National Treasury that was responsible for irrigation and water conservancy, the Commissioners of the Commission for Buddhist and Tibetan Affairs that was responsible for supervising the Buddhist clergies and governing Tibet, Commissioners of the Palace Provisions Commission that was responsible for providing food and drink for the imperial palace, and the principal officials of the Academy of Scholarly Worthies, the Hanlin and Historiography Academy, the Mongolian Hanlin Academy, the Commission for Ritual Observances, the Imperial Seals Commission, the Astrological Commission, the Imperial Academy of Medicine and the Imperial Manufactories Commission, etc. In addition, some religious leaders, prominent scholars and students of the Directorate of Education would follow the Emperor to Shangdu as well.

Keshig was the imperial guard of the Emperor. Originally set at 10,000 men, the actual number of the Keshikten usually exceeded this number. The entire Keshig was divided into four companies or the so calked "Four Shifts of Keshig." When the Emperor was in Dadu, they were responsible for the safety of the palace city; while the Emperor was in Shangdu, they served as the guard of the palace tent. They took turns to protect and provision the Emperor with all that he needed no matter in Dadu or in Shangdu. However, not all the Keshikten were to follow the Emperor to Shangdu every year. Some of them were left in Dadu to preside over the routine matters in the imperial palace, and some were to station in Shangdu during the winter to prepare for the arrival of the Emperor in the next spring.

To strengthen the centralized government, Qubilai established the Imperial Armies in the capital. By the late Yuan Dynasty, the Imperial Armies had expanded to over 30 Guards with a force of about 300,000 men. Soldiers in the Imperial Armies were grouped according to the races they belonged to. For example, there was the Chinese Guard, which was mainly draw from the Chinese Army and the Newly Submitted Army (consisted of the surrendered Southern Song soldiers), including the Front Guard, the Rear Guard, the Left Guard, the Right Guard, the Center Guard and the Militant Guard; the Semuren Guard, including the Tangut Guard, Qipchaq Guard, Asut Guard, Argyn Guard and the Russian Guard; the Mongol Guard which was drawn from the soldiers of the Allied Army; and the Zongren Guard which was comprised of the descendants

元代城市
生活长卷

The Urban Life of the
Yuan Dynasty

346

of the Mongol nomads. When the Emperor went to Shangdu, the Imperial Armies would sent a large number of soldiers to escort the Emperor and dispatch military troops to safeguard the important passes along the route to Shangdu. Besides, a body of about 10,000 soldiers from the Imperial Armies would be sent to guard the Emperor's camp during the trip to further guarantee the safety of the Emperor. When everything had been prepared, a mighty procession of miscellaneous guards of honor would set out for Shangdu.

The imperial procession would be headed by a bactrian camel with a black banner attached to its front hump and a smaller one to the other hump and a horse with a leather drum on the back. The camel "whose fur was formed into braids was decorated with many bronze bells and tiny minors. A little bronze drum was installed on its back, and every time in the imperial inspection tour the rider of the camel would beat the drum to warn the other pedestrians to get out of the road." As for the horse, its head, neck and hindquarters were "all decorated with red-tasseled bronze bells" and it was led by man walking in front of it. "During the imperial inspection tour, the horse with the drum and the camel with the black banners would proceed side by side in the front of the procession." (Section two, Record of Vehicles and Garments, Vol. 79, YS)

The royal guards of honor were composed of 22 companies of infantry and cavalry who respectively carried flags, drums, crossbows, knives and spears, etc. They included the Jingu Company, Qingyou Company, Cifei Company, Front Company Carrying Shu30, Front Cavalry Company, twenty eight Front Constellation Companies, Front Companies Consisted of the Left and Right Metropolitan Guards Carrying Huanghui Badges, Rear Company Carrying Shu, Left and Right Companies Carrying flags, Left and Right Dragon and Tiger Companies, twenty eight Rear Constellation Companies, Rear Cavalry Company, Rear Company Consisted of Left and Right Metropolitan Guards Carrying Huanghui

Badges, Left and Eight Guards Carrying Knives and Swords, Infantry Consisted of the Imperial Bodyguards, Armed Infantry of Imperial Guardsmen, Company of Standby Guard, Left and Right Armed Cavalry, Left Blue Armed Guard, Front Red Armed Guard, Central Yellow Armed Guard and Right White Armed Guard. Among all these companies and guards, the Armed Left, Front, Right and Center Guards were cavalry guards, each of which was led by a Chief Military Commissioner.

As has been introduced before, the Emperor traveled between the two capitals in the elephant-drawn carriage, while the Empress, Heir Apparent, other imperial princes and the courtiers usually traveled in carts drawn by horses or oxen or simply on horseback. And every nabo would provide such animals like horses and oxen for the imperial procession during the imperial inspection tour.

4

The annual Imperial Inspection tour involved a series of rituals in welcoming and seeing off the Emperor.

1. Picking an auspicious day. Every year an auspicious day would be picked by officials of the Astrological Commission for the Emperor to start his journey to the north.

2. Seeing the Emperor off at Dakou. Dakou was where the first nabo was located outside of Dadu. It was 20 li away from Jiande Gate of Dadu and marked the northern border of the Haidian District of modern Beijing. "When the Emperor set out for Shangdu, all the officials who came to see him off were supposed to stop here."

3. Reporting the itinerary to the Emperor at Longhutai. Longhutai was where the third nabo was situated outside of Dadu. It was located northwest to the Changping District and was 25 li away from the Juyong Pass and 100 li away from Dadu. Officials would report the itinerary to the

元代城市
生活长卷

The Urban Life of the
Yuan Dynasty

Emperor at Longhuitai Nabo, for they would soon enter the mountainous areas after Longhuitai.

4. Passing through the Juyong Pass at night. The mountain road of the Juyong Pass stretched for 30 li. So the imperial procession usually passed through the Juyong Pass at night. And when the imperial procession proceeded along the road with torches, it just resembled a fire dragon crawling over the mountains, which left a deep impression on the Yuan poets.

> From Changping the palace carriages set out in order,
> Whose lanterns rendered the capital into a city of flames.
> Having covered only several li of the Juyong Pass,
> She curled up the bead curtain to listen to the singing birds.

5. Welcoming the Emperor at Shaling. After a prolonged journey of over 300 li along the rugged mountain path, the imperial procession reached Shaling on the steppes where the Emperor would by welcomed by officials from Shangdu and a small-scale imperial banquet would be held in the nearby nabo.

6. Arriving in Shangdu. When the imperial procession arrived in Shangdu, all should dismount from the horse at Yutian Gate except the Emperor. The Emperor would then be ushered into the imperial palace by a group of singing and dancing court entertainers, who would form four large characters— "Tian Xia Tai Ping" (Peace reigns under heaven) in front of the steps of the imperial palace. Then a court assembly would be held by the Emperor and all the officials and imperial princes in Shangdu would come to pay their respects to the Emperor and extend their congratulations. After that a grand feast would be held.

7. Departing Shangdu. An auspicious day would also be picked, when the Emperor was to return to Dadu. On that day the imperial

procession would set out for Dadu after a banquet of koumiss.

8. Seeing the Emperor off at Nanpo. Nanpo, about 30 li away from Shangdu, was where the first nabo outside of Shangdu was located. It was at Napo that the officials who were to stay in Shangdu saw off the Emperor, and that the officials following the Emperor back to Dadu reported the itinerary to the Emperor.

9. Greeting the Emperor at Huailai. Some of the officials who had stayed in Dadu while the Emperor was away came all the way to wait for the Emperor at Huailai with the fruit wine. And a banquet would be held when the Emperor arrived at Huailai Nabo.

10. Welcoming the Emperor at Dakou. The imperial procession would continue to head south and pass through the Juyong Pass at night after Huailai. When they arrived at Dakou, they would be welcomed by the other officials of Dadu.

11. Returning to the imperial palace. After spending the night at Dakou Nabo, the Emperor together with the Heir Apparent and the Major Empress would set out for the palace city via Houzai Gate in the early morning followed by an extended procession of court carts that belonged to the other empresses and imperial consorts and concubines. Since there were so many horses and carts waiting to enter the imperial palace, those lining at the rear of the procession were only able to enter the imperial palace at night. "Hundreds of thousands of people of all walks, such as officials, maids, and servants, thronged Dadu on that day." Then several days after the Emperor's arrival in Dadu, an auspicious day would be picked by the Grand Councilors for the Emperor to hold the court assembly. (Annals, XJZJY)

5

Since every year the principal officials of the central government had to follow the Emperor to Shangdu where they had to stay and work for several months, branch offices of some pivotal government agencies were thus installed in Shangdu, such as the branch offices of the Secretariat, Censorate and the Hanlin and Historiography Academy.

As the Emperor and his courtiers had to spend almost half a year in Dadu and the other half in Shangdu every year, a postal relay system was established to deliver the important official documents, memorials to the throne and military intelligence between the two capitals. In the fourth lunar month of 1260, the first year of zhongtong, Qubilai had several postal relay stations installed between Yanjing and Kaiping, ordering "all the documents should be properly delivered in accordance with the old rules". The postal relay system was later institutionalized. "A postal relay station should be installed every 10, 15 or 25 li. Of every ten postal relay stations, there should be a Senior Official and each postal relay station should be staffed with five soldiers." (Postal Relay Stations, JSDD; YLDD, Vol. 14575) There were a total 82 postal relay stations strewn between Dadu and Shangdu.

The official mail delivered by the postal relay stations was packed in two ways. The urgent documents were contained in a box, while the ordinary ones were put in a paper bag. Further protection from a piece of oil satin, boards and a mailbag would also be added to the packed documents in delivery.

A set of strict rules and regulations was laid down to ensure the efficient delivery of the official documents and guarantee the safety of the mail. For example, "the rider-messengers should cover 400 li each day and night when delivering the mail. The attendants should work round the clock in the postal relay stations, ready to relay the mail at any moment. Thus "very postal relay station would be illuminated by candles throughout the night." Besides, the mail should all be registered, labeled and relayed without delay at the postal relay stations. If any mail was found opened, missing or damaged, the person in charge would be severely punished.

As the center of the politics of the Yuan Dynasty, Dadu and Shangdu naturally witnessed a series of political upheavals.

元代城市
生活长卷

The Urban Life of the
Yuan Dynasty

Chapter Two | The Underage Emperor from Jiangnan

The Southern Song Emperor together with his entourage was brought to the north for an audience with the Mongol ruler soon after his capitulation, which left many unforgettable stories to the people.

1

After the Yuan troops took the Southern Song capital Lin'an, the Mongol Commander urged the surrendered Southern Song Emperor and Empress Dowager to have an audience with the Mongol ruler in the north. They then headed north with a 3,000-man body of entourage which consisted of the Southern Song Palace Women, Palace Attendants, Music Masters and Students of the National University and the School for the Imperial Family. The Music Master Wang Yuanliang was also in the list of the entourage.

On March 28, 1276, the twelfth day of the third lunar month in the thirteenth year of zhiyuan, the seven-year old Emperor Zhao Xian set out for Shangdu. Grand Empress Dowager Xie remained behind due to illness, so he was accompanied to the north by Empress Dowager Quan, the imperial consorts and concubines and some Palace Women, altogether over 100 people. Meanwhile the Palace Attendants, Musicians including

Wang Yuanliang and students of the National University also left the capital for the north.

When the Emperor and his entourage were about to leave Lin'an, the entire city was shrouded by a desperate atmosphere mingled with people's loud lamentation. In great dismay and despair, Wang Yuanliang and his Song folks were taken to the north under the Mongol military escort. These scholars, weak and never wandering about in a desperate plight, soon got exhausted once they walked out of the city. But they gained no mercy from the Mongols; instead each of them was given three floggings by the escorting soldiers. A pail of porridge without eating utensils was provided by the Mongols for them when they were about to take boat by the canal. Extremely hungry and thirsty, the students of the National University all leapt at the porridge with the clam shells they picked at the riverside with no consideration for scholarly dignity. Different from the wealthy royal members and dignitaries who were able to bribe the Mongol soldiers in exchange of preferential treatment, these students of the National University, most of whom took with them nothing but books and some personal necessities, had no choice but to suffer the increasingly severe maltreatment from the Mongol soldiers. On their way to Dadu, quite a few students who couldn't endure such hardships died and their bodies were just left unburied in the wilderness. When they finally reached Dadu in the fifth lunar month, only 46 of the 99 students of the National University survived. Many Musicians and Palace Attendants also died en route, but Wang Yuanliang was able to struggle his way to Dadu with a deteriorating health.

Those imperial consorts and concubines as well as the Palace Women who followed Empress Dowager Quan and Zhao Xian to the north were all filled with a great sorrow on their way to the north, because they knew that there was no chance of ever returning to the south. Lady of Bright Deportment Wang Qinghui, for example, wrote a poem on the wall

of a postal relay station. The poem was soon discovered by others and began circulating among the people.

2

On May 29, the twenty-fourth day of the intercalary month following the third lunar month, Empress Dowager Quan and Zhao Xian as well as their entourage arrived in Dadu. After a rest of over half a month, they set out again for Shangdu to have an audience with the Yuan Emperor Qubilai who was escaping summer heat there at that time.

On second day of fifth lunar month, a ceremony was held in Shira Ordo, which was located about 10 li south of Shangdu, for Qubilai to meet the Southern Song Emperor. Qubilai, of course, would never expect a 7-year old to strictly observe all the rituals during the ceremony. They just went through the motions, for what Qubilai wanted was only a Southern Song emperor who had surrendered paying homage to him, the conqueror. Qubilai then conferred the title of Duke of Ying on Zhao Xian, and appointed him Commander Unequalled in Honor and Minister of Education.

As usual, Qubilai held a Jamah Banquet after the ceremony for celebration, and invited all the newly arrived Song people to it. They, of course, were deeply impressed by the magnificence of the banquet.

All were in high spirits and drank to their heart's content during the banquet expect the Song loyalists led by Empress Dowager Quan, which was easy to understand, and the Mongol Empress Chabui, which, however, greatly shocked Qubilai. Then he asked her why she was in such a low mood. Chabui answered, "no empire could last for ever. I only hope my children and grandchildren could be spared such misfortunes." And when Qubilai invited Chabui to the front of the hall to appreciate the treasures taken from Lin'an, She just walked to the displaying table, cast a glance at the treasures, shook her head and left without a word.

Qubilai immediately sent a Palace Attendant to ask her which treasure she would like to have. Chabui replied, "How could I take what was supposed to be the inheritance of the Song people, though they are unable to safeguard them and lost them to us?"

Every word of Chabui sounded sensible to Qubilai. Yes, one should stay vigilant in peace time, for it was easy to start an undertaking but difficult to sustain it. Even such sagacious emperors as Qin Shi Huang, Emperor Wu of Han, Emperor Taizong of Tang, and Emperor Taizu of Song inevitably had prodigal sons. How to sustain such a mighty empire was really a thorny question.

But Qubilai had already come up with a plan to settle the Southern Song Emperor, Empress Dowager and their entourage. They would receive preferential treatment under house arrest in the Yuan capital, lest they should be used by the Southerners in their anti-Yuan movement.

However two palace women surnamed Dong and Zhu and two palace servants committed suicide in their rooms after taking a bath and putting on clean clothes. A poem was found in the sleeves of the woman surnamed Zhu. Obviously they died for their country before the Mongols were able to extend the favored treatment.

Empress Dowager Quan and other Song imperial consorts and concubines, like Wang Qinghui, wanted to be nuns. Qubilai agreed to their requests but ordered that they should first be warmly received by him. And the Yuan court did show great hospitality to the Southern Song Emperor and Empress Dowagers.

Even so, Chabui still felt great sympathy for the Song people. Considering that Empress Dowager Quan, a southerner, was unaccustomed to the climet of the north, she repeatedly appealed to Qubilai to release her and let her continue to live in Jiangnan. But this request was declined by Qubilai who was more concerned about the political influence of this

元代城市
生活长卷

The Urban Life of the
Yuan Dynasty

356

Southern Song Empress Dowager than her life. He told Chabui, "Women are women. Have you ever considered that if they were sent back to Jiangnan, rumors against them would arise and they would be seriously endangered? If you truly care about them, just console them frequently and persuade them to accept the life here." Qubilai not only refused to release Empress Dowager Quan, but also took the Southern Song Grand Empress Dowager Xie Daoqing to Dadu. He then conferred the title Madam of Shouchun on her.

3

It was very hot and muggy in Dadu in the mid July of 1281, the late sixth lunar month of the eighteenth year of zhiyuan. And it was then that the Southern Song loyalist Wen Tianxiang who was imprisoned in Dadu wrote his masterpiece— Zheng Qi Ge (Song of Righteousness).

Wen Tianxiang, a native of Luling, Jizhou, styled Songrui, or Lüshan, and was known by his literary name Wenshan. In 1256, the fourth year of baoyou under Emperor Lizong of Song, he ranked first in the imperial examinations. In 1259, the first year of kaiqing, when Ezhou was besieged by the Mongol troops, he urged the Song court to execute Eunuch Dong Songchen who had suggested the Song court to move the capital to a more secure place, and to launch a defensive war against the Mongols. He subsequently took up several posts in the Southern Song government, including the Vice Minister of the Ministries of Justice and the Vice Minister of the Left Office of the Department of State Affairs, but was finally impeached and removed from office by the Censorate. Later he was appointed Directorate for Armaments and Provisional Auxiliary in the Institute of Academicians, but was impeached again for mocking Jia Sidao, a powerful official in the Song court, in drafting the imperial edict. In 1275, the first year of deyou, Wen established an Anti-Yuan

Volunteer Army when he served as Administrator of Ganzhou Prefecture and led his army to guard Lin'an. In the first lunar month of the next year, having been promoted to the Grand Councilor of the Right, Military Affairs Commissioner, and Commander-in-chief from Administrator of Lin'an Superior Prefecture, he was sent to the Yuan camps for a peace talk but was detains there, and was forced to accompany the Southern Song Peace Mission to the north. He then managed to escape to Fuzhou when the Peace Mission crossed the Yangtze River. Due to his discord with the then Grand Councilor Cheng Yizhong, he was dispatched to Jiangxi as Associate Commander-in-chief for Conscription. In the twelfth lunar month of 1278, the first year of xiangxing, Wen was defeated and captured in Wupoling (which is now located in the north of Haifeng, Guangdong) and was then taken by the Yuan troops to Yanshan Island where he witnessed the defeat of the last Song military force and uttered his famous line— " None since the advent of time have escaped death, may my loyalty forever illuminate the annals of history."

In then tenth lunar month of 1279, the sixteenth year of zhiguan, Wen Tianxiang was taken to Dadu under army escort. He was first lodged in a lavishly decorated house by the Bureau of Military Affairs. But he rejected the "offer" by staying up, facing the south day and night. Failed in their attempts to win him over, the Bureau of Military Affairs could only hand him to the Warden's Office of Dadu. And Wen was then imprisoned. In the jail Wen swore that he would never commit suicide even if he were to be cruelly slaughtered by the Mongols.

The prison of the Warden's Office in Dadu was walled by mud walls. It was not very large but imprisoned many criminals. In addition to the murders, arsonists and thieves, those who had breached the court prohibitions against illegal possession of weapons, illegal assembly for gambling, the sale of counterfeit medicines, and wander at night would also be captured and thrown into the jail by the Warden's Office

which was responsible for the general peace and order of Dadu. The jail consisted of three parts—the southern chamber, the northern chamber, both of which were large prison cells packed with all kinds of criminals, and a small cell facing the west where Wen Tianxing was imprisoned.

Like most houses in Dadu, the prison was made of pounded earth. Small, shabby and low-lying, the prison cells would become extremely damp and musty in rainy days and scorching under the burning sun. Besides, the overcrowded cells were usually filled with the stinking smells of sweat, feet, toilet, and the moldy smell of decayed grains wafted from the nearby storehouse. All these smells were then ironically referred to as "Seven Foul Smells" by Wen Tianxiang. He said, "although this mud house was taken over by the seven foul smells, I could resist them with "the vast vital energy" mentioned by Mencius. Such vast vital energy was actually the righteousness in the world. And my righteousness would definitely help me overcome the seven foul smells." And it was in such a mood that Wen wrote his famous poem—Song of Righteousness.

In the world there is the spirit of righteousness, taking many forms, bestowed on the over-changing things

Below they are the rivers and mountains; above they are the sun and stars.

With people it is called the spirit of honor and fearlessness, so vast it fills the universe.

When the empire is tranquil one pours forth harmony in the splendid court.

When times are extreme true fidelity is seen, and goes down in history case after case.

During the State of Qi it is the official historian's bamboo slats; during the State of Jin it is Dong Hu's pen.

During the Qin Dynasty it is Zhang Liang's hammer; during the

Han Dynasty it is Su Wu's ambassadorial staff.

It is General Yan's head; it is Imperial Attendant Ji's blood.

It is Zhang's teeth at Sui Yang; it is Yan's tongue at Chang Shan.

Or it is the Eastern Liao hat, the incorruptibility purer than ice and snow.

Or it is the Memorials to Embark on the Campaign—the courage and fierce loyalty make gods and spirits weep.

Or it is the oar during the River crossing—the fervency swallows up the barbarians.

Or it is the court tablet striking the villain, breaking the rebel rogue's head.

What is permeated by this spirit lives on forever revered.

It links up the cosmos, so how can life and death compare in importance?

The Corners of Earth depend on it to stand; the Pillars of Heaven depend on it to maintain their honor.

The Three Relationships really do determine one's life; moral righteousness is the root.

Sad that I met with the Yang Nine; the slaves really didn't exert themselves.

The head of the prisoners of war was tied up and sent on the transport cart to the extreme north.

The cauldron would have been sweet as syrup; I sought it but couldn't get it.

The dark room was silent with ghost fires; the spring garden was depressing with dark skies.

Cattle and the thoroughbred shared the same manger; the phoenix ate from the chicken's roost.

Should the dew and fog get to me one morning, my fate would have been that of a corpse cast into a ditch.

元代城市
生活长卷

The Urban Life of the
Yuan Dynasty

I lived that for another winter and summer, yet all the ailments stayed away from me.

How sad that a low, wet space is now my tranquil land!

There can be no other trickery; neither Yin nor Yang can steal from me.

With this in mind I am at peace; I look above to the floating white clouds.

My heart is sad but relaxed; don't tell me that the blue sky has an end.

The philosophers' days are far from us; our models are in the past.

Under the eaves I open the book and read; the ancient Way lights up my face.

Wen Tianxiang's patriotism didn't dwindle over years of imprisonment. He flatly rejected the Yuan court's enticement into submission and always angrily rebuked those former Southern Song officials who came to persuade him to surrender.

In the nineteenth year of zhiyuan, an anonymous letter appeared in Dadu, and rumor had it that two forces of soldiers would come to rescue Wen Tianxiang by setting the city walls of Dadu on fire. In the meanwhile, a man named Xue Baozhu, a native of Zhongshan, who claimed to be the Emperor of Song, also planned to rescue Wen Tianxiang and he had already had thousands of men under his command.

All such disturbing news forced Qubilai to make up his mind to execute Wen Tixanxing. On January 8, 1283, the eighth day of the twelfth lunar month of the nineteenth year of zhiyuan, Qubilai made his last futile effort to persuade Wen to pay homage to him by holding an audience with Wen. Wen simply said, "I am the Principal Graduate of the Palace Examination, and the Grand Councilor of Song. Now that Song has fallen, I have no reason to live on." He was taken to the execution ground in the next day, and the last thing he left to this world was another two poems.

4

Xue Baozhu was arrested by the Yuan troops in the first lunar month of the twentieth year of zhiyuan. He admitted having written the anonymous letter and was immediately executed. This event, however, didn't come to an end with the death of Xue Baozhu, because the fate of Zhao Xian, Duke of Ying, was also changed by it.

Zhao Xian and other Song royal remembers were first relocated from Dadu to Shangdu. On November 19, 1288, the twenty-fourth day in the tenth lunar month of the twenty-fifth year of zhiyuan, Zhao Xian was sent to the Tibet to study Buddhism in Sasijia Monastery. By sending the young emperor of the fallen Song Dynasty to a thinly populated region and having him controlled by his trusted monks, Qubilai could not only eliminate the Southern Song adherents' intention to rescue their emperor and thereby recover their country, but also project an image of a benevolent monarch who never maltreats his captives.

Zhao Xian, who had already grown up by that time, however, was indeed a born monk. He not only grasped Tibetan and translated some Buddhist works, but also became "Benbo Instructor" of the Sasijia Monastery. And he was honored as "Manzi Hezun". Influenced by the Mongols, Tibetans also called the Song people "manzi"; and "hezun" was the honorific title people gave to those royal members who gave up the throne for Kasaya.

In the fourth lunar month of 1323, the third year of zhizhi, a misfortune befell Zhao Xian, Duke of Ying—he was suddenly executed by Sudibala, Emperor Yingzong of Yuan. Sudibala was not a fatuous ruler; in fact, he had made many achievements during his reign. Then what made him decide to kill Zhao Xian, a captured emperor who had been a

元代城市
生活长卷

The Urban Life of the
Yuan Dynasty

362

monk for years and whose nation had lived in submission to the Mongols for 40 years? It remained a mystery even until the end of the Yuan Dynasty, which, however, gave rise to many speculations on the reason of his death.

The most popular one was that Zhao Xian's death was caused by a poem.

Please ask Lin Hejing for me,
How many times have the plums blossomed?
Held as a guest at the Golden Terrace,
Unlikely could I ever return to my home.

The poem was Zhao Xian's reflection on his life. The person named Lin Hejing in the poem was the Northern Song learned hermit Lin Bu, a native of Qiantang. He was famous for his poetic prose. Well-travelled in his early years, he later led a secluded life in a mountain by the West Lake for 20 years and never got married. The Golden Terrace was one of the Eight Sights of Dadu. Obviously, this poem was composed by Zhao Xian to express his nostalgia for his hometown, but it was later abused by others as his incitement to a revolt. Emperor Yingzong, therefore, had him executed. But this account somewhat lacks credibility, for according to the tone of the poem, it must be written by Zhao Xian when he was still in Dadu, to which he never returned after he had became a monk. And it would be very unlikely for Emperor Yingzong to sentence Zhao to death just because of a poem Zhao had composed decades ago.

According to the historical records written in Tibetan, Zhao was killed for another reason. At that time the astrologer of the Emperor predicted that the monks in Tibet would revolt to usurp the throne. Alarmed by this news, the Emperor immediately sent people to inspect in Tibet only to find that a majority of the populace there followed Zhao

Xian. To prevent the prophecy from coming true, he decreed that Zhao be beheaded. When Zhao was taken to the execution ground, he swore to get his revenge in the afterlife saying, "Why should I be executed when I have never plotted rebellion? I swear I would return and reclaim the throne in the afterlife!" After his death, he reincarnated as Zhu Yuanzhang, the first Emperor of the Ming Dynasty, and overthrew the Mongol rule.

This story is more credible except for the part of incarnation, because in third lunar month of the third year of zhizhi, some emissaries dispatched to Tibet by the Yuan court did get killed there by a group of monks.

In the late Yuan Dynasty, there circulated a more fantastic story about Zhao Xian. According to Geng Shen Wai Shi (Unofficial History of the Gengshen Period), the unofficial history written by a hermit called Quan Heng, Zhao Xian, the Duke of Ying, once married a Muslim woman in a emple in Ganzhou. The woman gave birth to a son on May 24, 1320, the sixth day of the fourth lunar month in the seventh year of yanyou, when Emperor Mingzong and Kuala accidentally passed the temple and noticed a dragon-shaped and five-colored propitious cloud hovering over the temple. They then entered the temple to find out what had happened and left with the woman and the newborn baby. And this baby was Toghun Temür, the last Emperor of Yuan.

In the yongle era of the Ming Dynasty, when Yongle Emperor of Ming was watching the portraits of the emperors of the previous dynasties, he noticed that Emperor Shundi of Yuan looked more like the emperors of the Song Dynasty than those of the Yuan Dynasty. He then asked his accompany Yuan Zhongche, who grew up in a family of astrologers, for the reason. But Yuan couldn't answer it at that moment. Soon after that Yuan learned about the legend that Emperor Shundi of Yuan was the son of Zhao Xian. He then embroidered the story and recorded it into his book

元代城市
生活长卷

The Urban Life of the
Yuan Dynasty

364

Fu Tai Wai Ji (Supplement to the Collected Works of the Chief Minister of the Seals Office).

The story that Zhao fathered Emperor Shundi was not brilliant and credible at all. It only took advantage of the fact that Emperor Wenzong of Yuan had once revealed that Toghun Temür was not the legitimate son and heir of Emperor Mingzong of Yuan, and reflected the Southern Song adherents' wish to recover their country. But its influence was far-reaching, especially after it was the embellished by the Ming people.

5

Xie Daoqing, Madame of Shouchun, had spent seven years in Dadu before she died of illness at the age of 74. Empress Dowager Quan later became a nun in Zhengzhi Monastery and finally died there. Wang Huiqing became a Taoist nun with the Taoist name "Chong Hua". She stayed in close contact with Wang Yuanliang and the like but only in terms of making poetry and listening to music.

Most of the eunuchs (or huozhe according to the Mongols) who had followed Zhao Xian and the Empress Dowager to the north were required to serve in the Yuan Imperial palace. Among them there was a native of Qiangtang named Luo Taiwu, who was later permitted to leave the imperial palace to live in Dadu due to health problems. After he moved out of the imperial palace, he indulged himself in reading and receiving guests. His nephew was also a eunuch in the Yuan imperial palace and came to power during the era of Emperor Taiding (1324-1328). Nobles and officials in the imperial court all mingled with him, but Luo Taiwu refused to meet his nephew. One day when his nephew came to visit him again, he only talked to him through the closed doors. "I'm sick and need rest, so just leave me alone. I don't expect you to kowtow to me. Others think that you are as powerful as the Mountain Tai, but in my eyes, you are only a paper tiger. I always warned you to stop but you never listen to me. If you really care for me, just tell the Empress Dowager that I am old and seriously sick. And I beg to be buried in my hometown. If you were to help me return to Hangzhou, you should do a great favor for me." His nephew then returned to the imperial palace and reported Luo's request to the Empress Dowager who permitted. Having packed all his books on a cart and warning his nephew not to throw his weight around any more, Luo drove his cart out of Dadu through Qihua Gate. When he was about to pass through Qihua Gate, he looked up at the city gate tower and said, "Farewell, Qihua Gate. I will never return gain!" Taiwu died of illness shortly after he returned to Hangzhou. And his nephew was later convicted of corruption and exiled to a far-away place. As for Wang Yuanliang, he was permitted to go back to Jiangnan after thirteen years of confinement in Dadu.

元代城市
生活长卷

The Urban Life of the
Yuan Dynasty

Chapter Three | **The Coup D'état in Dadu**

After the unification of China, Qubilai tried every means to rejuvenate the nation. But under this treacherous disguise of prosperity, there lurked sharp contradictions which finally gave rise to an astounding coup in Dadu.

1

Although Qubilai had many capable courtiers and valiant generals, Bayan was undisputedly the most prominent official in the Yuan imperial court.

Bayan of the Baarin had followed Hulagu, the younger brother of Qubilai, in the west military expedition to the Central Asia. In 1264, the first year of zhiyuan, he was sent as the envoy of Ilkhanate to the capital of the Yuan Dynasty. Bayan's talent deeply impressed Qubilai, who urged Bayan to stay. Bayan had served as Assistant Director of the Left of the Secretariat and Associate Administrator of the Bureau of Military Affairs. He was later appointed Commander-in-chief and was dispatched to South China by Qubilai to conquer the Southern Song Dynasty.

When Bayan seized the Southern Song capital Lin'an and returned with victory, he made a large banner with the words "peace reigns under heaven" written on it. All the officials in Shangdu welcomed Bayan outside the city on Qubilai's orders, which was the highest courteous reception an official could get from the imperial court. Manager of Government Affairs Ahmad, a Muslim, was more active than all the other officials. He covered an additional 10 li of road so as to be the first to meet Bayan. When he met Bayan, he started to pile compliments on Bayan. "Congratulations for your unparallel contributions to the imperial court, my Grand Councilor! It is really brave and resourceful of you to successfully take over Lin'an from the hands of the Song people without even shedding a drop of blood."

"The entire honor should be credited to my generals and soldiers." Bayan answered dryly. It seemed that Ahmad's flattery didn't work with Bayan.

Given the cold shoulder, Ahmad was dumbfounded all of a sudden. But he soon recovered himself. He forced a smile and whispered to Bayan, "There must be quite a lot of rare valuables in the Song imperial palace, isn't it?"

"Maybe, but I am not quite clear about that." Bayan was telling the truth, because Qubilai had already sent a special person to make an inventory of all the treasures in the Song imperil palace and transport them back to the capital. And he knew he'd better stay out of this matter.

"That's weird. Isn't it you that were in charge of everything in Lin'an? Ahmad couldn't believe his ears.

"I just worked for His Majesty. And you must have heard that His Majesty had already sent a man to make an inventory of all the treasures of the Song people?" Bayan retorted.

"Well, I know. What I mean is that when you were in the Song imperial palace, the Song people must have presented some priceless gifts to you."

"Gift? Who dare to receive gift? And who dare to violate the

rules of the court? Haven't you forgotten Yong Guer?" Bayan retorted again. Actually Chinggis Khan had already set up the rules that all should hand over the booty obtained from the enemy to the Khakhan, and that any embezzlers would be severely punished. When the Mongols had conquered the Jin Dynasty, Hu Duhu and Yong Guer and Qasar were sent to the Jin capital Zhongdu to make an inventory of treasures in the Jin imperial palace where Yong Guer and Qasar accepted the gifts presented by the Jin people. Soon Hu Duer reported them to Chinggis Khan who severely punished them and almost had them beheaded. This incident later was often mentioned by Qubilai as a negative example to warn his courtiers to be observant.

"Of course, how could I forget?" Ahmad answered, but all smiles had vanished from his face. "Your incorruptibility has always had my genuine admiration⋯" Ahmad continued with biting sarcasm.

"You really flattered me. But as for the treasures in the Song imperial palace, I dare not appropriate anything to myself." With these words, Bayan unhooked a jade ornament from his clothes and handed it over to Ahmad so as to send this nuisance away. "Thank you for riding all the way here to welcome me. This jade ornament was given by Abaqa Khan and now I'd like to give it to you."

Ahmad immediately blushed. He thought Bayan was embarrassing him, which Bayan didn't intend to. So he answered coldly, "Since Abaqa Khan has given it to you, you'd better keep it to yourself." With these words he mounted his horse, whipped it ferociously, and rode off at a gallop.

Bayan didn't expect things would turn out like this, but he couldn't find a better gift for Ahmad. So he just stood there shaking his head.

Bayan soon fell out of favor with Qubilai due to Ahmad's calumnies about him in front of Qubilai. Ahmad had secretly reported to Qubilai that Bayan had appropriated the peach-shaped jade cup from the Song imperial palace to himself when he was in Lin'an and that Bayan had claimed all the credit for himself in the pacification of the south China.

Qubilai was very angry. He sent a Palace Attendant to accuse Bayan. "It is I who raised you Bayan from a commoner to an official in the imperial court. And it is I who conferred high official ranks and all the titles on you. And you would never have conquered Jiangnan, were it not for the help of the late Grand Councilor Shi Tianze. But now you have all forgotten and even become swollen with pride!"

Bayan also replied to Qubilai through the Palace Attendant. "Don't worry, Your Majesty. A commoner is supposed to stay in a common place. Your Majesty can just take everything away from me. I will not complain. But I have never intended to steal the honor of subjugating Jiangnan from Grand Councilor Shi Tianze. That must be a conspiracy of the Song people who intended to drive a wedge between us. And I beg an in-depth investigation from Your Majesty. I dare not be complacent about myself and I don't consider it a fault to serve heart and soul for Your Majesty."

Hearing these words of Bayan, Qubilai felt he was too stern to Bayan. He thus sent a Palace Attendant to tell Bayan that he had no other intention but to warn Bayan not to be smug about his past achievements.

But hardly had this incident quiet down, when another one arose. Bayan was first secretly accused of having killed thousands of Song captives in Dingjiazhou and of keeping the Emperor in the dark about this massacre. He was also secretly denounced for refusing to employ those imperially appointed officials and for reserving all the important

元代城市
生活长卷

The Urban Life of the
Yuan Dynasty

and lucrative positions for his favorite. And someone even reported to the Emperor that in Jiangnan, everyone paid homage to Bayan instead of him.

Qubilai was furious this time. He immediately had Bayan imprisoned for investigation.

El-Temür, the Chief Commander of the Keshig, was shocked to learn Bayan's imprisonment. So he hurried to the imperial palace to intercede with the Emperor for Bayan. He said to Qubilai, "These rumors should not be taken as the evidence of Bayan's guilt. It is only too easy to execute Bayan, just as easy as mowing the grass. But if Bayan were really killed, people in Jiangnan should identify Your Majesty as a tyrant who was intolerant of his officials of merit. Your Majesty could even give lenient treatment to the Song Emperor and his officials, then why couldn't Your Majesty spare your most outstanding official of merit?"

Qubilai agreed and released Bayan. But his suspicion about him was not totally dismissed. He stripped Bayan of all the official titles and ordered him to shut himself up to reflect on his mistakes.

Soon several Mongol princes rebelled in the northeast and Qubilai needed someone to deal with this sudden crisis. After long deliberation, he decided to send Bayan to the north to command the troops. Bayan then was informed by a person sent by Qubilai of this military task and was told to set out on an auspicious day without the necessity of bidding farewell to Qubilai.

Although the mandate had been delivered to Bayan, Qubilai still felt concerned about this military expedition. He then sent a person to spy on Bayan. Soon the spy returned and reported to Qubilai that Bayan had set out at a low speed and that he had repeatedly complained to the courtiers who came to see him off that "never is there a general being dispatched like this."

Qubilai then immediately summoned Bayan for an audience in the imperial palace.

371

"Have you ever said the words 'never is there a general being dispatched like this'?" Qubilai asked Bayan in a stern voice. Bayan admitted and Qubilai continued to ask why.

Bayan replied, "As is known to all that we captured Jiangnan for Your Majesty. As is also known to all that I was thrown into the prison an innocent man, and that I was deprived of all the officials titles due to false accusations. Mongolia in the north was home to many imperial princes and high-ranking officials. Now Your Majesty send me, a notorious criminal, there to command them, how could they be willing to listen to me? Besides, they are all considered trustworthy by Your Majesty. If they should accuse me of treason or shunning enemies out of cowardice, I should definitely be dead. Never suspect the man you use and never use the man you suspect, which is the golden rule of choosing a person for a job. If Your Majesty is suspicious of me, please replace me with another man. If Your Majesty still trusts me, I should not be dispatched to the north in such a rash way. I couldn't go just like that. That's why I said those words. And I beg Your Majesty to reconsider the arrangement."

Touched by Bayan's straightforwardness, Qubilai immediately forgave Bayan. He then ordered to execute a subordinate of Bayan who had smeared Bayan and nearly plunged the entire army into chaos. And Qubilai sent Bayan to supervise his subordinate's decapitation.

Bayan left the palace but the convict had already been taken to the execution ground outside the city. When Bayan arrived there, he only poured a wine for his subordinate. After watched him drink the wine, Bayan left without a word. The executioner then reported it to Qubilai who summoned Bayan again and asked why he refused to supervise the execution

Bayan answered, "what he committed is the crime of undermining the morale of the army and deceiving Your Majesty. If I had supervised the execution, others would have thought that he was executed for framing

me up. And people would take this lawful execution as my personal revenge. Therefore I refused to supervise the execution. And I am here to beg Your Majesty's pardon."

Qubilai was favorably impressed by Bayan's way of handing affairs. He then issued an imperial edict to commend Bayan for his contribution to the pacification of the Southern Song Dynasty, and to purge him of all the false accusations. Then he appointed Bayan Associate Administrator of the Bureau of Military Affairs, and officially sent Bayan to quell the rebellion in the north.

Before long the peach-shaped jade cup was presented to Qubilai as tribute. Only then did Qubilai realize what had happened. He severely reproached Ahmad, repeatedly saying, "this trivial object nearly cost me my staunchest courtier!"

3

The military officials made conspicuous contributions to the unification of the Yuan Dynasty by successfully subjugating the southern China. The civil officials, unwilling to be outshone by them, also pitched in to help establish a prosperous country.

A group of Mongol students of National University submitted a joint petition to the Emperor about expanding the National University. They first illustrated the importance of education by quoting recorded utterances of Confucius, such as "only via education could people be cultivated and good social customs and habits be formed"; "Gems unworked form nothing useful; man without education is ignorant of the right way." They pointed out that all the emperors of the previous dynasties relied on education to rule the country. But the lamentable fact was that although the Emperor had subjugated the Song Dynasty and unified China, excelling all the emperors of Jin, Sui and Tang dynasties in military achievements, there still lacked a sound education system, in spite of the fact that the Emperor had established the National University for the Mongols to study Confucianism, to better serve the court out of the consideration that there were far fewer Mongols serving in the government than those of the other ethnic origins. Since the school system hadn't been established, the number of students in the National University remained small. Thus they proposed to establish schools all over the country with expanding the National University in Dadu as the first step. They suggested enrolling 100 Mongols aged between 10 and 15 and 100 children of officials and commoners into the National University, establishing the education system and employing those who were both high-minded and erudite to teach Confucian classics and doctrines in the school.

But Qubilai knew that these students were just expressing their dissatisfaction with Ahmad and the like, for schools and the National University had already been established and there had already been a group of learned students. Although it was inappropriate for Ahmad to denounce literati as useless people, those Neo-Confucians indeed amounted to nothing but haranguing. Qubilai would never introduce such an impractical style of work into his court. What he advocated was a down-to-earth attitude to work.

There were also proposals for restarting the imperial civil examination, on which Qubilai frowned. The Palace Attendant Dong WenZhong then severely reprimanded those proposers. He said, "As His Majesty has repeatedly mentioned, the Confucians only indulge themselves in chanting poems and making prose. That is of no use to cultivating one's character, let alone administering the country. Besides we only follow the doctrines of Confucius and Mencius instead of the so-called Neo-Confucianism. Now with His Majesty's advocacy of real learning some Confucians began to divert their attention to it. But some pedantic scholars still intend to revive the old practice of the

conquered nation by advocating the imperial civil examination and Neo-Confucianism. They are actually confusing His Majesty with these wicked ideas. And they fall far short of His Majesty's expectations!"

The Confucian Scholar Yang Gongyi was also on Dong Wenzhong's side, which pleased Qubilai a lot. Yang said, "His Majesty has criticized Confucian scholars for abandoning themselves to poetry and harangue instead of seriously studying the Confucian classics and the doctrines of Confucius and Mencius. This criticism is indeed an axiom that could guarantee the long-term stability of the country. As for selecting the Confucian scholars, we could just ask the local authorities to recommend those Confucian scholars who are both upright in character and well-read in classics. Thus it is not necessary to restart the imperial civil examination. If all the Confucian scholars should begin to focus on the real learning, the pompous society practices and folk customs could be refined. By that time, will it still be difficult for the imperial court to get access to talents?"

Indeed, the imperial civil examination which had lasted for hundreds of years resulted in more and more problems. Since memorizing commentary and subcommentary of Confucian classics and making poetry and poetic prose were the key to passing the examination, all the Confucian scholars concentrated on writing eight-part essays, a rigid literary form prescribed by the imperial civil service examinations, and learning commentary and subcommentary of Confucian classics by rote. Thus an imperial court that advocated the imperial civil examination was usually packed with Confucian scholars who were good at nothing but haranguing and writing pompous articles. Such state was destined to be destroyed by such Confucian scholars. And the Song Dynasty was a case in point. Since Dong and Yang criticized the proponents of imperial civil examination, no one else had mentioned the imperial civil examination in front of Qubilai again.

4

On the eleventh day of the sixth lunar month of thirteenth year of zhiyuan, Qubilai decided to carry out Liu Bingzhong's proposal for the revision of Da Ming Calendar. Thus people like Wang Xun and Guo Shoujing set about implementing the decision under Zhang Wenqian and Zhang Yi's direction.

Wang Xun then recommended Xu Heng to Qubilai, saying that the prominent Confucian scholar Xu Heng was one of the very few who were not only familiar with the calendrical principles but also proficient in calendrical calculation. In fact, Xu Heng had once served in the imperial court as a master of Neo-Confucianism. Three years ago, he left the capital for his hometown. Qubilai didn't urge him to stay, only telling the local authorities to take care of him. But now Qubilai agreed to recruit Xu Heng because this time he was introduced as an expert of calculation.

Guo Shoujing also proposed to make new observational devices. He argued, "test is indispensable to the revision of the calendar and observational devices are the most important testers. The armillary sphere we now use at the observatory was made over 200 years ago by the Song people in Bianliang. But it is no longer accurate and often entails a sharp declination of four degrees when measuring the North and South Poles. So it should not be used any more, nor are the sundials left by Song and Jin peoples." Guo's proposal to renew the old observational instruments to enhance observing efficiency and accuracy was approved Qubilai.

On the sixth day of the second lunar month of the sixteenth year of zhiyuan, Wang Xun and Guo Shoujing pleaded with Qubilai to install the new astronomical devices they had made in areas around Shangdu and Luoyang. And they proposed to staff each observatory with Astronomical Observers. Qubilai also approved.

Guo Shoujing applied his engineering skills to a batch of skillfully

元代城市
生活长卷

The Urban Life of the
Yuan Dynasty

contrived astronomical devices.

He revised the armillary sphere, whose three major rings representing the celestial equator, the meridian and the ecliptic were fixed together with up to 9 rings of different sizes huddled in the globe they formed, and devised the abridged armillary by simplifying the ecliptic ring and separating the ring of meridian from that of the celestial equator, making it more convenient to use.

Yang Yi (Projection Semi-sphere) was a creation by Guo Shoujing to observe the solar eclipse. The instrument is a metal semi-sphere resembling an upturned pot with its mouth carved with marks indicating the four directions and time, and its internal spherical surface with lines designating the latitude. A plate with a small hole supported by two sticks attached to the mouth of the pot would then be placed on the surface of the mouth with its hole just aiming at the center of the semi-sphere. When the sunlight goes through the hole, it will project the image of the sun onto the internal spherical surface. Then the observer can read the sun's position from the scale. Moreover, both the exact position and size of the eclipse at different times can also be measured.

Gui Biao (Gnomon) is the astronomical instrument used to observe the length of the shadow cast by the sun so as to determine the time of the vernal and autumnal equinoxes and the summer and winter solstices. The gnomon consisted of two parts, gui and biao. The "biao" is an upstanding post, while the "gui" is a south-north lying ruler or dial. The biao of the gnomon made in the Song Dynasty only measured 8 chi in length. To enhance the precision of projection, Guo Shoujing made a new gnomon called Gao Biao. He lengthened the biao to 36 chi and added a crossbar which was held by two bronze dragons over it. Thus the entire length of biao was prolonged to 40 chi, five times as long as the original one. He also improved the scale of gui, graduating it into millimeters.

In addition, Guo also revised and devised many other astronomical instruments, such as the Square Table, Pole-observing Instrument, Time-determining Instrument, and Suspended Standard Instrument.

Guo later advised Qubilai to carry out observational tests in different areas for astronomical changes. He said, "according to the historical record, monk Yi Xing in the Tang Dynasty established 13 observatories to observe the heaven. Now Your Majesty reins a territory far vaster than that of the Tang Dynasty. If we don't install observatories in those far-flung areas, we would never know the exact difference between areas in time, degree of the solar and lunar eclipses and the length of day and night. Therefore I beg Your Majesty to launch a large-scale project to measure the astronomical changes throughout the country."

Qubilai agreed and entrusted Guo Shoujing with the project. Guo then constructed a total 27 observatories throughout the country and staffed every observatory or every two observatories an Astronomical Observer. These observatories were located in Dadu, Shangdu, Xijing (modern Datong, Shanxi Province), Beijing (modern Ningcheng in Inner Mongolia), Taiyuan, Yidu, Dengzhou (modern Penglai in Shangdong Province), Daming, Dongping, Henan, Residence of Prince of Anxi (in modern Xi'an, Shanxi province), Chengdu, Yangzhou, Ezhou, and Leizhou, etc. Besides, Guo also installed observatories in the far north of the steppes, in the Uighur area in the west, in Korea in the east, in Yunnan and Tibet in the southwest and in Qiongzhou in the south.

At the winter solstice of the seventeenth year of zhiyuan, Xu Heng, Wang Xun and Guo Shoujing finally compiled the new calendar which synthesized the best of science at that time based on their astronomical observations and the previous celestial almanacs. On the twenty-sixth day of the eleventh lunar month of the same year, Qubilai issued an edict to promote the new calendar and named it "Shoushi Calendar".

元代城市
生活长卷

The Urban Life of the
Yuan Dynasty

5

After Qubilai's coronation, the Hanlin Academician Recipient of Edicts Wang E proposed that the historical records of the Liao and Jin dynasties as well as those of the early Mongolian rulers be collected. He said: "Since time immemorial, the achievements and errors of every emperor have been recorded into the history books, which enabled us to learn from the past. And if we didn't write a dynastic history now, all the remarkable feats accomplished by the previous emperors since Emperor Taizu would be forgotten over time. Although Shi Lu, the history of the Jin Dynasty which recorded quite a few good policies of the Jin emperors is still extent, many historical records of the Liao Dynasty have lost. We could destroy a country but not its history. If we didn't establish a History Office, people in the future would never know what really happened today."

Qubilai attached great importance to Wang E's proposal. In 1261, the second year of zhangtong, he established the Hanli and Historiography Academy to compose the dynastic history as well as the histories of the Liao and Jin dynasties. The Hanli and Historiography Academy mainly consisted of the Chinese Confucians. Its governing body was comprised of Hanlin Academician Recipient of Edict, Hanlin Academician, Hanlin Academician Reader-in-waiting, Hanlin Academician Expositor-in-waiting, and Hanlin Auxiliary Academician, who were assisted by such officials as Academician Awaiting Instruction, Hanlin Senior Compiler, Hanlin Provisioner and Hanlin Junior Compilor, etc. Apart from composing the dynastic history, the Hanlin and Historiography Academy was also responsible for drafting the imperial edicts and offering advices to the Emperor

Sheng Wu Qin Zheng Lu (Record of the Personal Campaigns of the Sagely Militant), composed in the early years of zhiyuan, recorded the feats achieved by Chinggis Khan and Ogedei Khan and in the meanwhile attested to the valuable contributions the Hanlin and Historiography

Academy had made to the dynastic history compilation. But the Academy was up against a serious problem, the problem of determining the legitimate predecessor of the Yuan Dynasty, when composing the histories of the previous dynasties. The problem had already caused great difficulty to the compilation of the histories of the Liao and Jin dynasties. It became all the more urgent when the Southern Song Dynasty had fallen and the compilation of the history of the Song Dynasty was also imminent.

The Confucian officials were called for a discussion of the problem by Qubilai. Soon there formed three different views. One group held it that the legitimate predecessor of Yuan should be the Song Dynasty because Yuan was founded after the conquest of Song, and that they derived from the same origin. The second group argued that they should follow the practice of the Tang Dynasty by classifying the Liao and Jin dynasties as the Northern Dynasty and Song as the Southern Dynasty, and that both would be the legitimate predecessors of Yuan. The third group rejected the eligibility of the Jin and Song dynasties for the legitimate predecessors of Yuan on the grounds that Yuan was already established before the fall of Jin and Song.

Every group tried to prove their point by quoting from the classics. And the discussion escalated into a fierce debate. Having found none of the three arguments plausible after careful consideration, Qubilai decided to put aside the question of legitimate predecessor and stop the futile discussion. He halted the compilation of the histories of the Liao, Jin and Song dynasties and at the same time, set the Hanli and Historiography Academy to compose the Ping Jin Lu (Pacification of the Jin Dynasty) and Ping Song Lu (Pacification of the Song Dynasty) and to collect the historical records of the Song, Liao and Jin dynasties. But the question of the legitimate predecessor of the Yuan Dynasty wasn't settled until the late Yuan Dynasty.

6

Jingim, the Heir Apparent of Qubilai Khan, was a tragic figure on the Yuan political stage.

Born the second son of Qubilai, Jingim had been tutored by such masters of the Neo-Confucianism as Yao Shu and Dou Mo ever since he was a child. Thus he was deeply influenced by the Chinese culture.

In the twelfth lunar month of 1262, the third year of zhongtong, Jingim was made Prince of Yan and concurrent Director of the Secretariat. In the next year, the Bureau of Military Affairs was established, and Jingim was appointed Military Affairs Commissioner.

In the seventh year of zhiyuan, Jingim toured the areas to the north of the Gobi Desert on Qubilai's orders, accompanied by an entourage including Bayan. On their way there, Jingim, the Imperial Prince Zha Lahu and their subordinates including Bayan and Sa Liman chattered about their mottos. Zha Lahu said, "Our ancestors have instructed that 'a tree should be measured from the top to the roots'. That probably means in doing anything, you must go through it from start to finish and never drop it half way." Bayan said, "As His Majesty (Qubilai) has instructed, deception and theft are the two most vicious crimes in the world. Because a deceiver would never be trusted again; and a theft would never have a clear conscience." Sa Liman said, "As Emperor Taizu has instructed, to cure the body, you should first cure the heart; before reprimanding others, you should first examine yourself." And Jingim started, "As His Majesty has instructed, never aim too high, for a vaulting ambition always goes before a fall. And I have noticed that Confucius had also expressed the same idea as His Majesty." (Biography of Emperor Yuzong, Vol. 115, YS)

Jingim, just as his motto has reflected, was very discreet. He not only was cultivated, modest, thrifty, and sympathetic with the people, but also knew well how to behave. Although he was made the head of the Secretariat and the Bureau of Military Affairs, he never interfered with the state affairs, for he knew only too well what he adopted were merely nominal positions.

In the tenth year of zhiyuan, Jingim was made Heir Apparent to succeed Qubilai. Before long the Eastern Palace was set up and the Imperial Guard of the Eastern Palace was established for him. At that time, someone proposed to build a fountain in the Eastern Palace, but it was immediately rejected by Jingim who found it reminiscent of the ancient tyrant's "Wine Pool and Meat Forest". Even though Jingim was officially appointed Heir Apparent, he still refused to participate in the state affairs for fear that he should arouse Qubilai's suspicion. So he simply concentrated on the discussion of the Confucian classics with the Confucian officials.

In the sixteenth year of zhiyuan, Qubilai decreed that Jingim should participate in the court administration, and that the Secretariat, the Bureau of Military Affairs, the Censorate and all the other government agencies should first report to the Heir Apparent and then to him. All the Confucian officials thrilled at the news, for they thought they could rely on Jingim to raise their status in the imperial court. Jingim, however, became all the more discreet, because he knew that sometimes appearances were deceptive.

And his presentiment soon became a reality. The Chinese officials in the imperial court were hostile of the Manager of Government Affairs Ahmad. They considered him villainous and accused him of profiteering, cronyism and monopolizing power. But their resentment against Ahmad only served to arouse a growing antipathy in Qubilai, who was always partial to Ahmad, towards them. These Han officials, therefore, decided to get rid of Ahmad.

In 1282, the nineteenth year of zhiyuan, Wang Zhu, a Chinese

元代城市
生活长卷

The Urban Life of the
Yuan Dynasty

382

Battalion Commander, and Gao Heshang (Monk Gao) developed a plot to kill Ahmad with the support of some Chinese officials. With Qubilai and Jingim departed for Shangdu, on the early morning of April 27, eighteenth day of the third lunar month, a cabal of Chinese conspirators suddenly arrived in Dadu, announcing that Jingim was returning for a matter of great urgency, and that Ahmad, the Regent in Dadu, should go to welcome him. Perplexed, Ahmad hurried to greet the false "Jingim", and was killed by Wang Zhu with a hammer who had pretended to be Jingim's retainer. Besides, Ahmad's cronies in Dadu were also killed in this coup d'état.

The citizenry of Dadu thrilled at the death of Ahmad. They celebrated by drinking and singing. And it is recorded that all the wine was sold out in the market in Dadu at that time.

But Qubilai was furious at the news. He immediately sent people to Dadu to capture the conspirators including Gao Heshang, Wang Zhu and the Chinese official Zhang Yi, all of whom were executed by Qubilai. Before his execution, Wang Zhu cried out to heaven, "today I die for eliminating the public scourge. Tomorrow I would be remembered in history." He was right. Shortly after his death, poems and prose were composed to commemorate him, such as the Yi Xia Xing (Hero).

Although Qubilai finally acknowledged Ahmad's treachery, he didn't probe into it. And although the Confucian officials finally turned Qubilai against Ahmad, they didn't win any favor from Qubilai who in fact became more indifferent to them. As for Jingim, the supporter of the Confucian officials, he was also affected by this event. Later a blundering official unwisely composed a memorial to the throne, in which he advised Qubilai to abdicate in favor of Jingim. It naturally infuriated Qubilai. Extremely frightened, Jingim fell ill and died in the twenty-second year of zhiyuan.

| **Mongol Princes Died Early**

Although the Mongol royal members had high political status and lived in affluence in the city under the care of Qubilai, a majority of them didn' t live long.

1

In the Yuan Dynasty, all the males of Chinggis Khan' s Golden Family became princes and all the female princesses. And the husbands of these princesses, mostly Mongol nobles, had the title "Commandant-escort".

The Mongol Imperial Princes, Imperial Princesses and Commandants-escort were of high standing. They not only had appanage and people of their own, but also could expect abundant awards from the Emperor.

Every year, the Emperor would accord gold, silver, money and a variety of silk to the Imperial Princes, Imperial consorts and concubines, Imperial Princesses and Commandants-escort. Such awards were called the annual grant. With the increase in the number of the royal members the total amount of the annual grant expanded dramatically. In 1260, the first year of zhongtong under Emperor Shizu, the total amount of the annual grant was 1,217 ding of silver, 3,050 bolts of satin, 141 ding of

元代城市
生活长卷

The Urban Life of the
Yuan Dynasty

paper money, 5,148 jin of silk, and 5,098 bolts of silk tabby. In 1289, the twenty-sixth year of zhiyuan, the total amount of the annual grant grew to 2,000 liang of gold, 252,630 liang of silver, 110,290 ding of paper money and 122,800 bolts of satin.

Apart from the annual grant, the Emperor would confer on them a wide range of other awards. Among them, the award given at the court assemblies, especially the Emperor's coronation was the most lavish.

For example, when Jingim's son Temür ascended to the throne after Qubilai's death, he was advised by an official of the Secretariat to quintuple the gold and triple the silver in the awards for the Imperial Princes and Commandants-escort. The proposal was approved by the new emperor. He awarded each Imperial Prince, such as the Xiping Prince, Ningyuan Prince and Zhennan Prince, 500 liang of gold, 5,000 liang of silver, 2,000 ding of paper money and 400 bolts of silk fabrics. And he awarded the Commandant-escort Man Zitai 76,500 liang of silver and the Commandant-escort Korguz 15,450 liang of silver. Even the King of Korea which was the vassal state of the Yuan Dynasty was awarded 30,000 liang of silver. A financial stringency ensued from the Emperor's generous awards. And before long he was faced with an urgent report from the Secretariat which told him "there was only 270,000 ding of paper money left after the coronation grant." (Section one, Biography of Emperor Chengzong, Vol. 18, YS)

When Temür, Emperor Chengzong died, Khayisan, Emperor Wuzong succeeded him. Khayisan then decreed that all the relatives of the imperial family be awarded on the scale of that of Emperor Chengzong. In fact, before his coronation in Shangdu, Khayisan had already awarded the Imperial Princes in Qara-qorum. Therefore some officials of Secretariat proposed to cancel the grant to those who had already been awarded in Qara-qorum. But Khayisan rejected the proposal. Soon he received a report from the Secretariat. It read, "we are facing a massive deficit! The annual revenue of the state is 4,000,000 ding of paper money, of which 3,800,000 ding goes to the imperial court and about 2,700,000 ding is used to cover the state expenditure. But now 4,200,000 ding of paper money has already been spent since the accession of Your Majesty and these is still an expenditure of 1,000,000 ding of paper money waiting to be covered. Faced with a plausible financial crisis, we had no choice but to report it to Your Majesty." Only until then did Khayisan cancel the large-scale awards. (Section one, Biography of Emperor Wuzong, Vol. 22, YS)

The coronation grant, however, grew increasingly lavish under the reign of the succeeding Yuan emperors. Taking Emperor Renzong for example, the awards he accorded during his coronation included 39,650 liang of gold, 1,849,050 liang of silver, 223,279 ding of paper money and 472,488 bolts of silk fabrics. This amount slightly dropped after the accession of Emperor Yingzong who awarded the Imperial Princes 5,000 liang of gold, 780,000 liang of silver, 121,100 guan of paper money, 57,364 bolts of satin, 49,322 bolts of other silk fabrics, 92,672 bolts of silk cotton and 23,398 bolts of cloth.

Such lavish grant not only undermined the state finances but also placed a heavy burden on the vast populace.

2

Historical sources reveal an evident decline in the longevity of the Yuan royal members. During the era of Mongol Empire, Chinggis Khan died at 66, Ogedei Khan at 56, Güyük Khan at 43, and Mongke Khan at 52. In the Yuan Dynasty, Qubilai, the only long-lived Yuan Emperor died at 80, Temür (Emperor Chengzong) made 42, Khayisan (Emperor Taiding) reached only 31, Ayurbarwada (Emperor Renzong) died at 36, Sudibala (Emperor Yingzong) died at 21, Yesün Temür (Emperor Taiding) at 36,

元代城市
生活长卷

The Urban Life of the
Yuan Dynasty

Khuslen (Emperor Mingzong) at 30, Tugh Temür (Emperor Wenzong) at 29, Rinchinbal (Emperor Ningzong) at only 7, and Toghun Temür (Emperor Shundi) at 51. Of all these Mongol emperors, no one, except Qubilai, lived longer than Chinggis khan, with many suffered a poor health such as Emperor Wuzong, Emperor Renzong, Emperor Wenzong and Emperor Chengzong whose Empress usually acted as a regent because of his ill health, some died unnatural deaths in the competition for the imperial throne such as Güyük Khan, Emperor Yingzong, Emperor Mingzong and some died prematurely, such as Emperor Ningzong.

A similar pattern could be observed with the other Mongol royal members. Taking the descendants of Qubilai for example, Jingim died at 43, his eldest son Gammala at 40, and his second son Darmabala at 29. And many Imperial Princes of the succeeding emperors after Emperor Chengzong died prematurely, such as Deshou who died 6 months later after he was made Heir Apparent in the sixth lunar month in 1305, ninth year of dade under Emperor Chengzong, the second son of Emperor Renzong, the four sons of Emperor Taiding, the three sons of Emperor Wenzong, and Emperor Shundi's son Zhengjin who died at only two.

Besides, the same thing also happened to the families of some Mongol and semuren dignitaries. For example, Muqali died at 54, his son Bo'al at 32 and Bo'al's son at 28. And very few of the descendants of Muqali lived up to 50.

Among the various causes of the truncated lives of the Mongol royal members and nobles, unacclimatization and consanguineous marriage are the two major objective reasons. The hot summer in the Central Plains and Jiangnan Region didn't agree with the Mongols who had grown up on the steppes. And even those Mongols who were born in the Central Plains or Jiangnan couldn't immediately adapt to the climate and lifestyle there. That's why the Yuan royal members would spend their summer in Shangdu every year. The Mongol tribes usually maintained a constant marital relationship with one another, which inevitably resulted in consanguineous marriages. And because of the consanguineous marriage, the population quality of the Mongol royal family decreased rapidly.

Some habits and customs the Mongol nobles kept also damaged their health. The Mongols were given to heavy drinking which ruined their health. Although some Mongols, having realized the harm of the wine, abstained from drinking, they still had to attend the feasts characterized by binge drinking held by the Emperor. For example, Baiju, the Grand Councilor of the Right under Emperor Yingzong, never drank. "He would frown whenever a Provisioner offered him the wine." "The other day he went to the imperial palace to attend the imperial feast, during which he was forced to drink by Emperor Yingzong who knew that Baiju didn't drink. When Baiju returned home, his mother said, "His Majesty urged you to drink only to test your drinking capacity. You should stay sober and be not addicted to alcohol." (Biography of Baiju, Vol. 136, YS) Baiju's mother was indeed a great mother, for very few Mongols would ask their children to abstain from wine. In addition, constant indulgence in hunting and sensual pleasures also ruined health. El-Temür, the powerful and domineering minister during the reign of Emperor Wenzong, was a typical example. He had many wives, concubines, and numerous sexual companies, and he finally died of excessive indulgence in sex.

3

Chinggis Khan once consulted the Quanzhen Taoist Qiu Chuji about immortality. Qiu said, "there is no pill of immortality. To achieve longevity, one should purify one's heart, reduce one's desires and restrain from killing. Qiu actually revealed the secret of keeping in good health for Chinggis Khan who readily accepted and even agreed to moderate hunting, an integral part of the Mongol traditional customs,

under the influence of Qiu Chuji.

The Chinese had developed a serious of theories and methods to maintain good health, but not the Mongols. Thus both the Mongol Empire and the Yuan Dynasty saw many works on keeping in good health, among which the Yin Shan Zheng Yao (Proper and Essential Things for the Emperor's Food and Diet) was the most famous. It was a cookbook written by the Uighur Hu Sihui who was an imperial dietary physician. Hu Sihui introduced many nutritional recipes in his book based on his eclectic knowledge of different dietary customs and also formed his own theory of how to maintain good health.

Much of the Yin Shan Zheng Yao was concerned with the nutritional value of food and recipes and proper and sanitary ways of eating. According to Hu Sihui, the reason for Qubilai's longevity lay in his imperial dietary physicians' proper arrangement of his food and drinking.

To change the Mongols' habit of excessive drinking, Hu Sihui especially expounded on the danger of binge drinking— "excessive indulgence in drinking paved the way to the hell." He also listed a series of don'ts after drinking, such as riding, jumping, shouting, drinking cold water, eating cheese, sleeping outside, taking a bath, etc.

Hu Sihui also highly valued the traditional way of keeping in good health which stressed the importance of both the living conditions and health protection. He then introduced several setting-up exercises to maintain good health, such as self-massage, washing the eyes, brushing the teeth and combing the hair, etc.

However, now matter how convincing Hu Sihui's laws of health sounded, very few Mongol nobles seriously followed them in their life.

Fierce court conflict, especially the internecine fighting caused by frequent changing of power since Emperor Chengzong, resulted in a lot of deaths among the royal members.

After Emperor Chengzong's demise, his Empress Bulugan attempted to set up Ananda, Prince of An'xi, but failed. When Emperor Wuzong ascended to the throne, Bulugan, Ananda and their retainers were all executed.

Emperor Yingzong began to reform the government with the help of the Grand Councilor of the Right Baiju after his coronation. Some of his reforms, however, threatened the interests of some Mongol and semuren nobles. Therefore a group of dignitaries headed by the Censor-in-chief Tegshi decided to plot against Emperor Yingzong and Baiju.

On September 4, 1323, the fourth day of the eighth lunar month of the third year of zhizhi, Emperor Yingzong and Baiju encamped at Nanpo on their way back from Shangdu to Dadu. In the night, Tegshi and his men with the help of the Asut Guard stormed the imperial camp and killed Emperor Yingzong and Baiju. Never had such incident in which the emperor was assassinated by his retainers happened before in the Yuan history. And it was later known as the coup d'état at Nanpo.

However, no conspirator of this coup came to a good end. After the accession of Emperor Taiding, all those who had participated in the assassination of Emperor Yingzong were arrested and executed.

A larger-scale internecine was triggered by the competition for the throne between the two capitals after the demise of Emperor Taiding.

In the first year of zhihe, Emperor Taiding made an imperial expedition tour of Shangdu in spite of illness and died on the tenth day of the seventh lunar month in Shangdu. His son Ragibagh succeeded to the throne in Shangdu with the support of Emperor Taiding's entourage,

元代城市
生活长卷

The Urban Life of the
Yuan Dynasty

390

such as the Assistant Director of the Left of Secretariat Dawlat Shah, Prince of Liang Wangchan, Prince of Liao Toktoghan. Meanwhile the Assistant Military Affairs Commissioner El-Temür of the Qipchaq, together with the Prince of Xi'an launched a coup d'état in Dadu. All the Regents in Dadu were taken prisoner by El-Temür who then sent emissaries to Jiangnan to invite Tugh Temür, the second son of Emperor Wuzong, to succeed the throne in Dadu.

A war soon broke out between the two forces. In the eighth lunar month of the same year, several military forces of Shangdu headed south to attack Dadu. And El-Temür dispatched the armies in Dadu to fight back. In the next month, Tugh Temür ascended the throne in Dadu, while Ragibagh enthroned himself in Shangdu.

The military forces of Shangdu launched several attacks on Dadu between the early ninth lunar month and the early tenth lunar month, taking such pivotal passes as Juyong Pass, Gubei Pass and Zijing Pass near Dadu. To ensure the safety of Dadu, El-Temür took command in person and fought off the repeated attacks.

The situation was suddenly reversed in the mid tenth lunar month when the Prince Qi Orlug Temür who was on Tugh Temür's side launched a surprise attack on Shangdu from the east of Liaoning Peninsula and forced Dawlat Shah to surrender. Dawlat shah was then taken to Dadu where he was executed. Dawlat Shah's death soon brought about the crushing defeat of all the other forces of Shangdu and, with that, the end of the civil war between the two capitals.

However, hardly had the civil war been stopped when another tragedy was staged between Tugh Temür and his brother Kuala.

While the two capitals were heavily engaged in war, Kuala chose to stay in areas to the north of the Gobi Desert, patiently watching the progress of the war. When the outcome was a foregone conclusion, Tugh Temür sent envoys to areas to the north of the Gobi Desert to invite Kuala to succeed the throne in Dadu. Kuala readily accepted the invitation and ascended the throne in Qara-qorum in the first lunar month of the next year, with Tugh Temür declaring abdication in Dadu at the same time. Two months later, Kuala left Qara-qorum for Shangdu. Meanwhile, he summoned Tugh Temür and El-Temür to Shangdu for an audience and asked them to prepare the grant he was to confer on the other imperial princes.

A new conspiracy, however, had come into being when Kuala expectantly headed south to Shangdu. Tugh Temür was actually unwilling to abdicate the throne and El-Temür also feared that he might be stripped of power. The two therefore conspired to murder Kuala to reclaim the throne. In the third lunar month, El-Temür left Dadu to bring the imperial seal to Kuala by way of welcome; and Tugh Temür also left Dadu for Shangdu to welcome Kuala. All these submissive gestures on the part of Tugh Temür and El-Temür served to fog Kuala's mind. The plan of the two Temürs worked out successfully. On the first day of the eighth lunar month, the indiscreet Emperor arrived in Ongghuchad; in the next day he had an audience with Tugh Temür. And on the sixth day, Kuala suddenly died. Tugh Temür was then escorted to Shangdu by El-Temür and restored to the throne on the fifteenth day of the eighth lunar month.

Tugh Temür, remorseful for what he had done to his elder brother Kuala, expressed his intention to pass the throne to the sons of Kuala on his deathbed. Kuala had two sons—Toghun Temür and Rinchinbal, a seven-year-old. Kuala's second son Rinchinbal was then installed by El-Temür because Toghun Temür was then far away from Dadu and, more importantly, too mature a puppet for El-Temür to control. However, Rinchinbal shortly died only two months after his enthronement. Thus Toghun Temür was summoned to Dadu by El-Temür who was pressured into doing it by the other courtiers. But El-Temür deliberately postponed the official investiture of Toghun Temür as Emperor for nearly half a year,

元代城市
生活长卷

The Urban Life of the
Yuan Dynasty

392

and during that time he became the de facto ruler of the imperial court. It was only after El-Temür's death that Toghun Temür was able to ascend the throne in Shangdu.

| **Parting the City in Tears**

When confronted with the powerful Ming armies, the Mongols were forced to abandon the city, retreat to the steppes and return to their former nomadic life. Only on the point of the departure did they realize how strong their attachment was to the city.

1

The Yuan Dynasty under the rule of Toghun Temür was on the wane, and everything about the government suggested a plausible collapse.

The factional struggle in the imperial court intensified even after the enthronement of Toghun Temür, for though El-Temür was dead, his family continued to monopolize prerogative in the imperial court with his daughter installed as the Empress of the new Emperor and his son Tanggisi an influential courtier. To free himself from the control of the family of El-Temür, Toghun Temür allied Bayan of the Merkid tribe and placed him in a post higher than that of Tanggisi. Infuriated by this gesture of Toghun Temür, Tanggisi decided to get rid of Bayan and dethrone Toghun Temür through a coup. He even clamored, "All under heaven belongs my family, how dare Bayan, a nonentity, ride roughshod over me!"

元代城市
生活长卷

The Urban Life of the
Yuan Dynasty

In the sixth lunar month of 1335, the first year of zhiyuan. Tanggisi started a coup d'état in Dadu, of which Bayan had already been aware. Thus Tanggisi instead got himself killed by Bayan in an ambush when he broke into the imperial palace. With Empress Danashri, the daughter of El-Temür, poisoned to death by Bayan after her brother's rebellion, the family of El-Temür was at last exterminated by Toghun Temür.

However, Bayan was no less autocratic when he was in power. According to the historical record, he came to hold an awesome range of concurrent official positions over important central organs and his official title consisted of as many as 246 letters. "A majority of articles of tribute to the imperial court and tax revenue flew to the family of Bayan. His partisans occupied the most important positions in the government. Every time after the court assembly, he would be escorted by big crowds of the other court officials as he left the hall." As Toghun Temür grew, he came to disfavor Bayan's autocratic rule. He then began to put his trust in Bayan's nephew Toghtogha by promoting him to important positions. In the second lunar month of 1340, the sixth year of zhiyuan, when Bayan was out hunting, he was removed from all his offices and banished by Toghun Temür.

Growing factionalism at the imperial court severely disintegrated the political cohesion of the Yuan court, and rampant corruption and exploitation intensified the social contradictions. All these together with a succession of natural calamities, such as droughts, floods especially those caused by the broken dikes of the Yellow River, and ensuing famines, led to several rebellions and uprisings. The Yuan Dynasty was by then on the very verge of collage.

In 1351, the eleventh year of zhizheng, the mansion of the Yuan Dynasty shattered in a wave of nationwide revolts that were triggered by an armed insurrection led by Han Shantong and Liu Futong in Yingzhou.

But the regular Yuan armies by this time had grown too decadent to defend the country from these upheavals. Just as someone has pointed out, "Nowadays the descendants of the Mongol generals tend to lead a luxurious and dissipated life. What they inherited from their ancestors is only an underserved title. They are good at nothing but singing, drinking and womanizing." (CMZ) The Yuan armies suffered heavy casualties after several large-scale but futile attempts to suppress the uprisings and became rather vulnerable to attacks.

2

Before long, the insurrectionary armies began to direct their attack at the Yuan capitals. In the twelfth lunar month of 1358, the eighteenth year of zhizheng, an insurrectionary army captured Shangdu. The imperial palace was burnt down during the war, which forced the Emperor to cancel his annual trip to Shangdu in summer.

The fall of Shangdu took a heavy toll on the Yuan Dynasty.

Toghun Temür, however, was not worried at all because he was at that moment indulging in the sexual rites of Tibetan Buddhism. And he chose many women throughout the country to "practice Buddhism" with him in the houses he especially built for such Buddhist rites. Beside, he also selected a hundred beauties who "were dressed in finery to play music, sing Buddhist scriptures and dance" for him. And the top sixteen girls of them were called the Sixteen Deities. When the officials in the court pleaded with Toghun Temür not to participate in such activities, he refused to listen and even constructed a tunnel between his sleeping quarters and the house where he secretly "practiced Buddhism". (GSWS)

Only when the Ming armies under the command of Zhu Yuanzhang began to press on towards Dadu in the intercalary seventh lunar month of the seventh year of zhizheng, did Toghun Temür realize what was really going on. On September 10, 1368, he summoned all the imperial consorts and concubines and the imperial princes to Qingning Hall for a discussion of a retreat from Dadu to the north. Unexpectedly, his proposal met with a lot of objection from the officials. One of them even said, "Your Majesty ought to defend the country with your life, because it is the country that was established by Emperor Shizu! We would go outside to fight against the rebels with our soldiers, people and the Keshikten, if only Your Majesty would stay in the capital with your people." (Section ten, Biography of Emperor Shundi, Vol. 47, YS) But Toghun Temür had already made up his mind to escape and he fled to the north in the same night via Jiande Gate with his consorts and concubines and Heir Apparent. On September 14, the second day of the eighth lunar month, the Ming armies occupied Dadu, marking the fall of the Yuan Dynasty.

3

Toghun Temür and his entourage escaped to Shangdu where they could only dwell in tents, for the imperial palace had already been destroyed. On July 20, 1369, the Ming armies captured Shangdu and Toghun Temür escaped to Yingchang. On his way to Yingchang, he bewailed over the loss of his country and the two capitals:

Dadu, a city of treasure, pure and elegant,
My Shangdu in sira tala, the summer camp of my ancestors,
My cool and homelike Shangdu in Kaiping,
My warm and beautiful Dadu.
...
Those foolish Noyans have all retreated to their countries,
Leaving me behind on his land like a new calf.
I wailed but what's the use of that?

The exquisite and eight-faceted white pagoda,

My elaborately constructed Dadu,

Telling the stories of the mighty Empire,

The rectangular Dadu,

The pride of my four million Mongol fellows,

Are now lost in my hands,

In the process of spreading Buddhism.

Oh, my lovely Dadu,

Please forgive my incompetence.

...

The holy Cane Palace,

Shangdu, the summer capital of Qubilai Khan,

Were all lost to the Han Chinese,

And I, Ukhaantu Khan, will be accused of being greedy.

My great Dadu which was built by my people,

Where I spent the winters,

Is now lost to the Han Chinese.

And I, Ukhaantu Khan, will be accused of despotism.

The elaborately constructed Dadu,

The summer resort Shangdu,

Are now lost to the Han Chinese due to my mistake.

And I, Ukhaantu Khan, will be accused of exile.

The mighty Khanate,

The lovely Dadu, founded by Se?en Qayan,

The sacrificial center of the world,

Are now lost to the Han Chinese.

The lovely Dadu,

The Golden Family of Chinggis Khan, the Son of Heaven,

The shrine of the embodiment of Buddha Se?en Qayan,

The embodiment of Buddha Uqayatu Qauan,

元代城市
生活长卷

The Urban Life of the
Yuan Dynasty

398

Are lost by the mandate of Heaven.

…

The lovely Dadu is lost due to my imprudence,

Hope the Buddhist religion left behind in Dadu,

Would flourish again in the later generations,

And Chinggis Khan's lineage would last for ever.

(HYMGHJSG, pp. 43-45)

No matter how remorseful he was, Toghun Temür could never return to the former magnificent Dadu and Shangdu. He died of illness in Yingchang a year later. Before long, the Ming armies came to attack Yingchang. The Heir Apparent hurriedly fled with some retainers and the Yuan remnants dispersed in panic. From then on, the Mongols ended their sedentary life in the city and resumed their nomadic life on the steppes.

1 Title of the chief of the Xiongnu in ancient China.

2 An earthen wine vessel in ancient China with a narrow mouth and a bulging midsection.

3 A bell-shaped percussion instrument with a long handle.

4 Here it refers to the zhongtong yunabao jiaochao (primary treasure exchange note of the zhongtong era) which was a paper currency issued in the Yuan Dynasty during the zhongtong period under Qubilai.

5 A long front cloth panel attached from the waist belt.

6 It was annotated by the author of the book.

7 The term "guan" traditionally is an umbrella term to encompass all forms of headgear which covers the hair of the wearer (whether partially or entirely). It makes use of a hairpin which goes across a topknot of hair to stabilize itself, and is coupled with a sash tied underneath the chin.

8 It is originally a guan for judges. Xiezhi is an abstraction for the

fabled goat which is reputed to be able to distinguish between good and evil, hence a fitting symbol for judges.

9 Liang Guan (ridged guan) is ridged according to the status of the official: seven ridges for the first rank, six for the second rank, five for the third rank, four for the fourth rank, three for the fifth rank, two for the sixth and seventh ranks, and one for the eighth and ninth ranks.

10 "Futou" refers to the head cloth used to wrap the head. It is fastened with an attached cloth sash that wraps around the top knot, and can be fastened to the back or in the front.

11 "Hu" refers to the tablet held before the breast b officials in ancient times when received in audience by the emperor.

12 The "jin" is a piece of headgear made from cloth, and is traditionally a turban wrapped around the top of the head or the topknot. The primary difference between jin and guan is that jin do not use a hairpin to stabilize itself. Instead it relies on the head itself, or a set of drawstrings (sashes) to wrap or tie itself around the head or topknot.

13 Jin with the use of frames could also be called "ze", and are deemed more formal than the unframed ones.

14 Zaju refers to a poetic drama flourishing in the Yuan Dynasty consisting of four acts called zhe, evolving form a type of comic show in the Song Dynasty.

15 A long full body garment.

16 It was also called "variety entertainments". It is a kind of drama performance interspersed with songs, dances, and acrobatics.

17 The hat baoli was a li resembling a bass cymbal.

18 A guan worn by high-ranking officials, square and with a zhantou (the frontal display portion where décor or ridges are displayed).

19 It was the unit of length employed by Egyptians. It was originally based on measuring by comparing to one's forearm length.

20 Pyramid-shaped dumpling made of glutinous rice wrapped in

bamboo or reed leaves, usually eaten during the Dragon Boat Festival.

21 Round flat cake.

22 Steamed dumpling with the dough gathered at the top.

23 Qi in Traditional Chinese Medicine refers to the vital energy of the body.

24 It is a kind of fiat money used in the Yuan Dynasty. "Zhongtong" was the reign title of Emperor Qubilai Khan; "yuan bao" referred to a kind of gold and silver coin upon which the paper currency was based; and "jiaochao" meant money.

25 Recall and Restore (to previously occupied post) is a term indicates that someone of official status and with a record of prior service, having been out of active service in formal mourning for a parent or sometimes other reasons, was called to service and restored to his most recent post and rank.

26 The tablet held before the breast by officials when received in audience by the emperor.

27 A general in the period of the Three Kingdoms.

28 It was a game played by the children before the New Year's Eve. Maimeng in Chinese means "selling naivety". In the game children would call anyone they saw in the street, but the person who was called was not supposed to answer them, because if he did he would be considered naive.

29 It was a type of song or tune popular in the Yuan, Ming and Qing dynasties.

30 An ancient weapon made of bamboo.

Author's Afterword

During the ten long years when I was sent to work and "be educated" in the countryside, never in a single day had I ceased thinking of the city where I was born and bred. In order to be able to "return to the city" I had made strenuous efforts. However, when I was at last resurrounded by the hustling city, I found part of me longing for the tranquility of the countryside.

Such mixed feelings about life of city and the countryside have been shared by people throughout history, and are definitely a subject worth writing.

People, especially those of a different ethnic or cultural background, have different understanding of the urban life, which is especially true in ancient times. Yet it is from the perspective of "exoticism" that the entire book tries to reveal the nomads' judgment of the value of city and the new look the city took on after their assimilation into the city in the Yuan Dynasty, which in turn shaped the city life of the Ming and Qing dynasties.

When writing this book, I received considerable support and help from Mr. Chen Gaohua from the Institute of History, CASS. Here I'd like to extend my sincere thanks to Mr. Chen, without whose in-depth studies of such aspects of the Yuan Dynasty as diet and recreation, I would never have been able to complete this book.

My heartfelt thanks also go to Mr. Zhou Liangxiao from the Institute of Modern History, CASS, and Mr. Bai Gang from the Institute of Politics, CASS. Mr. Zhou helped me coordinate with the press. And it is Mr. Bai's encouragement and assistance that help accelerate the writing

元代城市
生活长卷

The Urban Life of the
Yuan Dynasty

of the book after my transference to the Institute of Politics. Besides, there are Chen Baoliang from the China Social Sciences Press and Zhao Shiyu from the History Department of Beijing Normal University. They are respectively the authors of the Urban Life in Ming China and Urban Life in Qing China. They, too, had my thanks for their constant support and stimulation.

Last but not least, I'd like to thank the leadership and working staff of Hunan People's Publishing House for their hardworking in editing and publishing this set of books—The Urban Life in Ancient China.

The book is about to be published, yet I know it's only my initial attempt in this field. And I'm earnestly looking forward to criticism from the readers and experts to enhance my learning of the urban life, and even the entire social life of the Yuan Dynasty.

Shi Weimin

July 13, 1996
Beijing

Publisher's Postscript

Since its first publication in September 1996, this series of book has aroused active response from the reading public and it has won a Fourth Hunan Book Prize and a Fourth Editor's Prize awarded to the presses directly under the Hunan Provincial Bureau of Press & Publication. Even today, it enjoys a high reputation among its readers.

Now at the tenth anniversary of its first publication, with the approval of the author, we decide to present a second edition of this series. A fairly large number of illustrations, historical pictures and paintings are added and we believe it will attract our readers, both old and new.

It must be stated that when collecting pictures, we have endeavored to contact all the painters and photographers to get their authorization. However, due to a variety of reasons, some of them were not found. We sincerely hope they will contact us so that we can offer them the remuneration and our gratitude.

Hunan People's Publishing House

May, 2006

元代城市
生活长卷

The Urban Life of the
Yuan Dynasty

This book is the result of a co-publication agreement between Hunan People's Publishing House (China) and Paths International Ltd (UK).

Title: The Urban Life of the Yuan Dynasty
Written by Shi Weimin
Translated by Liao Jing and Zhou Hui

ISBN: 978-1-84464-355-4

Paths International Ltd
PO Box 4083
Reading
United Kingdom
RG8 8ZN

www.pathsinternational.com

CPSIA information can be obtained at www.ICGtesting.com
Printed in the USA
BVOW02*2325250214

346002BV00006B/30/P